Introduction to

DESIGN AND ANALYSIS

A Series of Books in Psychology

Editors: Jonathan Freedman
Gardner Lindzey
Richard F. Thompson

Introduction to
DESIGN AND ANALYSIS

A Student's Handbook

Geoffrey Keppel
William H. Saufley, Jr.

UNIVERSITY OF CALIFORNIA, BERKELEY

 W. H. Freeman and Company
San Francisco

Sponsoring Editor: W. Hayward Rogers

Project Editors: Nancy Flight and Larry Olsen

Manuscript Editor: Suzanne Lipsett

Designer: Sharon H. Smith

Production Coordinator: Fran Mitchell

Illustration Coordinator: Cheryl Nufer

Cover Design: Martha Geering

Compositor: Bi-Comp, Inc.

Printer and Binder: The Maple-Vail Book Manufacturing Group

Library of Congress Cataloging in Publication Data

Keppel, Geoffrey.
  Introduction to design and analysis.

  (A Series of books in psychology)
  Bibliography: p.
  Includes index.
  1. Psychometrics. I. Saufley, William H., joint
author. II. Title.
BF39.K46   150′.1′82   79-26166
ISBN 0-7167-1142-7
ISBN 0-7167-1143-5 pbk.

1 2 3 4 5 6 7 8 9

Contents

To the Student

We wrote this book to give students the opportunity to think extensively about analytical research designs and to gain familiarity with the basis of current research in psychology. Most undergraduates who enroll in an introductory statistics course have been exposed to the idea of experimentation and are ready to consider the statistical analysis of data generated by experiments. Consequently, this text begins with a discussion of statistical analyses in the context of meaningful experimental situations. Throughout the book, we stress the analytical use of an experiment to answer specific questions posed by the researcher. We use examples to show the relationships between research questions, the choice of specific treatment conditions, and the statistical analysis of the experiment. It is our experience that this approach is stimulating and interesting to students, for it demonstrates the direct relevance of the procedures for analyzing data.

Throughout this book our approach is to emphasize the job of a researcher trying to make sense of some aspect of nature. Our explanations of hypothesis testing and our discussions of the sources and uses of variability are primarily verbal rather than mathematical. We have introduced each new procedure with an intuitive explanation and then worked through an example step by step to illustrate the procedure in detail. As a result, students with no more than the basic mathematics prerequisites required for college should have no difficulty understanding this book. Any undergraduate with the patience to work through the procedures and the willingness to correct his or her errors can master the procedures covered in the text.

To gain maximum value from the book, first read about the procedure for a particular analysis and then work through the examples, checking each step to make certain you understand the various operations. Frequently, errors in calculation result from an incorrect substitution or the omission of a step in the analysis. Although we have indicated places where errors are likely to occur, the best safeguard you can develop against errors is a systematic format for working through an analysis. Using a neatly arranged worksheet will enable you to make certain you have performed each step of an analysis and to check your work for accuracy. Finally, to gain a more complete understanding of a section, you may find it helpful to completely reread the chapters involved. We hope you will take advantage of the various study aids we have prepared. You can read about them in the following section to the instructor.

You will find that hypothesis testing and the analysis of variance are remarkably valuable in the design and analysis of research. Still, as with any new techniques, students often tend to depend too heavily on these procedures, especially when they do not fully understand them. As you read this text, keep in mind that there is no substitute for knowledge of the subject matter you are investigating and common sense in research.

Throughout the text, we have provided relevant references to Keppel's advanced text *Design and Analysis* to permit interested students to pursue points of discussion in a more sophisticated and comprehensive book. The use of a notational system common to both books facilitates the continuing students' understanding of this more advanced graduate-level book.

We have adopted two notational systems in this book. The first is standard notation, which we use to express calculations necessary for problems in linear regression, correlation, and estimation. The second is a system of letters and combinations of letters used to represent the individual observations and the different sums needed for the analysis of variance. We have found that students have considerably more difficulty comprehending standard notation than the letter system in the analysis of variance. Students report that our system is easy to use and that they have no difficulty in switching between the two systems when necessary. Glossary 2, An Overview of the Notational System, is intended for instructors who do their statistical thinking in standard notation and for students who have been exposed to statistical procedures in other courses or statistics texts where standard notation has been employed.

We have included a number of study aids to assist students in working through this book. First, in the part introductions, we summarize the material covered in each of the five major parts of the book. Second, each chapter opens with a detailed outline that can serve as a study guide and a reference to specific sections of the chapter, and each chapter closes with a comprehensive summary. Third, we list the critical terms, concepts, and symbols at the end of each chapter to emphasize the new material just covered. Fourth, we present exercises to supplement the text discussion. Complete answers to all problems are given in Appendix B. Finally, the glossaries provide definitions of all critical terms and concepts (Glossary 1), an overview and summary of the notational system (Glossary 2), an explanation of symbols denoting various arithmetical operations and statistical calculations (Glossary 3), and a functional summary of computational formulas covered in the text (Glossary 4).

AN OVERVIEW

The first twelve chapters are devoted to the analysis of data from experiments. In contrast to other texts, our approach reflects the thinking of a researcher, and our explanations are verbal rather than algebraic or mathematical. Our aim is to provide students with an intuitive understanding of the basic procedures involved in designing and analyzing an experiment.

In Part I, we introduce students to the logic of experimentation (Chapter 1) and to the notion of central tendency and variability (Chapter 2).

Part II focuses on the analysis of single-factor experiments. We begin with a general discussion of the use of randomization to control unwanted nuisance factors and the fundamental logic of hypothesis testing (Chapter 3). We present this material in the context of the completely randomized single-factor design, assuming virtually no statistical knowledge on the part of the students. In Chapters 4 and 5, we explain in detail the procedures we follow to assess the significance of an experimental outcome. By focusing immediately on the multilevel experiment, we encourage students to think very early in terms of designs using more than two groups—designs that are more representative of current research reported in the literature.

In Chapter 6, we consider the detailed analysis of an experiment, stressing the analytical, meaningful analysis of the results of an experiment. Our students have been intrigued with the idea of planned comparisons and challenged by the possibility of conducting a creative independent research project. In Chapter 7, we discuss additional descriptive measures that students may find useful in examining and presenting their data—for example, alternative measures of central tendency and variability, the construction of tables and graphs, frequency distributions, and a measure of the magnitude of treatment effects (omega squared). In Chapter 8, we contrast different methods of reducing experimental error and concentrate on the within-subjects design, in which each subject serves in all the treatment conditions.

Part III covers the design and analysis of factorial experiments. As elsewhere, our emphasis is on an intuitive understanding of the material. We introduce the concept of interaction and the analysis of the completely randomized two-factor design in Chapter 9. In the next chapter, we indicate how researchers are able to extract detailed information from the results of a factorial experiment. To demonstrate, we use an example initially introduced as a single-factor manipulation in Chapter 6 and expanded into a factorial experiment in Chapter 9. This continuity enables students to see how theoretical expectations can be examined and evaluated in factorial designs. Finally, we present the analysis of the mixed factorial design, in which one independent variable represents a between-subjects manipulation and the other a within-subjects manipulation. We cover this design in detail, since its use in psychological research is widespread and it is frequently the choice of undergraduate students designing their own research projects.

Part IV covers linear regression and correlation. As a natural extension of the material covered in previous chapters, we introduce the concept of linear regression in the context of the single-factor experiment (Chapter 12). First, we develop the formulas for the best-fitting straight line relating the treatment means of an experiment and the levels of the independent variable. Significance of linear trend is tested by the general formula for single-df comparisons, presented initially in Chapter 6, and coefficients of orthogonal polynomials. We extend these concepts to the use of linear regression to describe relationships obtained from correlational data and to predict future performance on the basis of linear regression (Chapter 13). Also, we emphasize linear regression in terms of variance and illustrate how the significance of linear trend can be tested by the analysis of variance. In Chapter 14, we consider linear correlation, additional correlational procedures available to researchers, and the use of correlation in the analysis of experiments.

In Part V, we cover a number of topics that are usually included in introductory statistics courses. In Chapter 15, we present chi square, focusing on the analysis of experiments and the subdivision of the overall chi square statistic into a number of meaningful comparisons obtained by arranging the treatment conditions into different patterns. In Chapter 16, we consider standard scores and the construction of confidence intervals.

CLASSROOM USE

We have used earlier drafts of this book with undergraduates at the University of California, Berkeley, typically in the two-quarter sequence required of psychology majors. In the second quarter, students conduct research projects that are factorial in nature and usually involve repeated measures. Our approach works! We believe that the building-block nature of analysis of variance is responsible for this success. Ideas, concepts, and principles from earlier chapters are readily applied to later chapters. The result is a class of students who understand the nature of contemporary experimental research in psychology.

We have given a great deal of thought to the order in which the material is presented, and we encourage instructors to follow this order when using this book. However, we realize that not everyone will agree completely with our approach. Some instructors might want to introduce Chapter 7 (Additional Descriptive Measures and Techniques) immediately after Chapter 2 in order to emphasize the descriptive role of statistics. (We would advise postponing the last section of Chapter 7—on the magnitude of treatment effects—until students have completed at least Chapter 5 and preferably Chapter 6.) The estimation and construction of confidence intervals (Chapter 16) can be assigned after Chapter 2 if an instructor wants to cover estimation procedures before hypothesis testing.

For a shorter course, certain chapters will probably have to be omitted. The choice of which chapters to keep and which to delete will in large part depend on the goals and biases of individual instructors. If class time is extremely limited, an instructor might choose to omit repeated measures in the single-factor design (Chapter 8), analytical comparisons in the factorial designs (Chapter 10), within-subjects factorial designs (Chapter 11), and the analysis of frequency data (Chapter 15). If time is only somewhat limited, an instructor might only omit Chapters 10 and 11.

This book can profitably be used as a supplementary text for a course in experimental psychology and other courses requiring experimental-laboratory work. It is our impression that students are generally ill prepared for such courses, either because preliminary courses have failed to cover necessary procedures—for example, analysis of variance—or because students have failed to master the techniques. This book would certainly serve either of these two needs. The particular chapters chosen would depend on the background of the students and the scope of the course. Students with statistical background could skim Chapters 1–3 and begin formal study of the analysis of variance with Chapter 4. Students who have been exposed to single-factor analysis of variance could skim Chapters 1–5 and then focus on Chapter 6, where we discuss the analytical use of planned comparisons and the interplay between specific research hypotheses, experimental design, and statistical analysis. For most students, this material will be interesting new ground.

ACKNOWLEDGMENTS

We thank the students who urged us to write this book and those who encouraged us with thoughtful comments about the material in earlier versions. The book benefitted greatly from these suggestions as well as the detailed reviews we received from Dr. John J. Shaughnessy and Dr. Theodore J. Stolarz. We also thank W. Hayward Rogers of W. H. Freeman and Company for his enthusiasm and support, Nancy Flight for overseeing the editing of the manuscript, Suzanne Lipsett for her steady hand on the words and sentences that make up this book, and the production staff of W. H. Freeman and Company—especially the project editor, Larry Olsen—for their careful attention to details.

We wish to acknowledge our appreciation to the *Biometrika* Trustees for giving permission to reprint substantial amounts of material from the *Biometrika Tables for Statisticians,* Volume 1 (3rd edition), edited by E. S. Pearson and H. O. Hartley.

November 1979   Geoffrey Keppel
                                                       William H. Saufley, Jr.

Dedicated to the late Professor Jack Richardson,

a friend and professional colleague,
who offered advice and encouragement
when the book was simply a collection
of undeveloped ideas,

and to our parents,

Charles and Edetha Keppel
Bill and Olyn Saufley

EXPERIMENTAL DESIGN AND PRELIMINARY DATA ANALYSIS

We assume that most students reading this book are undergraduate majors in psychology or related disciplines and that the course of which this book is a part is probably a requirement of the major. As a psychology major, you will be expected to understand how the empirical basis of a science is created—how data are generated, collected, and summarized statistically—and you may even work with data yourself. To be able to contribute to the growth of an empirical science, no matter how modestly, you must be able to use the analytical methods and procedures of the science. In psychology, these consist of methods and procedures for manipulating a subject's internal and external environment and statistical techniques for isolating, measuring, and evaluating the effects of these manipulations on behavior.

Each research field within psychology has its own collection of methodological and statistical tools, and these tools change and develop continually as the field grows through new research. As your interests become more focused and you learn more about particular methods, you will begin to acquire a critical attitude toward the inferences that you and others are able to draw from experiments. Fundamentally, the quality of any fact, new or old, depends on the logic of the experiment that generated it in the first place. A familiarity with specific procedures and methods will enable you to evaluate the experiments you read and study and thus to weigh the significance of the reported results.

Basic to all experimentation is a working knowledge of statistics. While statistical techniques vary among different research areas within psychology, certain statistical methods are common to most if not all fields of psychology. These are the methods and procedures that are emphasized in this book. We are both researchers in the field of human learning and memory—not statisticians—and this fact accounts for the book's clear experimental bias. Our primary goal is to introduce you to the *analytical* side of experimentation. A knowledge of this subject will assist you in your reading of primary source material in psychological research journals and in designing research projects that reflect the sophistication of present-day experimentation in psychology.

We have found through our teaching of experimental design and statistical analysis that undergraduates have widely varying backgrounds, both in mathematics and in psychological experimentation. The two chapters in Part I are designed to make up for deficiencies you may have in these subjects and to set the stage for the systematic coverage of statistical analysis in later chapters.

In Chapter 1, we describe the critical features of an experiment and introduce some fundamental terms and concepts. The chapter is intended to help you think in terms of experimentation and to make clear how ideas are pursued through the critical testing ground of the experiment.

In Chapter 2, we discuss the processing of data. We introduce two fundamental descriptive statistical measures, of central tendency and of variability. As you will see, the required arithmetical operations for applying these measures consist only of the basic four functions: addition, subtraction, multiplication, and division. All you have to learn is when to perform each operation in a series of calculations. These calculations are expressed by formulas that are easily understood if you have at least a nodding acquaintance with simple algebra. (We do not assume any mathematical background beyond high school algebra.) In any case, we work through all the steps specified by a formula so you can follow each calculation when you feel rusty or become confused.

Introduction to Experimentation

1

The **experiment** is the primary means by which we are able to establish cause-effect relationships between certain events in the environment and the occurrence of particular forms of behavior. The basic notion is simple: At least two groups of subjects are treated exactly alike in all ways except one—the differential treatment. Any differences observed in the behavior of the two groups of subjects is then attributed to, or said to be caused by, the difference in the specific treatment conditions. We will consider this simple notion in some detail.

THE ANATOMY OF AN EXPERIMENT

We can describe the function of an experiment most clearly by covering each of its component parts in turn.

The Research Hypothesis

Few experiments are conducted out of the blue without any rationale. Experiments are based on previous observations, the results of other experiments, or deductions from theory. They also result from hunches and speculative thinking. A researcher sets out to discover something or to "prove" that a particular line of reasoning is correct or incorrect. In every research report, an introductory section presents background research to the problem, the reasoning leading up to the reported experiment, and, finally, the **research hypothesis**—a succinct statement of the purpose of the experiment.

The Treatment Conditions

As noted, an experiment consists of two or more **treatment conditions.** The actual treatment conditions in an experiment are usually determined by the manipulations specified in the research hypothesis. A research hypothesis may state, for example, that variations in the amount of a particular drug will have differential effects on behavior, or that different kinds of drugs will have differential effects on behavior. "Variations in amount," in the first example, and "different kinds of drugs," in the second example, are descriptive phrases referring to the treatment conditions included in the two experiments designed to test these hypotheses. However, these phrases are not detailed enough to define the treatment conditions sufficiently. The researcher would have to provide more information—specifying the dosage variations in the first example, naming the particular drugs to be administered in the second—to clearly delineate the different treatment conditions in these two experiments.

A number of different terms are used to refer to the treatment conditions included in an experiment. Most commonly, the treatment conditions are called, collectively, the **independent variable.** In the first of our examples, variations in amount constitute the independent variable of the experiment, while in the second, variations in drug type constitute the independent variable. The independent variable comprises the range of treatment conditions under the control of the experimenter. The term *under control* means *manipulated by* or *varied by* the experimenter. For this reason, the independent variable is also known as the **manipulated variable** or the **treatment variable.** Alternative terms are also used to refer to the treatment conditions themselves—that is, the differences in treatment administered to the subjects of the experiment. These terms are **treatments** and **levels of the independent variable.**

The Response Measure

The behavior observed by the experimenter in conjunction with the manipulation of the independent variable is called the **response measure.** Any behavior capable of being measured can be a response measure, for example, the speed of completing a task, the number of errors made, or even ratings on a scale. The response measure is often referred to as the **dependent variable.** The terms dependent variable, response measure, and **response variable** are used interchangeably.

A choice of response measures exists for most experiments. The experimenter's choice of which response measure to include depends on a number of factors. A response measure should be *readily observable, easily transformable into numbers,* and *economically feasible.* Also, a response measure must actually *measure the behavior* it is supposed to measure. Finally, the response measure must be *stable,* or *reliable,* known to show the least variation under constant experimental conditions. Mechanized recording procedures, which are usually not available for an undergraduate project, help to produce stability in the translation of behavior to some numerical index.

Researchers often "solve" the problem of choosing among response measures simply by including several response measures in an experiment. They follow this procedure in order to preserve some of the richness and complexity of the behavior being studied and to ascertain whether different aspects of the behavior are affected differently by the administration of the treatment conditions. In this book, we will only consider experiments that have a single dependent variable. In experiments in which two or more dependent variables are to be recorded and analyzed, results can be examined as deriving from *separate experiments,* one for each of the response measures.[1]

Method, Design, and Subjects

The specification of the research hypothesis and the identification of the independent and dependent variables provides only a skeletal outline of an experiment. Many specific details must be worked out before experimentation can actually begin. The decisions an investigator makes at this stage can be creative, challenging, and often frustrating. In reporting research, an investigator must fully describe the methods and procedures to be followed

---

[1] In fact, most researchers analyze an experiment with multiple response measures in this way. More appropriate multivariate procedures are available for analyzing experiments with more than one response variable, but these are complicated, generally require the assistance of a computer, and are beyond the scope of this book.

but at the same time be succinct enough to conserve the limited space usually allotted to accounts of individual experiments in journals. These detailed descriptions of the methods, design, and subjects of the experiment are found in the method section of a research report.

The actual *design* of the experiment is a topic about which we will have a great deal to say. In a statistics book, **experimental design** usually refers to a general plan for conducting an experiment. Experimental designs can differ in a number of ways, for example, in the number of independent variables to be manipulated. The most common design for an experiment in which two or more independent variables are manipulated is called the factorial design. Most experiments in the contemporary literature of psychological research employ factorial designs. As a consequence, we will discuss the analysis of such designs fully (in Chapters 9, 10, and 11) to enable you both to understand such experiments when you encounter them in your studies and to design them when you are ready to conduct independent research of your own. In the earlier chapters, however, we will focus on the *single*-variable experiment, because it is simpler to understand and it serves as an important building block for the more complicated factorial design.

A second major way in which experimental designs can differ is in the method of *assigning subjects* to the different treatment conditions. In the simplest procedure, and the one we consider first, an independent group of subjects is assigned to each of the treatments. At the other extreme is a design in which each subject serves in all the treatment conditions. In between are designs in which these features are combined, with the subjects serving in some but not all of the treatment conditions. All these designs are relatively common in psychology, and consequently we give them considerable attention in this book.

A final design consideration concerns the subjects included in the study. Generally, two questions arise at this point. First: What sort of subjects do we wish to study? Should we test animals or humans? Any particular sort of animal or human? Do we want subjects with a particular past history? Do we want individuals at a particular stage of development? In many cases, the primary factor is availability. Students usually test one another as well as friends and relatives, and researchers frequently select student "volunteers" from introductory psychology classes. In our own case, we defend our choice of subjects by noting that we want to study basic learning-memory processes, and that these factors are most easily observable in articulate individuals who have developed efficient skills in learning and in using what they have learned. If the nature of our research questions were to change and college students were no longer appropriate as subjects, we would choose other types of individuals. In addition to availability, then, theoretical considerations may also play a role in the selection of subjects.

The second question concerns the number of subjects needed in an experiment. The answer to this question is so simple it seems trite. An experimenter needs as many subjects as are necessary to provide a relatively sensitive test of the research hypothesis. (By sensitivity, we mean the ability to detect differences when they are present.) One way to increase the sensitivity in an experiment is to increase the number of subjects.[2] Given that the availability of subjects is generally limited, however, the experimenter attempts to test as many subjects as possible. Due to the nature of most psychological research, by and large the minimum number of subjects in an experiment is *five subjects per condition,* although the gain in sensitivity with ten or more subjects is considerable. Often, students are forced to conclude that their experiments have produced results that are "promising," that is, results that lean in the direction predicted but that do not have strong statistical support, since too few subjects were tested. To aid our own students in increasing the sensitivity of their experiments, we encourage them to work jointly on research projects so that they can both broaden the scope of their studies—by increasing the number of treatment conditions—and add to the number of subjects tested per treatment condition.

The relative lack of statistical sensitivity resulting from the use of small numbers of subjects—a problem that is usually beyond student experimenters' control—takes some of the fun out of conducting a student research project. You may have an interesting research idea and a perfectly good experiment and by all rights expect to be able to obtain unambiguous conclusions following the statistical analysis. But an insufficient number of subjects may render such conclusions impossible. We will return to the problem of sensitivity in later chapters.

Classification of Independent Variables

We turn now to a more detailed examination of independent variables and a brief discussion of the ways in which treatment variables are classified. We consider two such classifications: the nature and the source of the manipulation.

The Nature of the Manipulation. One common classification scheme concerns the nature of the manipulation. A variable in which the treatment levels differ in degree or in amount as measured by either a physical or a psychological scale is called a **quantitative independent variable.** A **qualitative independent variable,** on the other hand, is a variable in which the levels differ in kind

---

[2] Additional ways of achieving sensitivity are discussed in Chapter 8.

rather than in amount. We will discuss these distinctive types of manipulations in turn.

A quantitative variable can be any manipulation that represents variations in the *amount* of the independent variable. The number of hours of food deprivation for rats in a maze-learning experiment, the degree of background noise in a signal-detection task, the amount of money given as incentive in a problem-solving task are all examples of quantitative independent variables. In an experiment that has a quantitative independent variable, the variable is usually tested on several levels, or conditions, covering a relatively large range of variation. In the rat experiment, for example, a researcher might include conditions with 0, 1, 12, and 24 hours of food deprivation—and even longer intervals if there is reason to believe that additional changes will be observed after 24 hours. This strategy ensures that the relationship linking changes in the independent variable with changes in the dependent variable will be adequately determined in the experiment. (For further discussion of this concept, see *Design and Analysis,* pp. 113–117.[3])

Qualitative independent variables, as opposed to quantitative ones, are easy to recognize, since the specific treatment conditions chosen to define the independent variable cannot be ordered meaningfully on a quantitative scale. Types of drugs, variations in the instructions given to subjects, and differences in teaching methods are examples of qualitative variables.

The Source of the Manipulation. A second classification, which cuts across the qualitative-quantitative distinction, specifies the source of the treatment manipulation. One source of manipulation is the task; variations in some characteristic of the task itself constitute a **task variable.** Mazes differing in complexity and different types of conceptual problems are examples of task variables. A second type of independent variable is an **environmental variable.** In this case, the nature of the task is held constant, but some aspect of the experimental environment is manipulated. Obvious examples include the temperature, humidity, illumination, and other conditions prevailing in the testing situation.

A final source of manipulation is the *subject.* We discuss two types of such manipulation. The first consists of some sort of temporary psychological or physiological intervention. Giving differential instructions to human subjects is the typical way of manipulating subjects' set, or view, of the task. For example, in an experiment intended to determine whether guessing rate af-

---

[3] Citations refer to the references presented at the end of the book. The presentation of material in this book has been coordinated with that in *Design and Analysis,* by Geoffrey Keppel. To emphasize this fact, citations to this more advanced work utilize the title, rather than author's name.

fects speed of learning, a subject may be instructed to guess freely or to refrain from guessing. Inducing different hypnotic states is an extreme form of instructional manipulation. Drugs are commonly used to induce differential physiological states in subjects. The internal changes produced in the subjects by such manipulations are temporary in the sense that the subjects will quickly return to their "normal" selves after the experiment. Thus, we call such manipulations *temporary* subject variables.

The second is a different sort of manipulation, involving more or less permanent characteristics of subjects. The effect of intelligence on problem solving and the effect of biological sex on speed of learning are examples of this class of manipulation. Such variables are variously referred to as **subject variables,** classification variables, organismic variables, and individual-difference variables. In the context of an experiment, classification variables are manipulated through the *selection* of subjects on the dimension to be studied. To manipulate intelligence, for instance, we would have to obtain intelligence scores for a large number of individuals and then select subjects from this pool on the basis of these scores. The independent variable would then consist of subjects grouped together according to their IQ scores.

Manipulation of this sort—involving classification variables—does not constitute an experiment as we have defined it, however, since the "administration of the experimental treatments" is obviously not under the control of the experimenter. The manipulation consists of classifying the subjects—in our example, with regard to IQ. In an experiment, the independent variable is the only feature of the situation that is allowed to vary systematically from condition to condition. It is this characteristic of an experiment that permits the researcher to infer that a particular manipulation caused systematic differences in behavior observed among the different groups. But when a classification variable is manipulated, the subjects may also differ systematically from level to level with respect to characteristics other than the classification variable. Since such characteristics are not subject to the researcher's control, making an unambiguous statement about cause and effect is impossible where classification variables are involved.[4]

The Confounding of Variables

Description. The strength of the experimental method depends on our ability to guarantee that only the manipulated variable is permitted to vary system-

---

[4] Wood (1974, pp. 44–47) provides a clear discussion of this sort of design. Underwood (1957, pp. 112–125) considers in detail problems of inference resulting from the manipulation of subject variables. Underwood and Shaughnessy (1975, pp. 94–104) describe a research strategy for trying to deal with this problem.

atically from condition to condition. In cases where a second independent variable is unwittingly permitted to vary along with the intended one, we say that the two independent variables are **confounded.** If the confounding variable influences the behavior under study, we will not be able to distinguish the effects of the manipulated variable from the effects of the other. Thus, the confounding of variables usually ruins an experiment.

As an example, suppose we want to compare the effectiveness of three different methods of teaching arithmetic to elementary school children. For the experiment, we train a different teacher in each method, making sure that in all three methods exactly the same material is covered. The teachers then instruct their classes for two weeks using the method in which they were trained, and the performance of the students is assessed by a test made up by the experimenter. The methods of teaching arithmetic constitute the independent variable, and the scores on the proficiency test constitute the dependent variable.

How would you evaluate this experiment? We hope that you can see the rather serious flaws built into this example. Although the manipulated independent variable consists of the differences in the teaching methods, several other variables were at work, thus confounding the variable under study. One such variable is the ability of the students in the different classes. It is highly likely that the classes differed in average ability and training *before* the start of the two-week training period. Disentangling these differences from any differences produced by the three training methods would be impossible; thus, training and preexisting ability levels are confounded. Another confounding variable might consist of differences in the abilities of the three teachers. The teachers probably differ in teaching effectiveness, and discriminating these differences from the effects of the three training methods would also be impossible. Thus, teacher ability and training methods are confounded.

We made this example of confounding obvious in order to illustrate the concept. But even when the confounding is difficult to detect, its existence damages the experiment irreversibly. While part of your early training as a researcher should involve learning to identify and recognize confoundings in your work and in the work of others, you should realize that no one is immune to the problem. Every researcher has his or her favorite personal confounding to recount. One of the primary functions of the reviewers who assist editors of research journals is to assess carefully each study submitted for publication for possible confoundings. The high rejection rate for these journals is due in large part to the discovery of serious confoundings in the submitted experiments.

The obvious first step toward preventing confoundings in your own research is to be constantly aware of the problem. You should examine critically all phases of your planned research to discover possible flaws. Discussing your experiment with others is also often helpful. Kirk (1968, p. 8) suggests that researchers try to list all factors that might affect the behavior under study and to make sure that these are all controlled in some manner in the design of the experiment. Underwood and Shaughnessy (1975) offer the following suggestion:

> A confounding is most likely to occur among variables within the same class. When a task variable is being manipulated, it is most likely to be confounded with another task variable if a confound does exist; a subject variable is most likely to be confounded with another subject variable, and so on. This rule, viewed as a probabilistic rule, is a fairly valid one in guiding our attempts to design an experiment without a confounding (p. 30).

Unfortunately, however, there is no easy way to avoid creating a confounded independent variable.[5] All you can hope for is that you or someone else will discover a confounding before you have gone very far on your research project. Most confoundings can be eliminated through changes in experimental design, but only before the experiment is conducted and the data collected.

Intentional Confounding. Situations do exist in which a researcher deliberately confounds an independent variable, usually during the exploratory stages on a research problem, in which the independent variable is a complex combination of two or more potential factors. The strategy is to determine whether deliberate confounding of independent variables produces any changes in behavior. If this admittedly complex manipulation does produce changes, the researcher will follow the study with experiments designed to pinpoint the aspects of the original manipulation that produced the observed changes. Another example comes from the applied fields, where the primary goal is not to answer the question "Why?" but to ascertain, for example, which advertising campaign or which packaging or which training program among several is the most effective. In this sort of work, in which the goal is to exhibit large and clear differences among the treatment conditions, the confounding of a number of variables, each of which has its own little effect, is often employed as a strategy.

---

[5] Underwood's classical discussion of the problem (1957, pp. 85–173) has been helpful to many researchers. Other books by Underwood provide students with exercises designed to illustrate different types of confoundings (Underwood, 1966; Underwood and Shaughnessy, 1975, pp. 161–215). Also, the treatment by Campbell and Stanley (1966) is especially useful for researchers working in the social-science areas of psychology.

THE ANALYTICAL NATURE OF EXPERIMENTATION

Not long ago, the two-condition experiment was the typical experiment in psychology. Today, the multiple-condition experiment is dominant, and the simple two-condition study is rarely reported. One reason for this development is that contemporary researchers choose to study a range of treatment variations—variations either in kind (qualitative) or in amount (quantitative)—rather than to base their conclusions on an experiment with only two levels of an independent variable. We will illustrate this point briefly with respect to each kind of variable.

Quantitative Variables

In our discussion of the classification of independent variables, we noted that a quantitative independent variable is usually manipulated at more than two levels. The reason for including more than two levels is clear: The greater the number of points, or levels, along the independent variable included, the more accurately will be revealed the underlying functional relationship between the independent and dependent variables. (Choosing the specific levels of a quantitative independent variable to be examined is discussed in *Design and Analysis,* pp. 116–117.)

The research hypothesis associated with a quantitative manipulation consists of a statement that changing a particular independent variable quantitatively will produce a systematic change in the dependent variable. For example, the experimenter might ask, "Will increasing amounts of light affect the detection of a visual pattern?" or, "Will increasing amounts of a particular drug influence the speed of a motor response?" Entertaining such a speculation is sufficient reason for designing an experiment to provide this sort of information. The investigator making the speculation will then conduct analyses to determine the properties of this particular relationship. The analytical nature of such an experiment is reflected by the procedures involved in detailing and assessing the components or processes responsible for the observed relationship.

Qualitative Variables

An experiment containing a qualitative independent variable is generally made up of a number of **analytical comparisons,** or, if you will, a number of miniature experiments. Suppose, for example, that we have been asked to assess the usefulness of two different drugs in relaxing hyperactive children in the classroom. The most obvious approach would be to administer the two drugs to two groups of hyperactive children and to compare their relative effectiveness. The independent variable in this experiment is qualitative (kind of drug, not amount). Any difference observed in the classroom between the two groups after the drug is administered is attributed by the researcher to the differential effectiveness of the two drugs. Most investigators would not be satisfied with this simple experiment, however. They would probably include a third level in the experiment, a control condition in which a third group of subjects is given no drug at all. This control group (or placebo group, as it is often called) adds valuable information to the experiment. More specifically, the control condition helps to rule out the operation of *psychological* factors associated with the experience of serving in an experiment. Let's consider this point in more detail.

The addition of the control group results in three different treatment conditions and the possibility of obtaining answers to several analytical questions from the results of the experiment. Consider three possibilities:

Comparison 1: Control versus drug A

Comparison 2: Control versus drug B

Comparison 3: Drug A versus drug B

You will note that each comparison is in essence a separate two-group experiment incorporated into the design of the overall experiment. Comparison 3, drug A versus drug B, represents the information available from the original two-group experiment we considered initially. Comparisons 1 and 2 both involve the control condition and provide information that would not have been available from the simpler design. That is, comparison 1 permits us to determine whether drug A has a *positive* effect (produces relaxation in the subjects), a *negative* effect (increases hyperactivity), or *no effect* whatsoever (in which case no differences would be discovered between the drug A group and the control group). Comparison 2 assesses the same three possible outcomes with drug B.

Let us summarize the important advantages of including the control group in this experiment. First, the control condition will lead us to the appropriate conclusion if the two drugs are *equally effective* in reducing hyperactivity. The two-group experiment, on the other hand, would lead us to conclude that the two drugs do not differ, but we would be unable to tell whether the drugs were equally effective or equally ineffective in controlling hyperactivity. The addition of the control condition provides us with a means of distinguishing between these two possibilities.

Second, the control condition will give us information about the nature of the two drug effects if the two drug conditions *do* produce a difference on the dependent variable. Suppose drug A is found to be more effective than drug B. Does this mean that drug A has a positive effect and drug B has no effect? No, all we are able to conclude is that drug A is more effective than drug B. In reality, drug A may have no effect, while drug B has a negative effect, that is, drug B increases hyperactivity. The control condition allows us to determine which of these different possibilities is correct.

This example demonstrates how we can increase the analytical power of an experiment by including more than two conditions in an experiment. As you will see, this form of qualitative manipulation can be applied to most of the experiments we will encounter. In Chapter 6 we will introduce statistical procedures by which these kinds of analytical comparisons can be assessed directly. In this section, we set the stage for Chapter 6 by illustrating how informationally rich even a relatively simple experiment can be, and by emphasizing that in the design and analysis of experiments a researcher can exercise his or her imagination, individuality, and creative powers to the fullest. No two investigators will design an experiment in exactly the same way. Some researchers design experiments that yield important insights, while others construct studies that are less creatively designed. The challenge is to create meaningful and analytically powerful experiments that excite your imagination. Learning how to use an experiment analytically will permit you to enter this rewarding arena, in which new knowledge about behavior is continually being sought and discovered.

While the execution of a research project allows the full expression of imagination and creativity, the success or failure of the whole operation still depends on the proper exercise of *logic* at all stages of the study. First, the research hypothesis must follow logically from the empirical-theoretical background of the study. Next, the specific treatment conditions must adequately reflect the critical elements of the research hypothesis. Third, the experiment must be designed so that only the differential treatments are permitted to vary systematically across the conditions, that is, confoundings must be avoided. Also, the statistical analyses must be conducted so as to provide a comprehensive assessment of the results; and, finally, the investigator must draw correct inferences in interpreting the statistical analyses and integrating these new findings with existing knowledge and theory.[6]

Despite these caveats, it is worth remembering that statistical procedures and analyses are only of secondary importance in the discovery of knowl-

---

[6] The subjects of theory building and construction and the role of theory in experimentation are fascinating topics for discussion and study. Unfortunately, we do not have the space to consider these topics properly. The discussion by Underwood and Shaughnessy (1975, pp. 123–160) is an interesting introduction to the nature and use of theory in psychological research.

edge and that statistical procedures are neutral with respect to the quality of the experiment under analysis. A poorly designed experiment can be just as impeccably and competently analyzed as one that is well designed. In this regard, researchers often view statistics and statistical analyses as tools to assist them in drawing statistically justifiable conclusions from a set of data. Success in using these tools is dependent on the underlying logic and creative construction of the experimental design.

NONEXPERIMENTAL RESEARCH APPROACHES

In the experimental approach to research, the administration of the different treatment conditions is under the investigator's direct control. The establishment of a difference between two treatment conditions, and the monitoring of behavior within the context of the experiment, permit the investigator to infer causality. That is, a researcher can conclude that the critical difference between two conditions was responsible for (or caused) the differences in behavior observed in the experiment. The **nonexperimental research** methods described in this section are of use to psychologists, but do not permit them to infer causation with the certainty that is possible in a properly designed experiment.

Observational Research

Observation in the laboratory is important, but those aspects of behavior that can be measured are limited. Moreover, the independent variables chosen and the methods for manipulating them are relatively contrived compared with the "manipulations" produced by the natural occurrence of events. An observer can learn a great deal by conducting **observational research**—that is, by watching and recording behavior as it unfolds in the natural environment. Certain scientific fields such as astronomy and geology are based primarily on the use of observational techniques, and the development of these fields is impressive evidence of the utility of these methods in science. The study of animal behavior (ethology) and the clinical use of case histories are examples of enterprises within psychology that rely heavily on detailed observation.

Most observational research requires that the observer be completely neutral. Since the behavior of both animals and humans changes when they are aware of being observed, investigators often go to great lengths to conceal themselves from their subjects. Observers must be trained to recognize key features of the environment and behavior and to record these details neutrally, that is, without interpreting it. The behavior under study is usually observed by at least two investigators, whose independent summaries of the flow of events must be in close agreement. In the first stages of such research, the investigators are usually unrestricted in their observations in order that they may examine and assess the target behavior fully without any preconceived bias. Once a researcher has examined the data and more fully understands the nature of the behavior, the scope of the observation may be restricted.

The major shortcoming of purely observational methods is their inability to establish causal relationships between observed events. In an experiment, the researcher controls the occurrence or administration of the independent variable. With observational research, on the other hand, the observer goes to great pains to avoid influencing the research setting. Thus, any changes in the environment impinging on the subject are introduced by nature, independent of the researcher. As a consequence, we can never unequivocally infer cause and effect from an observational study in which all potential independent variables are completely free to vary—and to influence behavior. The close and repeated occurrence in time of a change in the research setting and the occurrence of a particular behavior may suggest a causal relationship, but is not sufficient to allow a definitive conclusion. Coming to such a conclusion requires that a researcher design an experiment that focuses on the particular change in the research setting, thus bringing it under the control of the experimenter. In short, observational research helps to identify possible causes of behavioral change while the experimental method permits the establishment of such relationships.

Do not underestimate the value of observational methods, however. While they lack the inferential power of experimental methods, they do provide guidelines for further experimental work. Experiments tend to elicit behavior that is artificial, restrictive, and "pale" in comparison with the rich flow of behavior observed in the unrestricted, natural setting. The obvious solution to this problem is to make use of both techniques. Careful and detailed observation can provide us with fruitful research hypotheses to be tested in the laboratory, and offers a behavioral perspective against which we should always compare the behavior elicited in carefully controlled experiments.

Correlational Research

Correlational research in psychology consists of the search for consistent relationships between two (and sometimes more) characteristics of individuals. These characteristics can be biographical (for example, age, sex, education, or personal income), physiological (height, weight, blood pressure, or other "medical" characteristics), psychological (measures of intelligence, personality, or attitudes and opinions), or behavioral (any characteristic of behavior that can be observed and measured). Once a consistent relationship has been established, a researcher can predict one of these characteristics of an individual from a knowledge of the other characteristic. For example, a common use of prediction using correlational methods is the selection of individuals for some future activity—for example, college, skilled jobs, professional schools, and so on—based upon information such as school grades and aptitude tests of various sorts.

Correlational information is useful in all areas of psychology. Some subfields, such as personality psychology, are almost entirely based on correlational data. Even when prediction is not an issue, correlational information is useful to the researcher who is making a thorough analysis of his or her data. We discuss the analysis of correlational data in Chapters 13 and 14.

The distinction between correlational research and observational research is blurred and difficult to express, primarily because both approaches involve the study of relationships between naturally occurring phenomena. In observational research, one is usually interested in demonstrating a relationship between naturally occurring changes in the environment and changes in the behavior of the subjects under observation. In correlational research, on the other hand, one is usually interested in establishing a relationship between two different characteristics of individuals. Both endeavors involve the identification of relationships between naturally occurring events, that is, events (or characteristics) that are not under the control of the investigator. This shared characteristic is critical, of course, since it is responsible for our inability to establish unambiguously causal relationships with these two types of research techniques.

These nonexperimental approaches often permit us to study phenomena that are not amenable to experimental research, either because finding an experimental analogue of the natural events is too difficult or because the manipulations are harmful to the well-being of the subject. For these reasons, observational and correlational approaches occupy an important place in psychological research even though they are limited in their ability to establish cause-effect relationships.

SUMMARY

The establishment of facts and the testing of theory in psychology are dependent on careful and imaginative experimentation. While other research approaches such as observational and correlational techniques occupy an important place in our discipline, the experiment is a tool we can use to establish factors that cause behavior.

An experiment begins with the formulation of a research hypothesis. A research hypothesis often represents a test of an existing theory, but other reasons exist for conducting an experiment. For example, investigators may undertake experiments to add to our factual knowledge, to investigate a new independent variable, or to study a new phenomenon, while showing little or no concern for theory testing or even theoretical development. In any case, the research hypothesis provides the focus for the experiment: It dictates the nature of the independent variable to be manipulated, and it probably suggests the nature of the dependent variable as well. Other decisions influence the design of an experiment, for example, the specific methods and procedures to be employed, the type of experimental design to be used, and the subjects to be tested.

The greatest failing of experiments is the inadvertent confounding of independent variables. Confounding occurs when uncontrolled factors vary in conjunction with the manipulation of the independent variable. If any possibility exists that such factors may have influenced the behavior under study, then the experiment is usually ruined and the findings are uninterpretable.

Almost any feature of the task and of the subject's external and internal environment can be manipulated in an experiment. Also, researchers are able to study the effects of psychological variables by giving different instructions to different subjects designed to induce differential sets and motivations. Even relatively permanent characteristics of subjects can be varied in an experiment—these are subject or classification variables—but since in such cases the "manipulations" are not directly under the control of the experimenter, this approach is basically correlational, not experimental.

Most experimental manipulations are carefully crafted by a researcher to provide answers to the analytical questions posed by research hypotheses. If the manipulation is quantitative in nature, the research hypothesis often includes some speculation concerning the anticipated nature of the function relating the dependent variable to the quantitative manipulations. If the manipulation is qualitative, the research hypothesis generally consists of a number of specific questions that use the data from the different treatment conditions in various combinations. Each of the combinations is designed to shed some light on specific analytical questions.

Observational and correlational, as opposed to experimental, techniques often provide indications of independent variables that might fruitfully be manipulated in an experiment. Observations of naturally occurring behavior, free from the intrusion or intervention by a researcher, provide us with an important perspective from which to interpret the results of experiments. Correlational techniques offer ways to express the degree to which freely changing features of subjects and of the environment are interrelated or vary together. In comparison with the experimental approach, both methods are limited in their ability to establish cause-effect relationships.

TERMS AND CONCEPTS

experiment
research hypothesis
treatment conditions
independent variable
treatment variable
levels of the independent variable
response measure
dependent variable
response variable
experimental design

quantitative independent variable
qualitative independent variable
task variable
environmental variable
subject variable
confounding of variables
analytical comparison
nonexperimental research
observational research
correlational research

Preliminary Data Analysis

2

In the preceding chapter, we described the general nature of psychology experiments. In this chapter, we introduce procedures that transform the results of an experiment (the so-called "raw data") into a manageable and useful form. This stage can be thought of as a preliminary analysis of the data, that is, an initial examination of how the experiment "turned out." To accomplish this preliminary analysis, the researcher uses the individual data points—the basic scores or observations—to calculate certain quantities that summarize the fundamental characteristics of the results. This process of "refinement" has been called **data reduction,** since it results in the reduction of a large number of observations to a much smaller number of **statistical indices.** These indices—numbers derived from the raw data—are used as indicators or measures to describe and summarize the different sets of scores produced by the experiment.

We introduce two statistical indices that are particularly useful in summarizing data and in drawing inferences from the results of experiments. The measure we discuss first is used to specify what we might call the "typical" score—a score that is representative of all of the scores in any set under consideration. This index is a measure of the centrality, or the **central tendency,** of a set of scores. When obtaining a measure of central tendency, we make a simple assumption, which, given past experience, appears to be a safe one: Even though the scores vary, they do gravitate around a point that best describes the data in question. The second index provides a measure of this "gravitation" or irregularity in a set of scores. This index is a measure of the **variability**—the differences among scores—in a given set. As you will see in later chapters, we use this measure of variability to estimate the degree to which chance factors are responsible for any differences observed among the treatment conditions of an experiment.[1]

THE MEAN AS A MEASURE OF CENTRAL TENDENCY

Definition of the Mean

The arithmetic mean, or **mean** for short, is the primary index of central tendency used in the analysis of experiments. It is defined thus:

$$\text{mean} = \frac{\text{sum of the scores}}{\text{number of scores}} \ . \qquad (2\text{-}1)$$

Computationally, the mean is simple, especially if you have a hand-held calculator. The scores do not have to be arranged in any particular order, but can be summed just as they are listed in front of you.

Most people are familiar with the concept of the mean due to the averages reported by the media at every flip of a channel or turn of a page. The average score on a midterm examination, the average income of a college graduate, and the team batting averages of baseball players are all common examples of the mean. Conceptually, the mean represents the score value *per subject* or *per observation*. This property of means makes possible the comparison of individuals or groups of individuals on a *common base* or reference point.

---

[1] Other methods are available to describe central tendency and variability, but these are generally used when the primary motivation of the researcher is to describe rather than to test hypotheses through experimentation. These alternative procedures are discussed in Chapter 7.

Other Characteristics of the Mean

Suppose each score is expressed as a discrepancy (or difference) from the mean. Thus, scores smaller than the mean would take on negative values, while scores greater than the mean would take on positive values. A unique property of the mean is that the sum of the negative discrepancies *exactly equals* the sum of the positive discrepancies. As a consequence, the sum of the discrepancies—keeping in mind the positive and negative signs—equals zero. We will illustrate this characteristic below using the data presented in Table 2-1.

Three other characteristics of the mean are of interest to us. First, the mean is influenced by all scores or observations gathered in an experiment. A change in only one of the numbers will change the value of the mean. Second, since the mean is a calculated value, it is usually not an actual score present in the set of scores, but some fractional value in between. Finally, in comparison with other measures, the mean is the most consistent measure of central tendency.[2]

Symbolic Representation of the Mean

Some Comments About Notation. While presenting the formulas for various calculations, we will also introduce some notation. The notation is merely a shorthand that refers to certain operations; it serves as a way of identifying quickly just what number or set of numbers is involved. Notational systems can become quite specific and are often adapted to suit the goal of authors. As a result, different textbooks often exhibit variations in what is called "standard notation," particularly where the analyses are complicated. Keep in mind that these variations are not intended to confuse, but to clarify the ideas presented.

Since we are interested in the experimenter's view of statistics rather than that of the statistician, we have purposely avoided the standard system and developed one that highlights the required calculations in a simple manner. In this chapter, we use notation that does not veer far from the standard notation. Our intention is to avoid confusing students who have been exposed to these calculations in other courses. In subsequent chapters, however, in which we consider the analysis of experiments, we assume that the

---

[2] Consistency is a theoretical concept that refers to the variability of a measure. Variability in this case is based on means calculated from independent sets of data drawn in an unbiased fashion from a much larger collection of scores. The mean varies less from set to set than do other measures of central tendency, and in this sense, the mean is more consistent.

reader is totally unfamiliar with the subject matter and thus introduce a special system. This system is less useful to mathematicians than standard notation, but it is almost self-explanatory as applied to experimental data. Any system requires that one pay attention to the rules with which the arithmetical operations are coded or represented. We advise you to study carefully each complication to the system as it is introduced so that you fully understand the new formulas and the calculations that follow.

The Formula. We have already defined the mean in words as the sum of the scores divided by the number of scores. The next step is to demonstrate how these arithmetical operations can be represented symbolically. In order to construct a formula, we need to represent the scores by a set of symbols and to introduce other symbols to indicate the summing operation and the number of scores. The formula must be written in such a way that it will apply to any set of scores, no matter how large or small. Since you may be unfamiliar with expressions of this sort, we will construct the formula for the mean step by step.

We start with the representation of the set of scores from which the mean will be calculated. The capital letter X is used to symbolize a score or observation, and a numerical subscript is used to designate a *particular* score. Thus, X_1 refers to the first score in a set, X_2 to the second score in a set, and so on. To refer to all the X scores *in general* but to no one score in particular, we use the letter i as a subscript instead of a number: X_i.

Next, we designate the addition of the X scores by means of the symbol Σ, which is the Greek letter *sigma* and means *sum*. We usually "read" this symbol as "take the sum of ...," and follow this expression with whatever quantities we want to add. In the case of the mean, we want to take the sum of all the X scores. Symbolically, this intention is represented by

$$\Sigma X_i \quad ,$$

which states, "take the sum of the X_i scores." Finally, we will represent the number of scores by a lower-case s, since s is an obvious symbol for *s*cores or *s*ubjects. Putting all this together, we can write the formula for the arithmetic mean, $\overline{X}$. (With this notation, $\overline{X}$ is the symbol for a mean and is read as X *bar*. Usually, any symbol with a bar over it indicates a mean.) Thus, the formula is

$$\overline{X} = \frac{\Sigma X_i}{s} \quad . \tag{2-2}$$

Again, in words this formula states that the mean is defined as the sum of the scores divided by the number of scores.

TABLE 2-1   A Numerical Example

Basic Observation		Deviation from the Mean ($\overline{X}$)	
Symbol (X_i)	Score	Symbol ($X_i - \overline{X}$)	Deviation
X_1	6	$X_1 - \overline{X}$	$6 - 5 = +1$
X_2	3	$X_2 - \overline{X}$	$3 - 5 = -2$
X_3	4	$X_3 - \overline{X}$	$4 - 5 = -1$
X_4	9	$X_4 - \overline{X}$	$9 - 5 = +4$
X_5	3	$X_5 - \overline{X}$	$3 - 5 = -2$

In most situations, the use of the i subscript is superfluous, however, and conveys no additional information. When this is the case, we drop the subscript and write the formula more simply as

$$\overline{X} = \frac{\Sigma X}{s} \ . \tag{2-3}$$

Numerical Example. A set of five scores (that is, $s = 5$) is presented on the left side of Table 2-1. Each score is designated by a number subscript representing the ordinal position of the score in the set. The sum of these scores is represented by

$$\Sigma X = X_1 + X_2 + X_3 + X_4 + X_5 \ .$$

When the scores are substituted, the formula becomes

$$\Sigma X = 6 + 3 + 4 + 9 + 3 = 25 \ .$$

Substituting in equation (2-3), we calculate the mean as follows:

$$\overline{X} = \frac{\Sigma X}{s}$$

$$= \frac{25}{5} = 5 \ .$$

The right side of Table 2-1 presents the calculations needed to demonstrate that the sum of the deviations from the mean equals zero. In symbols,

$$\Sigma(X - \overline{X}) = 0 \ . \tag{2-4}$$

Substituting in equation (2-4), we obtain

$$\Sigma(X - \overline{X}) = (X_1 - \overline{X}) + (X_2 - \overline{X}) + (X_3 - \overline{X}) + (X_4 - \overline{X}) + (X_5 - \overline{X})$$
$$= (6 - 5) + (3 - 5) + (4 - 5) + (9 - 5) + (3 - 5)$$
$$= 1 - 2 - 1 + 4 - 2 = 0 \ .$$

Rounding. In the numerical example provided in the preceding section, the mean was intended to come out evenly, without decimals. With actual data, however, the mean is not usually a round number. Now that nearly everyone has access to a hand-held electronic calculator, it is possible with minimal effort to produce answers to a large number of decimal places. On the other hand, such accuracy and precision is usually unnecessary in our work, and we drop, or **round off,** these excess digits. Generally, for purposes of calculating and reporting, the value of the mean (and other statistics) is rounded to two or at the most three decimal places. In this book, we round each calculation we report, whether a substep in a longer calculation or a final answer, to two decimal places, that is, to the nearest hundredth.[3]

Authors (and researchers) differ in the particular method they use in rounding numbers. For the sake of simplicity, we have adopted the method that is programmed into most pocket calculators. The only difference is that we will round answers to the second decimal place while most calculators round to the limits of the numerical display regardless of the number of decimal places appearing in the answer. The rounding rules are simple:

1. **If the digit in the third decimal place is less than 5, leave the digit in the second place** *unchanged;* **and**

2. **If the digit in the third decimal place is equal to or greater than 5,** *raise* **the digit in the second place by 1.**

These two rules will become clear as you follow through the calculations appearing in this book. Rounding has the advantage of making the arithmetical operations easier to comprehend, especially when the calculations are complex. In nearly all cases, rounding to the nearest hundredth will have no practical effect on our ultimate statistical decisions.

THE VARIANCE AS A MEASURE OF VARIABILITY

We have seen that one way to characterize a set of scores is to calculate the mean. This index of central tendency can then be used as a basis for compar-

---

[3] Technically, we should carry all substeps to three decimal places and round to two only in the last step. This has proved to be confusing to students in the past, and the precision afforded by such a procedure for our purposes is minimal. If you choose to be more precise and carry your calculations out further, you may find that your final answers differ from ours by 1–2 percent at the most.

ing different sets of scores. We will be making such comparisons when we begin to analyze experiments. A second way to characterize a set of scores is to determine the extent to which the scores differ from one another. As noted earlier, this characteristic is usually referred to as the variability of a set of scores, but other terms—for example, deviation, dispersion, spread, and scatter—are often used interchangeably. While not immediately apparent, these two characteristics—central tendency and variability—provide independent information about the nature of a set of scores.

Definition of the Variance

While several measures of variability exist, the variance is the most critical for the statistical analysis of experiments. The **variance** is essentially an average of the dispersion, or scatter, contributed by each of the scores in a set. The dispersion of each score is expressed as a **deviation from the mean.** The more widely scattered the scores in a set are, the larger these deviations will be.

Unfortunately, however, a straightforward average of these deviations will be of no use to us, since the sum of the deviations from the mean will be zero for any set of scores no matter how variable they may be. (We illustrated this property of the mean with the data in Table 2-1.) The solution to this problem is to remove the positive and negative signs associated with this index of dispersion by *squaring* each of the deviations *before* taking the average.[4] Thus,

> the variance is defined as an average of the squared deviations from the mean.

We will now consider the formulas with which the variance can be calculated.

Sum of Squares

The first step in obtaining the variance involves the calculation of the sum of the squared deviations from the mean, or the **sum of squares** (abbreviated as SS). Two formulas are commonly given for calculating SS. The formula

---

[4] The sum of the squared deviations do not cancel each other, since squaring eliminates the negative deviations. Moreover, the sum will be zero only when there is absolutely no variability, that is, when all the scores have the same value.

termed the **defining formula** will be presented first, since it preserves perfectly the verbal definition of the sum of squares. The other, the **computational formula,** is used for calculation, as it involves less computational effort and has a wider application in the analysis of experiments. The disadvantage of the computational formula is that it loses some of the intuitive meaning of the sum of squares.

Defining Formula. The defining formula can be written directly from the verbal definition of a sum of squares. Again, the sum of squares is defined in the following way:

$$SS = \text{the sum of the squared deviations} \atop \text{of all of the scores from the mean} \qquad (2\text{-}5)$$

Since we already have available symbols for the mean ($\overline{X}$) and for an individual score (X_i), we can let

$$X_i - \overline{X}$$

represent the deviation of any score from the mean. If we introduce the symbol for summation, Σ, we can write the following expression:

$$SS = \Sigma(X_i - \overline{X})^2 \quad .$$

Again, we can drop the unnecessary subscript and write the formula more simply as

$$SS = \Sigma(X - \overline{X})^2 \quad . \qquad (2\text{-}6)$$

Make sure that you can "read" this formula. The first symbol, Σ, means "take the sum of," and the expression that follows designates the squared deviation of an X score from the mean ($\overline{X}$). Combining these two expressions and reading from left to right, we have "the sum of squares equals the sum of the squared deviations from the mean."

As a numerical example, consider the set of scores in column 2 of Table 2-2. The calculations specified in equation (2-6) are enumerated step by step in the table. First, we need the mean. Substituting in equation (2-3), we find

$$\overline{X} = \frac{\Sigma X}{s}$$

$$= \frac{16 + 2 + 4 + 2 + 11}{5} = \frac{35}{5}$$

$$= 7.00 \quad .$$

Second, we subtract the mean from each score in order to obtain the required deviations. This step is made explicit with symbols in column 3 of

TABLE 2-2   The Steps in the Calculation of a Sum of Squares

Basic Observation		Deviation from the Mean ($\overline{X}$)		Squared Deviation from the Mean	
1. Symbol (X_i)	2. Score	3. Symbol ($X_i - \overline{X}$)	4. Deviation	5. Symbol ($X_i - \overline{X}$)^2	6. Squared Deviation
X_1	16	$X_1 - \overline{X}$	$16 - 7 = +9$	$(X_1 - \overline{X})^2$	$(+9)^2 = 81$
X_2	2	$X_2 - \overline{X}$	$2 - 7 = -5$	$(X_2 - \overline{X})^2$	$(-5)^2 = 25$
X_3	4	$X_3 - \overline{X}$	$4 - 7 = -3$	$(X_3 - \overline{X})^2$	$(-3)^2 = 9$
X_4	2	$X_4 - \overline{X}$	$2 - 7 = -5$	$(X_4 - \overline{X})^2$	$(-5)^2 = 25$
X_5	11	$X_5 - \overline{X}$	$11 - 7 = +4$	$(X_5 - \overline{X})^2$	$(+4)^2 = 16$

Table 2-2 and with numbers in column 4. You will note—as specified in equation (2-4)—that the sum of these deviations is zero, that is,

$$\Sigma(X - \overline{X}) = 9 - 5 - 3 - 5 + 4 = 0 \quad .$$

Third, each deviation is squared, as shown with symbols in column 5 and with numbers in column 6. Finally, all the squared deviations are summed. Substituting these squares in equation (2-6), we obtain

$$SS = \Sigma(X - \overline{X})^2$$
$$= 81 + 25 + 9 + 25 + 16 = 156 \quad .$$

Computational Formula. As we stated earlier, the defining formula is usually not used to calculate the sum of squares. Some computational steps in the defining formula can be quite tedious, especially when the mean is not a whole number as it was in our example. The computational formula, which we consider next, requires fewer steps and avoids this problem by dealing directly with the basic raw scores. In this form, the sum of squares is calculated by

$$SS = \Sigma(X)^2 - \frac{(\Sigma X)^2}{s} \quad . \tag{2-7}$$

With this formula, the raw scores are used to obtain two different sums:

1. The sum of the scores themselves, ΣX.

2. The sum of the *squares* of these scores, $\Sigma(X)^2$.

The latter quantity is new, and you should be certain that you understand completely what is involved. To be more explicit,

$$\Sigma(X)^2 = (X_1)^2 + (X_2)^2 + (X_3)^2 + \text{etc.}$$

TABLE 2-3   A Numerical Example of the
Computational Formula

Basic Score		Square of the Basic Score	
Symbol (X_i)	Score	Symbol $(X_i)^2$	(Score)^2
X_1	16	$(X_1)^2$	256
X_2	2	$(X_2)^2$	4
X_3	4	$(X_3)^2$	16
X_4	2	$(X_4)^2$	4
X_5	11	$(X_5)^2$	121

Each score is first squared and then the squares are summed. This operation is distinctly different from that specified in the numerator of the second term on the right side of equation (2-7), $(\Sigma X)^2$. This latter operation involves a squaring also, not of the individual scores, but of their sum, or total.

Students frequently confuse these two different calculations, and consequently they have difficulties in obtaining correct values for sums of squares. It is important that we not lose you at this point. You must understand sums of squares both conceptually and computationally. We make this emphatic pronouncement because sums of squares are calculated in nearly all of the statistical analyses we consider in this book. Thus, sums of squares are vital for your future health and welfare, both as a neophyte researcher and a struggling student.

The calculations themselves, specified in equation (2-7), are not complicated. They involve only the simple arithmetical operations of addition, subtraction, multiplication (in the form of squaring), and division. The one step that students identify as the most confusing is the translation of the abstract symbols in the computational formula into the concrete arithmetical manipulations of actual data. In fact, a relatively simple pattern lies behind the computational formulas of *all* sums of squares. However, we will not elucidate this pattern until Chapter 4, when it will be more evident than it would be now. At this point, we will describe—first with symbols and then with numbers—the calculation of the two quantities specified in equation (2-7) that are required to obtain the sum of squares.

We will use the data from Table 2-2 again as a numerical example to compare the defining and computational formulas. For convenience, the data are presented again on the left side of Table 2-3. On the right side of the table, each score is squared. We are now ready to use the basic scores and the square of these scores to obtain the sum of squares.

With reference to equation (2-7), we will calculate the two quantities on the right first and then subtract them as indicated to obtain the sum of squares. That is,

$$\Sigma (X)^2 = (X_1)^2 + (X_2)^2 + (X_3)^2 + (X_4)^2 + (X_5)^2$$

$$= (16)^2 + (2)^2 + (4)^2 + (2)^2 + (11)^2$$

$$= 256 + 4 + 16 + 4 + 121$$

$$= 401;$$

$$\frac{(\Sigma X)^2}{s} = \frac{(X_1 + X_2 + X_3 + X_4 + X_5)^2}{s}$$

$$= \frac{(16 + 2 + 4 + 2 + 11)^2}{5}$$

$$= \frac{(35)^2}{5} = \frac{1,225}{5}$$

$$= 245.00; \text{ and}$$

$$SS = \Sigma (X)^2 - \frac{(\Sigma X)^2}{s}$$

$$= 401 - 245.00$$

$$= 156.00 \quad.$$

Using the computational formula, we have calculated the same value we obtained using the defining formula in the preceding section.

The basic operations involved in the calculation of the sum of squares are at times tedious but are really relatively simple. These operations are repeated over and over in the analysis of simple as well as complex experiments. The calculation of ΣX and of $\Sigma (X)^2$, called "summing and squaring," is relatively easy when performed on a calculator designed for statistical use. With this type of calculator, one just enters the basic scores individually, presses the summation button, and both sums, the sum of scores and the sum of the squared scores, are cumulated automatically. The use of such a calculator, which is relatively inexpensive, greatly reduces the agony usually associated with statistical calculations. Even a simple (and less expensive) four-function calculator cuts calculation time considerably. Since the simpler calculator has no memory, the user has to supply the memory and perform the necessary operations in a series of three steps:

1. Sum the scores to obtain ΣX.

2. Square each score and record each result on a worksheet.

3. Sum these squares to obtain $\Sigma (X)^2$.

With a calculator that cumulates numbers in memory, you can eliminate the second step by entering each squared score into the memory store. When you have finished squaring all of the scores, a press of the memory-recall button will give you $\Sigma (X)^2$, the sum of the squared scores.

Variance

The variance is an average, just as the mean is an average. While the mean is calculated by dividing the sum of the scores by the number of scores, s, the variance is calculated by dividing the sum of squares (SS) by a slightly smaller number, the number of scores minus 1, that is, $s - 1$. In symbols,

$$\text{variance} = \frac{SS}{s - 1} \quad . \tag{2-8}$$

The divisor is called the **degrees of freedom** (abbreviated as df). Thus, the variance can be defined as

$$\text{variance} = \frac{SS}{df} \quad . \tag{2-9}$$

We will discuss the concept of degrees of freedom more fully in Chapter 4. For the time being, we ask you to accept this definition of variance and not to worry about why we divide the sum of squares by $s - 1$ rather than by the more "natural" s.[5]

We can illustrate the calculation of the variance using the data from Table 2-3. From the calculations summarized in the last section, we can substitute directly in equation (2-8), that is,

$$\text{variance} = \frac{SS}{s - 1}$$

$$= \frac{156.00}{5 - 1}$$

$$= \frac{156.00}{4} = 39.00 \quad .$$

---

[5] Situations exist in which it is appropriate to divide by the number of scores in calculating variance, but these are rarely found in psychological experimentation. These generally occur when one merely wants to describe the variability of a set of scores and has absolutely no interest in extending the findings to any larger group of individuals. In fact, there is a growing trend among applied statisticians to disregard this distinction and to use equation (2-9) to define the variance regardless of the ultimate use of the information. The only time we will use the alternative form of the variance is when we consider standard scores in Chapter 16.

Standard Deviation

The **standard deviation** is often reported instead of the variance. This statistical index is equal to the square root of the variance, that is,

$$\text{standard deviation} = \sqrt{\text{variance}} \quad . \qquad (2\text{-}10)$$

The primary advantage of using the standard deviation is that the variability of a set of scores is expressed in terms of the original units of measure. The variance requires that the basic deviation scores be squared, changing the units of measure to a squared quantity. "Unsquaring" the variance by taking the square root restores the measure to a form that is more easily understood and assimilated. We consider some useful applications of the standard deviation in Chapter 16.

SOME COMMENTS ON DATA DESCRIPTION

In our desire to move directly to statistical analysis and hypothesis testing, we may have created the impression that the only purpose of the mean and the variance is to serve these admittedly important functions. On the contrary, the primary role of descriptive statistics, of which the mean and the variance are parts, is describing "what happened" in an experiment. In addition to examining the means from the treatment conditions and testing hypotheses about differences among the means, researchers usually spend much time and effort looking at their data from a variety of different angles. They construct tables and graphs, examine distributions of individual scores, and conduct detailed analyses on additional response measures. If you could follow an experienced researcher through the analysis of an entire experiment, you would be amazed at the amount of information that can be extracted by someone who is experienced in working with data. It is difficult to convey the nature and extent of this activity in an abstract discussion. Thus, we can only encourage you to become exposed to concrete examples of experimentation in your studies. If the current course requires you to analyze data collected by you and your classmates, you will soon find that you are inundated with information. If you have the opportunity to conduct your own research, either as a final project in this course or as an independent study, your introduction to data analysis and research will be even more thorough.

In Chapter 7, we will consider some methods and procedures that may prove useful in describing a set of data. For the time being, however, we will continue with our primary goal by focusing on the statistical analysis of experiments.

SUMMARY

An experiment produces a large amount of "raw" data that, without being "refined" to some degree, will not convey quickly and accurately the findings of the experiment nor permit the statistical evaluation of the research hypotheses. In this chapter, we considered at some length two measures that abstract most of the information present in a set of scores, the mean (a measure of central tendency) and the variance (a measure of variability). Not only do these two measures provide a succinct description of a set of scores, but they permit the assessment of hypotheses formed about the possible outcome of an experiment.

The mean is defined as the sum of a set of scores divided by the number of scores in the set. The mean is a point at which the deviation of scores above the mean and the deviation of scores below the mean are perfectly balanced. The variance is defined as an average of the squares of these deviation scores. In the process of calculating the variance, we described the calculation of the sum of squares, a procedure employed often throughout this text.

TERMS, CONCEPTS, AND SYMBOLS

---

data reduction

statistical indices

central tendency

variability

mean

rounding

variance

deviation from the mean

sum of squares

defining formula

computational formula

degrees of freedom

standard deviation

X_i

ΣX

s

$\overline{X}$

$X - \overline{X}$

$\Sigma (X)^2$

$(\Sigma X)^2$

SS

df

EXERCISES

---

1. Calculate the means of the following three sets of scores.

A	B	C
3	10	6
5	12	10
2	9	4
8	15	16
1	8	2
5	12	10

   What is the relationship between the scores of columns A and B? Between columns A and C? What is the effect on the means?

2. Find the deviations from the mean for the three sets of scores in problem 1. Verify that the sum of each set of deviations is zero.

3. Calculate the sums of squares using the computational formula, equation (2-7), for the three sets of scores of problem 1. (Using the deviations from

problem 2, you can confirm for yourself that the sum of the squared deviations from the mean is equal to the sum of squares determined by the computational formula.)

4. Using the sums of squares from problem 3, calculate the three variances and standard deviations.

THE ANALYSIS OF SINGLE-FACTOR EXPERIMENTS

II

In this part, we present a detailed discussion of the analysis of experiments. We focus on designs in which a single independent variable (or factor) is manipulated in the experiment.

Chapter 3 is a general discussion of the logic governing the evaluation of research hypotheses. The principles of hypothesis testing covered in this chapter are applied throughout the book—wherever we assess the reliability of a set of results. At first, the logic of this procedure may seem strange, especially if you are unfamiliar with the topic. Thus, we have avoided introducing formulas and numbers in order to concentrate on the overall logic of the operations. We review this logic in later chapters, in the hope that repetition in the context of concrete examples will aid you in integrating the procedure into your general thinking about experimentation.

In Chapters 4 and 5, we concentrate on the statistical analysis of the most basic experimental design, a design in which one independent variable is manipulated and subjects are randomly assigned to the different treatment conditions. The analysis of this design will serve as a building block for the analysis of more complex—and more typical— experimental designs. Chapter 4 covers the formation of an index that reflects the presence of the effects of the different treatment manipulations, a process known as the analysis of variance. Chapter 5 discusses the methods for determining whether the observed differences among the treatment means can be reasonably attributed to the influence of the independent variable or to the operation of chance factors, which can never be completely eliminated from any experiment.

In Chapter 6, we concentrate on the analytical function of hypothesis testing. That is, in Chapters 4 and 5, we concern ourselves with detecting differences among the treatment conditions, but not with determining which treatments are responsible for the observed effects. The means by which differences among specific treatment conditions can be examined individually are covered in Chapter 6.

Chapter 7 presents several useful methods and techniques for describing the results of an experiment. This material is intended to supplement the descriptive information already provided by the mean and the variance (or standard deviation). Included in this chapter are methods for calculating alternative measures of central tendency and variability, constructing tables and graphs, tabulating frequency distributions, and estimating the magnitude or size of treatment effects. While these various techniques are not used in the analysis of every piece of research, they are frequently applied in a large number of research contexts.

In the final chapter of this section, Chapter 8, we consider two types of experimental designs that attempt to reduce the operation of chance factors. One of these designs accomplishes this goal through the use of subjects matched on characteristics assumed to be strongly related to performance on the dependent variable. The other type of design achieves this goal by using the same, rather than different, subjects in each of the treatment conditions. The second type of design is widely used in psychological experimentation, especially in its more complex forms. We examine in detail the way in which this important experimental design "works," because it is likely that you will actually choose this sort of design or some variant of it for a class project, an independent study, or an honors thesis.

The Logic of Hypothesis Testing

3

In Chapter 1, we called your attention to a number of details that must be considered in the design of an experiment. Underlying the whole process is the requirement that only the independent variable be permitted to vary systematically from treatment condition to treatment condition. Without elaboration, we simply asserted that this requirement was necessary to prevent a confounding of variables and did not discuss how this critical condition is in fact met. The present chapter deals with this problem, as well as with the general logic of hypothesis testing. The ideas, concepts, and arguments developed in this chapter are extremely important for an understanding of the statistical analyses covered in subsequent chapters. You may have to read this chapter several times before you feel comfortable with the topics covered, but this additional study will facilitate your mastery of the later material. The chapters that follow translate this relatively abstract discussion into the concrete arithmetical operations applied to the data generated by an experiment.

THE CONTROL OF POTENTIAL
SYSTEMATIC BIAS

In any experiment, many variables exert measurable effects on the dependent variable. In the simplest experiment, we single out one of these potential independent variables for manipulation and attempt to neutralize the systematic variation of all the others. Since in the context of the experiment we are not interested in these other variables, and must take steps to prevent them from damaging our results through systematic biasing, or confounding, they are often called **nuisance variables.** Although various ways of controlling nuisance variables exist, we will consider only two: control through holding a nuisance variable constant, and control through spreading the effect of the nuisance variable randomly over the treatment conditions.

Holding Nuisance Variables Constant

Common nuisance variables are background characteristics in the experimental situation—temperature, level of illumination, humidity, and the like. The experimenter can nullify the effects of these potential variables by holding them physically constant throughout the duration of the experiment, that is, by applying them equally to all the treatment conditions. Other factors, such as characteristics of the experimental task—for instance, the learning material, the rate at which the material is presented, the instructions read to the subject—can be easily maintained from condition to condition. In fact, no one would seriously entertain changing these features during the course of the study. Characteristics of subjects could be held constant by using subjects of the same sex, of the same intelligence level, from the same economic background, and so on.[1]

There is no question that holding potentially variable characteristics of the experiment at constant levels prevents the confounding of variables in an unambiguous and straightforward manner. Unfortunately, however, we are not able to "handle" all potential nuisance variables in this way. This happens because we find it difficult or impossible to control many nuisance variables during the course of an experiment and because we are usually not able even to identify all potential nuisance variables in order to hold them constant.

---

[1] Various forms of matching are discussed in Chapter 8, including a design in which "perfect" matching is achieved through the use of the same subject in all of the treatment conditions.

Neutralizing Nuisance Variables Through Randomization

Randomization is one of the most important concepts in experimentation. We will discuss first the advantages of randomizing subject variables.

Subject Variables. Suppose we want to study as a research project the running speed of rats under different degrees of food deprivation. We decide to form three treatment conditions consisting of low, medium, and high levels of food deprivation, and to test a total of fifteen rats, five in each of the treatment conditions. How can we assign the animals to the different groups to prevent confoundings with other variables—in this case subject variables? While many characteristics of rats would probably affect running speed, we will concentrate on one at first, namely, body weight. Unless the weight of the rats assigned to the different conditions is controlled in some manner, this factor could potentially confound the independent variable. That is, without some control, any differences in average running speed observed among the treatment groups are as likely to be due to differences in the weights of the rats assigned to the groups as to the differences in food deprivation.

What can be done about this serious problem? An obvious solution would be to employ some form of **matching** of the weights of the animals assigned to the different conditions, but for the purposes of extending this example to cover nonmeasurable nuisance variables, we will assume that we have no adequate way of determining an animal's weight before the start of the experiment. Thus, matching is out as a solution to this problem.

What if we assigned each rat *at random* to the treatment conditions? (By *random* we mean that each subject has an equal chance of being assigned to any one of the treatment conditions.) One thing can be said about this alternative: It is improbable that the groups will be perfectly matched by this method of assignment. The groups will still differ in the average weights of the rats assigned to them in a random manner. What sort of solution is this?

The miraculous answer is that randomization *is* the solution in most experimental designs! The differences in the average weights introduced by the random assignment of the rats to the three conditions are typically small, and—most important—these differences can be specified statistically to provide a *baseline* against which we can assess the effect of the independent variable. The method for establishing this baseline is discussed later in this chapter.

Note carefully that by assigning subjects at random to the treatment conditions we have used the "roulette wheel" of experimentation to spread the weight differences more or less equally among the treatment conditions. Once we have randomly assigned the subjects, we can introduce statistical procedures to assess the degree to which the average differences resulting from randomization can reasonably account for the observed differences in behavior.

So far we have only considered a single subject variable, weight. But subjects, even rats, vary in a number of ways, and at least some of these will affect the dependent variable, running speed. If we deal with each subject variable one by one, advancing the argument we offered for the weight variable, we can show that the random assignment of rats to the treatments will "guarantee" that any difference among the groups on each subject characteristic will still reflect only chance factors. Since random assignment of subjects to conditions "works" for all subject variables individually, a single random assignment should be sufficient to neutralize all the effects at the same time.

Other Variables. What about the influence of other types of nuisance variables—for example, time of day, temperature, and the like—that might possibly influence the behavior under study? Consider time of testing. It is known that the performance of rats changes during the course of the day (or night). We could control this factor by running our animals at only one time or by following a schedule that would balance all times of testing equally across the treatment conditions. As an alternative, we could make up a testing schedule based on the times convenient to us, assigning these times at random to the treatment conditions. (*Random* in this case refers to a method that gives each treatment an equal chance of being assigned to a particular time period.) Time of day would then exert only a random influence on the treatment conditions in our experiment. We could treat other factors in a similar manner in order to transform their influence into random or chance fluctuation as well. Let's see how all of this randomization can be accomplished in practice.

Randomization in an Experiment. In order to permit randomization to "work,"

it is necessary to subject *all* nuisance variables that are not controlled by other means to a process of random assignment to the treatment conditions.[2]

---

[2] Random assignment is also a theoretical necessity for the hypothesis testing to follow. Many experiments fail because this necessity is not strictly adhered to.

Random assignment is sometimes conducted in two stages, one for the randomization of subject nuisance variables and one for the randomization of other types of nuisance variables. First, subjects are assigned at random to the treatment conditions with the usual restriction that an equal number of subjects are to be placed in each of the conditions. According to the reasoning described in the preceding section, this step will "equate" the treatment conditions on all subject variables within a tolerance that can be specified statistically. Second, a testing schedule is constructed and the subjects—along with their assigned treatments—are assigned randomly to the days and times specified in the schedule. All factors associated with the different testing times are thus "spread" in a random fashion over the treatment conditions.

Methods of Randomization. Any procedure that will generate a series of events, usually numbers, in such a way that the events have equal chances of occurring at each point in the series can be used to randomize the influence of nuisance variables in an experiment. The most common way of introducing randomization into an experiment is through the use of **random number tables.** These tables consist of strings of single-digit numbers (1, 2, . . . , 9, and 0) usually produced by a computer programmed to generate strings of random numbers. A portion from a much larger random number table can be found in Table 1 of Appendix A. In order to use this table, we must number the subjects and code the treatments to be randomized numerically. We will consider several ways this can be done.

Suppose we want to assign a pool of twenty subjects known to us ahead of time—for example, students in a class, or animals in a breeding colony—to four treatment conditions. The only restriction is that an equal number of subjects (five) must be assigned to each treatment. One way to make the random assignments is to start with an arbitrary listing of the subjects first and to use the numbers 1–4 to stand for the four treatments, enter the random number table "blindly," and begin reading single-digit numbers in a left-to-right direction. (Actually, the table produces a random string of numbers in any direction.) As the critical digits, that is, the coded treatment conditions, appear in the table, we assign them to the subjects as they appear on the list. When we come to the end of a row of numbers, we scan the next row for the code numbers (up or down—either direction is acceptable). In order to meet the condition that an equal number of subjects be assigned to each condition, we eliminate a critical digit (that is, a condition) as soon as five subjects have been assigned to that condition.

Table 3-1 is an example of this method of randomization. Twenty subjects are listed by number from 1 to 20 on the far left of the table. The next column

TABLE 3-1   An Example of Random Assignment of Twenty Subjects to
Four Treatment Conditions

Subject	Random Assignment		Conditions	Code
S_1	1		Treatment 1	1
S_2	2		Treatment 2	2
S_3	1		Treatment 3	3
S_4	4		Treatment 4	4
S_5	1			
S_6	4			
S_7	2			
S_8	3		Subject Assignment to Treatments	
S_9	4			

Subject	Random Assignment	Treatment 1	Treatment 2	Treatment 3	Treatment 4
S_{10}	4	S_1	S_2	S_8	S_4
S_{11}	2	S_3	S_7	S_{15}	S_6
S_{12}	1	S_5	S_{11}	S_{16}	S_9
S_{13}	1	S_{12}	S_{17}	S_{19}	S_{10}
S_{14}	4	S_{13}	S_{18}	S_{20}	S_{14}
S_{15}	3				
S_{16}	3				
S_{17}	2				
S_{18}	2				
S_{19}	3				
S_{20}	3				

shows the order in which the numerically coded treatment conditions appeared in the table of random numbers. (The numerical code is indicated on the right side of the table.) That is, the first relevant number found in the random number table was 1 and was assigned to S_1; the second number was 2 and was assigned to S_2; the third number was 1 and was assigned to S_3; and so on. A summary of the subject assignments is presented at the bottom of the table on the right.

Next, to assign subjects to the time schedule, we code the subjects with two-digit numbers—for example, 01, 02, ..., 19, and 20. Then we enter the table of random numbers from a new starting point, and begin reading successive pairs of digits, searching for the subjects' code numbers. Subjects are assigned to the time schedule in the order in which they ''turn up'' in the sequence of random numbers. That is, the first subject so identified is tested first, the second subject is tested second, and so on.

What happens if we run out of random numbers? One obvious solution is to find more extensive tables. Most statistics and experimental psychology texts contain other tables, and books of random numbers, such as Moses and Oakford (1963), are also available. Another solution is to work out a number-coding system that allows us to use the table more efficiently, for example, by using more than one number to code the conditions or more than one pair of numbers to code the subjects.[3]

The procedure we have described is appropriate when we know who the subjects are *before* the start of the experiment. What if we do not know who the subjects will be until they show up individually in the laboratory? One solution is to assign the conditions an appropriate number code, enter the random number table, and list the conditions as they appear in the sequence of random numbers. This sequence of numbers, translated back to the treatments, becomes the assignment schedule. Subjects are assigned the treatments as they show up in the order specified by the treatment schedule. Since it is equally likely that each subject will be assigned to any one of the conditions, and since it is equally likely that each condition has been assigned a particular time in the testing schedule, all nuisance variables associated with subjects and with time of testing are neutralized through randomization.

Most researchers use a variant of this procedure called **block randomization.** With this method, the treatment schedule is arranged in blocks, with each block containing (usually) each treatment once. If we have four conditions and plan to test a total of twenty subjects, we would have *five* blocks, the first block containing a random ordering of the four conditions, the second block containing an independent random ordering of the four conditions, and so on. Table 3-2 is an example of block randomization of four treatment conditions and twenty subjects (five subjects per condition). Each random sequence (or random permutation) of the four treatments obtained from the table of random numbers makes up a separate block. Within a block, each treatment condition appears once. From the table you can see that the first subject tested in the experiment will be given treatment 3; the second subject will be given treatment 2; the third subject will be given treatment 1; and so on. A summary of the subject-treatment assignments is given on the right side of the table.

Notice the difference between the two procedures. With the first method, the number of subjects is balanced at the very *end* of the testing schedule,

---

[3] For example, in assigning the 4 conditions to the twenty subjects, we used the numbers 1, 2, 3, and 4 to code the conditions and disregarded the other digits (5, 6, 7, 8, 9, and 0). A more efficient use of the table would be to use *two* digits to represent each treatment, e.g., 1 and 2 for the first condition, 3 and 4 for the second condition, and so on. In assigning the twenty subjects to the testing schedule, we used only twenty two-digit numbers (the numbers 01 to 20) out of the one hundred different two-digit numbers in Table 1. A more efficient use of the table would be to represent each subject by *five* two-digit numbers rather than one. For example, the first subject could be represented by the numbers 01, 02, 03, 04, and 05; the second subject could be represented by the numbers 06, 07, 08, 09, and 10; and so on. Both examples increase the efficiency of any table of random numbers by increasing the number of digits or pairs of digits that stand for the entities to be randomized.

TABLE 3-2   An Example of Block Randomization of Four Treatments for Twenty Subjects

Blocks	Treatment Sequence	Subjects	Subject Assignment to Treatments			
			Treatment			
			1	2	3	4
Block 1	3	S_1	S_3	S_2	S_1	S_4
	2	S_2	S_7	S_8	S_6	S_5
	1	S_3	S_{10}	S_{12}	S_9	S_{11}
	4	S_4	S_{14}	S_{15}	S_{13}	S_{16}
			S_{17}	S_{20}	S_{19}	S_{18}
Block 2	4	S_5				
	3	S_6				
	1	S_7				
	2	S_8				
Block 3	3	S_9				
	1	S_{10}				
	4	S_{11}				
	2	S_{12}				
Block 4	3	S_{13}				
	1	S_{14}				
	2	S_{15}				
	4	S_{16}				
Block 5	1	S_{17}				
	4	S_{18}				
	3	S_{19}				
	2	S_{20}				

when the number of subjects must be the same in the four conditions. With block randomization, on the other hand, the number of subjects is balanced at the end of each block, not just at the end of the schedule of conditions.

There are good reasons for using block randomization. The nuisance variables we are trying to control often follow a cycle or a pattern. The fluctuation of temperatures during the day is an obvious example. Less obviously, the flow of subjects volunteering for an experiment may also follow some cycle. Subjects who volunteer early in the school term may be more anxious, more curious, or smarter than those who volunteer later—who knows? Block randomization capitalizes on the cyclic nature of certain nuisance variables and the fact that these variables will tend to have similar effects on the subjects appearing within a given block. Since each block usually contains one instance of each treatment condition, block randomization will also reduce the variation of nuisance variables from condition to condition and thus increase our chances that the randomization procedure will be successful.

Synopsis

Researchers create experiments by treating independent groups of subjects differently. A fundamental challenge to an investigator is conducting an experiment in such a way that only the independent variable is permitted to vary systematically from condition to condition. If this challenge is not met, the influence of the independent variable becomes entangled with the systematic variation of so-called nuisance variables, and discriminating the influence of one from that of the others is generally impossible. In some cases, the researcher controls nuisance variables by holding them constant for all subjects and thus eliminating completely their potential for systematic variation. In most cases, however, experimenters control nuisance variables by assigning subjects randomly to the different treatment conditions, transforming any potential systematic variation of nuisance variables into relatively "harmless" unsystematic, or random, variation. As we will see, this method is not without difficulties, but these problems can be solved through statistical means. In the next two sections, we consider the logic and rationale that underlie these helpful statistical procedures.

AN INDEX OF THE TREATMENT EFFECTS

In principle, you are now ready to design and conduct an experiment. All you would have to do is propose a research hypothesis, translate it into a set of manipulations, select a dependent variable, locate some subjects, minimize the influence of nuisance variables either by holding them constant during the experiment or by spreading their composite effects randomly over the treatment conditions, and, finally, collect the data. After arranging the data in a convenient form for calculations, you would obtain the means of the treatment conditions and ponder their implications. In doing so, you would ask yourself a number of questions: Did the differences among the means turn out as you predicted? Did any interesting differences appear that you did not predict? How will you integrate these new findings with the findings of others? What experiments are necessary for resolving the new questions raised by the data? Experimenters are exhilarated rather than disturbed by such questions; it is only natural to be excited and stimulated by the results of a new experiment. So much time elapses between the moment an experiment is conceived and that in which the final piece of data is collected that the question "What now?" is one to be savored.

    Once you had calculated the means of the treatment conditions, doubts would begin to surface. How would you determine whether the differences you observed were produced by the differences in the independent variable? Presumably, you would have avoided all serious confoundings of relevant variables and neutralized the effects of nuisance variables through appropriate randomization procedures. Wouldn't these precautions guarantee that the differences on your summary sheet reflected the effects of your independent variable and that variable alone?

Unfortunately, the answer is no. Chance factors are present in every experiment. It is *always* possible that the differences observed among the treatment means are due entirely to the influence of these chance factors and not to the differential effects of the treatment conditions. Said another way, the outcome of any experiment can always be due to the operation of chance factors alone; differences that seem to be the result of differences in treatments may actually be reflecting the fact that randomization never results in the complete elimination of nuisance variables.

To ascertain that the results of an experiment are not attributable to chance, we need an index that reflects the effects of the treatments relative to the effects that could reasonably be due to chance. Consider the kinds of information an experiment makes available. First, we have the differences among the treatment means. Using procedures that will be outlined in the next chapter, we can express these differences in terms of a measure of variability. This **treatment-group variability,** the variability among the treatment means, reflects the operation of two factors:

1. The effect of the differential treatments.

2. The effect of chance factors.

We will refer to the first source of variability as the **treatment effects** and the second source of variability as **experimental error.**[4] Thus,

$$\text{treatment-group variability} = \\ (\text{treatment effects}) + (\text{experimental error}) \quad .$$

Next, consider another source of variability obtainable from an experiment. We have concentrated, for obvious reasons, on the differences among

---

[4] Experimental error consists of all uncontrolled sources of variability in an experiment. As we have already indicated, individual differences represent the most important source of experimental error. Variations in the various features of the testing environment represent a second source. Another source of experimental error is measurement error—the misreading of a dial, a misjudgment that a particular behavior occurred, an error in recording a response, and so on. A final source of experimental error is the variability with which the experimental treatments are administered. Any given treatment cannot be administered identically to all subjects in that condition. The apparatus might move in and out of adjustment, an experimenter will inevitably read instructions differently each time, experimenter-subject interactions will be different with different subjects, and so on.

the treatment means. *But* the scores of the subjects who supply the individual data points for each treatment group also differ. Since all subjects within any given treatment group have been given the same treatment condition, they can vary only as a result of the same chance factors that are at least partially responsible for the treatment-group variability. That is, they will vary because of the differences—in ability, motivation, time of testing, and temperature—that were partially neutralized in the random assignment of the subjects to the treatment conditions. Thus, a measure of variability that takes into consideration the *variation of subjects treated alike*—the **within-group variability**—will provide an estimate of the residual effect of the randomized nuisance factors, or experimental error. That is,

$$\text{within-group variability} = \text{experimental error} \quad .$$

By taking advantage of these two measures of variability, which focus on different aspects of the same data—differences among the treatment means in one case and differences among subjects treated alike in the other case—we can form a useful index of the treatment effect, namely,

$$\text{Treatment Index} = \frac{\text{treatment-group variability}}{\text{within-group variability}} \quad . \qquad (3\text{-}1)$$

In subsequent chapters, we will refer to the **Treatment Index** as the *F* **ratio.**[5]

Considering the sources that influence the numerator and denominator terms of equation (3-1), we can see that the Treatment Index is responsive to the presence or absence of treatment effects. More specifically, if our treatments were completely ineffective, producing the same effects for all treatment groups, the ratio would consist of one estimate of experimental error (based on the variability among the treatment means) divided by another estimate of experimental error (based on the variability of subjects treated alike). Under these circumstances, the ratio would become

$$\frac{\text{experimental error}}{\text{experimental error}} \quad ,$$

and would be approximately equal to 1.0. If our treatments actually produced differential effects, the ratio would consist of

$$\frac{(\text{treatment effects}) + (\text{experimental error})}{\text{experimental error}} \quad ,$$

and would have a value *greater* than 1.0.

---

[5] Some authors define the Treatment Index as a ratio of systematic variability, reflecting in part any systematic effects of the different treatment conditions, to nonsystematic, or error, variability, reflecting the operation of unaccounted for or randomly varying nuisance variables.

Summary. The Treatment Index consists of a ratio of treatment-group variability relative to within-group variability. The former is based on the differences among the treatment means, and the latter is based on the variability of subjects treated alike. As we have seen, the Treatment Index provides a numerical index that is sensitive to the existence of treatment effects. More specifically, the index approximates 1.0 when treatment effects are completely absent and is greater than 1.0 when they are present. This index provides the baseline for chance effects (1.0) against which observed differences among treatment means can be compared. In the next section, we discuss the use of the Treatment Index in testing hypotheses concerning the outcome of an experiment.

HYPOTHESIS TESTING

Having introduced the Treatment Index, which reflects the presence or absence of effects of experimental treatments, we can turn to the actual **testing of hypotheses.** We begin by describing the statistical hypotheses to be tested, then go on to evaluate these hypotheses, and finally consider the construction of the relatively arbitrary rules by which a hypothesis can or cannot be rejected.

Statistical Hypotheses

The heart of any experiment is the research hypothesis. This construct represents the rationale of an experiment and specifies the kinds of information required to support the hypothesis. To evaluate a research hypothesis *statistically,* however, the researcher forms a set of **statistical hypotheses.** For reasons embedded in statistical theory, the statistical hypotheses are the ones that are assessed and evaluated in the actual statistical analysis. While the distinction between research and statistical hypotheses may not be clear at this point, be assured that the decision to reject or not to reject a statistical hypothesis has direct relevance for the status of the research hypothesis.

Statistical hypotheses as applied to any given experiment refer to the hypothetical outcome of the experiment were it administered to an infinitely large number of individuals. (This would never happen, of course, but the situation represents the sort of hypothetical conditions within which statistical theory must operate.) Let's assume that each of these individuals is randomly assigned to one of the treatment conditions. The set of scores obtained from subjects receiving the same treatment is called a **treatment population.** There is a different treatment population for each condition of the experiment. The mean of a treatment population is called a **population treatment mean** and is designated by the Greek letter μ (pronounced *mu*). A subscript is usually added so that we can designate a particular treatment condition. Thus, μ_1 is the population mean for treatment 1, μ_2 is the population mean for treatment 2, and so on. The symbol μ_i is used to represent any one of the population treatment means.

The differences among the population treatment means—the effects of the independent variable observed in these hypothetical treatment populations— are called the **population treatment effects.** Statistical hypotheses are thus statements concerning the hypothetical state of affairs in the treatment populations. For statistical purposes,

> **an experiment is assumed to consist of samples drawn** *randomly* **from the treatment populations.**

Viewed in this way, the experiment we actually conduct is used to obtain some idea of what the population treatment means are. We must say again that the concept of treatment populations and the differences among the population treatment means are based on statistical theory, and not a situation we will ever observe or measure. We can still think about the possibility and consider the implications of conceiving of an experiment as consisting of random samples drawn from different treatment populations.

We use the outcome of an actual experiment to tell us which characterization of the population, as specified by the statistical hypotheses, is the most reasonable. Though it may not be immediately obvious, our primary interest as experimenters is the nature of the population treatment effects. To elaborate, we generally wish to extend our results beyond a single experiment and to state that a particular outcome exists in the population, that is, that the effect will be obtained if the experiment is repeated once or many times. Because of the random variation of nuisance variables, our experimental results will reflect an imperfect picture of the population treatment means. For this reason, our inferences about the population will be subject to some degree of uncertainty and our conclusions concerning the population will be tentative and expressed in terms of probability.

Two statistical hypotheses are involved in the decision-making process called hypothesis testing. Taken together, they encompass all possible arrangements of the population treatment means. One of these hypotheses is called the **null hypothesis,** and it specifies only *one* of the possible arrangements, namely, the case when the population means are *equal*. (Obviously, there is only one way this can happen since the means are identical!) The null hypothesis specifies the *complete absence* of differences among the treatment means, that is, the absence of treatment effects. The null hypothesis is usually designated as H_0, H for hypothesis and 0 for null, and is stated in symbols as

$$H_0: \mu_1 = \mu_2 = \mu_3 = \mu_i \quad , \tag{3-2}$$

or more simply as

$$H_0: \text{All } \mu_i\text{'s are equal.} \tag{3-2a}$$

The other statistical hypothesis, referred to as the **alternative hypothesis** and designated as H_1, specifies all the remaining ways that the population treatment means might be arranged. In symbols, the alternative hypothesis is represented as

$$H_1: \text{Not all } \mu_i\text{'s are equal.} \tag{3-3}$$

This statement encompasses an extremely large number of possibilities, namely, all the possible ways a set of population treatment means can differ. Somewhere among these various possibilities we will find our research hypothesis, but at least it is included in the alternative hypothesis! (In Chapter 6, we discuss the ways in which the field of alternative hypotheses can be narrowed drastically so the investigator can focus more directly on the specific analytical questions originally posed for the study.)

Evaluation of the Null Hypothesis

Though ultimately our interest lies in the status of the alternative hypothesis, in this section we concentrate on the evaluation of the null hypothesis, since our decision concerning the null hypothesis has direct implication for the alternative hypothesis. The reason for this interconnectedness is that we have placed all possible outcomes into one or the other of two categories, the null category and the alternative category, the latter of which contains our research hypothesis. In order to gain support for our research hypothesis, therefore, we must *reject the null hypothesis*, thereby concluding that the alternative hypothesis reflects the state of affairs among the population treatment means. What follows is a general overview of the way in which the null hypothesis is evaluated.

Refer back to equation (3-1) and the so-called Treatment Index. You will recall that this index becomes approximately 1.0 when treatment effects are completely absent in the population. This value is obtained because the measures of treatment-group variability and of within-group variability both reflect the operation of experimental error, and

$$\frac{\text{treatment-group variability}}{\text{within-group variability}} = \frac{\text{experimental error}}{\text{experimental error}} = 1.0 \quad .$$

You will also recall that the null hypothesis specifies the *absence* of treatment effects. Thus, if the null hypothesis is true, the Treatment Index should be approximately 1.0. Consider what happens to the Treatment Index when the null hypothesis is false, and thus treatment differences exist in the population. Under these circumstances, the Treatment Index will be greater than 1.0, since the numerator term is affected by two factors, while the denominator term is affected by only one of these factors, that is,

$$\frac{\text{treatment-group variability}}{\text{within-group variability}} = \frac{(\text{treatment effect}) + (\text{experimental error})}{(\text{experimental error})} \quad .$$

Superficially, our course of action now seems obvious: to reject the null hypothesis whenever the Treatment Index is greater than 1.0, since the ratio will exceed this value only when treatment effects are present. Unfortunately, however, deciding which hypothesis is supported is not so simple. Evaluating the null hypothesis—that is, deciding whether it should be rejected or not—is much more complicated than determining whether the value of the Treatment Index is greater than 1.0.

The complication lies in the nature of the two estimates of experimental error. While both are estimates of the same theoretical quantity, experimental error, they are based on independent information derived from the same experiment. More specifically, one estimate is obtained from the variability among the *means* of the treatment groups and the other is obtained from the *scores* of subjects treated alike. Because of the chance factors operating in any experiment—stemming primarily from the random assignment of subjects to the treatment conditions—these two estimates will rarely be identical; rather, the numerator estimate will be larger approximately half of the time and smaller the other half of the time. Consequently, we cannot expect to be able to reject the null hypothesis whenever the Treatment Index is greater than 1.0, that is, when the numerator is larger than the denominator.

The solution to this difficulty is to determine the frequencies with which different values of the Treatment Index are expected to occur by chance and to base our decision to reject or not to reject on this information. Luckily, a great deal is known about the Treatment Index and how it varies in size when the null hypothesis is true. In general, as the Treatment Index increases beyond 1.0, the frequency with which larger values occur by chance decreases rather drastically. That is, **the larger the value of the Treatment Index, the smaller is the likelihood that it will in fact have occurred by chance** (and increasingly likely that a treatment effect is actually present).

What sort of evidence would prompt us to reject the null hypothesis? How large and how rare must the Treatment Index be before we feel confident in concluding that the null hypothesis is probably wrong? In principle, each researcher must make this decision individually. In practice, however, most researchers in psychology agree that a frequency of 5 times out of 100—that is, a probability of $5/100 = .05$—is a reasonable cut-off point. Thus, whenever the Treatment Index exceeds a critical value, which, theory tells us, will occur by chance only 5 percent of the time, we will consider such evidence to be incompatible with the null hypothesis. By rejecting the null hypothesis, we conclude in effect that the alternative hypothesis represents a more accurate description of the hypothetical population.

Decision Rules in Hypothesis Testing

The actions to be taken by an experimenter can be summarized as a set of **decision rules**—unambiguous statements, prepared before the experiment is begun by the researcher—that indicate under exactly what circumstances the null hypothesis will be rejected and under what circumstances it will not. The general form of the decision rules can be stated as follows:

> **If the Treatment Index equals or exceeds a value of _____, reject the null hypothesis; otherwise, do not reject the null hypothesis.**

In Chapter 5, we explain how this critical value of the Treatment Index is obtained. At this point, it is sufficient to say that the value in question is the value of the Treatment Index that will be exceeded only 5 percent of the time when the null hypothesis is true.

Once the decision rules have been written, the actions that follow are mechanical: calculation of the value of the Treatment Index and following the procedures outlined by the decision rules. With the latter step accomplished, the statistical operations involved in testing a research hypothesis are concluded, but there remains the important process of assimilating the findings into the body of literature relevant to the topic under investigation. For a researcher, the phase in which the results are interpreted—which occurs after the statistical procedures are completed—is the most critical; all the preceding operations are merely necessary steps in the entire analytical process of experimentation. In this sense, experimental design and statistical analysis are the analytical tools the researcher uses to establish new facts, evaluate (that is, support, reject, or revise) old theories, and create new ones.

Synopsis

To ensure that you understand the logic of the analytical process of experimentation, we pause in our discussion to summarize the steps:

1. A research hypothesis is generated as a deduction from theory or from an interesting idea or speculation.

2. Treatment conditions (the independent variable) and a response measure (the dependent variable) are chosen to provide a test of the research hypothesis.

3. An experiment is designed to demonstrate that a relationship exists (or doesn't exist) between the independent variable and the dependent variable.

4. The null and alternative hypotheses are formulated.

5. Decision rules are stated that specify exactly the circumstances under which the null hypothesis will or will not be rejected.

6. The experiment is conducted, and the Treatment Index is calculated.

7. If the obtained value of the Treatment Index exceeds the critical value specified by the decision rules, the null hypothesis is rejected, and the investigator concludes that treatment effects are present.

8. If the obtained value of the Treatment Index is smaller than the critical value, the null hypothesis is not rejected.

An Additional Comment

In this chapter, we have presented the basic steps involved in the statistical evaluation of the outcome of an experiment. Purposely, we have not introduced formulas, numbers, and numerical examples—these will come in the chapters that follow. Our point was to describe hypothesis testing in purely verbal terms in order to explain carefully the logic behind the process. Students tell us that this is not an easy chapter to assimilate—that the concepts are new and the logic underlying hypothesis testing is strange if not ''twisted.'' Many find that they do not fully comprehend the process until they are exposed to specific mathematical operations and concrete numerical examples. However, we feel that hypothesis testing should be understood on both the abstract and the concrete levels. There is a value to the abstract approach taken in this chapter in that you are forced to concentrate on the logic and are not distracted by the manipulation of numbers. The logic outlined in this chapter is general and applies throughout the book in a variety of experimental contexts and in other statistical procedures.

SUMMARY

The first step in testing a research hypothesis is to design an experiment in which the influence of known and of unknown variables is minimized. If uncontrolled, such variables could result in a systematic bias, that is, a confounding with the independent variable. While it is possible to control nuisance variables by holding them constant, the most common procedure is to spread their effects randomly over all the treatment conditions.

Due to the use of randomization to control the operation of nuisance variables, which is nearly unavoidable in experimentation, any differences observed among the treatment means are influenced to some extent by chance factors. The experimenter must decide whether the differences associated with the treatment conditions are entirely or just partially due to chance. As a first step in solving this problem, the experimenter determines the value of the Treatment Index, which will serve as a baseline against which to evaluate the presence or absence of treatment effects. The investigator calculates the Treatment Index by dividing an estimate of the variability among the treatment means, which is assumed to reflect the operation of potential treatment effects and experimental error, by an estimate of the variability of subjects given the same treatment condition, which is assumed to reflect the operation of experimental error alone. When treatment effects are present, the Treatment Index should be greater than 1.0; when they are not, the Treatment Index should be approximately equal to 1.0.

Next we considered in some detail the formulation of two statistical hypotheses, the null hypothesis, which states that the population treatment means are equal, and the alternative hypothesis, which states that not all of the means are equal. The experimenter tests the adequacy of the null hypothesis by applying a set of decision rules that specifies the circumstances under which the null hypothesis will be rejected—and the alternative hypothesis accepted—and the circumstances under which it will not be rejected. These rules give a critical value of the Treatment Index that divides all possible experimental outcomes into two categories, or regions, one in which they are reasonably likely to have occurred by chance and one in which they are likely to have been caused by the treatment differences. If the value of the Treatment Index exceeds the critical value assigned to it in the decision rule, the null hypothesis is rejected and the alternative hypothesis is accepted. Under these circumstances, the experimenter concludes that treatment effects are present. On the other hand, if the index is less than the critical value, the null hypothesis is not rejected. In the latter case, the experimenter is left with differences that are best interpreted in terms of chance factors.

TERMS, CONCEPTS, AND SYMBOLS

nuisance variable	F ratio	μ
randomization	hypothesis testing	μ_i
matching	statistical hypotheses	H_0
random number table	treatment population	H_1
block randomization	population treatment mean	
treatment-group variability	population treatment effects	
treatment effects	null hypothesis	
experimental error	alternative hypothesis	
within-group variability	decision rules	
Treatment Index		

The Calculation of the *F* Ratio

4

We are now ready to consider the statistical analysis of the simplest experimental design, in which a single independent variable is administered to groups of subjects who have been randomly assigned to the treatment conditions. It is common to refer to a single independent variable as factor A and to call this sort of arrangement a **completely randomized, single-factor design.** Our goal is to determine from an experiment a value for the Treatment Index and to compare the magnitude of this quantity against the results that might reasonably be expected to occur by chance if the null hypothesis were true. The calculation of the Treatment Index and the process of comparison are referred to together as the **analysis of variance.** The analysis of variance is an apt name since the procedure compares measures of variability (variances) that are adapted to our needs in hypothesis testing.

We use two chapters to cover the analysis of variance. In this chapter, we develop the procedures needed to calculate the Treatment Index, which

59

from this point on we call by its technical name, the **F ratio.**[1] In Chapter 5, we cover the statistical evaluation of the null hypothesis.

Taken together, these two chapters cover the basic operations we described more generally in Chapter 3. As we noted, an understanding of these procedures is critical in any discussion of the design and analysis of experiments. Keep in mind that the material covered in these two chapters will be applied repeatedly in other data analyses.

We suggest that in your approach to this critical material you read Chapters 4 and 5 over quickly first in order to establish an overall frame of reference. Try not to get too involved with specific points on this first reading; save this kind of attention for your more careful second reading of the material.

PARTITIONING THE TOTAL SUM OF SQUARES

In this section, we examine the very heart of the analysis of variance, the process by which different sources of variation are identified and isolated for use in hypothesis testing. The idea is fundamental to an understanding of the analysis of experimental data. Briefly, we calculate two sums of squares, one that reflects treatment effects and experimental error and one that reflects the operation of experimental error alone. The isolation of these sources of variability is most easily seen in the single-factor design, although the same basic logic underlies the analysis of the more complicated experimental designs considered in later chapters.

The Basic Design

A representation of the completely randomized, single-factor design is presented in Figure 4-1. Each column represents one treatment condition—the **levels** of factor *A*—and each cell within each given column represents one of the subjects randomly assigned to that treatment condition. A lower-case *a* is used to designate the number of treatment levels in an experiment, and a lower-case *s* is used to designate the number of subjects assigned randomly to each treatment level. (We are assuming that an equal number of subjects—also known as the **sample size**—appears in each treatment condi-

---

[1] The *F* ratio is named after Sir Ronald A. Fisher, who developed the analysis of variance.

Treatment Conditions
(Factor A)

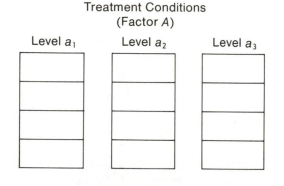

Figure 4-1. A Representation of the Completely Randomized Single-Factor Design. Each cell represents one subject. In this design, there are twelve subjects; four are assigned randomly to each of the three treatment conditions.

tion.[2]) In the example in Figure 4-1, $a = 3$ treatment conditions, and $s = 4$ subjects per condition. A subscript is used with the a to designate a particular treatment level: a_1 refers to the treatment associated with the first-listed condition, a_2 to the second, and so on. If we want to refer to any one of the levels without being specific, we will use the letter i as the subscript; thus, level a_i refers to any one of the three treatment conditions in this example.

Some Additional Notation

Consider the nature of the data to be analyzed on completion of an experiment. Since the specific treatments will have been administered in a random fashion to the subjects, the first step will be to rearrange the scores so that we can begin to make sense of them. The simplest and most obvious method is to segregate the scores according to the different treatment conditions and to arrange them in columns for subsequent calculations. These calculations will involve the computation of means for each of the treatment conditions and of various measures of variability to be used in constructing the F ratio.

---

[2] Although equal sample size is not a requirement in the single-factor design, experiments are usually designed this way. The use of equal sample sizes gives equal weighting (that is, attention) to the treatment means in the statistical analysis, a condition that makes the most sense in experimentation. We can compensate for unequal sample sizes in various ways, but it is best to design experiments with equal sample sizes.

To summarize the calculations necessary to perform the analysis of variance, we need symbols of some kind that designate clearly and unambiguously the arithmetical operations to be performed and the quantities on which they will be performed. If we were presenting the analysis in person, we could show you the necessary calculations by pointing to individual numbers or sets of numbers from an experiment and indicating what you should do with them. Since we must provide this instruction at a more abstract level, however, we must use words and symbols to make the operations explicit.

Any notational system is essentially a code. The symbols constitute a shorthand for specifying the operations to be performed on the data of an experiment. The notational system we use for the analysis of variance is different from the one we introduced in Chapter 2. While we could expand on that particular system to deal with our present and future needs, we consider it more confusing than the system we are about to present.[3] As you will see, this new system uses different capital letters to stand for the quantities required for the analysis. In the analysis of the single-factor design, we need to designate *three* basic quantities: the grand sum of the scores, or observations, the subtotals for each treatment condition, and the individual scores. We will consider each of these in turn.

The Grand Sum. We designate the **grand sum** of the scores—that is, the sum of all of the scores in the experiment—as T. Thus,

$$T = \text{the total sum of the scores}\quad.$$

When we translate this sum into a mean (the **grand mean**), the mean is designated as $\bar{T}$. We calculate $\bar{T}$ as we would any arithmetic mean, by dividing the sum of the scores by the number of scores. Since there are s scores in each of the a treatment groups, the total number of scores is $a \times s$, or $a(s)$, and

$$\bar{T} = \frac{T}{a(s)}\quad. \tag{4-1}$$

The Treatment Sums. Second, it is necessary to calculate the sums for each of the treatment groups, or the **treatment sums.** We use A to designate a treatment sum. That is,

$$A = \text{the sum of the scores in a treatment condition}\quad.$$

[3] This specialized notational system may be difficult to follow if you have been exposed to analysis of variance in another course or book in which standard notation was employed. If such is your background, we urge you to examine Glossary 2 at the end of the book.

A minor problem arises here in that there are several treatment sums in an experiment, and we need to distinguish among them. (We did not have this problem with the grand total, T, since by definition there is only one such quantity.) A simple solution is to use a numerical subscript to indicate the particular treatment condition we wish to specify. Thus, A_1 is the treatment sum for level a_1; A_2 is the treatment sum for level a_2; and so on. To designate a treatment sum without specifying any sum in particular, we use A without a subscript, or occasionally with an i as subscript, A_i. Both constructions refer to a nonspecified treatment sum.

To obtain a numerical summary of the outcome of the experiment, we use the treatment sums to calculate the **treatment means.** We obtain the treatment means, $\overline{A}$, by dividing each treatment sum by s, the number of subjects in each of the conditions. That is,

$$\overline{A} = \frac{A}{s} \quad . \tag{4-2}$$

To refer to specific treatment means, we use the number subscript. For example, the mean for level a_1 is

$$\overline{A_1} = \frac{A_1}{s} \quad ;$$

the mean for level a_2 is

$$\overline{A_2} = \frac{A_2}{s} \quad ;$$

and so on.

The Basic Observations. Finally, we designate the individual scores—the **basic observations**—on which the treatment sums and the grand sum are based with the special two-letter symbol AS, to emphasize the fact that each score represents a particular subject (the S portion) who receives a particular treatment (the A portion). Note that the two capital letters do *not* specify multiplication. They are merely a symbol, or descriptive label, used to represent a subject's score. To specify a particular subject in a particular condition, we use numerical subscripts just as we did with the treatment sums and the treatment means. In this case, however, two subscripts are required, one to indicate the treatment condition and the other to indicate the particular subject within that treatment condition. Thus, AS_{12} refers to the second subject listed under treatment level a_1, and AS_{21} refers to the first subject listed under treatment level a_2. Clearly, the order of the subscripts is important, the first subscript referring to the treatment condition and the second to

TABLE 4-1 A Summary of the Notational System

Value Being Designated	Factor A		
	a_1	a_2	a_3
Basic Observations	AS_{11} AS_{12} AS_{13} AS_{14}	AS_{21} AS_{22} AS_{23} AS_{24}	AS_{31} AS_{32} AS_{33} AS_{34}
1. Sums	A_1 +	A_2 +	A_3 = T
2. Number of Subjects	s +	s +	s = $a(s)$
3. Means	$\bar{A}_1 = \dfrac{A_1}{s}$	$\bar{A}_2 = \dfrac{A_2}{s}$	$\bar{A}_3 = \dfrac{A_3}{s}$ $\quad \bar{T} = \dfrac{T}{a(s)}$

the subject. The order of these subscripts, treatment first and subject second, is identical to the order of the two capital letters AS. To refer to a score without specifying any particular one, we use the two letters without a subscript, AS, or occasionally with letters as subscripts, AS_{ij}.[4]

Summary. The notational system is summarized in Table 4-1 using the experimental design in Figure 4-1 as an example. Four AS scores are listed for each of the three treatment conditions. The numerical subscripts identify each score explicitly. For example, for all the AS scores at level a_1, the first subscript is 1, indicating membership in that particular treatment group, but the second subscript is another number, indicating its place—first, second, third, or fourth—in the column of scores. Thus, each score is specified individually. The scores listed in the other two columns follow the same pattern, the first subscript designating treatment membership and the second

---

[4] Initially, you may find it helpful to separate the two subscripts, placing them next to the appropriate capital letter—for example, A_1S_2 and A_2S_1—until you feel comfortable with the notation. Alternatively, some students report that using a comma between the two subscripts is helpful at the beginning, as in $AS_{1,2}$ and $AS_{2,1}$. We introduce a comma between the two subscripts whenever one subscript takes on a value greater than 9, as occurs in Table 4-2. Thus, for example, the tenth subject in the second treatment group is denoted $AS_{2,10}$ rather than AS_{210} to indicate unambiguously which part of the subscript refers to the level of factor A and which refers to a particular subject. We also use a comma to ensure that the subscripts are clearly identifiable, as in Figure 4-2 and in the text accompanying the figure. Usually, however, the comma is not needed.

subscript designating serial position in the column listing. This arrangement of the scores is called the *AS* **matrix.**

We sum each set of scores to obtain the treatment totals (*A*). As you can see by examining row 1 in the lower portion of the table,

$$A_1 = \text{the sum of the scores at level } a_1$$

$$A_2 = \text{the sum of the scores at level } a_2$$

$$A_3 = \text{the sum of the scores at level } a_3$$

Row 3 specifies the corresponding treatment means, which we obtain by dividing each treatment sum by the number of scores (*s*).

Finally, we obtain the grand sum, or total, (*T*) either by summing all the individual scores in the *AS* matrix or, as indicated in row 1 of the table, by summing the three treatment totals. We find the grand mean by dividing the grand sum by the total number of scores in the experiment, *a*(*s*).

Basic Deviations

The data in Table 4-2 are from a hypothetical experiment. There are $s = 10$ subjects in each of the $a = 2$ treatment conditions. Below these scores are listed the treatment sums, the treatment means, the grand sum, and the grand mean. The steps in calculating these quantities are as follows:

$$A_1 = 5 + 3 + 4 + 4 + 6 + 1 + 3 + 4 + 6 + 4 = 40 \quad ;$$

$$A_2 = 13 + 9 + 10 + 8 + 9 + 12 + 8 + 12 + 10 + 9 = 100 \quad ;$$

$$\overline{A}_1 = \frac{A_1}{s} = \frac{40}{10} = 4.00 \quad ;$$

$$\overline{A}_2 = \frac{A_2}{s} = \frac{100}{10} = 10.00 \quad ;$$

$$T = A_1 + A_2 = 40 + 100 = 140; \quad \text{and}$$

$$\overline{T} = \frac{T}{a(s)} = \frac{140}{2(10)} = \frac{140}{20} = 7.00 \quad .$$

At this point, we can chart the two sets of data in a systematic manner.[5] Suppose we use a small square to represent each score, using squares with solid lines for scores from treatment level a_1 and squares with dashed lines for scores from treatment level a_2. We can arrange each square on a number

---

[5] This display is an example of a frequency distribution. The formal construction and use of frequency distributions is covered in Chapter 7.

TABLE 4-2   Basic Data from a Hypothetical Experiment

a_1	a_2
$AS_{11} = 5$ $AS_{12} = 3$ $AS_{13} = 4$ $AS_{14} = 4$ $AS_{15} = 6$ $AS_{16} = 1$ $AS_{17} = 3$ $AS_{18} = 4$ $AS_{19} = 6$ $AS_{1,10} = 4$	$AS_{21} = 13$ $AS_{22} = 9$ $AS_{23} = 10$ $AS_{24} = 8$ $AS_{25} = 9$ $AS_{26} = 12$ $AS_{27} = 8$ $AS_{28} = 12$ $AS_{29} = 10$ $AS_{2,10} = 9$
Treatment Sum $(A_1) = 40$	Treatment Sum $(A_2) = 100$
$s = 10$	$s = 10$
Mean $(\bar{A}_1) = 4.00$	Mean $(\bar{A}_2) = 10.00$
Grand Sum $(T) = A_1 + A_2 = 140$	
Grand Mean $(\bar{T}) = 7.00$	

line (called the baseline) according to the value of each score on the dependent variable. For example, the first score from a_1, $AS_{11} = 5$, would appear as a solid square above the baseline at 5, while the first score from a_2, $AS_{21} = 13$, would appear as a square with dashed lines above the baseline at 13. All the scores listed in Table 4-2 have been plotted in this fashion in Figure 4-2. Scores with the same value have been stacked on top of each other. You will notice that arrows below the baseline point to the values (locations) of the two treatment means and the grand mean. The sixth score from level a_1, $AS_{1,6} = 1$, is also indicated. (We have added a comma between the two subscripts for this score in order to facilitate your understanding of the important argument that follows.)

The purpose of this arrangement of the two sets of scores is to demonstrate geometrically an important relationship between an individual score, its relevant treatment mean, and the grand mean. More specifically,

the deviation of any score from the grand mean can be divided into two different deviations, one reflecting the deviation of the score from its treatment mean and the other consisting of the deviation of the treatment mean from the grand mean.

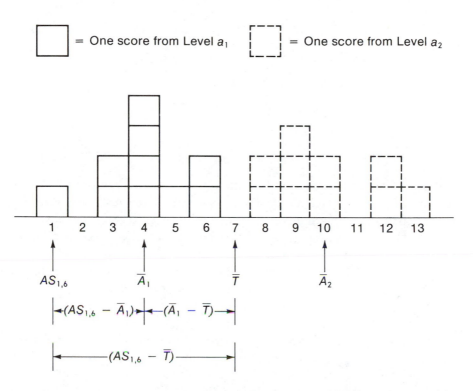

Figure 4-2. A Systematic Arrangement of Scores from Table 4-2. The components of deviation for a single score ($AS_{1,6}$) from the grand mean ($\overline{T}$) are shown beneath the baseline.

This relationship for one score ($AS_{1,6}$) is depicted at the bottom of Figure 4-2. The bottom line of the figure is a representation of the deviation of this score from the grand mean:

$$AS_{1,6} - \overline{T} \quad .$$

Above this deviation we have represented two other deviations, that is, the deviation of this score from its treatment mean,

$$AS_{1,6} - \overline{A}_1 \quad ,$$

and the deviation of the treatment mean from the grand mean,

$$\overline{A}_1 - \overline{T} \quad .$$

You can readily see that the first deviation ($AS_{1,6} - \overline{T}$) is equal to the sum of the other two deviations ($AS_{1,6} - \overline{A}_1$ and $\overline{A}_1 - \overline{T}$). This particular relationship holds for any score in any treatment condition, and as we will soon see, forms the basis for the analysis of variance.[6] The "truth" of this relationship can also be demonstrated by means of some simple algebra:

$$AS_{1,6} - \overline{T} = (AS_{1,6} - \overline{A}_1) + (\overline{A}_1 - \overline{T})$$
$$= AS_{1,6} - \overline{A}_1 + \overline{A}_1 - \overline{T}$$
$$= AS_{1,6} - \overline{T} \quad .$$

Sums of Squares

The preceding discussion contains hints as to how a Treatment Index is developed. The two **component deviation scores** in the last section reflect exactly the sorts of variability we want to capture for the Treatment Index. That is, the deviation of subjects from their treatment means reflects what we called "experimental error" in the last chapter—the variation attributable to subjects treated alike, that is, subjects given the same treatment condition. In contrast, the deviation of treatment means from the grand mean would reflect the joint influence of treatments *and* experimental error. You saw in the preceding section that the deviation of a particular score from the grand mean (the **total deviation**) is made up of two component deviations, one based on the deviation of the score from its treatment mean (**within-group deviation**) and the other based on the deviation of the treatment mean from the grand mean (**treatment-group deviation**). That is,

total deviation = within-group deviation
+ treatment-group deviation   .

We can extend this relationship, which holds for every score in the experiment, to the sum of the squares of these three sets of deviations. In words, it is the case that

the sum of the squared total deviations equals the sum of the squared within-group deviations plus the sum of the squared treatment-group deviations.

If we use *SS* to designate the sum of the squared deviations from a mean, this statement becomes

$$SS_{total} = SS_{within-group} + SS_{treatment-group} \quad . \tag{4-3}$$

In an even simpler shorthand notation, we have

$$SS_T = SS_{S/A} + SS_A \quad , \tag{4-3a}$$

---

[6] See *Design and Analysis* (pp. 48–50) for a demonstration of this fact.

where the subscript T stands for "total," S/A for "subjects within the A treatment groups," and A for the "variability among the A treatment means."[7] We turn now to a consideration of the computational formulas that permit us to calculate these three basic sums of squares with relative ease.

Computational Formulas

The computational formulas for the required SSs are neither intrinsically difficult nor complex. Each formula consists of two ratios, one of which is subtracted from the other. Moreover, each ratio has the same underlying form. Specifically, the numerator term for each ratio involves the *squaring* of either a score or a sum, and then the *summation* of these squared quantities if more than one is present. The denominator term for each ratio is simply a number that can be calculated easily from the formula. In short, all terms in the computational formulas for SSs have the following form:

$$\frac{\Sigma \ (\text{score or sum})^2}{\text{divisor}} \ . \tag{4-4}$$

We refer to this sort of ratio as a **basic ratio.**

Basic Ratios. Only three ratios are needed for calculating the three required sums of squares: SS_T, SS_A, and $SS_{S/A}$. Each ratio uses a different quantity, which is either a score or a sum. To emphasize the critical nature of these basic ratios, we will use a distinctive symbol to designate basic ratios and to distinguish among them. This symbol consists of a pair of brackets enclosing a letter code specifying the scores or sums involved in the calculation of a basic ratio. The special symbols for the three basic ratios and the quantities needed for the calculations are given below:

Special Code	Score or Sum
[AS]	AS (the basic observations or scores)
[A]	A (the treatment sums)
[T]	T (the grand sum)

We will consider these basic ratios in the order listed above and illustrate each set of calculations with a numerical example.

Starting with the basic score, AS, and substituting in equation (4-4), we obtain

$$\frac{\Sigma \ (\text{score})^2}{\text{divisor}} = \frac{\Sigma \ (AS)^2}{1} \ .$$

---

[7] You will frequently see the treatment-group sum of squares referred to as the *between-group* sum of squares. These designations are interchangeable, although in subsequent discussions we generally use the letter designations in equation (4-3a).

Since the divisor in this case is 1, the basic ratio may be written more simply as

$$\Sigma (AS)^2 \quad ,$$

the sum of all the squared scores in the experiment. If we add the special code for basic ratios, the equation becomes

$$[AS] = \Sigma (AS)^2 \quad . \tag{4-5}$$

This formula tells us to add all the squared AS scores. That is, the scores are to be first squared and then summed.

As a numerical example, consider the data presented in Table 4-2. Substituting the scores from the table into equation (4-5), we have, step by step,

$$\begin{aligned}
[AS] &= \Sigma (AS)^2 \\
&= (5)^2 + (3)^2 + (4)^2 + (4)^2 + (6)^2 + (1)^2 + (3)^2 + (4)^2 \\
&\quad + (6)^2 + (4)^2 + (13)^2 + (9)^2 + (10)^2 + (8)^2 + (9)^2 + (12)^2 \\
&\quad + (8)^2 + (12)^2 + (10)^2 + (9)^2 \\
&= 25 + 9 + 16 + 16 + 36 + 1 + 9 + 16 + 36 + 16 \\
&\quad + 169 + 81 + 100 + 64 + 81 + 144 + 64 + 144 + 100 + 81 \\
&= 1,208 \quad .
\end{aligned}$$

It is usually most convenient to perform this operation in two steps:

1. Square the AS scores and then sum the squared scores for each treatment group separately.

2. Add together these subtotals.[8]

Substituting the treatment sum, A, in equation (4-4). we obtain

$$\frac{\Sigma (\text{sum})^2}{\text{divisor}} = \frac{\Sigma (A)^2}{s} \quad ,$$

the sum of all of the *squared treatment sums* in the experiment divided by the sample size, s. Using the special symbol, we have

$$[A] = \frac{\Sigma (A)^2}{s} \quad . \tag{4-6}$$

---

[8] Some calculators permit users to obtain the sum of a set of numbers and the sum of the square of these numbers in the same operation. Thus, using such an aid you would be able to obtain both sums for each treatment condition separately. You would then use the treatment sums to calculate $[A]$ and the sums of the squared observations to calculate $[AS]$.

This formula tells us to sum all the squared A totals and to divide by the sample size.[9] The steps in the calculations require first the squaring of the A sums and then their summation. Substituting the treatment sums from Table 4-2 in equation (4-6), we find

$$[A] = \frac{\Sigma (A)^2}{s}$$

$$= \frac{(40)^2 + (100)^2}{10}$$

$$= \frac{1,600 + 10,000}{10} = \frac{11,600}{10}$$

$$= 1,600.00 \quad .$$

Finally, substituting the grand total, T, in equation (4-4), we obtain

$$\frac{(\text{sum})^2}{\text{divisor}} = \frac{(T)^2}{a(s)} \quad ,$$

the *squared grand total*, divided by the total number of observations (that is, subjects) in the experiment, namely, $a(s)$. No summation is necessary in the numerator term, since only one grand total exists and no summation is possible. Using the special symbol, we have

$$[T] = \frac{(T)^2}{a(s)} \quad . \tag{4-7}$$

Substituting the grand sum presented in Table 4-2 in equation (4-7), we find

$$[T] = \frac{(T)^2}{a(s)}$$

$$= \frac{(140)^2}{2(10)}$$

$$= \frac{19,600}{20} = 980.00 \quad .$$

Sums of Squares. You will recall from an earlier discussion that the deviation of each score (AS) from the grand mean $(\bar{T})$ is divided into two deviations, namely, the deviation of each score from the treatment mean $(\bar{A})$ and the

---

[9] Some students have been confused by this step. The difficulty seems to be in the division by s after the squared treatment sums have been added together. We could have divided each squared treatment sum individually and then added together the results of these separate divisions. Either way, we would obtain the same answer. The procedure specified by equation (4-6) is much simpler, however, since it involves fewer steps and reduces rounding error.

deviation of the treatment mean from the grand mean. The analysis of variance consists of transforming these deviations into sums of squares, variances, and then the F ratio. We will now indicate how the three sums of squares based on the three sets of deviations can be calculated from data by means of the basic ratios. More specifically, each of the basic ratios defined in the preceding section will be used twice in the calculations. The ratio used and the direction of the sign (positive or negative) are designated by the basic deviations used to define the particular sums of squares. To amplify, the total sum of squares (SS_T) is based on the following deviation:

$$AS - \bar{T} \quad .$$

The computational formula combines the two ratios designated by this deviation as follows:

$$SS_T = [AS] - [T] \quad , \qquad (4\text{-}8)$$

or, more completely,

$$SS_T = \Sigma\, (AS)^2 - \frac{(T)^2}{a(s)} \quad . \qquad (4\text{-}8a)$$

Substituting the quantities we calculated in the last section, we find

$$SS_T = [AS] - [T]$$
$$= 1,208 - 980.00 = 228.00 \quad .$$

The treatment sum of squares, SS_A, is based on the deviation of the treatment means from the grand mean, namely,

$$\bar{A} - \bar{T} \quad .$$

The computational formula combines the two ratios designated by this deviation as follows:

$$SS_A = [A] - [T] \quad , \qquad (4\text{-}9)$$

or, more fully,

$$SS_A = \frac{\Sigma\, (A)^2}{s} - \frac{(T)^2}{a(s)} \quad . \qquad (4\text{-}9a)$$

Substituting the quantities calculated previously, we find

$$SS_A = [A] - [T]$$
$$= 1,160.00 - 980.00 = 180.00 \quad .$$

Finally, the within-group sum of squares, $SS_{S/A}$, is based on the deviation of individual observations from the relevant treatment mean; in other words,

$$AS - \bar{A} \quad .$$

The computational formula combines the two ratios designated by these deviations as follows:

$$SS_{S/A} = [AS] - [A] \quad , \tag{4-10}$$

or,

$$SS_{S/A} = \Sigma (AS)^2 - \frac{\Sigma (A)^2}{s} \quad . \tag{4-10a}$$

Substituting the quantities from the last section, we obtain

$$SS_{S/A} = [AS] - [A]$$
$$= 1,208 - 1,160.00 = 48.00 \quad .$$

As a computational check and as a demonstration of the relationship among these three sums of squares, we will apply equation (4-3a) to our calculations:

$$SS_T = SS_{S/A} + SS_A$$
$$228.00 = 48.00 + 180.00$$
$$= 228.00 \quad .$$

That is, the total sum of squares (SS_T) is made up of two component sums of squares, the sum of squares based on the variability of subjects treated alike ($SS_{S/A}$) and the sum of squares based on the variability of the treatment means (SS_A).

A Summary of the Calculations

The arithmetical operations required by the computational formulas for the three sums of squares are summarized in Tables 4-3 and 4-4. Table 4-3 specifies the way in which the individual observations are "processed" in the initial steps of calculating the sums of squares. Each row in Table 4-3 concentrates on a different quantity and the calculations that are performed on those particular quantities. Row 1 focuses on the basic observations, AS_{ij}. As an example, four scores—two for level a_1 and two for level a_2—are listed in column 1. Row 2 focuses on the treatment sums, A_i, which are obtained, of course, from the individual observations listed in the first row. In this example, two treatment sums, A_1 and A_2, are listed in column 1 of the table. Finally, row 3 focuses on the grand sum, T, which is obtained either from the scores in row 1 or from the treatment sums in row 2. This quantity is also listed in column 1 of the table.

We have already indicated that column 1 contains three different kinds of quantities: basic observations (AS), treatment sums (A), and the grand sum

TABLE 4-3   The Arithmetical Operations Performed on Scores or Sums

	1. Basic Score or Sum	2. Squaring	3. Summing (If Relevant)	4. Dividing (If Required)	5. Coding
1. Basic Observations	$\begin{array}{c\|c} a_1 & a_2 \\ \hline AS_{11} & AS_{21} \\ AS_{12} & AS_{22} \end{array}$	$(AS_{11})^2 \quad (AS_{21})^2$ $(AS_{12})^2 \quad (AS_{22})^2$	$\Sigma\,(AS)^2$	$\Sigma(AS)^2$	$[AS]$
2. Treatment Sums	$A_1 \qquad A_2$	$(A_1)^2 \qquad (A_2)^2$	$\Sigma\,(A)^2$	$\dfrac{\Sigma\,(A)^2}{s}$	$[A]$
3. Grand Sum	T	$(T)^2$	$(T)^2$	$\dfrac{(T)^2}{a(s)}$	$[T]$

TABLE 4-4 Computational Formulas for SS_A, $SS_{S/A}$, and SS_T

Source of Variability	Basic Deviation	Computational Formula
Treatment Means (SS_A)	$\overline{A}_i - \overline{T}$	$[A] - [T]$
Subjects Treated Alike ($SS_{S/A}$)	$AS_{ij} - \overline{A}_i$	$[AS] - [A]$
Both Components Combined (SS_T)	$AS_{ij} - \overline{T}$	$[AS] - [T]$

(T). The remaining columns designate the actual arithmetical operations performed on these quantities and the order in which they are performed, that is, *squaring* (column 2), *summing* (column 3), and *dividing* (column 4).[10] The *coding* step (column 5) is used to simplify the expression of the formulas for the sums of squares. Look carefully at this table and at the consistent pattern with which the different numbers are manipulated. To review, we start in row 1 with the basic AS scores, first squaring and then adding them. (The third step of division is not needed, since the sum of the squared AS scores are implicitly divided by 1, as noted on p. 70.) To create the next set of quantities, those in row 2, we sum the basic scores for each treatment condition separately to produce what are termed the A treatment totals. We then subject these subtotals to the same pattern of arithmetical processing, namely, squaring, summing, and dividing. We create the final quantity, which appears in row 3, by first summing the treatment totals to produce the grand sum (T), and then subjecting this sum to the same processing, that is, squaring and dividing (summing is not necessary in this case). If you recognize the consistency with which these quantities are processed, you will generate a certain rhythm in your calculations that will help to demystify the entire calculation process involved in the analysis of both simple and complex experimental designs.

---

[10] The divisors specified in column 4 actually follow a simple computational rule:

Divide by the number of observations contributing to the quantity in the numerator.

For example, since each AS score is based on a single observation, we divide by 1, which, of course, does not have to be expressed in the computational formulas. Each A sum, on the other hand, is based on s observations, so the divisor is s; the grand sum T is based on $a(s)$ observations, so the divisor is $a(s)$. As you will see, this rule holds for more complex designs as well.

In Table 4-4, the final steps in the calculation of the three sums of squares are summarized. Each row in this table specifies one of the three sources of variability, first the two component sources (SS_A and $SS_{S/A}$), and then the combination of the two sources (SS_T). The columns of the table indicate the basic deviations on which these sources of variability are based and the computational formulas for the sums of squares expressed in coded form.

If you have understood the rationale governing the use of the basic deviations, and have followed the various steps involved in the calculation of the three sums of squares, you are over the worst! The remaining steps in the analysis of variance are relatively simple arithmetically and follow the logic we discussed in Chapter 3.

THE ANALYSIS OF VARIANCE

Calculating Variances

The sums of squares discussed in the last section are not directly usable in the calculation of the Treatment Index, since each of the component sums of squares is affected by the *number* of deviations. The solution to this problem is to adjust each sum of squares for this difference. This *average* sum of squares defines a *variance,* but it is called a **mean square** (abbreviated *MS*) when the sum of squares comes from an analysis of variance. The general formula for a mean square is

$$MS = \frac{SS}{df} \quad , \tag{4-11}$$

where *df* refers to the number of **degrees of freedom** associated with the sum of squares (*SS*). A mean square is still an average, but one that adjusts for the number of degrees of freedom rather than for the number of squared deviations.

Degrees of Freedom

The concept of degrees of freedom can be understood on a number of levels depending on one's interests, background, and formal training in statistics. Most researchers are unfamiliar with the statistical theory and argument used to justify the division of a sum of squares by its degrees of freedom. As a result, they have learned to be satisfied with an understanding of the concept at a less rigorous and demanding level and to accept equation (4-11) for the simple utilitarian reason that it lends them statistical advantages. We are encouraging you to adopt a similar philosophy here and to accept the correctness of this definition of a mean square with a considerable amount of faith. We take this approach because a great deal is known about the theoretical properties of mean squares and ratios of mean squares and because we will use this important information in the evaluation of the null hypothesis.

Because of its importance in the process of statistical inference, however, we must say a few words about the concept of degrees of freedom itself. It can be shown that the degrees of freedom associated with a particular variance estimate reflect the number of independent pieces of information entering into the calculation of the corresponding sums of squares (see *Design and Analysis*, pp. 567–575). In general, degrees of freedom can be defined in terms of the number of scores in a set that are free to vary, meaning that they are not "fixed" by some restriction placed on them. Suppose we select a set of scores randomly from some larger population. Presumably, each of these scores is free to vary, to take on any of the values present in the population. But what happens when we begin the process of statistical inference and calculate a sum of squares from these scores? Under these circumstances, all the scores in the set are *not* completely free to vary, since a particular restriction has been placed on them. This restriction is most easily understood by a simple example.

Suppose we randomly select three numbers from a population, for example, 2, 6, and 7. Since each score is free to vary, there are $s = 3$ degrees of freedom. But what happens to the information present in this set of scores when the population mean is estimated from the mean of the sample? In this example, the mean is

$$\frac{2 + 6 + 7}{3} = \frac{15}{3} = 5 \quad .$$

How many of the scores are now free to vary once the mean has been estimated? Only two, since for the mean to equal 5, the sum of these scores must be 15, and once two scores have been selected randomly—in other words, are free to vary—the last is already known by subtraction. That is,

last score = 15 − (sum of the first two scores)   .

In this example,

$$\text{last score} = 15 - (2 + 6)$$
$$= 15 - 8 = 7 \quad .$$

Thus, once we estimate the population mean from the sample data, only $s - 1$ degrees of freedom—pieces of independent information—are left for the estimate of the variance.

The general rule for computing the df for any sum of squares is

$$df = \begin{pmatrix} \text{number of} \\ \text{independent} \\ \text{observations} \end{pmatrix} - \begin{pmatrix} \text{number of} \\ \text{population} \\ \text{estimates} \end{pmatrix} . \qquad (4\text{-}12)$$

If there are s observations in a sample, one degree of freedom is lost when we estimate the population mean. Application of equation (4-12) indicates that

$$df = s - 1 .$$

In the following subsections, we apply this definition to the three sources of variability obtained in the analysis of variance.

SS_A. The sum of squares SS_A is based on the deviation of each treatment mean ($\overline{A}$) from the grand mean ($\overline{T}$). There are a observations contributing to this source of variance. As a result of our estimating the overall population mean from the means of the treatment groups, the value of one of the group means is "fixed," and one df is lost. In symbols,

$$df_A = a - 1 . \qquad (4\text{-}13)$$

$SS_{S/A}$. The sum of squares $SS_{S/A}$ is based on the deviation of each individual score (AS) from the appropriate treatment mean ($\overline{A}$). For any *one* treatment group, there is a total of s observations. Since one df is lost as a result of estimating the population treatment mean from the mean of the treatment group,

$$df = s - 1 .$$

However, in this sum of squares, the separate sums of squares are pooled together for each of the treatment groups. We find the degrees of freedom, therefore, by pooling together the dfs associated with each of the different treatment groups. That is,

$$df_{S/A} = (s - 1) + (s - 1) + (s - 1) \ldots \text{ etc.}$$

Since there are a treatment groups, each with $df = s - 1$, we can simplify the formula to read

$$df_{S/A} = a(s - 1) . \qquad (4\text{-}14)$$

SS_T. The sum of squares SS_T is based on the deviation of each individual score (AS) from the grand mean ($\overline{T}$). There are $a(s)$ observations in the total experiment. As a result of our estimating the overall population mean from the grand mean, which we obtained by summing all the scores in the experiment, the value of one subject's score is "fixed," and one df is lost. Thus,

$$df_T = a(s) - 1 . \qquad (4\text{-}15)$$

TABLE 4-5   A Summary of the Analysis of Variance

Source of Variance	Sum of Squares $(SS)^a$	Degrees of Freedom (df)	Mean Square (MS)	F Ratio
Treatments (A)	SS_A	$a - 1$	$\dfrac{SS_A}{df_A}$	$\dfrac{MS_A}{MS_{S/A}}$
Subjects Within Groups (S/A)	$SS_{S/A}$	$a(s - 1)$	$\dfrac{SS_{S/A}}{df_{S/A}}$	
Total (T)	SS_T	$a(s) - 1$		

^{a} See Tables 4-3 and 4-4 for computational formulas.

An alternative formula for df_T derives from the fact that the sum of the component degrees of freedom (df_A and $df_{S/A}$) must equal the total degrees of freedom, df_T, just as the sum of the component sums of squares must equal the total sum of squares. In symbols,

$$df_T = df_{S/A} + df_A \quad .\tag{4-15a}$$

Computational Formulas

Table 4-5 gives the computational formulas for the analysis of variance.[11] Each row of the table provides a formula for one of the three sources of variance. The first column of the table lists these three sources. The second column lists the sums of squares associated with these sources. (See Tables 4-3 and 4-4 for the computational formulas for these sums of squares.) The third column shows the degrees of freedom associated with the sources of variability. The fourth column gives the formulas for the two component mean squares, MS_A and $MS_{S/A}$. (A mean square based on the total sum of squares is not needed and is normally not calculated.) The fifth column gives the formula for the Treatment Index, now appropriately referred to as the F ratio. The F ratio is formed by

$$F = \frac{MS_A}{MS_{S/A}} \quad ,\tag{4-16}$$

an estimate of treatment variability divided by an estimate of the variability of subjects treated alike. This latter term, $MS_{S/A}$, is frequently called the

---

[11] For a comprehensive summary of this analysis of variance, see Glossary 4 at the end of the book.

TABLE 4-6   The Summary Table for the Analysis
of Variance

Source	SS	df	MS	F
A	180.00	1	180.00	67.42
S/A	48.00	18	2.67	
Total	228.00	19		

error term of the *F* ratio, the term that provides an estimate of the experimental error influencing the differences among the treatment means.

Numerical Example. We can now complete the analysis of variance for the data in Table 4-2. The sums of squares, calculated earlier, are presented again in Table 4-6.

The next step is to calculate the degrees of freedom for the three sums of squares. For this example, there are $a = 2$ treatment conditions and $s = 10$ subjects in each of the treatment groups. Thus,

$$df_A = a - 1 = 2 - 1 = 1 \;\;;$$
$$df_{S/A} = a(s - 1) = 2(10 - 1) = 2(9) = 18 \;\;; \text{ and}$$
$$df_T = a(s) - 1 = 2(10) - 1 = 20 - 1 = 19 \;\;.$$

These values are listed in the *df* column of the summary table. You should note that

$$df_T = df_A + df_{S/A}$$
$$= 1 + 18 = 19 \;\;,$$

which must hold for the calculations to be correct.

To obtain the two mean squares we divide the two sums of squares by the appropriate degrees of freedom. That is,

$$MS_A = \frac{SS_A}{df_A} = \frac{180.00}{1} = 180.00 \;\;, \text{ and}$$

$$MS_{S/A} = \frac{SS_{S/A}}{df_{S/A}} = \frac{48.00}{18} = 2.67 \;\;.$$

These quantities are entered into the summary table.

The final step in the calculations is to form the *F* ratio. From equation (4-16),

$$F = \frac{MS_A}{MS_{S/A}} = \frac{180.00}{2.67} = 67.42 \;\;.$$

Given the logic surrounding the evaluation of the F ratio, you probably suspect that the null hypothesis will be rejected when the F value is this large. While this suspicion is correct, forming decision rules with which to evaluate the null hypothesis formally is still necessary. This step is covered in the next chapter.

Construction of a summary table of the analysis as presented in Table 4-6 is an essential part of completing the analysis of variance. You should develop the habit of constructing such a table whenever you undertake an analysis.

THE LOSS OF SUBJECTS

As we have noted, in most experimental designs an equal number of subjects is assigned to each of the treatment conditions. This procedure ensures that equal weight is given to each of the treatment levels in the calculation of the between-group sum of squares (SS_A). But what happens when inequality of sample sizes is forced on the researcher through the inadvertent loss of subjects during the course of experimentation? We will consider the implications of this unfortunate circumstance in some detail.

Subjects are lost (or discarded) from an experiment for various reasons. In animal studies, for example, subjects are frequently lost through sickness and death. In human studies in which testing is to continue over several days, subjects are discarded when they fail to complete the entire experimental sequence. In a memory study, for instance, some subjects may fail to return a week after the first phase for their final retention test, perhaps because of illness or an unforseen appointment. Subjects may also be lost when the experimental procedures require that all subjects meet a common performance criterion, such as a certain level of mastery. In this sort of experiment, subjects who fail to meet the previously determined performance criterion are dropped. Another source of losses is the failure of subjects to produce responses that meet the criteria established for the response measure. Suppose we are interested in the speed with which correct responses are made. A subject who fails to give a correct response cannot contribute to the analysis. Or suppose we want to determine the percentage of times in which the errors produced on a task are of a particular type. A subject who fails to make any errors cannot contribute to the analysis. In such situations, then, subjects are eliminated from the experiment because they fail to give scorable responses.

When subject losses occur, it is of critical importance to the analysis of the data that we determine their implication. After all, we have assigned our subjects to the experimental conditions randomly so that we can attribute any differences among the groups at the start of the experiment to chance factors. We are not concerned with the loss of subjects per se, but with this question: Has the loss of subjects, for whatever reason, resulted in a loss of randomness? If randomness has been lost, we must either find a way to restore it or simply junk the experiment. No form of statistical juggling will rectify the situation if randomness cannot be restored. If randomness may still be safely assumed, or if it has been restored, we can proceed with the statistical analysis of the data.

In each situation, we must determine whether the reason for the subject loss was in any way associated with particular treatments. In animal research, for instance, certain treatment conditions (such as surgery, drugs, high levels of food or water deprivation, exhausting training procedures) may actually be responsible for the loss of the subjects. In such a case, only the strongest and healthiest animals would survive, and the result would be an obvious confounding of subject differences and treatment conditions: The difficult conditions would contain a larger proportion of healthy animals than the less trying conditions. Replacing the lost subjects with new animals drawn from the same population would not be an adequate solution, since the replacement subjects would not "match" those lost. But if the researcher can show that the loss of subjects was approximately the same for all the treatment conditions or that the loss was not related to the specific treatments, the analysis can continue.

The second source of subject loss—through subjects' failure to reach a criterion of mastery—poses similar problems. Clearly, subjects who fail to learn the task in an experiment are by definition poorer learners than those who do learn it. If one group suffers a greater loss through failure of mastery, which may very well happen if the conditions differ in difficulty, the subjects in the difficult condition who meet the predetermined criterion will be better learners than those completing the training in the easier conditions. Replacing subjects lost in the difficult condition would not solve this problem, since the replacement subjects would not match the ability of the lost subjects.

Clearly, then, the loss of subjects is of paramount concern to a researcher. If the loss of subjects is related to the phenomenon under study, it destroys the neutralization of nuisance variables normally achieved by randomization, thus potentially adding a systematic bias to the differences among the means that cannot be disentangled from the influence of the treatment effects. This problem is one of experimental design, and must be solved by the researcher if the data are to have meaning. It is here that knowledge of the subject matter being studied and the practice of others can be helpful. In cases where subject loss has occurred but the researcher is convinced that no bias has resulted, statistical procedures that adjust for the loss of subjects are available for the analysis of the data.[12]

SUMMARY

The process of analyzing completely randomized, single-factor experiments begins with the isolation of two sources of variation in the data: one source reflecting the effects of the treatments (if any) and the unavoidable effects of experimental error, and the other source reflecting the effects of experimental error alone. We first express these sources as deviations from means and then use formulas to calculate the two variances, known as mean squares (MS_A and $MS_{S/A}$), from the data. The ratio of the MS_A to the $MS_{S/A}$ forms the Treatment Index—the F ratio—which we will use in evaluating the null hypothesis. In the next chapter, we describe how this final, but critical, last step is accomplished.

The loss of subjects for any reason in any experiment is a potential source of damage to the interpretation of results. Although such loss can be compensated for, the researcher has the responsibility to determine a sensible course of action and explain it to others.

---

[12] For a discussion of the statistical analysis of experiments with unequal sample sizes, see *Design and Analysis* (pp. 345–355).

TERMS, CONCEPTS, AND SYMBOLS

---

completely randomized,
  single-factor design
analysis of variance
F ratio
levels
sample size
grand sum
grand mean
treatment sum
treatment mean

basic observation
AS matrix
component deviations
total deviation
within-group deviation
treatment-group deviation
basic ratio
mean square
degrees of freedom
error term

Notation and Basic Calculations

$$
\begin{array}{cccc}
T & (T)^2 & [T] & \overline{T} \\
A & \Sigma\,(A)^2 & [A] & \overline{A} \\
AS & \Sigma\,(AS)^2 & [AS] & \\
& a,\ s,\ a(s) & &
\end{array}
$$

Terms in the Analysis of Variance

$$
\begin{array}{cccc}
SS_A & df_A & MS_A & F \\
SS_{S/A} & df_{S/A} & MS_{S/A} & \\
SS_T & df_T & &
\end{array}
$$

EXERCISES

---

1. Suppose a researcher is interested in the effects of various chemical additives to foods on activity levels in children determined to be hyperactive.
   An experiment is designed in which the two conditions consisted of food
   without the additives and the same food but with the additives. Data for

the two groups of nine children consisted of a response measure developed especially for the research. The following data were obtained:

No Additives		Additives	
AS_{11}	31	AS_{21}	30
AS_{12}	33	AS_{22}	28
AS_{13}	25	AS_{23}	36
AS_{14}	28	AS_{24}	41
AS_{15}	24	AS_{25}	29
AS_{16}	30	AS_{26}	32
AS_{17}	31	AS_{27}	27
AS_{18}	26	AS_{28}	35
AS_{19}	30	AS_{29}	36

  a. Calculate the basic ratios.
  b. Find the sums of squares for A, S/A, and T.
  c. Write the df statements and determine the degrees of freedom.
  d. Calculate the mean squares.
  e. Construct the summary table and calculate F. (Save this information for problem 1, Chapter 5, p. 112.)

2. Before making a decision about his advertising campaign, a publisher ran an experiment to discover whether readers' responses to certain ads differed. He wanted to test responses to three kinds of ads: ads with a color picture, ads with a black and white picture, and ads with no picture. Each ad was inserted with other material intended to draw attention away from the material being evaluated. Subjects rated the critical ad on an 11-point scale where the higher the number, the greater the preference for the ad. Results for the twenty-one subjects (seven subjects in each condition) are given below.

Color	Black and White	No Picture
3	4	10
3	7	7
7	5	8
6	3	5
8	9	9
1	8	7
5	7	6

Complete all the necessary calculations for the construction of an analysis summary table. (Save your calculations for problem 2, Chapter 5, p. 112.)

The Evaluation of the F Ratio

5

It may be useful at this point to review the basic logic behind the evaluation of the null hypothesis. We start with an experiment in which subjects are assigned randomly to different treatment conditions. From the scores of the subjects on the dependent variable, we calculate two variance estimates, one reflecting the variation among the treatment means (MS_A) and the other reflecting variation among subjects treated alike ($MS_{S/A}$). The MS_A is affected by the effects of the treatment conditions—if any—in addition to the presence of experimental error. The $MS_{S/A}$, on the other hand, is affected by the presence of experimental error alone. A set of two statistical hypotheses is formed, the null hypothesis, which states that the population treatment means are equal—that is, no treatment effects exist—and the alternative hypothesis, which states that not all of the population means are equal, or treatment effects do exist. The *F* ratio—MS_A divided by $MS_{S/A}$ (the so-called error term)—provides a useful way to test the null hypothesis. If the null hypothesis is true, both mean squares will reflect the operation of experimental error, and the value of *F* will be approximately equal to 1.0. If the null hypothesis is false, the MS_A will reflect the operation of an additional factor—treatment effects—and the value of *F* will be greater than 1.0.

We know that values of *F* greater than 1.0 can be expected to occur by chance even when the null hypothesis is true, although larger values occur with increasingly smaller frequencies. Given this fact, we choose a value of *F* above which only a small proportion of *F*'s will occur by chance when the null hypothesis is true. If the obtained *F* equals or exceeds this critical value, we will reject the null hypothesis. Rejection of the null hypothesis permits us to accept the alternative hypothesis and conclude that at least some differences among the treatment means exist in the population.

THE SAMPLING DISTRIBUTION OF *F*

Suppose we were able to conduct the same experiment over and over, each time with a different set of subjects. Suppose further that the null hypothesis were true, and no differences existed among the treatment means in the population. Each experiment would yield a perfectly valid value of *F*. Suppose we arranged these *F*s in size from small to large and noted the frequencies with which each value occurred over an extremely large number of these experiments. We would be able to plot this information in a graph, measuring off the values of *F* on the horizontal axis and the frequency of occurrence on the vertical axis. The result would be the **sampling distribution** of this particular *F* statistic.

An Empirical Determination of a Sampling Distribution

Consider an example of just such a series of experiments conducted by Lewis F. Petrinovich and Curtis D. Hardyck.[1] These investigators did not

---

[1] We wish to thank Drs. Petrinovich and Hardyck for making available the results of these experiments. Experiments using this method are often referred to as "Monte Carlo experiments."

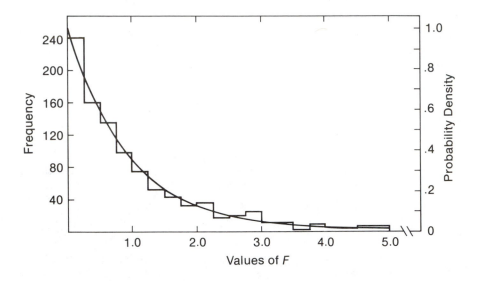

Figure 5-1.   A Sampling Distribution of F from Simulated Experiments (Bar Graph) with a = 3 (Groups) and s = 15 (Scores Each). The smooth curve is the theoretical sampling distribution of F corresponding to this example.

actually perform real experiments, but simulated them with a computer by drawing forty-five scores randomly from a population of six thousand scores stored in the memory of the computer. They then divided the forty-five scores randomly into a = 3 "treatment" groups of s = 15 scores each, and performed an analysis of variance on these data. The forty-five scores were then replaced in the population, and a new sample of forty-five scores was randomly chosen. The second group of scores was divided randomly into three groups, and the procedure was repeated until one thousand such "experiments" had been conducted and analyzed.

Since each of the three "treatment" conditions represented a random sample from the *same* underlying population, the null hypothesis is true—that is, the three population "treatment" means are identical. The one thousand values of F, arranged and grouped according to size, represent a sampling distribution of this F statistic. The distribution obtained is plotted in Figure 5-1. For comparison, the *theoretical* sampling distribution of this F statistic, which is mathematically determined, is superimposed over the results of the sampling study.

The first point to note is the close correspondence between the theoretical sampling distribution (the smooth curve) and that obtained from experimentation. Second, the average value of F is approximately equal to 1.0 (F = 1.09), which is what should occur if the null hypothesis is true.

Finally, as you can see, the frequency of F's declines rapidly as the values of F get larger and larger. (We cut the distribution off at $F = 5.0$, because cases of larger values occur so infrequently. The theoretical distribution actually extends to $F = $ infinity.)

Consider the ways in which we can use this information. Although large values of F can and do occur by chance when the null hypothesis is true, still they do not happen all that frequently. For example, the largest F obtained by Petrinovich and Hardyck in their sampling experiment was 8.50. On the basis of their experiment, we can conclude that an F this large or larger occurs by chance once in one thousand sampling experiments.[2] What would happen if we obtained an F of 8.50 in an *actual* experiment where we did not know whether the null hypothesis was true? Remember, we would only know the result of the sampling experiment, which would tell us what to expect when the null hypothesis was true. Would we conclude that the null hypothesis was in fact true, since an F this large could occur by chance (and did in the illustration) under these circumstances? Or would we note that an F of 8.50 or larger is an *extremely rare event,* and conclude that the null hypothesis is far more likely to be false?

In fact, the decision to reject the null hypothesis would be justified in such a case. It is simply not reasonable to hold on to the null hypothesis when the probability is so small that a particular F could have occurred by chance under the null hypothesis. One time out of a thousand (a probability of $p = .001$) certainly qualifies as an infrequent event. For this reason, we are willing to conclude that an F of 8.50 is evidence that—in a word—is *incompatible* with the null hypothesis.

In this discussion, we focused on the largest F obtained from the sampling experiment. As noted in Chapter 3, most researchers would find a probability level of $p = .001$, which this example reflects, too stringent a test of the null hypothesis. They would be willing to accept smaller values of F as critical evidence against the null hypothesis.

Given the results of the sampling experiment, we could start counting the values of F beginning with the largest ($F = 8.50$) and moving toward the smallest until we had tabulated 5 percent of the one thousand F ratios (5 percent of $1,000 = 50$). You will recall that this particular percentage (5 percent) is the standard against which most researchers assess the null hypothesis. In this example, the critical value of F representing the fiftieth case is 3.23. If we were to conduct an experiment with the same number of subjects randomly assigned to three different treatment groups, this value of F would define the beginning of a region within which the null hypothesis

---

[2] The theoretical probability is $p = .0008$—making this an even rarer event than the sampling experiment suggests.

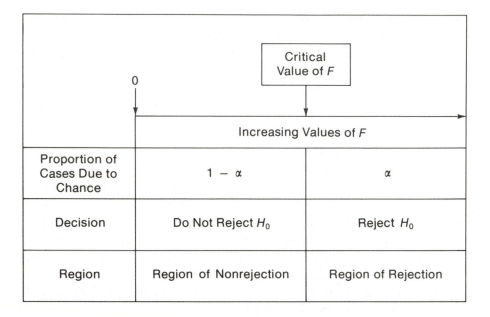

Figure 5-2. Terms Associated with Hypothesis Testing.

would be rejected. Any value of F below this point would fall into a region within which the null hypothesis would not be rejected.

A Summary of Terms. Several terms commonly used to refer to different aspects of hypothesis testing are defined graphically in Figure 5-2. At the top of the figure lies a number line representing all possible values of the F statistic; this scale runs from zero to extremely large numbers. The critical value of F is placed on this number line and extended down to the bottom of the figure. The **critical value** is determined by a researcher's personal definition of evidence considered to be incompatible with the null hypothesis, that is, values of F that cannot be reasonably attributed to the operation of chance factors when the null hypothesis is true. This definition of incompatibility is usually stated as a percentage, a proportion, or a probability, and is referred to as the **significance level.** This probability is generally designated by the Greek letter α (**alpha**). We will use F_α as shorthand when referring to the critical value of F.

The first row of terms in Figure 5-2 shows the critical value of F as a point dividing the sampling distribution of F into two parts. If $\alpha = .05$, the critical value of F is such that the proportion of Fs occurring *at or above* the critical value is .05. By subtraction, the remaining proportion of Fs falling *below* the critical value is $1.0 - .05 = .95$. In symbols, the proportion of cases at or above the critical value is α and below the critical value is $1.0 - \alpha$.

The second row in the figure indicates the relationship between the significance level and a researcher's decision concerning the status of the null hypothesis. That is, if the observed F equals or exceeds the critical value of F, we reject the null hypothesis; if not, we do not reject the null hypothesis. Finally, the third row gives names to the two categories of F defined by the critical value: the **region of rejection**—also known as the critical region—for the range of F values within which the null hypothesis will be rejected, and the **region of nonrejection** for the range of F values within which the null hypothesis will not be rejected.

DETERMINING THE CRITICAL VALUE OF F

Determining the critical value of F is relatively easy when the sampling distribution is available, but what do we do when it is not? This problem is increased immeasurably by the fact that a different sampling distribution of F exists for every possible combination of the number of treatment conditions (a) and sample size (s).[3] Although the theoretical sampling distributions for these different situations are known to statisticians and could be made available to researchers in that form, a book containing this information would be enormous. You may have noted that we do not need to plot the entire sampling distribution to determine the beginning of a rejection region—only the critical value. Thus, if some agreement exists among researchers concerning acceptable significance levels (and it does), tables of critical values—called an F **table**—can be constructed for all possible combinations of a and s in a relatively small space. Table 2 in Appendix A is such a table.

Using the F Table

To find a critical value in the F table, you need three pieces of information:

1. The degrees of freedom for the numerator of the F ratio

2. The degrees of freedom for the denominator of the F ratio

3. The significance level (α)

---

[3] The shapes of these different F distributions can be quite different from the one depicted in Figure 5-1, depending both on the number of treatment conditions and the number of subjects per condition.

Look at Table 2 in Appendix A. You will find that numerator df's are listed in the columns and denominator df's are listed in the rows. You may notice that not all combinations of df's are available in this table. Most F tables are abbreviated in some way or another in order to conserve space. Little is lost, however, since deletions occur only where changes in critical values of F are small, with increases in either numerator or denominator degrees of freedom.[4] Within each row, a choice exists of two significance levels, $\alpha = .05$ or $.01$. Critical values of F are listed in the body of the F table. (Values for the most commonly chosen significance level, $\alpha = .05$, are printed in boldface type.)

FORMING THE DECISION RULES

The **decision rules** represent a formal statement of the exact conditions under which the null hypothesis will be rejected. Once stated, a researcher merely needs to apply the rules to the F obtained from an experiment. The decision rules take the following form:

> **If the obtained value of F equals or exceeds F_α = _____ , reject the null hypothesis; otherwise, do not reject the null hypothesis.**

The critical value of F (F_α) is obtained from the F table. As we saw, this value depends on the degrees of freedom associated with the numerator and denominator terms of the F ratio and the significance level (α). This information can be communicated easily as follows:

$$F(df_{num.}, df_{denom.}) = \underline{\quad\quad} \text{ at } p = \alpha \quad ,$$

where all the vital information is presented compactly and unambiguously. (The letter p stands for the word *probability*.)

As an example, consider the analysis of variance we conducted on the data from Table 4-2 (summarized in Table 4-6, p. 80). In this example, $a = 2$ and $s = 10$. The degrees of freedom associated with the numerator term of the F ratio (MS_A) were found to be $df_A = 1$, and the degrees of

---

[4] When the critical value of F falls between two rows (or columns) of the table, most researchers follow the practice of choosing the row (or column) with the smaller number of degrees of freedom. This choice results in a critical value of F that is slightly larger than it should be. The consequence is a reduced rejection region (and a smaller value for α). Other options are available if this procedure seems unreasonable, for example, linear interpolation (see Lindman, 1974, pp. 18–19) or the use of more extensive tables of F (for example, Pearson and Hartley, 1970). This problem is not serious, however, and only becomes relevant when the obtained value of F lies very close to the critical value.

freedom associated with the denominator term $(MS_{S/A})$ were found to be $df_{S/A} = 18$. If we set the significance level at $\alpha = .05$, we have all the information we need to determine F_α.

Turning now to the F table, the first step is to find the point at which the appropriate column listing $df_{num.} = 1$ and the appropriate row listing $df_{denom.} = 18$ intersect. The two critical values of F are found in this cell of the table, one for $\alpha = .05$ (in boldface type) and the other for $\alpha = .01$. The value we want is $F_\alpha = 4.41$. Thus, the critical value of

$$F(1, 18) = 4.41 \text{ at } p = .05 \quad .$$

This value can now be substituted in the general decision rule:

If the obtained value of F equals or exceeds $F_\alpha = 4.41$, reject the null hypothesis; otherwise, do not reject the null hypothesis.

Consulting Table 4-6, we see that the obtained value of $F = 67.42$ clearly exceeds the critical value of F. Thus, we reject the null hypothesis and conclude that the two population treatment means are different. In a research report, we would omit the lines of reasoning with which investigators are very familiar and simply state that "the F is significant at $p = .05$." If we wanted to convey more information, we could say, "the $F(1, 18) = 67.42$ is significant, $p = .05$." This more complete statement gives all the relevant information the *reader* needs to make his or her own decision, and indicates what decision the researcher has made, that is, that the null hypothesis is rejected with $\alpha = .05$.

Some Comments on Format

For a class report, you would probably be expected to include a summary table for any analysis of variance you performed on your data. (Table 4-6 is an example of such a summary.) Such tables are usually omitted from research reports found in the literature, however, unless the analysis is complex. Instead, the outcome of the statistical analysis is generally reported in the text of an article. In addition, researchers are often expected to report the value for the denominator of the F ratio—the error term—in order to permit readers to perform their own statistical analysis of the data. Using the analysis reported in Table 4-6 as an example, we can report the error term, $MS_{S/A}$, as $MS_e = 2.67$.

A common mistake made by students is to omit the presentation of the treatment means. This omission is serious, since without the treatment means the results of an experiment are incomplete and relatively uninformative. If the experiment is a simple one, as in the example of Table 4-6, the means can be reported in the body of the text along with the summary of the statistical test. If the experiment is more complex, the means should be presented in a table, properly labeled with regard to the nature of the treatments, or, if the treatment conditions consist of a *quantitative* manipulation, in a figure.[5]

Reporting Significant Results. As you begin to read articles in the research literature, you will find that the statistical outcomes of analyses are reported in various ways. A recent practice in some journals is to require a researcher to state at the beginning of the results section the particular level of significance adopted, for instance $\alpha = .05$. Once this standard is stated, the outcome of any statistical analysis is then reported as being "significant" or "nonsignificant." More typically, however, the results of statistical tests are reported in symbols and numbers. Since you will need to understand the meaning of these statements when you come across them in your reading, we pause in our discussion of the analysis of variance to explain some frequently encountered terms. We consider first statements designating significant statistical tests.

Significance is often reported by means of $<$, the symbol for *less than,* in conjunction with a probability statement. For example, the statement that a particular analysis is "significant at $p < .05$" indicates that the obtained value of F falls within the rejection region established for the 5 percent level of significance. We will use this particular format in this book.

Often, significant results are reported with probabilities other than .05. For example, a test might be declared to be "significant at $p < .01$" or even "significant at $p < .001$." Such expressions rarely mean that the researcher has set his or her personal probability at these smaller values of α. They simply allow the few researchers who *have* adopted these smaller values of α to determine at a glance whether *they* will reject the null hypothesis. It should be noted that if an F can be rejected at an α level *smaller* than .05—for instance, .01—it would necessarily be rejected at $\alpha = .05$ as well. Thus, the use of this particular format provides information that is useful to the researcher who has adopted the more common 5 percent significance level and to the relatively rare investigator who prefers to use a significance level smaller than 5 percent.[6]

---

[5] The construction of tables and graphs is discussed in Chapter 7.
[6] In this regard, you will occasionally see reported what is called the "exact probability" of an F statistic. This probability, obtained from most computer calculations and certain "exotic" pocket calculators, refers to the proportion of the sampling distribution of the F statistic falling at or above the F obtained from an experiment. An $F(2, 45) = 6.39$, for example, has an exact

The habit of some researchers to report different probability levels (.05, .01, .001, and so on) while maintaining a personal probability level of $\alpha = .05$ (which most researchers do) leads to some problems of misinterpretation as to exactly what can be concluded following a test of significance. For example, many researchers have a tendency to assume that a finding that is significant at $p < .01$, say, is actually *more* significant than one that is significant at $p < .05$. Given the logic outlined in Chapter 3, a finding is either significant or it is not. The results of two experiments cannot be measured against each other in this manner.[7]

A similar misunderstanding can arise when a researcher reports a finding to be "highly significant," or even "very highly significant," rather than merely "significant." If these adverbs are intended as the verbal equivalents of the probability statements $p < .01$ and $p < .001$, respectively, then there is no problem. But often the researcher is implying with these words that a finding is actually "more significant" than one that is "only" significant at $p < .05$. Again, only *two conclusions* are possible in the reasoning we follow in rejecting null hypotheses, namely, significance or nonsignificance. *Degrees* of significance (for example, significant, highly significant, and very highly significant) are not included in the possible conclusions.

In summary, then, the term *significance* has a very precise meaning when applied to statistical tests. A test is statistically significant if the obtained F (or any other statistic, for that matter) falls within the rejection region determined by a researcher's choice of significance level. *Significance* is not to be interpreted as *importance,* however—a common error among individuals who are unfamiliar with these concepts. The importance of a finding depends on a number of additional factors, including its usefulness in both a practical and a theoretical sense. More information than the outcome of a statistical test is necessary for determining the importance of results from an experiment.

Reporting Nonsignificant Results. Nonsignificance is often denoted by $>$, the symbol for *greater than,* in conjunction with a probability statement. For

---

probability of $p = .0036$. Knowing this, one can simply apply his or her chosen significance level, for example $p = .05$, and reject the null hypothesis if the exact probability is smaller (which it is in this example) or not reject the null hypothesis if it is larger. This method of reporting the results of statistical tests has considerable merit, since it results in a clear distinction between an accurate description of the F test provided by the exact probability and a researcher's own decision to reject the null hypothesis or not. Since few readers of this book will have the means readily available to obtain exact probabilities, we will continue to use the "old-fashioned" F table until this situation changes!

[7] We discuss a measure that does permit an estimate of the size, or magnitude, of the treatment effects in Chapter 7. With this measure, one can compare the size of the treatment effects from one experiment with those from another. Such a comparison is difficult to make by observing the size of the F test alone.

example, the statement that a particular analysis is "not significant, $p > .05$" indicates that the obtained value of F falls within the region of nonrejection established at the 5 percent level of significance.[8] Also, the results of a statistical analysis are sometimes reported as "$F < 1$." Since no F smaller than 1.0 can be significant, this is a shorthand way of stating that a particular result is not significant.

ASSUMPTIONS OF THE ANALYSIS

We used the sampling distribution of F—by means of the F table—to find the critical value of F that marks the beginning of the rejection region. In our theoretical justification of this procedure, we assume that several conditions are met by the data being subjected to statistical analysis. This concept will require a bit of explaining. We start with the notion of treatment populations—extremely large numbers of individuals randomly subjected to the different treatment conditions. There is a different treatment population for each treatment condition. A population treatment mean is an average of the scores obtained from the subjects in a given treatment population. As we saw in Chapter 3, the null and alternative hypotheses are statements concerning the relationship among these population treatment means. That is, the null hypothesis states that the population treatment means are equal, and the alternative hypothesis states that not all the population treatment means are equal.

The assumptions underlying the use of the sampling distribution of F consist of statements about additional characteristics of these treatment populations. More specifically, we make three assumptions regarding the individual scores of the subjects present in these hypothetical treatment populations:

1. That they distribute themselves normally

2. That they show the same degree of variability from treatment population to treatment population

3. That they are independent from one another both within each treatment population or across populations

---

[8] Occasionally, you will see a statement that an outcome is not significant at a probability greater than .05, that is, $p > .10$ or $p > .25$. Such an expression means that the null hypothesis would not be rejected even if one adopted a relatively lax significance level, for example, $\alpha = .10$ or .25, respectively.

The first assumption is concerned with the particular shape of the frequency distribution of the scores in the population. This shape, which is defined mathematically and is known as the **normal distribution,** is commonly observed in nature, especially when characteristics being measured are influenced by a large number of independent factors. (The normal distribution is bell-shaped and is familiar to anyone who has read an introductory psychology text or has taken a course that was graded "on the curve.") The second assumption specifies that the different sets of treatment scores be equally variable, that is, have the same variance. This is known as the assumption of **homogeneity of variance.** The final assumption ultimately refers to the absence of systematic bias resulting from nuisance variables operating in the experiment.

How well does a typical experiment bear out these assumptions, and to what extent do deviations from them jeopardize the procedures we employ in evaluating a null hypothesis? The assumption of independence is generally satisfied through the random assignment of subjects to the treatment conditions. However, the other two assumptions—normality and homogeneity of variance—frequently are not satisfied in psychological experimentation. Fortunately, however, it appears that even relatively severe deviations from the conditions assumed have little effect on the evaluation process. In short, while it is important that we be aware of the assumptions underlying the statistical tests we perform, deviations from the conditions assumed have little consequence for the researcher using the completely randomized experimental design.

A COMPLETE NUMERICAL EXAMPLE

The Experimental Design

In this section, we work through a second numerical example to demonstrate all the calculations required for the analysis of variance. Consider a hypothetical experiment designed to study the effects of social environment on the sexual behavior of male hamsters. For two weeks preceding the critical testing day, subjects are housed in a cage either alone or with another hamster. The effects of three sorts of cage mates are to be studied, namely, a male hamster, a female hamster, and an ovariectomized, sexually unresponsive female hamster. A total of twenty sexually naive male hamsters are assigned randomly in equal numbers ($s = 5$) to the $a = 4$ treatment conditions.

TABLE 5-1   Preliminary Calculations for the Analysis of Variance

Treatment Conditions	Factor A (Type of Cage Mate)			
	Control (none) a_1	Male a_2	Female a_3	Female (unre-ceptive) a_4
Basic Observations	3	2	3	0
	5	1	0	4
	4	3	3	2
	3	5	1	7
	0	6	0	3
1. Sum of Scores	15	17	7	16
2. Sum of Squared Scores	59	75	19	78
3. Number of Observations	5	5	5	5
4. Mean	3.00	3.40	1.40	3.20
5. SS	14.00	17.20	9.20	26.80
6. Variance	3.50	4.30	2.30	6.70
7. Standard Deviation	1.87	2.07	1.52	2.59

On the critical testing day, each animal is placed in a new cage with a normal female hamster who has been housed separately and out of contact with any other animals in the experiment. The dependent variable consists of the number of sexual advances made by the male hamster within the first ten minutes of testing. The scores from this hypothetical experiment are presented in Table 5-1.

Preliminary Calculations

As a first step, certain preliminary calculations are performed, including the determination of the treatment sums (row 1), the sum of the squared observations (row 2), and the treatment means (row 4). For convenience, the numbers of observations per condition are listed in row 3. An examination of the means suggests that the sexual response of male hamsters to female strangers is depressed after they have been housed for two weeks with normal females ($\bar{A}_3 = 1.40$) when compared with the control condition ($\bar{A}_1 = 3.00$). In addition, housing the animals with other males ($\bar{A}_2 = 3.40$) or with sexually unresponsive females ($\bar{A}_4 = 3.20$) seems to have had relatively little effect on their sexual behavior relative to the control.

   As part of the preliminary calculations, most researchers would also obtain some measure of variability, for example, the variance or the standard deviation for each treatment condition. These measures of variability may be calculated from the summary information appearing in rows 1–3 of Table 5-1. The first step is to calculate the sum of squares (SS) for each treatment group. For any given set of scores,

$$SS = (\text{sum of the squared scores}) - \frac{(\text{sum of the scores})^2}{s} \quad .$$

Sums of squares for each of the treatment conditions appear in row 5 of the table. As an example of the calculations, the sum of squares for the control condition is equal to

$$SS = 59 - \frac{(15)^2}{5}$$

$$= 59 - \frac{225}{5} = 59 - 45.00 = 14.00 \quad .$$

Once the sum of squares is calculated, finding the variance and the standard deviation is easy. You will recall from Chapter 2 that the

$$\text{variance} = \frac{SS}{df} = \frac{SS}{s - 1} \quad .$$

For the control condition,

$$\text{variance} = \frac{14.00}{5 - 1} = \frac{14.00}{4} = 3.50 \quad .$$

The variances for each treatment condition are presented in row 6 of the table. Finally, the standard deviation of a set of scores is defined as

$$\text{standard deviation} = \sqrt{\text{variance}} \quad .$$

For the control condition,

$$\text{standard deviation} = \sqrt{3.50} = 1.87 \quad .$$

The standard deviations for the different treatment conditions are given in row 7 of the table. The main reason for calculating measures of variability for each treatment condition is to determine whether or not the groups show comparable degrees of variability. While an inspection of rows 6 and 7 of the table indicates some differences in variability from group to group, these differences are well within the range of values one would expect if chance factors alone were operating.[9]

Calculating Basic Ratios

The second step is the determination of the sums of squares, beginning with the calculation of the key quantities, namely, $[AS]$, $[A]$, and $[T]$. The computational formulas for these quantities are found in Table 4-3 (p. 74). Substituting in the formula for $[AS]$, we find

$$[AS] = \Sigma \, (AS)^2$$
$$= (3)^2 + (5)^2 + (4)^2 + (3)^2 + (0)^2$$
$$+ (2)^2 + (1)^2 + (3)^2 + (5)^2 + (6)^2$$
$$+ (3)^2 + (0)^2 + (3)^2 + (1)^2 + (0)^2$$
$$+ (0)^2 + (4)^2 + (2)^2 + (7)^2 + (3)^2$$
$$= 231.$$

Next, in calculating $[A]$, we find

$$[A] = \frac{\Sigma \, (A)^2}{s}$$
$$= \frac{(15)^2 + (17)^2 + (7)^2 + (16)^2}{5}$$
$$= \frac{225 + 289 + 49 + 256}{5} = \frac{819}{5}$$
$$= 163.80 \quad .$$

Finally, we must obtain $[T]$. For this calculation we need the grand total, which is most conveniently obtained by adding together the treatment sums appearing in row 1 of the table. That is,

$$T = \Sigma A = 15 + 17 + 7 + 16 = 55 \quad .$$

Now we can calculate

$$[T] = \frac{(T)^2}{a(s)}$$
$$= \frac{(55)^2}{4(5)}$$
$$= \frac{3,025}{20} = 151.25 \quad .$$

[9] Most advanced statistics texts present procedures for determining the significance of differences among treatment variances. For example, see Winer (1971, pp. 205–210).

TABLE 5-2   Analysis of Variance Summary Table

Source	Calculations	SS	df	MS	F
A	$[A] - [T] = 163.80 - 151.25 = 12.55$	3	4.18	.995*
S/A	$[AS] - [A] = 231 - 163.80 = 67.20$	16	4.20	
Total	$[AS] - [T] = 231 - 151.25 = 79.75$	19		

*$p > .05$.

Calculating the Sums of Squares

The three quantities calculated in the preceding section are now used to form the three sums of squares. From the formulas listed in Table 4-4 (p. 75),

$$SS_A = [A] - [T] = 163.80 - 151.25 = 12.55;$$

$$SS_{S/A} = [AS] - [A] = 231 - 163.80 = 67.20; \text{ and}$$

$$SS_T = [AS] - [T] = 231 - 151.25 = 79.75 \quad .$$

These values are recorded in the summary table (Table 5-2). As an arithmetical check, we should verify that

$$SS_T = SS_A + SS_{S/A}$$

$$79.75 = 12.55 + 67.20$$

$$= 79.75 \quad .$$

The Analysis of Variance

The final steps in the analysis (see Table 4-5, p. 79) are summarized in Table 5-2. First, the degrees of freedom are calculated:

$$df_A = a - 1 = 4 - 1 = 3;$$

$$df_{S/A} = a(s - 1) = 4(5 - 1) = 4(4) = 16; \text{ and}$$

$$df_T = a(s) - 1 = 4(5) - 1 = 20 - 1 = 19 \quad .$$

They are then subjected to an arithmetical check:

$$df_T = df_A + df_{S/A}$$

$$19 = 3 + 16$$

$$= 19 \quad .$$

Next, the two mean squares are obtained:

$$MS_A = \frac{SS_A}{df_A} = \frac{12.55}{3} = 4.18, \text{ and}$$

$$MS_{S/A} = \frac{SS_{S/A}}{df_{S/A}} = \frac{67.20}{16} = 4.20 \quad .[10]$$

Finally, we are able to find the value of the F ratio:

$$F = \frac{MS_A}{MS_{S/A}} = \frac{4.18}{4.20} = .995 \quad .$$

An examination of the F table shows the critical value of $F(3, 16)$ at $p = .05$ to be 3.24. The decision rules can now be stated formally:

If the obtained value of F exceeds or equals $F_\alpha = 3.24$, reject the null hypothesis; otherwise, do not reject the null hypothesis.

Applying these rules to the data of the experiment, where the obtained $F = .995$, leads us to the nonrejection of the null hypothesis. This decision is recorded as a footnote to the summary table stating that $p > .05$. (We could also have indicated simply that $F < 1$, since the F statistic cannot be significant if it is less than 1.)

ERRORS OF STATISTICAL INFERENCE

We have hinted in our discussion of hypothesis testing that researchers make wrong decisions from time to time. We can now be even more emphatic:

We can never be certain—one way or another—whether we have made the right decision after applying the decision rules to the results of an experiment.

---

[10] It is possible to calculate the $MS_{S/A}$ in an alternative way by averaging the individual variances obtained for each of the treatment groups. Using the variances appearing in row 6 of Table 5-1, we find

$$MS_{S/A} = \frac{3.50 + 4.30 + 2.30 + 6.70}{4} = \frac{16.80}{4} = 4.20 \quad ,$$

which is identical to the value for the $MS_{S/A}$ obtained in the normal fashion. In addition to providing a useful arithmetical check, this equivalency illustrates the fact that the $MS_{S/A}$ is actually an average of the separate within-treatment variances, each of which provides an estimate of experimental error for that condition.

Students often find this rude fact disillusioning and rather hard to accept; they would much prefer to deal with certainties. Unfortunately, however, complete certainty is unknown in psychological research, and, for that matter, in any other field of science that utilizes methods of statistical inference in its day-to-day operations. We tolerate this reality by determining as accurately as possible the *extent* of our uncertainties, that is, the magnitude of our errors of statistical inference. In this section, we are concerned with the nature of the error surrounding the process of hypothesis testing.[11]

In hypothesis testing, we make dichotomous, yes-no decisions. The decision rules we follow in evaluating the null hypothesis ultimately tell us to do one of two things—either to reject or not to reject the null hypothesis. Also, as we have noted, the statistical basis for these decisions is essentially probabilistic, which means that we take a calculated risk of being wrong with every decision we make. Two such risks, or errors of hypothesis testing, are discussed in this section. These are unimaginatively called type I and type II errors, due evidently to the order in which they were discovered and amplified.

Type I Error

Type I error is the easiest both to understand and to control. In discussing the sampling distribution of the F statistic (see Figure 5-1, p. 88), we noted that an important relationship exists between the frequency of occurrence by chance and the size of the F ratio: Expected frequencies decrease as the size of F increases. In order to reject the null hypothesis, which is the primary way we establish new facts from experiments, we must select a critical value of F, thereby dividing the range of all possible values of F into two regions. One of these, the region of nonrejection, extends from the lowest possible value of F (zero) to the critical value, and contains the range of values of F that we are willing to attribute to the operation of chance factors. The values in this region represent differences among treatment means that might very well have occurred by chance. If the value of F falls within this region, we do *not* reject the null hypothesis. The other region, the region of rejection, extends from the critical value to the largest possible value of F (infinity) and contains the range of values of F that we are not willing to attribute to the operation of chance factors. When the F falls within this region, we reject the null hypothesis.

If we follow this procedure every time we wish to compare two or more means, will we ever make a mistake when we reject the null hypothesis? The

---

[11] To supplement this simplified discussion, see *Design and Analysis* (pp. 65–68 and 525–529).

answer is yes. We will make a mistake whenever the null hypothesis is *true and* we *reject* the null hypothesis. That is, if the population treatment means are in fact *equal* (that is, if the null hypothesis is true), we will be in error if we reject the null hypothesis and conclude that they are *not all equal* to one another. In such a case, the decision to reject the null hypothesis will be the wrong decision. This error of inference is called the **type I error** and has been described as "seeing too much in the data" (Anderson, 1966, p. 72).

Most of the time we will not make this error, however. We will do so only when the null hypothesis is true and the *F* falls within the region of rejection. The reason for the comparative rarity of type I error is that the theoretical probability with which *F* will fall *by chance* in the rejection region is relatively small (usually $\alpha = .05$). Thus, we will make a type I error a small percentage of the time—the exact amount being specified by our significance level. We will make the *correct* inference, that is, no error, the rest of the time.

In summary, type I error is the logical consequence of hypothesis testing. It can occur only when two situations are *both present,* namely,

1. When the null hypothesis is true, *and*

2. When we reject the null hypothesis.

The magnitude of type I error is determined by the significance level chosen for the experiment by the researcher. In this sense, then, the probability with which a type I error will occur—that is, the size of the type I error—is directly under our control. If we are greatly concerned about making this particular error, we can simply lower the rejection probability, for example, from $\alpha = .05$ (5 times in 100) to $\alpha = .01$ (1 time in 100). The price we pay for being particularly concerned about type I error, however, is an increase in the size of another kind of error—the type II error.

Type II Error

While the focus of type I error is the *null* hypothesis, the focus of type II error is the *alternative* hypothesis. Suppose the alternative hypothesis is *true,* which means that some differences among treatment means do exist in the population. Given this happy event, can anything go wrong if we follow the procedures for testing the adequacy of the null hypothesis? Again, unfortunately, the answer is yes. Suppose some differences exist among the population treatment means (that is, the alternative hypothesis is *true*). Under these circumstances, we will make a mistake whenever the alternative hypothesis is *true and* we *fail to reject* the null hypothesis. In this case, we should reject the null hypothesis and conclude that some differences exist, but we fail to do so and therefore make the wrong decision. We will make a type II error whenever two situations are *both present:*

1. When the alternative hypothesis is true, *and*

2. When we *fail* to reject the null hypothesis.

Type II error, then, is an error caused by our failure to reject the null hypothesis when the alternative hypothesis is true. This type of error has been described as "not seeing enough in the data" (Anderson, 1966, p. 72).

Beta and Power. Some special terms are used to describe type II error. The size of the error is designated by the Greek letter β **(beta).** Type II error is usually expressed in terms of a probability, based on the frequency with which this error would be made if the experiment were repeated over and over a large number of times. **Power** refers to the converse side of type II error, the probability with which a *correct* decision will be made, that is, rejection of the null hypothesis when the alternative hypothesis is true. In symbols,

$$\text{power} = 1 - (\text{type II error})$$
$$= 1 - \beta \ . \tag{5-1}$$

The relationship between power and β is obvious: Any *decrease* in type II error will result in an *increase* in power.

Control of Type II Error. The magnitude of type I error is controlled directly through the choice of significance level (α). Type II error, on the other hand, is controlled indirectly through a variety of means. What these procedures accomplish is to increase the size of the F ratio relative to what it would have been otherwise. Any increase in the size of F increases a researcher's chances of rejecting the null hypothesis and thereby avoiding a type II error. Generally, a researcher achieves this increase by taking certain steps in designing the experiment. The following is a list of four such techniques and their means of increasing the F ratio.

1. *Increasing the number of subjects assigned to the treatment conditions.* Increasing sample size leads to an increase in the size of the numerator term relative to that of the denominator term of the F ratio and, consequently, to an increase in the size of the obtained F. An increase in sample size also increases the number of degrees of freedom for the denominator term—$df_{S/A} = a(s - 1)$—which leads to a smaller critical value of F. (You can verify this for yourself by turning to the F table and seeing what happens to the critical values of F as you move *down* any column.) While the benefits of increasing

sample size are obvious, this method of decreasing type II error is often difficult to implement because of (*a*) cost, especially when the subjects are animals; (*b*) availability, if the number of subjects with which to conduct the research is limited; or (*c*) time, since testing more subjects takes more time.

2. *Increasing the size of treatment effects.* In choosing specific treatment conditions, one can try to select treatments that are most likely to produce big differences. When this technique is used successfully, the numerator term of the *F* ratio is increased as a result of an increase in the size of the observed differences among the treatment means.

3. *Decreasing the amount of experimental error.* A decrease in the amount of experimental error present in an experiment produces an increase in the size of the *F* ratio by decreasing the size of the denominator term relative to the numerator term. A researcher generally accomplishes this result by attempting to restrict the variation of nuisance variables that will be controlled through the random assignment of subjects to conditions. A common example is the use of homogeneous subjects, subjects who are matched on relevant subject variables.

4. *Using a more sensitive experimental design.* In general, increasing the sensitivity of experiments leads to larger *F* ratios through a reduction in the size of the denominator term of the *F*. We will have more to say about this particular way to decrease type II error in Chapter 8.[12]

Comments and Clarification

Decision and Type of Error. You should now understand what we meant by stating that a certain degree of uncertainty surrounds hypothesis testing. Researchers make errors of inference, but fortunately they make correct decisions as well. Table 5-3 summarizes the circumstances under which errors and correct decisions occur. Hypothesis testing is concerned with two theoretical possibilities:

1. The treatment means in the population are equal—that is, the null hypothesis (H_0) is true.

2. At least some of the means are different—that is, the alternative hypothesis (H_1) is true.

---

[12] See *Design and Analysis* for a general discussion of power (pp. 525–546) and for an elaboration of the ways a researcher may increase the sensitivity, or the power, of an experiment (pp. 521–525).

TABLE 5-3   Experimenter Decision and the Nature of
the Population

Experimenter Decision	Nature of the Population	
	H_0 Is True (All μ_i's Are Equal.)	H_0 Is False (Not All μ_i's Are Equal.)
Reject H_0.	Type I error	Correct decision
Do not reject H_0.	Correct decision	Type II error

Taken together, these two hypotheses encompass all the possible ways in which the treatment means exist in the population. These two hypotheses are represented in the last two columns in Table 5-3.

Hypothesis testing results in one of two decisions: Either the null hypothesis is rejected or the null hypothesis is not rejected. These two decisions are represented in the last two rows in the table.

Depending on the status of the treatment means in the population, which of course we do not know, we will either make an error or we will make a correct decision.

If the hypothesis we decide on reflects or describes the population, our decision is correct; if it does not, an error is made.

First consider the consequences of rejecting the null hypothesis (see the row labeled "Reject H_0"). With respect to the situation in the population indicated in the first column—that H_0 is true—we would make a type I error by rejecting H_0; in other words, the hypothesis we chose (the alternative) does not describe the population. On the other hand, regarding the situation indicated in the second column—that H_0 is false—we would be making a correct decision in rejecting H_0; the hypothesis we chose (the alternative) describes the population.

Next, examine the consequences of not rejecting the null hypothesis (see the row labeled "Do not reject H_0"). If the situation indicated in the first column is correct (H_0 is true), the decision not to reject would be correct; the hypothesis we chose (the null) describes the population. On the other hand, if the situation indicated in the second column were correct (H_0 is false), we would have made a type II error, because we did not reject H_0 when it was false; the hypothesis we chose (the null) does not describe the population.

This table makes clear the fact that it is not logically possible to make *both* errors in testing a null hypothesis. We are permitted to make only one decision in hypothesis testing—either to reject or not to reject H_0. Once we have made that decision, we are susceptible to only *one* of the types of errors: a type I error if we have rejected the null hypothesis (the first row) or a type II error if we have not rejected the null hypothesis (the second row).

The Meaning of Proof in Hypothesis Testing. Clarification of the statement "to reject the null hypothesis" may prove useful at this point. Earlier we stated that to reject the null hypothesis is to accept the alternative hypothesis. This does not mean we have unequivocally proved that the alternative hypothesis is true, however. In the first place, when we reject the null hypothesis, we do so with the full knowledge that such a decision will be in error a small but still a finite percentage of the time (type I error). Second, while a particular theory may have predicted the differences observed in an experiment, rejection of the null hypothesis does not necessarily prove that theory. Other theories might make the same prediction. As Underwood and Shaughnessy (1975) put it,

> the results may be said to confirm or support the deduction from the theory, or they may be said to be consonant with theoretical expectations, but a theory is never said to be proved by a result (p. 154).

For these reasons, *proof* is generally considered too strong a word to refer to the rejection of the null hypothesis and acceptance of the alternative hypothesis.

The statement "do not reject the null hypothesis" is also frequently a source of confusion. You may have noted that we have avoided saying "*accept* the null hypothesis." Why are we inconsistent with our terminology? If the alternative hypothesis can be accepted, why not the null hypothesis? The answer is the near impossibility of "proving" that no differences in treatments exist in the population. Our experiment may have been insufficiently sensitive to detect the differences in the population. Perhaps if we had used more subjects, employed a more sensitive design, exerted more precise controls over the nuisance variables, chosen different levels for our independent variable, and so on, we would have rejected the null hypothesis.

By saying that we "do not reject the null hypothesis," we are in essence admitting to the logical possibility that a more powerful, or sensitive, experiment would have detected differences in the population treatment means and would have resulted in the rejection of the null hypothesis. When we accept the alternative hypothesis, we know how often we will be wrong— that is, we know the magnitude of the type I error. When we fail to reject the null hypothesis, we cannot accept that hypothesis under the same terms.[13] For this reason, we generally want to remain tentative in our decision. We will wait for additional information from more powerful experiments to provide a more adequate test of the null hypothesis. Once such experiments have been conducted, researchers are often willing to act as if they have in fact accepted the null hypothesis—by revising theory or by turning to a different problem—even though they are still confronted with the logical problem of demonstrating unequivocally that differences do not exist.

SPECIAL ANALYSIS WITH TWO TREATMENT CONDITIONS

Most experiments in psychology consist of more than two treatment conditions, although there was a time when the typical experiment contained only two different treatments. As you now know, the analysis of variance can be used to analyze experiments with any number of conditions, including, of course, the two-group experiment. In those early years, however, researchers used a statistical test called the Student t test, or t test, to analyze the results of two-group studies. In fact, researchers did not know about the analysis of variance until much later.

The interesting point is that the t test is a special case of the F test. To be more specific, if you were to conduct a t test and an F test on the data from the same two-group experiment, you would obtain *exactly the same information*. The reason the results would be identical is that the two statistical tests are algebraically equivalent, that is,

$$F = (t)^2 \text{ and } t = \sqrt{F} \ \ .$$

Due to this equivalency, we decided not to develop the t test in this book. The F test can be applied to almost any situation in which the t test can be used, but it can also be applied in situations where the t test cannot be used. We mention the t test here to aid you in understanding references to the t test in your reading of the research literature. Whenever you see reference to a t test, simply remind yourself that the test is equivalent to F. If the t is significant, F is significant; if t is not significant, F is not significant.

You will occasionally come across what are called *one-tailed* and *two-tailed*

---

[13] The reason is that the magnitude of the type II error requires knowledge about the differences among the population treatment means, which, of course, we do not have. See *Design and Analysis* (pp. 529–541) for a discussion of ways of overcoming this problem.

or *directional* and *nondirectional t* tests. These terms refer to two different sets of statistical hypotheses that can be used in the analysis of a two-group experiment. The statistical hypotheses we have used,

$$H_0 : \mu_1 = \mu_2, \text{ and}$$
$$H_1 : \mu_1 \neq \mu_2 \quad ,$$

do not specify whether μ_1 is larger than μ_2 or the reverse, but simply that the two means are not equal ($\neq$). Rejection of the null hypothesis permits the conclusion that the two means are different *regardless* of the direction of the difference. Such a test is a **nondirectional (two-tailed)** statistical test. The second kind of statistical hypothesis specifies a particular direction for the difference, either $\mu_1 < \mu_2$ or $\mu_2 < \mu_1$, and represents a **directional (one-tailed)** statistical test. We will say nothing more about directional tests. Their use is controversial, and most researchers employ instead the non-directional test we have presented in this book.[14]

SUMMARY

The final steps in the analysis consist of the evaluation of the F ratio. From the tabled values of the F statistic, which are based on theoretical sampling distributions of F, we are able to obtain the critical value of F. This value sets the lower boundary of the range of Fs within which we will reject the null hypothesis. If the F we obtain from an analysis falls within this range—if it is equal to or greater than the critical value of F—we reject the null hypothesis and conclude that some treatment effects are present in the population. If the observed F is smaller than the critical value, we do not reject the null hypothesis.

Application of the decision rules will lead to errors of statistical inference at least part of the time. One such error, type I error, is that committed when the null hypothesis is falsely rejected. The magnitude of this error is called the significance level and is set by the researcher at a fairly low value (for example, $\alpha = .05$) before the start of the experiment. The other error is the type II error, that committed when the null hypothesis is not rejected and the alternative hypothesis is true. The researcher controls this error indirectly by designing the experiment to be reasonably sensitive to the existence of treatment effects in the population.

---

[14] See Kirk (1972, pp. 276–290) for a sampling of the opinions that have been expressed in psychological journals regarding directional and nondirectional alternative hypotheses.

Both sorts of errors are expected to occur in experimentation, although not at the same time, and both contribute a certain degree of uncertainty to the conclusions stemming from any investigation. This uncertainty can be reduced, however, when subsequent studies support the original conclusions. Through statistical analysis, a researcher reaches a tentative decision concerning the sorts of results that would be obtained if the experiment were repeated a large number of times. This tentative decision is a shortcut used to avoid the actual repetition of an experiment. Although one could argue that such repetitions should be conducted much more frequently than they are in psychological research, the fact remains that repetition of an experiment is not undertaken as generally as it should be. Type I and type II errors represent the price we pay for using a single experiment to provide information about treatment effects in the population.

TERMS, CONCEPTS, AND SYMBOLS

---

sampling distribution of F t test
critical value   two-tailed (nondirectional) test
significance level   one-tailed (directional) test
alpha α
region of rejection F_α
region of nonrejection $F(df_{num.}, df_{denom.})$
F table p
decision rules MS_e
normal distribution $p < .05$
homogeneity of variance $p < .01$
type I error $p < .001$
type II error $p > .05$
beta $F < 1$
power β
                                            t

EXERCISES

---

1. For problem 1, Chapter 4 (p. 84), find the critical value of F from the F Table (Appendix A, Table 2). Is the obtained F significant statistically?

2. Do the same for problem 2, Chapter 4 (p. 85).

3. In this experiment subjects were asked to rate each of twenty-four words on a specified attribute. After the words were rated, each subject wrote down as many of the words he or she could remember. The data consist of the number of words recalled by each subject. Block randomization was used in the formation of four groups of sixteen subjects each. The subjects in a_1 rated each word on how pleasant its meaning was; in a_2 each word was rated on frequency of usage in the language; in a_3 each word was rated on how pleasant its sound was; and in a_4 each word was rated

on how frequently each subject thought its syllables were used in the language. The investigators were interested in whether the differences in the rating tasks would lead to differences in the numbers of words recalled. The results of the study are given below. Conduct an analysis of variance and determine if the different treatments had an effect on the word recall. To assist you in your calculations, we have indicated the sorts of summary calculations you will need to make to complete the analysis. Though they are not needed for the F ratio, the mean, variance, and standard deviation are requested for each treatment condition. (Save your calculations for problem 1, Chapter 6, p. 145, and for problem 2 of Chapter 7, p. 173.)

Pleasantness of Meaning	Frequency of Word	Pleasantness of Sound	Frequency of Syllables
11	7	8	3
11	3	2	4
12	10	8	3
9	7	8	2
10	7	9	5
13	4	4	2
11	8	6	5
9	7	7	5
10	5	7	2
6	7	1	8
13	8	9	4
7	11	3	8
12	8	6	5
12	10	5	7
9	9	11	7
10	8	8	5

Sum of Scores	_____	_____	_____	_____
Sum of Squared Scores	_____	_____	_____	_____
Mean	_____	_____	_____	_____
SS	_____	_____	_____	_____
Variance	_____	_____	_____	_____
Standard Deviation	_____	_____	_____	_____

4. A student was interested in comparing the effects of four kinds of reinforcement on children's performance in a visual discrimination task. The

four reinforcements used were praise for correct responses, a jelly bean for correct responses, reproof for mistakes, and silence. A block randomization procedure was used to assign the children to the four groups, with seven children in each condition. The measure of performance given below is the number of errors made during the course of the testing.

Praise	Jelly Bean	Reproof	Silence
68	78	94	54
63	69	82	51
58	58	73	32
51	57	67	74
41	53	66	65
40	52	61	80
34	48	61	73

Analyze the data with an analysis of variance and determine whether the treatments had an effect. (Save your calculations for problem 2 of Chapter 6, p. 146.)

Analytical Comparisons in the Single-Factor Design

6

In the last chapter, you saw how the F ratio and the theoretical sampling distribution of the F statistic are used in the evaluation of the adequacy of a null hypothesis, which states that the population treatment means are equal. To evaluate this hypothesis, we obtain the MS_A, which reflects the presence of treatment effects in the population in addition to experimental error. The fact that each treatment condition contributes to the calculation of the MS_A suggests that this mean square represents a sort of *average* of the differences among the treatment means. For this reason, the F ratio formed to evaluate this null hypothesis is often called the overall, or **omnibus, F test.**

We considered these statistical procedures in detail, since they constitute the first in a series of building blocks leading to the analysis of more complicated experimental designs. However, the test of this particular null hypothesis is of limited value to most researchers. A rejection of it indicates very little about the adequacy of the research hypotheses that generated the experiment in the first place. For example, suppose we have four treatment means and find a statistically significant F ratio based on the deviation of these means. The significant omnibus F test indicates that at least two means are significantly different. We do not know, however, which means are significantly different from each other or even if more than one such difference is significant.

In this chapter, we concern ourselves with the evaluation of more specific null hypotheses, hypotheses that correspond directly to the research hypotheses. We refer to these more focused statistical tests as **analytical comparisons** to stress the fact that they are analytical. While the procedures described in the last chapter can lead to the conclusion that some differences among the treatment means are present in the population, they do not enable us to determine which means are different or which means are the same. Analytical comparisons do permit us to discover such information, and for this reason they provide the researcher with an extremely valuable tool for pinpointing the source or sources of differences observed in an experiment.

THE NATURE OF ANALYTICAL COMPARISONS

An analytical comparison can be defined as a statistical test in which the number of means to be compared is smaller than the total number of treatment groups.[1] The most common form of analytical comparison is one in which two treatment means are compared. Such comparisons are performed because of their obvious specificity, that is, the difference between these two specific treatments. As we will explain, however, in certain situations it is

---

[1] A more accurate definition can be given in terms of the degrees of freedom associated with the numerator term in the omnibus F ratio, that is, $df_A = a - 1$. Specifically, an analytical comparison is defined as a statistical test in which the numerator degrees of freedom are less than df_A.

informative to involve more than two means in an analytical comparison, either by averaging together two or more treatment conditions or by assessing the variation among a subset of treatment means taken from the larger number of treatments represented in the experiment.

Planned versus Unplanned Comparisons

Analytical comparisons permit researchers to assess the research hypotheses formed in the planning stages of an experiment. Such comparisons are usually called **planned comparisons,** because they are in fact planned before the start of the experiment. The primary requirement is that an analysis plan be formulated *before* the data are collected. Since most researchers form, or at least imply, an analysis plan when they specify their research hypotheses and design experiments to test them, this approach is really the modal way of analyzing the results of an experiment.

In contrast, **unplanned comparisons,** also known as **post-hoc** or **multiple comparisons,** are comparisons that are suggested after the data are examined. Such comparisons are not specifically predicted before the start of an experiment and are, in this sense, unplanned. Unfortunately, little agreement exists among researchers as to the "appropriate" way to evaluate the significance of unplanned comparisons. Though we do not discuss the problem in detail, we do cover the issues involved and offer some recommendations in the final section of this chapter.

AN EXAMPLE OF THE RELATIONSHIP BETWEEN RESEARCH HYPOTHESES AND ANALYTICAL COMPARISONS

An Experiment

As an example, consider a hypothetical experiment based on a study proposed by a student as a possible research project.[2] The purpose of this experiment is to study the effects of odors from other animals on the exploratory behavior of kangaroo rats. It is known that many rodents depend on scent markings to establish territory and to identify friend or foe. Kangaroo rats are ideally suited for study, since they spend a great deal of time depositing scents on objects in their environment and seem to be highly

---

[2] We wish to thank Kay Holekamp for suggesting this example.

dependent on scents in their every-day behavior. The general plan of the experiment is to place a rat in an artificial burrow system made of plexiglass tubing and to measure the amount of time the rat spends exploring the new surroundings. The treatment conditions are differentiated by the different odors introduced in the artificial burrow from sawdust taken from the cages of other kangaroo rats.

Three Research Hypotheses. Three research hypotheses are to be tested in this experiment:

1. Kangaroo rats will avoid environments in which the odors of unfamiliar kangaroo rats are present.

2. Kangaroo rats will avoid environments in which the odors come from kangaroo rats with whom they have lost a territorial battle.

3. Kangaroo rats will forget the smells of previous winners of the territorial battles.

The Experimental Design. The experiment is designed around these three hypotheses. To test the first hypothesis, two treatments are to be contrasted: a control condition, in which sterile sawdust is placed in the testing apparatus, and a condition in which the sawdust is taken from a cage that housed a kangaroo rat who had never been in contact with the rat being tested. We will refer to these two treatments as the *control condition* and the *unfamiliar condition.* To test the second hypothesis, a third condition is introduced in which the sawdust is taken from the cage housing a rat with whom the rat being tested had just fought a territorial battle and lost. We will refer to this treatment as the *familiar-immediate condition.* The contrast most relevant to the second research hypothesis is between the *familiar-immediate* and the *unfamiliar conditions.* [3]

In order to test the third hypothesis—that a rat will forget the smell of a previous winner of a territorial fight—the experiment must include at least two "familiar" conditions, differing only in the time elapsed between territorial defeat and testing. Any difference in the exploratory behavior of the animals in these two conditions will be attributed to the forgetting of the

---

[3] While a comparison between the familiar-immediate condition and the control condition is possible, it lacks the analytical focus of the one proposed. That is, a difference observed between the familiar-immediate and the control conditions could be attributed entirely to the odor of another kangaroo rat, and not to the specific experience associated with that particular rat. The proposed comparison removes this ambiguity from the contrast and focuses on the effects of the negative experience, independent of the effects of the odor from another kangaroo rat.

presumably negative experience. Resources permitting, it would be advisable to include several delay groups in the experiment, one sufficiently long to guarantee that forgetting—if it occurs—will be observed, and others with intermediate delays to indicate the nature of the forgetting function, that is, the shape of the function relating exploratory behavior and time since contact. Is forgetting gradual over the total interval? Does it occur rapidly at first and slow down with more time? Or, alternatively, is it gradual at first and rapid later on? The use of intermediate delay conditions would help the investigator to distinguish among these three possible descriptions of the forgetting process. For this example, we have included two delay conditions, one with a delay of two weeks (*the familiar-two-weeks condition*) and the other with a delay of four weeks (*the familiar-four-weeks condition*). It is predicted that after four weeks, the rats will have forgotten the unsuccessful battle and treat that previously familiar odor as an unfamiliar one.

Summary of the Conditions. Each research hypothesis involves a different portion of the experimental design. The first hypothesis is tested by the comparison of the control and unfamiliar conditions. The second is tested by the comparison of the unfamiliar and familiar conditions. The third research hypothesis, like the others, only requires two treatment conditions, but given the arguments in the preceding paragraph, it will be tested by the comparison of the three familiar conditions (immediate, two-weeks, and four-weeks). You may have noticed that two of the treatment conditions are involved in the evaluation of more than one research hypothesis. That is, the unfamiliar condition is used to test the first two research hypotheses, while the familiar-immediate condition is used to test the last two research hypotheses. The possibility that specific treatment conditions can be shared among two or more research hypotheses means that fewer treatment conditions have to be included in the experiment. This multiple use of treatment conditions saves time, energy, and other resources.

The complete experimental design is summarized in Table 6-1. We refer to the five treatment conditions either as the levels of the experiment—a_1, a_2, and so on—or by their descriptive titles. In an actual experiment, equal numbers of kangaroo rats would be assigned at random to the different treatment conditions.

Analytical Comparisons

Corresponding to each research hypothesis is an analytical comparison, which can be represented in terms of a set of statistical hypotheses. This

TABLE 6-1　A Summary of the Experimental Design in the Kangaroo-Rat Study

Level	Condition	Treatment
a_1	Control	Sterile sawdust in apparatus
a_2	Unfamiliar	Sawdust from a rat "stranger"
	Familiar	Sawdust from a familiar dominant rat
a_3	Familiar-Immediate	Immediately after fight
a_4	Familiar-Two Weeks	Two weeks after fight
a_5	Familiar-Four Weeks	Four weeks after fight

relationship is made explicit in Table 6-2. Consider the first research hypothesis, that kangaroo rats will tend to avoid environments in which the odor of an unfamiliar kangaroo rat is present. The analytical comparison consists of a contrast between the control and unfamiliar conditions (level a_1 versus level a_2). The null hypothesis associated with this comparison states that the two population treatment means are equal:

$$H_0: \mu_1 = \mu_2 \quad .$$

If the null hypothesis is rejected, we will accept the alternative hypothesis that the two means are different, namely,

$$H_1: \mu_1 \neq \mu_2 \quad .$$

Accepting this alternative hypothesis permits us to conclude that the two means are different, but the nature of the hypothesis does not specifically tell us the direction of the difference, that is, which mean is larger or which mean is smaller. For this information, we simply look at the treatment means and note which mean is larger than the other.[4]

It is instructive to consider again the nature of the conclusion we can come to when we reject the overall, or omnibus, null hypothesis, which you learned to evaluate in Chapter 5. You will recall that rejection of the overall null hypothesis,

$$H_0: \mu_1 = \mu_2 = \mu_3 = \mu_4 = \mu_5 \quad ,$$

---

[4] This set of statistical hypotheses is sometimes called a *nondirectional test* in that differences in either direction (μ_1 larger than μ_2 and μ_1 smaller than μ_2) will be evaluated in the statistical test. It is possible to use a *directional test* that specifies a difference in only one of these directions, but this type of statistical test is somewhat controversial in psychological research. You may recall that we discussed these two types of statistical tests in Chapter 5 when we considered the use of the *t* test in the analysis of experiments that included only two treatment conditions (see pp. 109–110).

TABLE 6-2   Three Research and Statistical Hypotheses

Research Hypotheses	Statistical Hypotheses
1. Rats avoid unfamiliar odors.	$H_0: \mu_1 = \mu_2$ $H_1: \mu_1 \neq \mu_2$
2. Rats avoid familiar odors.	$H_0: \mu_2 = \mu_3$ $H_1: \mu_2 \neq \mu_3$
3. Rats forget familiar odors.	$H_0: \mu_3 = \mu_4 = \mu_5$ $H_1:$ Some means are different

leads to the acceptance of a *nonspecific* alternative hypothesis,

$$H_1: \text{ not all } \mu\text{'s are equal} \quad .$$

Thus, rejection of the omnibus null hypothesis merely tells us that some differences exist in the population. In contrast, as we saw in the last paragraph, rejection of a null hypothesis associated with an analytical comparison permits a much more specific conclusion, namely, that the control and unfamiliar treatments differ.

The second research hypothesis and the corresponding set of statistical hypotheses are presented in row 2 of Table 6-2. Rejection of the null hypothesis that compares that unfamiliar and familiar-immediate conditions would allow us to conclude that these two treatments differ in the population.

The third research hypothesis presents a null hypothesis of a different sort, a statement that the three "familiar" conditions are equal:

$$H_0: \mu_3 = \mu_4 = \mu_5 \quad .$$

The companion alternative hypothesis,

$$H_1: \text{ Some means are different} \quad ,$$

states that differences exist among the means, but does not specify which ones. While the conclusion afforded by rejecting this null hypothesis is not as specific as those associated with the other two research hypotheses, it is still analytical when compared with the omnibus null hypothesis. Rejection of the omnibus null hypothesis only permits us to conclude that some differences exist among the *five* treatment means, while rejection of this particular null hypothesis allows us to conclude that some differences exist among the *three* familiar treatment means. This reduction in possible outcomes represents a clear increase in specificity and analytical power.

If this third comparison is significant, we will probably want to test additional hypotheses to determine the nature of the differences responsible for the rejection of the null hypothesis. We discussed this point earlier when we considered the design of this experiment. To reiterate, in addition to answering the question of whether or not familiar odors are forgotten, we also want to ask something about the specific changes occurring with time: Does forgetting continue at a steady pace over the four-week interval or does it occur abruptly, either early or late during the time period studied?[5]

Synopsis

The omnibus F test is an indirect way of testing the explicit research hypotheses that occupy a central position in the design of most experiments. In contrast, planned comparisons provide a direct assessment of these research hypotheses. We are now ready to consider how analytical comparisons can be evaluated statistically in the analysis of variance. We will restrict our attention to the analysis of the difference between two means, since this is the type of analytical comparison most frequently encountered in the psychological literature.[6]

THE ANALYSIS OF THE DIFFERENCE BETWEEN TWO MEANS

As noted, the statistical analysis of the difference between two means is the most common type of analytical comparison. The two means being compared can either be the means from single treatment conditions or averages of means from two or more conditions. The justification for the averaging comes from the logic of the research design. In either case, the comparison involves a contrast between two means. Because two means are compared, the variability associated with them is based on two deviations, as would be true in a single-factor experiment with two treatment conditions. Conse-

---

[5] These sorts of questions are best analyzed by means of a method called a *trend analysis*. We will discuss trend analysis in Chapter 12.

[6] Moreover, analyzing a comparison such as the one specified by the third research hypothesis is relatively easy. We can treat the subset of conditions as an experiment in its own right and then use the standard formula for the SS_A from Chapter 4. In this example, there would be three conditions (a_3, a_4, and a_5). The treatment sums are A_3, A_4, and A_5; the grand sum is $T = A_3 + A_4 + A_5$; sample size is s; and $a = 3$. The error term for this comparison is the $MS_{S/A}$ obtained from the overall analysis based on *all* the treatment conditions.

quently, the mean square based on the difference between the two means has associated with it a single degree of freedom, $df = 1$. Thus, we often refer to such comparisons as **single-df comparisons.**

The only difficult part of the statistical analysis is in the calculation of the sum of squares. The other steps in the analysis are relatively straight-forward. We will consider the calculation of the sum of squares fully so that you can understand the computational formula and the means of modifying the formula to suit specific needs precisely. The technique for analyzing the difference between two means will prove to be a useful and flexible tool for extracting meaningful information from your data.

Our coverage of this technique consists of several steps. First, we intro-duce a way of expressing the difference between two means that will facili-tate the calculation of the sum of squares for a comparison. Next, we explain how you can adapt this method to your own analytical comparisons. Finally, we present the complete computational formula for calculating the needed sum of squares. In the remainder of this section, we consider the statistical evaluation of analytical comparisons and two numerical examples to illus-trate the entire process.

Using Coefficients to Express the Difference Between Two Means

The heart of the computational formula for the sum of squares representing the difference between two means is a special set of numbers called **coeffi-cients.** The coefficients specify how each treatment mean enters into the determination of the difference being evaluated. Treatments specifically in-volved in a comparison will have either positive or negative coefficients, while treatments not involved will have coefficients equal to zero.

The computational formula we will use to calculate the sum of squares for a comparison expresses the difference between two means as the sum of all the treatment means "weighted" by the coefficients. That is,

difference between two means
= sum of the weighted treatment means   .

We obtain each **weighted treatment mean** by multiplying each mean by the appropriate coefficient. That is,

weighted mean = (coefficient)(mean)   .

In our experience, students initially feel that expressing a single-df compari-son in terms of coefficients is awkward and inefficient. It is important to realize that the real advantage of this procedure is that it results in a convenient formula for calculating the sums of squares for these comparisons. Before presenting computational formulas, however, we will first indicate how the weighting process works and, in the next section, how to construct weighting coefficients for any single-df comparison you may choose to make.

A Simple Comparison. Let's examine the weighting process in a simple comparison between two means, $\bar{A}_1$ and $\bar{A}_2$. The coefficients for the two means are designated as c_1 and c_2, respectively. If we let $c_1 = +1$ and $c_2 = -1$, the two weighted means, obtained by multiplying each mean by the appropriate coefficient, are

$$(c_1)(\bar{A}_1) = (+1)(\bar{A}_1), \text{ and}$$
$$(c_2)(\bar{A}_2) = (-1)(\bar{A}_2) \quad .$$

The **sum of the weighted treatment means** becomes

$$(+1)(\bar{A}_1) + (-1)(\bar{A}_2) \quad ,$$

which is algebraically equivalent to

$$\bar{A}_1 - \bar{A}_2 \quad ,$$

the difference between the two treatment means. By reversing the signs of the two coefficients—letting $c_1 = -1$ and $c_2 = +1$—we express the difference in the "opposite" direction, that is, $\bar{A}_2 - \bar{A}_1$.

If instead of two means in an experiment we had three, we could still represent the difference between $\bar{A}_1$ and $\bar{A}_2$ in this manner by assigning a coefficient of *zero* to the mean not entering the comparison. In this example, then, $c_3 = 0$, and the sum of the three weighted means becomes

$$
\begin{aligned}
(c_1)(\bar{A}_1) + (c_2)(\bar{A}_2) + (c_3)(\bar{A}_3) &= (+1)(\bar{A}_1) + (-1)(\bar{A}_2) + (0)(\bar{A}_3) \\
&= (+1)(\bar{A}_1) + (-1)(\bar{A}_2) + 0 \\
&= \bar{A}_1 - \bar{A}_2 \quad ,
\end{aligned}
$$

the same basic difference in which we are interested.

Summary. We hope you have some understanding of how the weighting of means with the coefficients is used to express the difference between two means. As we have just shown, coefficients can be used to draw out two means and reduce them to a simple difference. Obviously, the smaller the difference revealed in this manner, the smaller the chances of finding a significant difference; conversely, the larger the difference the greater the chances of finding a significant effect. The difference extracted in this manner is the source of a sum of squares that can be evaluated with an F test.

As you will see in the next section, where we consider a more complicated comparison, the coefficients serve not only to isolate the means to be compared but also to average sets of means when several are grouped together in the comparison. We consider next how a set of coefficients is constructed for any single-*df* comparison of interest in an experiment. The discussion will be followed by a presentation of the computational formula for the sum of squares for these comparisons and the remainder of the statistical analysis.

Constructing the Coefficients

The procedure described here for constructing a set of coefficients for any single-*df* comparison is foolproof. At first you will probably be dependent on it, but as you gain experience you will find that you are able to write the coefficients directly from the research hypothesis or its associated null-hypothesis statement.

We will present the construction rules in the context of an example. Suppose an experiment has the following $a = 6$ treatment conditions:

Drug A		Drug B			No Drug
Batch 1 a_1	Batch 2 a_2	Batch 1 a_3	Batch 2 a_4	Batch 3 a_5	Control a_6

The first two conditions consist of two samples or batches of drug A obtained from a pharmaceutical supplier. The next three conditions consist of three batches of another drug (drug B), and the last condition is a no-drug control group. Suppose we want to compare drug A with drug B. Thus, we will compare the mean of the two drug A conditions (a_1 and a_2) with the mean of the three drug B conditions (a_3, a_4, and a_5); the mean for the control condition (a_6) will not enter this particular comparison. Coefficients for this comparison may be constructed by means of the following set of rules:

1. *Verbalize the comparison.* We start with a verbal statement of the research hypothesis. For this example, the statement could be this: "We predict that drug A and drug B will differ in their effects on performance."

2. *Write the null-hypothesis statement (H_0).* In this step, we translate the verbal description of the comparison into a null-hypothesis

statement, which provides a clear and unambiguous statement of the nature of the comparison under consideration. For this example,

$$H_0: \frac{\mu_1 + \mu_2}{2} = \frac{\mu_3 + \mu_4 + \mu_5}{3} \quad .$$

3. *Isolate the coefficients.* We can use the null-hypothesis statement to determine a set of coefficients appropriate for this—or any—comparison. We will obtain three sets of coefficients: (*a*) one set to be used with all the means on the left of the equal sign, (*b*) another set to be used with all the means on the right of the equal sign, and (*c*) a third set to be used with means that do not appear in the null-hypothesis statement. For either set of means listed in the null-hypothesis statement, the coefficient is equal to the fraction

$$\frac{1}{\text{number of means}} \quad .$$

In addition, we will arbitrarily give the coefficient for the means on the left a *positive* value and the coefficient for the means on the right a *negative* value. (The signs can be reversed without affecting the statistical assessment of a comparison.) Thus, the coefficient for each of the *two* means on the left is $+1/2$ and the coefficient for each of the *three* means on the right is $-1/3$. The coefficient for means not entering into a comparison is *zero*. Thus, the entire set of coefficients is

$$c_1 = +\frac{1}{2}, \ c_2 = +\frac{1}{2}, \ c_3 = -\frac{1}{3}, \ c_4 = -\frac{1}{3}, \ c_5 = -\frac{1}{3}, \text{ and } c_6 = 0 \quad .$$

While these coefficients can be used to calculate the sum of squares for the comparison, transforming the fractional coefficients into whole numbers is generally more convenient in order to avoid rounding errors. This transformation is accomplished in the final step.

4. *Eliminate Fractional Coefficients.* We remove the fractional coefficients by multiplying the set obtained in the last step by the *lowest common denominator* (the smallest number divisible by all the denominator terms) of the set of fractions. In this example, the lowest common denominator is 6. To obtain whole numbers, we simply multiply each of the fractions by 6. The two different fractional coefficients thus become

$$(6) \left(+\frac{1}{2} \right) = +3 \text{ and } (6) \left(-\frac{1}{3} \right) = -2 \quad .$$

Finally, we can write the complete set of coefficients:

$$a_1 \quad a_2 \quad a_3 \quad a_4 \quad a_5 \quad a_6$$

$$c_i: \quad +3 \quad +3 \quad -2 \quad -2 \quad -2 \quad 0 \quad .$$

Review and Check. This system will permit you to obtain a set of coefficients with which to extract the desired information from your data.[7] One important characteristic of a set of coefficients is that the individual coefficients must sum to zero. That is,

$$\Sigma c_i = 0 \quad . \tag{6-1}$$

Thus, as a check on our calculation, we substitute the coefficients in equation (6-1) to verify that they actually do sum to zero:

$$\Sigma c_i = (+3) + (+3) + (-2) + (-2) + (-2) + (0)$$
$$= 0 \quad .$$

The coefficient-construction scheme is really only needed for complex comparisons, as in the example cited. When a comparison consists of a simple contrast between two treatment means where no averaging of means is involved, developing a set of coefficients is unnecessary. For these comparisons, the coefficients are of the form $+1$, -1, 0, 0, 0, etc., where the nonzero coefficients ($+1$ and -1) are assigned to the two treatment conditions involved in the comparison, and the zero coefficients are assigned to all the remaining treatment conditions.

The Computational Formula for the Comparison Sum of Squares

Having detailed the construction of coefficients, we can present the computational formula with which is calculated the sum of squares associated with any comparison between two means. Although means could be used, using sums makes the calculations easier. For this reason, the formula for sums of squares associated with single-df comparisons is generally written with treatment sums rather than treatment means. Specifically,

$$SS_{A_{comp.}} = \frac{[\Sigma\,(c_i)(A_i)]^2}{s[\Sigma\,(c_i)^2]} \quad . \tag{6-2}$$

---

[7] This is not the only set that will serve this function, however. We could also use, for example, the fractional coefficients obtained in step 3. On the other hand, we need only one set of coefficients, and this particular set has the computational advantages of avoiding fractions while producing the smallest products, which in turn give us smaller numbers in our calculations.

Since many students have trouble "reading" this important formula, we will translate it into words.[8] But first, notice that all the quantities referred to in equation (6-2) are familiar: c_i represents the coefficient associated with a particular treatment sum (A_i), and s refers to the number of subjects in each of the treatment conditions.

It is convenient to consider the numerator and the denominator of this formula separately. Beginning with the "center" of the numerator term and working "outward," we have

$(c_i)(A_i)$ = the product or weighted treatment sum formed by multiplying a coefficient (c_i) by the relevant treatment sum (A_i) ;

$\Sigma\,(c_i)(A_i)$ = $(c_1)(A_1) + (c_2)(A_2) + (c_3)(A_3)$ + etc.

= the sum of the treatment totals *weighted* by the appropriate coefficients; and

$[\Sigma\,(c_i)(A_i)]^2$ = the square of the sum of the weighted treatment totals .

In words, the numerator term of equation (6-2) consists of the square of the sum of the weighted treatment totals.

In the denominator term, we have

s = the number of subjects per treatment condition ;

$(c_i)^2$ = the square of each coefficient (c_i) ;

$\Sigma\,(c_i)^2$ = the sum of the squared coefficients; and finally ,

$s[\Sigma\,(c_i)^2]$ = the sum of the squared coefficients times the number of subjects per treatment condition .

We will return to these operations with actual calculations from a numerical example. But first we will complete the entire testing process by considering the evaluation of any difference revealed by a comparison.

Evaluating the Null Hypothesis

The mean square for a comparison is given by this formula:

$$MS_{A_{comp.}} = \frac{SS_{A_{comp.}}}{df_{A_{comp.}}} \quad . \tag{6-3}$$

For comparisons assessing the difference between two means,

$$df_{A_{comp.}} = 1 \quad . \tag{6-4}$$

---

[8] Some students have reported difficulty in understanding the notation used to designate a comparison. The symbol $A_{comp.}$ is a shorthand way of referring to an analytical comparison involving the treatment levels of factor A. When appended to another symbol, for example SS, the resulting symbol, $SS_{A_{comp.}}$ is read as "the sum of squares for an analytical comparison involving the A treatment means."

The null hypothesis is evaluated by means of a *comparison F* ratio, which takes the following form:

$$F_{comp.} = \frac{MS_{A_{comp.}}}{MS_{S/A}} . \tag{6-5}$$

Note that the error term ($MS_{S/A}$) is the same mean square that is calculated in the overall analysis of variance. The reason is that the comparison mean square is assumed to reflect two sources of variation, namely, the comparison itself and experimental error. The within-groups mean square is influenced by experimental error alone, and provides an estimate of experimental error that is based on all the information available from the experiment. Thus, when the null hypothesis is true and the two comparison means are equal in the population, the comparison *F* ratio specified in equation (6-5) is expected to approximate 1.0. On the other hand, if the two comparison means are different, $F_{comp.}$ should be greater than 1.0.

Following the same line of argument that we used for the evaluation of the omnibus null hypothesis, we form a set of decision rules specifying the values of $F_{comp.}$ that will and will not permit the rejection of the comparison null hypothesis. More specifically,

> **If the obtained values of $F_{comp.}$ equals or exceeds F_α = _____, reject the null hypothesis; otherwise, do not reject the null hypothesis.**

In this statement, we obtain the critical value of F (F_α) from the F table in the usual manner, namely, by looking up the F listed under the appropriate numerator and denominator degrees of freedom and the significance level α we have chosen to use in our research. In this case, $df_{num.} = 1$ and $df_{denom.} = df_{S/A}$. We now turn to a numerical example of the use of analytical comparisons.

A Numerical Example

Some hypothetical data for the kangaroo-rat study are presented in Table 6-3. The dependent variable is the amount of time (in minutes) that each animal spent exploring the artificial burrow during a sixty-minute testing period. There are $s = 7$ subjects in each of the $a = 5$ treatment conditions.

Overall Analysis of Variance. Since we have made some explicit predictions concerning the outcome of this experiment (see Table 6-2, p. 121), we are not particularly interested in the significance of the overall F test. Even so, most researchers would still perform these calculations for ease of obtaining the

TABLE 6-3   A Numerical Example

Treatment Conditions	Control a_1	Unfa-miliar Smell a_2	Familiar Smells		
			Imme-diate a_3	Two-Week Delay a_4	Four-Week Delay a_5
Basic Observations	33	33	6	11	22
	31	19	0	4	15
	33	34	0	12	30
	38	21	10	15	24
	47	20	8	6	23
	42	22	12	12	21
	37	24	5	22	27
Sum of Scores	261	173	41	82	162
Mean	37.29	24.71	5.86	11.71	23.14
Sum of Squared Scores	9,925	4,507	369	1,170	3,884

error term, $MS_{S/A}$, and readers might want the information. Thus, we set forth the necessary calculations, though without comment:

$$[AS] = \Sigma\,(AS)^2$$
$$= 9{,}925 + 4{,}507 + 369 + 1{,}170 + 3{,}884$$
$$= 19{,}855 \quad ;$$

$$[A] = \frac{\Sigma\,(A)^2}{s}$$

$$= \frac{(261)^2 + (173)^2 + (41)^2 + (82)^2 + (162)^2}{7}$$

$$= \frac{68{,}121 + 29{,}929 + 1{,}681 + 6{,}724 + 26{,}244}{7} = \frac{132{,}699}{7}$$

$$= 18{,}957.00;\ \text{and}$$

$$[T] = \frac{(T)^2}{a(s)}$$

$$= \frac{(261 + 173 + 41 + 82 + 162)^2}{5(7)}$$

$$= \frac{(719)^2}{35} = \frac{516{,}961}{35}$$

$$= 14{,}770.31 \quad .$$

TABLE 6-4   A Summary of the Analysis of Variance

Source	SS	df	MS	F
A	4,186.69	4	1,046.67	34.97*
S/A	898.00	30	29.93	
Total	5,084.69	34		

*$p < .05$

To obtain the sums of the squares, we combine the value of the three basic ratios:

$$SS_A = [A] - [T] = 18,957.00 - 14,770.31 = 4,186.69 \quad ;$$
$$SS_{S/A} = [AS] - [A] = 19,855 - 18,957.00 = 898.00; \text{ and}$$
$$SS_T = [AS] - [T] = 19,855 - 14,770.31 = 5,084.69 \quad .$$

And we check our calculations in this way:

$$SS_T = SS_A + SS_{S/A}$$
$$5,084.69 = 4,186.69 + 898.00$$
$$= 5,084.69 \quad .$$

We enter the three sums of squares in the summary of the analysis, Table 6-4.

The final stages of the analysis are summarized in Table 6-4. The F of 34.97 exceeds the critical value of F required to be significant at $\alpha = .05$, $F(4, 30) = 2.69$.

Comparisons: Preliminary Steps. Before we consider the analysis of single-df comparisons, it will be useful to reexamine equation (6-2), with which we will be calculating the sums of squares for these comparisons, to identify the quantities needed for the calculations:

$$SS_{A\ comp.} = \frac{[\Sigma\ (c_i)(A_i)]^2}{s[\Sigma\ (c_i)^2]} \quad .$$

Although the formula has only three basic components—the coefficients (c_i), the treatment sums (A_i), and the sample size (s)—these elements are combined in a fairly complicated fashion. We have found that the best way to proceed is to perform the required calculations systematically in order to avoid making unfortunate errors during the process of substitution in the formula.

Consider the computational plan outlined in Table 6-5. Listed in the four columns are all the quantities (except sample size) needed for the formula: the treatment sums, the coefficients, their products, and the squared coeffi-

TABLE 6-5   Computational Plan for Single-*df* Comparisons

1. Treatment Sums (A_i)	2. Coefficients (c_i)	3. (Coefficient) $\times$ (Sum) (c_i)(A_i)	4. Squared Coefficients (c_i)^2
A_1	c_1	$(c_1)(A_1)$	$(c_1)^2$
A_2	c_2	$(c_2)(A_2)$	$(c_2)^2$
A_3	c_3	$(c_3)(A_3)$	$(c_3)^2$
A_4	c_4	$(c_4)(A_4)$	$(c_4)^2$
A_5	$\underline{c_5}$	$\underline{(c_5)(A_5)}$	$\underline{(c_5)^2}$
Sum	$\Sigma\, c_i = 0$	$\Sigma\, (c_i)(A_i)$	$\Sigma\, (c_i)^2$

cients. The sum at the bottom of column 3 provides the sum of the weighted treatment totals, the quantity we will substitute within the brackets appearing in the numerator of equation (6-2), while the sum at the bottom of column 4 provides the quantity we will substitute within the brackets appearing in the denominator of equation (6-2). All we have left to do once we have made these substitutions is to follow the indicated arithmetic correctly.

A "Simple" Comparison. We will illustrate these calculations by evaluating two comparisons, one involving the difference between two treatment means (a **"simple"** comparison) and the other the difference between a treatment mean and an average of several means (a **"complex"** comparison). The first example provides a test of the first research hypothesis, "Kangaroo rats will avoid environments in which the odors of unfamiliar kangaroo rats are present," a comparison between the control and unfamiliar conditions. Since this comparison involves two treatment means, the coefficients consist of $+1$ and -1 for the two treatment conditions being compared and are zero for the others. That is,

$$c_i: +1, -1, 0, 0, \text{ and } 0 \quad .$$

These coefficients and the treatment sums from Table 6-3 are presented in Table 6-6.

All the preliminary calculations for the sum of squares associated with this comparison are specified in columns 4 and 5 of the table. Substituting the sums from these two columns in equation (6-2), we find

$$SS_{A\text{ comp.}} = \frac{[\Sigma\, (c_i)(A_i)]^2}{s[\Sigma\, (c_i)^2]}$$

$$= \frac{(+88)^2}{7(2)} = \frac{7,744}{14}$$

$$= 553.14 \quad .$$

TABLE 6-6   The Difference Between Control
and Unfamiliar Conditions (Preliminary Calculations)

1. Levels (a_i)	2. Treatment Sums (A_i)	3. Coefficients (c_i)	4. Products $(c_i)(A_i)$	5. Squared Coefficients $(c_i)^2$
a_1	261	+1	$(+1)(261) = +261$	$(+1)^2 = 1$
a_2	173	-1	$(-1)(173) = -173$	$(-1)^2 = 1$
a_3	41	0	$(0)(41) = \quad 0$	$(0)^2 = 0$
a_4	82	0	$(0)(82) = \quad 0$	$(0)^2 = 0$
a_5	162	0	$(0)(162) = \quad 0$	$(0)^2 = 0$
Sum		0	$\Sigma\,(c_i)(A_i) = +88$	$\Sigma\,(c_i)^2 = 2$

Equation (6-3) gives the mean square for this comparison:

$$MS_{A_{comp.}} = \frac{SS_{A_{comp.}}}{df_{A_{comp.}}}$$

$$= \frac{553.14}{1} = 553.14 \quad.$$

Finally, we obtain the F by substituting in equation (6-5) the value for the mean square we just calculated and the value for $MS_{S/A}$ from Table 6-4. That is,

$$F_{comp.} = \frac{MS_{A_{comp.}}}{MS_{S/A}}$$

$$= \frac{553.14}{29.93} = 18.48 \quad.$$

We determine the decision rules by finding the critical value of $F(1, 30)$, at $\alpha = .05$, which is 4.17. The rules are stated thus:

If the obtained value of $F_{comp.}$ equals or exceeds $F_\alpha = 4.17$, reject the null hypothesis; otherwise, do not reject the null hypothesis.

Since the F for this comparison, 18.48, clearly exceeds the critical value of F_α, we reject the null hypothesis,

$$H_0: \mu_1 = \mu_2 \quad,$$

and accept the alternative hypothesis,

$$H_1: \mu_1 \neq \mu_2 \quad.$$

The direction of the difference between the means of the two treatment conditions, control > unfamiliar smell, allows us to conclude that kangaroo

TABLE 6-7   The Difference Between Unfamiliar and Combined
Familiar Conditions (Preliminary Calculations)

1. Levels (a_i)	2. Treatment Sums (A_i)	3. Coeffi-cients (c_i)	4. Products $(c_i)(A_i)$	5. Squared Coefficients $(c_i)^2$
a_1	261	0	$(0)(261) =\quad 0$	$(0)^2 =\quad 0$
a_2	173	$+3$	$(+3)(173) = +519$	$(+3)^2 =\quad 9$
a_3	41	-1	$(-1)(41) =\quad -41$	$(-1)^2 =\quad 1$
a_4	82	-1	$(-1)(82) =\quad -82$	$(-1)^2 =\quad 1$
a_5	162	-1	$(-1)(162) = -162$	$(-1)^2 =\quad 1$
	Sum	0	$\Sigma\ (c_i)(A_i) = +234$	$\Sigma\ (c_i)^2 = 12$

rats avoid environments containing the odors of strange or unfamiliar members of the same species.

A "*Complex*" *Comparison.* The comparison of the unfamiliar condition with
the combined familiar conditions offers a more complicated example.[9] Since
this comparison involves a mean based on an average of several treatment
conditions, we must construct a set of coefficients that will extract the necessary information from the data. An application of the computational rules
given previously produces the following set of coefficients for this
comparison:

$$c_i: 0,\ +3,\ -1,\ -1,\ \text{and}\ -1\quad.$$

(You should verify for yourself that this is the correct set of coefficients.)

All the preliminary calculations for the sum of squares are enumerated in
Table 6-7. Substituting the sums from columns 4 and 5 in equation (6-2), we
obtain

$$SS_{A\ comp.} = \frac{[\Sigma\ (c_i)(A_i)]^2}{s[\Sigma\ (c_i)^2]}$$

$$= \frac{(+234)^2}{7(12)} = \frac{54,756}{84}$$

$$= 651.86\quad.$$

---

[9] You may have noticed that we did not present this comparison in our earlier discussion of this
experiment. Instead, we considered a related comparison, the difference between the unfamiliar
and the familiar-immediate conditions. We use this more complicated comparison as a numerical
example to broaden your experience with this procedure.

To calculate the F ratio, we first compute the mean square for this comparison,

$$MS_{A\text{ comp.}} = \frac{SS_{A\text{ comp.}}}{df_{A\text{ comp.}}}$$

$$= \frac{651.86}{1} = 651.86 \quad,$$

and then divide by the $MS_{S/A}$, that is,

$$F_{\text{comp.}} = \frac{651.86}{29.93} = 21.78 \quad.$$

Since this F is associated with the same numbers of degrees of freedom as those in the last example, the same decision rules apply. The obtained F of 21.78 exceeds the critical value of $F_\alpha = 4.17$, and the null hypothesis is rejected. We are permitted to conclude, therefore, that kangaroo rats avoid the smells of rats to whom they have lost in a territorial battle.

Synopsis

The analytical procedure explained in this section permits you to statistically assess meaningful comparisons generated by the underlying logic of an experimental design. The omnibus F test merely tells us that at least one difference between means is significant, but does not specify how many or which ones. In contrast, analytical comparisons focus directly on differences between means that make sense in terms of the treatment conditions and of the theoretical rationale for including these conditions in the design of the experiment.

A researcher should always have an analysis plan in mind in designing an experiment. Table 6-2 (p. 121) illustrates the plan for the ficticious kangaroo-rat study used as an example in this section. In an actual experiment, we would probably have included a number of comparisons in addition to those listed in Table 6-2 to increase the analytical power of the experimental design. For example, we would have examined the nature of the differences among the three familiar conditions, determining whether or not a straight line could be used to describe the recovery of exploratory behavior over the four-week period between the territorial fight and the eventual test.[10] In addition, we would have compared the unfamiliar condition with the longest

---

[10] This type of analysis is discussed in Chapter 12 (pp. 307–311). As a sidenote, we mention that the set of coefficients $0, 0, -1, 0$, and $+1$ will produce a sum of squares that reflects the degree of linear trend exhibited by these data.

delay condition (familiar-four weeks) to see if the recovery was complete, that is, whether the passage of four weeks was sufficient to allow the rats to behave as if the familiar smell had become unfamiliar. (The coefficients for this comparison are 0, +1, 0, 0, and −1.) We probably would *not* have compared the unfamiliar condition with the combined familiar conditions as we did in the second numerical example. Instead, we would have chosen to test the second research hypothesis as specified in Table 6-2, with the more specific and less ambiguous comparison afforded by the contrast between the unfamiliar and the familiar-immediate condition. (The coefficients for this comparison are 0, +1, −1, 0, and 0.)

To give you a sense of the results of the kangaroo-rat study, we will summarize the main findings that were revealed by the analytical comparisons specified in the last paragraph as applied to the data in Table 6-3 (p. 130) and offer the following conclusions, without the analyses, derived from the pattern of statistical outcomes:

1. Kangaroo rats tend to avoid an environment containing the smells of an unfamiliar kangaroo rat.

2. They are additionally inhibited when the environment contains the smells of the successful protagonist in a previous territorial fight.

3. They appear to get over this inhibition gradually, however, at a more or less steady (linear) rate.

4. The recovery is "complete" after approximately four weeks, when they seem to be influenced by the previously familiar smell in the same way they are influenced by an unfamiliar one.

In an actual report, each of these conclusions would be supported by reporting the statistical evidence as well.

Another type of analysis plan is considerably less specific than the one just described. Namely, in situations where the researcher entertains no specific hypotheses ahead of time, the omnibus F test will be conducted first. If this test is significant, additional analyses are then conducted in an attempt to pinpoint the source or sources of the significant omnibus F. Such a plan is commonly used in applied research where the primary purpose is to determine which treatments are alike and which are different.

We do not mean to imply that applied research never involves planned comparisons or that nonapplied research always does. These two approaches toward comparisons characterize applied and nonapplied research *in general*, not as a rule. The distinction between these two methods of making comparisons will become clearer in the next section, where we consider in some detail the different ways in which the two types of analyses are evaluated statistically.

TYPE I ERROR AND ANALYTICAL COMPARISONS

We have defined type I error (α) as the probability of rejecting the null hypothesis when in fact the null hypothesis is true. While we did not stress the point earlier, this probability applies specifically to the particular statistical test under consideration. The proper term for denoting this probability is **per comparison type I error;** other terms are *type I error rate per comparison* or *type I error rate per statistical test*. To be more specific,

> **per comparison type I error refers to the probability of committing a type I error for an *individual* statistical test.**

The test referred to can be the omnibus null hypothesis discussed in the last chapter or an analytical null hypothesis of the type discussed in the present chapter.

Experimentwise Error

Another kind of type I error becomes relevant when more than one statistical test is to be performed on the data of an experiment—**experimentwise type I error.**

> **Experimentwise error refers to the probability of committing type I errors over a *set* of statistical tests.**

Consider, for example, a situation in which we conduct two statistical tests in the analysis of an experiment. Assuming that we have set $\alpha = .05$ in both cases, the probability is .05 that we have committed a type I error on the first test, and the probability is .05 that we have committed a type I error on the second test. This is what is meant by per comparison type I error—each test is considered separately and independently from the others. The point of reference for this error is the *individual statistical test*.

But what if we shift our point of reference to the set of two comparisons and to the probability that a type I error is committed in this set? Experimentwise type I error occurs whenever a type I error is made on any of the tests in the set. Where two statistical tests are conducted, experimentwise error can occur in three possible ways: namely, as a type I error on the first test only, on the second test only, or on both tests. With three or more statistical tests in the set, the number of such possibilities increases dramatically.

The Relationship Between Per Comparison and Experimentwise Errors

Experimentwise error is directly related to the number of statistical tests included in an experiment. With the probability of a per comparison type I error set at α for each of the statistical tests considered separately,

> **experimentwise error is approximately equal to the sum of the separate per comparison probabilities.**

With two tests, experimentwise error is approximately equal to $.05 + .05 = .10$; with three tests, experimentwise error is approximately equal to $.05 + .05 + .05 = .15$; and so on. While the exact relationship between the number of statistical tests and experimentwise error is relatively complicated (which explains why we use the word *approximately*), the general thrust of the concept is simple:

> **experimentwise error increases as the number of statistical tests increases.**

The greater the number of tests conducted, the greater are the chances that at least one type I error has been committed somewhere in the set.[11]

The point of this chapter has been to provide the rationale for using analytical comparisons in the analysis of experiments. We hope that you are convinced that to be valuable an experiment will usually include a number of analytical comparisons. But you should be aware that when more than one statistical test is included in an experiment, the problem of experimentwise type I error becomes relevant and of concern to researchers. We turn now to a consideration of the options available for controlling such error.

Controlling Experimentwise Error

Most solutions to the problem achieve control of experimentwise error by reducing type I error for the individual tests. To elaborate, per comparison

---

[11] See *Design and Analysis* (pp. 87–88) for a discussion of this relationship.

type I error is the probability of falsely rejecting the null hypothesis at the level of the individual statistical test. Suppose we make it more difficult to reject the null hypothesis for a comparison, for example, by lowering the significance level from 5 percent to 1 percent. Two consequences will result: a reduction in the probability of type I error for each comparison, and a necessary decrease in experimentwise type I error. This decrease occurs because of the direct relationship between per comparison and experimentwise type I errors; a decrease in the first produces a decrease in the second.

Many different techniques have been proposed for reducing experimentwise error, including the straightforward reduction of the significance level, used as an example in the last paragraph. Each technique has a particular set of features that distinguishes it from the others, but a detailed discussion of these techniques is beyond the scope of this book; this topic is covered in most advanced statistics books.[12] However, since these procedures are reported in the research literature, you should be familiar with their names so that you will be aware when a correction has been made for experimentwise error. Listed in order of increasing reduction of experimentwise error, these techniques are the Fisher test, the Duncan test, the Newman-Keuls test, the Tukey test, and the Scheffé test. A specialized technique, the Dunnett test, is used for controlling experimentwise error when a single control condition is to be compared with a number of experimental conditions.

This general solution to the problem of experimentwise error—that is, a reduction of type I error for the individual tests—is not without its cost, however. By following the decision rules of hypothesis testing, we can conclude that differences among the treatment conditions exist in the population only by rejecting the null hypothesis. If we make it more difficult to reject the null hypothesis—which is what happens when we control experimentwise error—we necessarily increase our failures to detect actual differences in the population. A failure to reject the null hypothesis when the alternative hypothesis is true is, by definition, a *type II error*. Thus, the cost of reducing experimentwise error is an increase in type II error.

There is no clear way around this problem, which is one of the reasons why so many techniques for controlling experimentwise error have been developed. A researcher must be concerned with both types of error, of course. Consequently, any plan of analysis represents a conscious balancing of the two types of error. At the moment, we cannot offer an easy technique for achieving this balance; in fact, this issue is a highly controversial

[12] See, for example, the discussion in *Design and Analysis* (pp. 135–152) and in Kirk (1968, Chapter 3).

topic for investigators in most fields of research. Given the introductory nature of this book, we will not discuss these complications, but offer instead a simplified—and reasonable—method for selecting statistical procedures based on whether a comparison is planned before the start of an experiment or unplanned, that is, suggested by the data following experimentation.

A RESEARCH STRATEGY

Planned Comparisons

Fortunately, researchers generally agree on the way to treat type I error with respect to planned comparisons:

> **Ignore the theoretical increase in experimentwise error and reject the null hypothesis at the usual *per comparison* probability level.**

This course of action represents the level of tolerance for experimentwise error that is acceptable to researchers in the field of psychology. It is based on the assumptions that planned comparisons were really formulated during the planning stages of a piece of research, and that the number of planned comparisons in any given experiment will be reasonably small. Some experts suggest that the number should not exceed the number of degrees of freedom associated with the MS_A, that is, one less than the number of treatment conditions. A "natural" limit to the number of planned comparisons is imposed by the implied requirement that a comparison be meaningful. Designs do differ in their analytical power—the number of meaningful questions they can answer—but the number is still limited.

In any case, planned comparisons occupy an honored place in the analysis of an experiment. They are tested directly regardless of the statistical significance of the omnibus null hypothesis, and they are each evaluated on their own merits, independently of the others, at the uncorrected significance level, that is, the per comparison probability, α. The critical value of F for planned comparisons, F_α, is determined by the α level chosen, the $df_{num.}$ associated with the comparison, and the $df_{denom.}$ associated with the error term ($MS_{S/A}$).

Unplanned Comparisons

Unplanned comparisons do not usually occupy the same favored position that planned comparisons enjoy. Unplanned comparisons are considered "opportunistic" in the sense that they can capitalize on chance factors that side with one condition over another. As a consequence, many researchers take precautions against becoming overly "zealous" in declaring that a particularly attractive difference between means is significant. Such precautions reflect the researcher's realization that a larger number of unplanned comparisons could have become "interesting" if chance factors had operated differently.

Thus, it is with respect to unplanned comparisons that adjustment techniques to control experimentwise error are generally applied. As we have indicated, such techniques "work" by inhibiting the researcher from asserting that unexpected comparisons, unplanned when the experiment was designed, are significant. We have also indicated that this sort of control necessarily increases type II error. The plan we offer in the following sections, while not elegant, at least accounts for a researcher's concern for the effects of the two types of error. One part of this plan controls experimentwise type I error by subjecting unplanned comparisons to a correction of some sort. The other part is an attempt to reduce the magnitude of the second problem, namely, the increase in type II error stemming from the control of experimentwise error. We consider the control of experimentwise error first.

The Scheffé Test. The technique known as the **Scheffé test** allows a researcher to conduct any and all comparisons while preventing experimentwise error from exceeding some arbitrarily chosen level. That is, if $\alpha = .05$ (the level chosen by most researchers), the Scheffé test guarantees that experimentwise type I error will not exceed $p = .05$, no matter how many comparisons a researcher may choose to make.

The Scheffé test is quite simple to apply. An F for any comparison is evaluated against a special critical value of F, which we will refer to as F_S. This critical value is given by the following formula:

$$F_S = (a - 1)F(df_A, df_{S/A}) \quad , \tag{6-6}$$

where a is the number of treatment conditions in the experiment and $F(df_A, df_{S/A})$ is the critical value of F for the overall, or omnibus, analysis of variance. The critical value for this F is found in the F table for $df_{num.} = df_A$, $df_{denom.} = df_{S/A}$, and $\alpha = .05$ (usually).

Suppose we use the kangaroo-rat study as an example. In order to use equation (6-6), we must find the value of F with $df_A = 4$ and $df_{S/A} = 30$ at $\alpha = .05$. An examination of the F table indicates that $F(4, 30) = 2.69$. Substituting in equation (6-6), we obtain

$$F_S = (5 - 1)(2.69)$$
$$= 4(2.69) = 10.76 \quad .$$

For any comparison to be significant with the Scheffé test, the value of the F statistic must equal or surpass $F_S = 10.76$.

If we contrast F_S with the critical value of F for a single-df planned comparison, $F(1, 30) = 4.17$, you can see that it will be considerably more difficult to reject the null hypothesis with unplanned comparisons than it is with planned comparisons. That is, an unplanned comparison must produce an F ratio equaling or exceeding $F_S = 10.76$, while a planned comparison must produce an F ratio equaling or exceeding $F_\alpha = 4.17$. This difference in the size of the two critical values of F is what is responsible for the control of experimentwise type I error. More specifically, the use of a larger critical value of F ($F_S = 10.76$) means that fewer unplanned comparisons will be declared significant and, consequently, that fewer type I errors will be made. This reduction in the number of type I errors for the set of unplanned comparisons represents a control of experimentwise type I error.

As already noted, a control of experimentwise error produces an "automatic" increase in type II error: If we reject fewer null hypotheses (that is, reduce type I error), we will detect fewer real differences—thus increasing type II error—as a consequence. In the following section, we attempt to formulate a compromise between these conflicting concerns about type I and type II errors.

A Modified Decision Rule. The usual decision rules specify two mutually exclusive decisions, either the rejection or the nonrejection of the null hypothesis. The modified decision rules introduce a third possible decision, namely, **suspension of judgment** for those values of F affected by the Scheffé correction. By suspending judgment, we avoid committing either type of error, and simply conclude that the evidence is not sufficiently strong to justify either one of the usual conclusions.[13] This may appear to be a cowardly approach, but at least it does sensibly resolve the conflict. In fact, many researchers suspend judgment in effect when they take note of "potentially significant" comparisons detected during routine combing of the data and suggest directions for future research based on these findings. Thus, though judgment is suspended, interesting and unexpected findings are not buried by a Scheffé or other correction technique. This simple modification of the decision rules alleviates the danger that real differences will go undetected due to attempts at controlling experimentwise error.

Specifically, the modified decision rules read as follows:

if $F_{\text{comp.}}$ **equals or exceeds** $F_S =$ _____, **reject the null hypothesis; if** $F_{\text{comp.}}$ **falls between** $F_\alpha =$ _____ **and** $F_S =$ _____, **suspend judgment; otherwise, do not reject the null hypothesis.**

---

[13] A similar three-option rule has been proposed by Hays (1973, pp. 350–353) to apply to the overall F test.

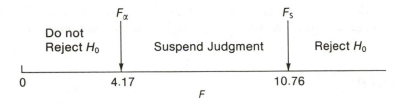

Values of F

Figure 6-1. The line represents increasing values of F and the two critical values F_α and F_S.

Thus, this new set of rules specifies the conditions under which we can safely reject the null hypothesis, not reject the null hypothesis, and suspend judgment.

Once more we return to the kangaroo-rat study to illustrate the use of the modified decision rules. Earlier, we found that $F_S = 10.76$ and $F_\alpha = 4.17$ in this example. The modified decision rules for evaluating unplanned comparisons read thus:

If $F_{comp.}$ equals or exceeds $F_S = 10.76$, reject the null hypothesis; if $F_{comp.}$ falls between $F_\alpha = 4.17$ and $F_S = 10.76$, suspend judgment; otherwise, do not reject the null hypothesis.

These rules can be expressed by means of a number line, as shown in Figure 6-1. The line represents increasing values of F and the two critical values of F: F_α and F_S.

In summary, the purpose of the preceding sections was to convey a sense of the complexity surrounding type I error and analytical comparisons. In conducting your own research, you should feel free to evaluate your planned comparisons in the usual manner. Difficulties only begin to arise when you sift through your data and discover meaningful but still unplanned comparisons. It is at this stage in the analysis of an experiment that experimentwise type I error becomes a concern. However, since reducing experimentwise error produces an increase in type II error, a researcher must be concerned with keeping *both* types of error as low as possible. The solution proposed, use of the Scheffé test in conjunction with suspension of judgment, represents one way to deal with the problem. Other ways exist, but they are outside the scope of this book. You are beginning to do research, and we have taken care not to confuse you unduly by adding too much complication at this point in your training. The main points we have stressed include the notion of experimentwise type I error, the status of planned comparisons in the analytical analysis of an experiment, and one way to deal with the complications arising from the analysis of unplanned comparisons.

SUMMARY

As you know, experiments are usually designed to answer a series of analytical or meaningful questions. Background considerations such as fact, theory, and speculation lead a researcher to form a number of research hypotheses. An experiment is then designed to provide meaningful and relevant answers to these questions. In this chapter, we discussed analysis techniques that permit the statistical evaluation of these particular hypotheses.

We differentiated two types of analytical comparisons in this chapter: those based on the differences between two means and those based on the differences among three or more means. While both types of comparisons are useful, the former is conducted much more frequently than the latter and consequently was discussed more fully in this chapter.

Comparisons between two means are accomplished by means of a formula in which a set of coefficients is constructed for obtaining the particular variation desired. All F ratios are formed with the within-groups mean square obtained from the overall analysis of variance as the denominator.

A problem inherent in the use of analytical comparisons is that the greater the number of statistical tests performed, the greater is the probability that at least one type I error will be committed. Most researchers agree that when comparisons are meaningful and planned in accordance with preexperimental hypotheses, they should be evaluated without concern for the contribution they make to experimentwise type I error. On the other hand, many investigators feel that experimentwise type I error should be controlled when comparisons are unplanned, suggested and conducted only after the data have been examined. One method of dealing with this complicated and difficult problem is the use of the Scheffé test combined with a modified decision rule allowing for the option of suspended judgment.

TERMS, CONCEPTS, AND SYMBOLS

---

omnibus (overall) F test

analytical comparison

planned comparison

unplanned comparison

post-hoc comparison

multiple comparison

single-df comparison

coefficient

weighted treatment mean

sum of weighted treatment means

"simple" comparisons

"complex" comparisons

per comparison type I error

experimentwise type I error

Scheffé test

suspended judgment

c_i

$SS_{A_{comp.}}$

$(c_i)(A_i)$

$\Sigma \, (c_i)(A_i)$

$[\Sigma \, (c_i)(A_i)]^2$

$df_{A_{comp.}}$

$MS_{A_{comp.}}$

$F_{comp.}$

F_α

F_S

$F(df_A, \, df_{S/A})$

EXERCISES

---

1. This problem involves the data from problem 3, Chapter 5 (p. 112). Suppose that the researcher had intended to make the following planned comparisons:

   Comparison 1: A comparison of the two "pleasantness" ratings (meaning and sound) with the two "frequency" ratings (word and syllable)

   Comparison 2: The "meaning" treatment versus the other three

   Comparison 3: Word frequency versus syllable frequency

   a. Construct the coefficients (c_i's) appropriate for the comparisons.
   b. Form the summary table and evaluate the comparisons to determine whether the differences are significant statistically.

c. If the comparisons named above were unplanned and the Scheffé test were used, what would be the outcome?

2. This problem uses the data from problem 4, Chapter 5 (p. 113). Two comparisons were planned in this experiment. The first was a comparison of the silence treatment versus the other three. The second was a comparison of the praise treatment versus the reproof treatment. (a) Determine whether these planned comparisons indicated significant differences. (b) After inspecting the data, the investigators observed that certain other comparisons should have been conducted. Accordingly, they made a decision to compare the reproof condition with the combined praise and jelly bean conditions. Finally, they examined a comparison of the silence condition versus the praise condition. Since these were unplanned comparisons, they used F_S to avoid making excessive experimentwise type I error and the modified decision rules to reduce type II error. Conduct these comparisons and draw conclusions.

Additional Descriptive Measures and Techniques

7

INTRODUCTION

Statistics have several functions in research. One function, common in all fields, is to describe or summarize the salient features of a set of data. When statistics are used in this fashion, the summary measures employed are called **descriptive statistics.** We have seen how the mean and the variance can be used to reduce the data of an experiment to a reasonable and comprehensible set of numerical indices. In this chapter, we introduce additional methods and procedures that serve this useful function.

Inferential Statistics

Most research is more than purely descriptive in function. Researchers usually undertake experimentation in order to make inferences concerning certain characteristics of individuals most of whom have *not* been tested or studied by them. In these cases, the investigator views the data from a study as a **sample** drawn from a much larger *population* and uses characteristics of the sample (called **statistics**) to make estimates concerning corresponding characteristics of the population (called **parameters**). When statistics are used in generalizations from sample to population, they are referred to as **inferential statistics.**

We have already considered one aspect of this inferential function in our discussion of hypothesis testing. To reiterate, the *F* statistic is used in the evaluation of (that is, the making of inferences about) two hypothetical statements about the treatment populations: the hypothesis that the population treatment means are the same (the null hypothesis) and the hypothesis that they are not all the same (the alternative hypothesis).

Another important area of inferential statistics is concerned with the actual **estimation of population values** rather than the testing of hypotheses about these populations. Estimation is most commonly found in survey research and other applied fields of the behavioral sciences. Estimation is discussed in Chapter 16.

Descriptive Statistics

In addition to analyzing the data from an experiment, researchers summarize the major results. Summary descriptions of data serve two important functions. First, they inform others about the outcome of an experiment in a concise manner. Second, they provide the researchers performing the study with as much information as possible about the nature of the phenomenon under study. Generally speaking, the more you as an investigator know about the data from one experiment, the better equipped you will be to carry out and analyze future experiments. Usually, the data from a study suggest many questions that are not readily answered by hypothesis testing. Such questions can lead to the creation of research hypotheses for subsequent experiments.

ALTERNATIVES TO THE MEAN AND THE VARIANCE

Occasionally, alternative measures of central tendency and of variability are reported in the research literature. While these measures are not usually utilized in the evaluation of research hypotheses, they can serve useful descriptive functions nevertheless. Because they are of value to the researcher, you should understand these measures and be able to recognize instances in which they might be used in preference to the mean and the variance (or standard deviation).

Measures of Central Tendency

Consider the set of numbers in the first column of Table 7-1. These numbers, which seem to be presented haphazardly, are actually the ages of the students in a laboratory section listed in the order they were reported to us. Although we must be wary of drawing conclusions from a "reading" of the data, a cursory examination of the scores reveals that certain ages, 19 and 20, are repeated frequently; one age, 42, is noticeably different from the others, and the remainder mostly hover around 19 and 20. The mean of these scores is 22.10. We will now calculate two alternative measures of central tendency, the mode and the median.

The Mode. The **mode** is the score that occurs most frequently in the set. We find the mode by counting to see which score occurs most frequently. For the data in Table 7-1, the mode is 20, which appears a total of six times. More students in the section were 20 than any other age. The mode is extremely easy to calculate once the data have been arranged in order of magnitude, which has been done in the second column of Table 7-1. Complications arise when two or more scores tie for the highest frequency of occurrence. If the scores occupy adjacent positions on the scale of measurement, we can calculate the mode by averaging the tied score values. If the two scores are separated by other scores, the set of scores is said to be bimodal. Bimodality usually occurs when a set of scores contains responses from two widely divergent groups of subjects.

The Median. The **median** is the score at or above which one-half of the scores lie. (The median can also be defined in terms of the other half of the scores—as the point at or *below* which one-half of the scores lie.) To find the

TABLE 7-1 Ages
from a Laboratory
Section

1. Age	2. Ordered Ages
19	18
20	18
22	19
20	19
21	19
23	19
18	20
19	20
26	20
34	20
21	20
20	20
19	21
20	21
42	21
18	22
20	23
20	26
21	34
19	42

median, we list the scores in order of magnitude. The median is the middlemost score of this ordered set. If the number of scores is odd, the median is the score located in this middlemost position. Thus, where there are twenty-one scores, the median will be the score located in the eleventh position; ten scores lie above that score and ten scores lie below it. Where the number of scores is even, no single score is middlemost; rather, two scores are middlemost, and the median falls between them. For example, where there are twelve scores, the median will be an average of the scores falling in the sixth and seventh positions.

As an example of the calculations, consider the data presented in Table 7-1. Column 2 lists the scores in order of magnitude, which is necessary in order to calculate the median. Since twenty scores are listed, there are two middlemost scores, one in the tenth position and one in the eleventh position. If we begin counting from the top, we find that the tenth and eleventh scores are both 20. Averaging the two scores is unnecessary; we would have to do so only if the scores were of different values. Thus, the median score is 20, and we can say that one-half of the class is 20 or younger and the other half of the class is 20 or older.[1]

The median is not influenced by the presence of extreme scores on either side of the dividing point. The only scores that are critical in the determination of the median are those on either side of the median—the remaining scores beyond these two transitional points have no direct effect on the median value. The mean, on the other hand, *is* influenced by extreme scores, since its value is affected directly by the values of all the scores in the set.

Researchers use the median when they feel that extreme scores would tend to obscure the central tendency exhibited by the large majority of the scores if the mean were calculated. For example, when social scientists report the average income of a group of individuals, they usually choose the median as a more representative measure of central tendency than the mean. They make this choice to minimize the influence of a small number of extremely high incomes that would have a distorting effect on the mean.

Experimenters also use the median when obtaining a score for each of the subjects in an experiment is impossible—for example, in a problem-solving experiment where the response measure is the time to solve a problem, and some subjects never solve the problem. Under these circumstances, the mean would actually be incalculable, because solution-time scores would not be available for all subjects. The median usually would be calculated, however, as it does not require the actual values of these extreme and unavailable scores.

Comparison of the Mean, Median, and Mode. Calculating each measure of central tendency requires different amounts of information from the data— the mean requires the most, and the mode the least. As already noted, the mean plays an essential role in the statistical analysis of experiments, and for this reason we have stressed it most heavily as a measure of central tendency. The median can be used in the testing of research hypotheses, but its applications are not as extensive as those associated with the mean. In purely descriptive research—for example, survey research, demographic research, and the like—the median may actually be more descriptive than the mean

---

[1] A problem arises in the determination of the median when several scores fall at the median value, as they do in this example. Under these circumstances, it is usually necessary to use *linear interpolation* to obtain the precise value of the median. Using this method, we find that the median is 20.17. We will not discuss this method, however, since we will have little need to calculate medians with the analyses we cover in subsequent chapters. If you ever need to use linear interpolation to calculate a median, you can find excellent treatments in most introductory statistics texts.

because of its relative insensitivity to extreme scores and to missing or incomplete data. The mode is generally not used to summarize the results of an experiment.

Measures of Variability

While alternative measures of variability are available to the researcher, they are rarely reported in the literature. In fact, usually researchers only bother to calculate an alternative measure of variability when they need to create an index of variability quickly, with a minimum of calculation. Thus, we will describe these measures only briefly, providing just enough information to permit you to identify them. You are most likely to encounter the alternative measures in relatively old research literature and in literature from other fields.

The Range. The **range** is the difference between the highest and lowest scores in a set of data. The range thus defined is called the exclusive range; this definition is the one most commonly presented in introductory statistics texts. Another measure, the inclusive range, is one score unit larger than the exclusive range; it is based on the real limits of the two extreme scores. (Real limits are discussed later in this chapter.) The range is easy to calculate and is frequently used with the mode to give immediate but admittedly rough indications of variability and central tendency, respectively.

The Semi-Interquartile Range. The **semi-interquartile range** is often used in conjunction with the median as a measure of variability. It is defined in terms of the **interquartile range.** The interquartile range refers to the difference between two scores: that representing the point below which 75 percent of the scores fall (known as the *third quartile* or the *seventy-fifth percentile*) and that representing the point below which 25 percent of the scores fall (known as the *first quartile,* or the *twenty-fifth percentile*). The semi-interquartile range is equal to one-half the interquartile range. The semi-interquartile range is of value when the data *require* the median as a measure of central tendency, which is often the case with survey data. However, the measure finds limited application in the statistical evaluation of experiments.

TABLES AND GRAPHS

Two common and efficient ways to display summary data from an experiment are by means of tables and graphs. Not being statistics, tables and

TABLE 7-2   Mean Number of Minutes (and Standard Deviations) Spent Exploring by Kangaroo Rats During the Sixty-Minute Test ($s = 7$)

Type of Smell	Mean Minutes	Standard Deviation
Control	37.29	5.68
Unfamiliar smell	24.71	6.21
Familiar smell		
Immediate	5.86	4.63
Two-week delay	11.71	5.91
Four-week delay	23.14	4.74

graphs may seem out of place among statistical procedures. In truth, they are such simple and convincing devices for summarizing the results of research that we cannot get along without them. Since they are essential for describing data, we offer some advice on their use and construction.[2]

Examples of tables and graphs in published reports and texts (including this one) vary in content and format. Any kind of measure can be displayed in tables and graphs, and no strict rules govern the construction of data displays. The student's best source of ideas for arranging descriptive statistics is the published literature in the field.

Tables

Tables are simply organized collections of summary information. Even when the object is to construct a graph, the investigator first makes a table from which to work. Of course, when only a few means are to be reported, including them in the text along with the explanations may make more sense than preparing a formal table. When several pieces of summary data are to be reported, listing them in tabular form is a good choice. As you probably know from your reading, tables can include means, standard deviations, variances, correlations, proportions, frequencies, and even F ratios when a large number of comparisons or a complicated analysis is reported.

Table 7-2 is an example of a table. This table is a summary of the data presented as an example in Chapter 6 and given in Table 6-3. The functions of

---

[2] Most research reports present a given set of data either in a table or a figure, but not both. The restriction on duplicating information is made to conserve journal space by eliminating information that would otherwise be redundant.

some features of this display may seem obvious to you, but many students frequently fail to make use of these basic features when learning to make up tables. First, the title of the table indicates the table's contents and, in general terms, the source of the data. Even the number of data points for each of the means is given sómewhere in the table, in this case in the title.[3] The group designations are given as brief descriptions of the particular treatment condition. Students are often tempted, in constructing a table, to use group designations from the analysis, such as a_1, a_2, a_3, and so on. These labels are appropriate for specifying the details of the analysis, but not for describing the data to others. In working with the data, you will become familiar with the groups and use your own shorthand to refer to them, sometimes forgetting that others do not have this same familiarity. Thus, we stress the need for providing descriptive labels in a table.

The arrangement of the groups in a table conveys information about the design of the experiment. In Table 7-2, for example, the arrangement of the familiar conditions emphasizes the fact that all three received the "familiar treatment," but differed with respect to the time elapsed following the treatment. Occasionally, when the experimental design is complex, a table can be useful for outlining the experimental design and showing the sequence of events.

Two advantages of tables are the clarity and succinctness with which critical summary data can be presented. Frequently, journal editors favor an efficiently constructed table over a written report of the data to conserve space. Another advantage is the accuracy of the information, which permits readers to conduct statistical analyses not reported in the paper but of interest to them nevertheless.

Graphs

Graphs, which depict relationships between independent and dependent variables with lines and points, are also concise summaries of experimental results. Their advantage is that they permit a reader to skim the summary rapidly to identify relationships and trends in the data.[4] Thus, graphs have high impact value—that is, their meaning can be apprehended almost instantly—which is why they are used so frequently in newspapers, magazines, and television. The main disadvantage of graphs is that the

---

[3] We have designated sample size by s, which is part of the overall notational system used in this book. Sample size is usually referred to as n or N in the research literature.

[4] In this regard, graphs are ideal for displaying an interaction of two independent variables. The importance of this function will become clear in Chapter 9.

information they provide is not as accurate as that presented in tables and usually does not include variability. Consequently, conducting additional statistical analyses is difficult if not impossible when the means are only presented graphically.

Conventions for Graphical Displays. The primary criterion for assessing a graph is the clarity with which it displays the data. In standard graphs, the independent variable is represented on the horizontal axis (or abscissa) and the dependent variable along the vertical axis (or ordinate). The axes must be labeled clearly, and some form of legend or key should be provided to distinguish points that might be confused. (See Figure 7-2 below for an example of a legend.) As with tables, the title of the figure should tell the reader just what the figure contains. In addition to these conventions, certain others have been more or less adopted in the field of psychology:

1. The length of the vertical axis is approximately three-quarters of the length of the horizontal axis. Deviations from this "formula" can result in distortions of meaning—an exaggeration of the treatment differences where the vertical axis is unduly expanded, and a minimization if the vertical axis is unduly compressed.

2. The scale for the dependent variable (and the independent variable if the manipulation is quantitative) is assumed to begin with zero, at the left-hand intersection of the horizontal and vertical axes. If the graph includes some "dead space," a break in the scale is often introduced to condense this area. Such breaks must be clearly designated in the figure or the results may be misleading.

3. It is a good idea to enclose the graph on all four sides with the vertical axis on the right marked off in the same units as the vertical axis on the left. This permits a reader to estimate the data points more accurately from the printed version of the figure.

4. Standard deviations can be expressed by a vertical band centered over each data point. Each deviation above and below the mean represents the size of one standard deviation for that condition.

Graphing Quantitative Variables. A quantitative variable is an independent variable that consists of a series of points selected from some quantitative dimension. The primary purpose of plotting a quantitative variable is to reveal the *shape* of the function describing the relationship of the independent and dependent variables. Is the relationship approximated by a straight line or is a curve more appropriate? The example in Figure 7-1A is best described as a downward-sloping straight line, or linear function, while that

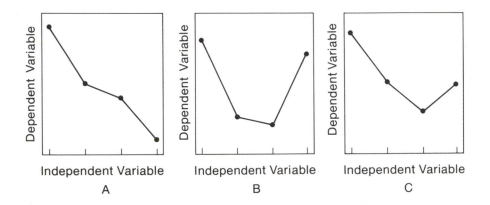

Figure 7-1. Three Examples of the Outcome of a Quantitative Independent Variable.

in Figure 7-1B is a so-called U-shaped, or curvilinear, function. Figure 7-1C represents a mixture of both linear and curvilinear trends. (The statistical assessment of these two types of trends is discussed in Chapter 12.)

Certain conventions govern the graphing of the results of quantitative manipulations. First, intervals depicting treatment conditions are spaced along the baseline in direct proportion to the scale values associated with each of them. For example, if the values chosen for the independent variable were 2, 4, 6, and 8, the distance between successive points on the horizontal axis—including the origin (0)—would be the same, namely, 2 units each. On the other hand, if the values were 1, 3, 9, and 18, the distances between them on the baseline would be proportional to the differences in the numerical values of the treatment conditions—that is, between 0 (the origin) and 1, 1 unit; between 1 and 3, 2 units; between 3 and 9, 6 units; and between 9 and 18, 9 units. Second, successive points are connected by straight lines. This type of graph is often called a **line graph.**

Once the independent and dependent variables have been arranged on a piece of graph paper, we are ready to plot the data points. To plot the data obtained from any given treatment condition, we start at the location of this condition on the horizontal axis—the point on the horizontal axis representing the numerical value of the independent variable administered to the subjects. Next, we move vertically from this point until the appropriate value of the dependent variable—for example, the treatment mean—is reached on the vertical axis. We place a mark at this point on the graph. After all the data points have been plotted, we connect successive points by straight lines. To "read" a graph, we simply note the values on the independent and dependent variables for each point plotted on the graph.

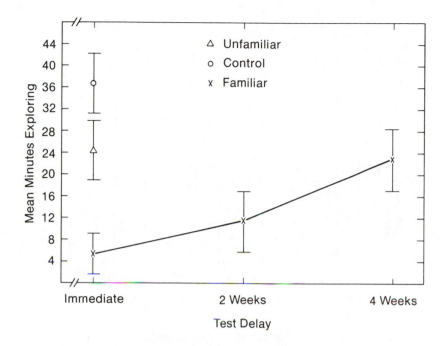

Figure 7-2. Mean Number of Minutes of Exploration Spent by Kangaroo Rats during the 60-Minute Test. Brackets indicate ± 1 standard deviation. Based on $s = 7$ subjects per condition.

The data from Table 7-2 have been plotted in Figure 7-2 as an example of a line graph. The first important feature of this graph is that three points are connected with straight lines while two of the groups stand alone. The connected points link the three familiar-smell groups where the time of the test (immediate, after 2 weeks, or after 4 weeks) is a quantitative variable (time). The other two groups do not share a common dimension, and are therefore unconnected to the means of the other treatments. Completing the picture are the standard deviations for each treatment condition; the upper brackets represent one standard deviation above the mean and the lower brackets one standard deviation below the mean.[5]

Graphing Qualitative Variables. A different sort of graph is used to depict results involving qualitative independent variables—a form of **bar graph.** Consider a hypothetical experiment as an example. Subjects are exposed to

---

[5] It would make more sense to plot confidence intervals—covered in Chapter 16—since they reflect more directly the extent of chance error operating in each treatment condition, but this is not what is commonly done. In any case, the type of range presented in the graph should be clearly indicated in the figure legend.

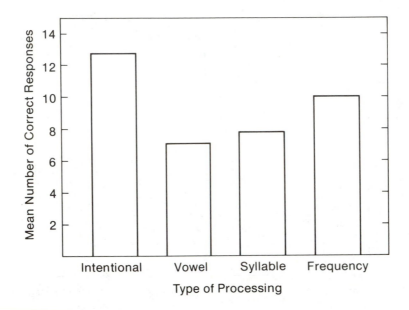

Figure 7-3. Mean Number of Correct Responses (out of 30) for the Four Processing Conditions. Based on $s = 26$ subjects per condition.

a list of common words and instructed to "process" the material in different ways. One group is asked to study the words for a memory test, while the other three groups are not explicitly instructed to memorize the words. One group is asked to report the number of vowels in each word; another group, to report the number of syllables in each word; and a third group, to give a "pleasantness" rating for each word. A total of 30 words is presented at a rate of 5 seconds per word. After exposure, subjects are asked to recall the words. The results of the experiment are presented in Figure 7-3.

The independent variable (type of processing) is a qualitative manipulation—the treatment conditions reflect differences in *kind* rather than in amount. One criterion for determining whether a variable is qualitative or quantitative is that the order in which the treatment conditions are arranged is *not* critical for a qualitative variable, though it is with a quantitative variable. In this example, the four conditions could be arranged in any of the twenty-four possible orders. In Figure 7-2, however, which involved a quantitative variable, the conditions are ordered and spaced in the only way possible, namely, that which reflects the underlying ordered dimension of time.

The distinguishing feature of a bar graph is the use of rectangles to depict the value on the dependent variable. The reader obtains the plotted value for each condition by measuring the top of each rectangle against the vertical axis. Despite the fact that bar graphs are appropriate for summarizing data obtained from a qualitative manipulation, most researchers prefer to use line graphs for this purpose. Usually, such data can be presented in a line graph with no problem unless this alternative way of plotting the data could confuse a reader. Bar graphs and related displays are favored in the pictorial representation of results from opinion surveys and other forms of survey research.

FREQUENCY DISTRIBUTIONS

The mean and the variance abstract important characteristics from a set of scores, but tend to obscure individual features, for example, the presence of some unexpectedly deviant scores. A **frequency distribution** is an arrangement of a set of observations that provides additional information concerning the nature of the differences present within the set. If the observations consist of *numerical values* on some response measure, the frequency distribution focuses on the relationship between particular scores and the frequency with which they occur. If the observations consist of response categories—for instance, preferences expressed by voters for different candidates—the frequency distribution relates these categories of preference and the frequency with which they occur in the set of observations. In this section, we consider frequency distributions of the first type; distributions of the second type are discussed in Chapter 15.

Ungrouped Frequency Distributions

Table 7-3 presents eighty-seven scores on a reading-comprehension test obtained from a sample of school children in the fourth and fifth grades. It is difficult to obtain much of a "feel" for the data from this random listing of the scores. The situation improves slightly if we order the scores from high to low and group identical scores together, as in Table 7-4. Such an arrangement is called an **ungrouped frequency distribution,** which is something of a misnomer since identical scores have in fact been grouped. This ambiguity will be resolved when we consider the grouped frequency distribution below.

The ungrouped frequency distribution does help us to find the center of the distribution of scores and to assess the degree and nature of the variabil-

TABLE 7-3   Scores on a Reading Comprehension Test for $s = 87$

28	31	53	41	77	60	53	40	58
34	28	68	80	78	57	23	43	36
61	63	15	67	27	54	37	57	56
61	45	51	59	41	50	29	43	34
93	39	49	51	76	29	43	41	54
36	73	78	44	46	65	43	53	35
63	72	37	61	37	54	38	50	23
78	55	54	42	62	65	69	59	—
47	75	58	50	47	71	47	62	—
56	37	44	50	68	48	72	62	—

ity present. Usually, however, this type of display is of limited value. All the frequencies in Table 7-4 are relatively small (none is greater than $f = 4$), and no single modal value (most frequent score) is revealed. Rather the scores 37, 43, 50, and 54 all have frequencies of $f = 4$, and for many scores $f = 0$.

Grouped Frequency Distributions

Generally, reporting the frequency of occurrence of every score in a set of data results in a very long list, and, as we have seen, many scores in such a list will have a frequency of 0. A way of avoiding unnecessary detail and smoothing out the distribution is to group the scores into sets of **class intervals.** A class interval is a range of scores. The frequency of each score within the interval is determined, and the total number is listed as the frequency of the scores within the interval. The number and size of intervals are chosen to suit the convenience of the researcher. A frequency distribution based on class intervals containing two or more contiguous score values is called a **grouped frequency distribution.**

The steps in constructing a grouped frequency distribution are relatively simple:

1. Find the range of the scores (the difference between the highest and lowest scores).

2. Select a convenient number of intervals (usually between eight and fifteen intervals are useful).

3. Find the size of the interval by dividing the range by the number of intervals chosen.

4. List the intervals in either increasing or decreasing order of score values.

TABLE 7-4   Ungrouped Frequency Distribution of Reading
Comprehension Scores (f = frequency)

Score	f	Score	f	Score	f	Score	f
93	1	69	1	45	1	21	0
92	0	68	2	44	2	20	0
91	0	67	1	43	4	19	0
90	0	66	0	42	1	18	0
89	0	65	2	41	3	17	0
88	0	64	0	40	1	16	0
87	0	63	2	39	1	15	1
86	0	62	3	38	1	14	0
85	0	61	3	37	4	13	0
84	0	60	1	36	2	12	0
83	0	59	2	35	1	11	0
82	0	58	2	34	2	10	0
81	0	57	2	33	0	9	0
80	1	56	2	32	0	8	0
79	0	55	1	31	1	7	0
78	3	54	4	30	0	6	0
77	1	53	3	29	2	5	0
76	1	52	0	28	2	4	0
75	1	51	2	27	1	3	0
74	0	50	4	26	0	2	0
73	1	49	1	25	0	1	0
72	2	48	1	24	0	0	0
71	1	47	3	23	2	—	—
70	0	46	1	22	0	—	—

5. Classify each score in one of the intervals.

6. Count the number of tally marks within each interval to obtain the frequencies.

7. As a check, make sure that the sum of the frequencies (Σf) equals the total number of scores (s).

Let us follow these steps constructing a grouped frequency distribution of the eighty-seven reading scores presented in Table 7-3.

1. Find the range: $93 - 15 = 78$.

2. Select the number of intervals: 9.

3. Divide the range by the number of intervals: $78/9 = 8.67$ (round to 9).

4. List the intervals: See column 1, Table 7-5.

TABLE 7-5   A Grouped Frequency Distribution of Reading Scores

1. Interval	2. Midpoint	3. Tally Marks	4. Frequency
86–94	90	I	1
77–85	81	卌	5
68–76	72	卌 IIII	9
59–67	63	卌 卌 IIII	14
50–58	54	卌 卌 卌 卌	20
41–49	45	卌 卌 卌 III	17
32–40	36	卌 卌 III	12
23–31	27	卌 III	8
14–22	18	I	1
			$\Sigma f = \overline{87}$

5. Tally the scores: See column 3, Table 7-5.

6. Determine the frequencies: See column 4, Table 7-5.

7. Sum the frequencies: $\Sigma f = 87 = s$.

Column 2 in Table 7-5 lists the **midpoints** of each class interval. The midpoint is the center of an interval, and is used in graphs of grouped frequency distributions. The midpoint is easily calculated by the following formula:[6]

$$\text{midpoint of an interval} = \frac{\text{lower limit} + \text{upper limit}}{2} \quad .$$

For example, the midpoint for the interval defined by the score value of 14 and 22 is

$$\text{midpoint} = \frac{14 + 22}{2} = \frac{36}{2} = 18 \quad .$$

Plotting Frequency Distributions

One more set of definitions is necessary before we can consider the graphical display of frequency distributions: the **apparent limits** (or score limits) of the

---

[6] More precisely, the formula for the midpoint is defined in terms of the real limits of the interval (see p. 163). That is, midpoint = (lower real limit + upper real limit)/2. For this example, midpoint = (13.5 + 22.5)/2 = 36/2 = 18. Both formulas give the same result.

intervals and the **real limits** (or true limits). In Table 7-5, the apparent limits of the highest interval are 86 and 94. The real limits extend beyond these values by .5 units, to 85.5 and 94.5. Similarly, the real limits of the next interval are 76.5 and 85.5. Real limits have practical value when some of the scores are themselves fractional values. Sometimes a score will fall exactly on the division of two intervals—in this example, 85.5, the upper limit of the second highest interval and the lower limit of the highest—and a choice has to be made as to where the score will be assigned. You could divide all such scores equally and assign any "odd" scores by a flip of a coin.

One way to graph a frequency distribution is by means of a **histogram.** A histogram is a type of bar graph in which the bar is as wide as the real limits of the interval and as high as the frequency of scores in the interval. Figure 7-4A is a histogram of the frequencies from Table 7-5. Technically, each bar should extend from the lower real limit to the upper real limit of each interval. For convenience, however, the intervals are marked by the lower score limits given in Table 7-5 (14, 23, 32, and so on) rather than by the more cumbersome real limits (13.5, 22.5, 31.5). The vertical axis is, of course, the frequency with which individual scores fall within any given interval.

A second way to graph a frequency distribution is to use a **frequency polygon.** A frequency polygon is formed when the frequencies are plotted in conjunction with the midpoints of the respective intervals and adjacent points are connected with straight lines. Figure 7-4B is the frequency polygon that corresponds to the histogram in Figure 7-4A. Note that the two endpoints of the frequency polygon (midpoints of 18 and 90) are connected to the baseline at the midpoints of the next lower (9) and higher (99) intervals. This convention is followed to "anchor" the frequency polygon to the horizontal axis.

When properly constructed, the histogram and the frequency polygon convey the same information, since the areas included under the two "curves" are equal in size. Both methods of graphing frequency distributions are used by researchers. For the most part, the choice is based on personal preferences, although the frequency polygon is the better method when two or more distributions are to be compared in the same figure. Graphs can convey a great deal about the distribution of scores quickly. We can determine at a glance if the scores tend to clump together and where or if they spread out, and we can tell if they center around one point or more than one point. We can even see if they distribute themselves in a balanced, symmetrical fashion on either side of the mean (a **symmetrical** frequency distribution) or in a somewhat asymmetrical, lopsided fashion (a **skewed** frequency distribution).

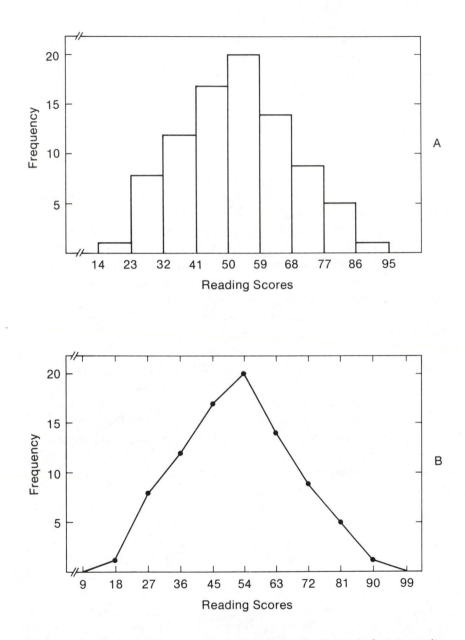

Figure 7-4. Types of Graphs. (A) A Histogram. Each bar is 9 score units wide and centered over the interval it represents. (B) A Frequency Polygon. The points on the horizontal axis are the midpoints of each interval.

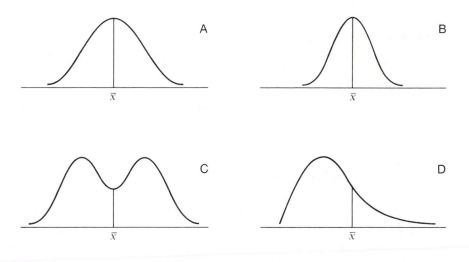

Figure 7-5. Examples of Various Distributions. (A) Normal (with Considerable Variance). (B) Normal (with Less Variance). (C) Biomodal. (D) Skewed.

Common Types of Frequency Distributions

Certain shapes of distributions occur often enough that you should become familiar with them. Figure 7-5 shows four frequency distributions. The curves are smoothed because they represent ideal forms of the distributions rather than portrayals of actual data. Figures 7-5A and 7-5B are both "bell-shaped" symmetrical curves, examples of the **normal curve.**[7]

The precise form of a normal curve is specified by a rather complicated mathematical expression. The shape is determined by the variability of the scores. Highly variable scores produce a normal curve that is spread out; less variable scores produce a normal curve that is narrow in comparison. Figure 7-5A is a "prototypical" normal curve, the sort generally used in psychology texts to illustrate the normal distribution. Relative to Figure 7-5A, 7-5B reflects less variability. The normal distribution has a rather central and honored place in statistics. We will have more to say about the normal distribution in our discussion of standard scores in Chapter 16.

Figure 7-5C shows a **bimodal distribution,** so named because it has two modes rather than one as in the other examples. A bimodal distribution can

---

[7] Normal curves are generally found when measureable features of biological organisms are obtained from a large number of individuals. Bailey (1971, pp. 199–205) offers an interesting discussion of factors "responsible" for normal distributions.

result when responses from two widely divergent groups of subjects happen to be mixed together. Suppose, for example, that we measured and plotted the heights of students in the tenth grade of high school. A plot of the heights would probably be bimodal, the higher peak reflecting the greater concentration of boys (boys tend to be taller) and the lower peak reflecting the greater concentration of girls. A researcher is often forced to examine the data carefully in an attempt to identify the "cause" of the bimodality when it occurs. And the presence of bimodality is difficult to detect unless the frequency distribution is actually plotted; measures of central tendency and of variability alone do not necessarily draw one's attention to the possibility of a bimodal distribution.

Figure 7-5D is an example of a skewed distribution. Note that the distribution is not symmetrical about the mean, but has a "tail" that strings out in one direction. The figure is an example of **positive skew**—the curve strings out with the larger numbers. (A curve with a **negative skew** is one that strings out with smaller numbers.[8]) The median is often used as a measure of central tendency with data that are severely skewed.

Sampling Distributions

A frequency distribution is simply a distribution of the number of times different scores occur; no restriction is placed on the nature of the scores involved. If the scores are actually statistics derived from a large number of random samples drawn from a population of scores, the frequency distribution is called a **sampling distribution** of that statistic. Sampling distributions are indispensible for problems of statistical inference. The concept was introduced in Chapter 5, where we discussed the sampling distribution of the F statistic, a theoretical distribution used to determine whether an obtained F is significant. We discuss other uses of sampling distributions in Chapter 16.

THE MAGNITUDE OF TREATMENT EFFECTS

To set this topic in a relevant context, imagine the following situation. You are just completing the data analysis for a project that you and a partner have

---

[8] An objective way to determine the direction of skew is to compare the mean, median, and mode plotted on the frequency distribution. If a distribution is symmetrical, all three measures will be equal. With a positive skew, the mode with be the smallest, followed by the median, and then the mean; with a negative skew, the ordering of the three indices will be reversed.

been working on for a course requirement. You have done all the calculations carefully, and have finally obtained the F for the most important part of your study. Turning quickly to the table of F values, you find that the null hypothesis can be rejected at $p < .05$, the level of significance you chose at the outset of the study. Relief sets in and then a bit of self-satisfaction at having produced a significant effect. A classmate walks in and asks how your project turned out, and you report that you found significant results for your major hypothesis at $p < .05$. You ask in turn, "How did you do?" She replies, "We got significance at the .001 level!"—whereupon your smile disappears and the glow of $p < .05$ fades in comparison with $p < .001$.

As we pointed out in Chapter 5, comparing outcomes in terms of probability levels is an inappropriate use of hypothesis testing. Since such comparisons are made frequently in the research literature, however, there is reason to stress the point. For example, a report may contain such phrases as "a highly significant F," used not only to substitute for "$p < .01$," but also as a thinly disguised code for "big" or "highly important." At times, a researcher trying to convince a skeptic of the importance of an effect might even add, "It was significant beyond the .001 level."

Unfortunately, level of significance tells us nothing about the magnitude or the importance of a particular set of treatment effects. It would be convenient if the F statistic worked in this way, but it does not. As we indicated in Chapter 5, the level of significance is the risk one takes in being wrong when rejecting the null hypothesis. We also noted that investigators often report the table level nearest to the F value obtained, whether it be .025, .01, or .001, but only as a courtesy to readers who might have a more stringent rejection region for the particular problem. No other reason exists for reporting rejection regions other than that chosen for the analysis (generally .05).

The Problem with the F Ratio

The F test provides important and necessary information concerning the presence or absence of treatment effects—differences among treatment means—in the population. A significant F ratio permits the inference that treatment effects are present—that the null hypothesis is *false*. The primary problem with the F ratio is that its size is directly related to sample size:

The size of the F ratio increases as sample size increases.

We suggested earlier that a relatively easy way to increase the sensitivity of an experiment is to increase sample size. This recommendation holds true as long as a researcher is primarily concerned with the status of the null hypothesis. But if he or she is also interested in the magnitude of the treatment effects, a different index is necessary, one not directly affected by the number of subjects in the different treatment conditions.

Estimate of Treatment Magnitude

The index most commonly used to estimate the **magnitude of treatment effects** consists of a ratio relating the variability attributed to the experimental manipulations to the total variability in the experiment.[9] To obtain this ratio, we have to estimate population variances from the data of an experiment.[10] The ratio itself is relatively simple to express. If we let

$\hat{\sigma}_A^2$ = the estimated population treatment effects,
$\hat{\sigma}_{S/A}^2$ = the estimated population *error* variance, and
$\hat{\sigma}_T^2$ = the estimated population *total* variance,

then the estimate of treatment magnitude may be expressed by the following formula:

$$\text{estimated magnitude of treatments } (\hat{\omega}_A^2) = \frac{\hat{\sigma}_A^2}{\hat{\sigma}_T^2}$$

$$= \frac{\hat{\sigma}_A^2}{\hat{\sigma}_A^2 + \hat{\sigma}_{S/A}^2} . \qquad (7\text{-}1)$$

Note: $\hat{\omega}_A^2$ is called **omega squared;** the symbol above each of the quantities in equation (7-1) is called a *caret,* and is used to designate an *estimate* of a population characteristic.

Estimates of Population Variances. You will recall that the treatment mean square (MS_A) is influenced by two theoretical components, population treatment effects and error variance, and that the within-treatments mean square ($MS_{S/A}$) is influenced only by experimental error. If we subtract $MS_{S/A}$ from MS_A, we obtain a quantity that reflects the effects of the treatments with the influence of experimental error "removed." That is,

$$MS_A - MS_{S/A} = [(\text{treatment component}) + (\text{experimental error})]$$
$$- (\text{experimental error})$$
$$= \text{treatment component}$$

---

[9] See *Design and Analysis* (pp. 547–552) for a more detailed discussion of this index.
[10] A detailed discussion of estimation procedures occurs in Chapter 16. A familiarity with these procedures is not necessary to an understanding of the nature of this index or its use in the analysis of experiments.

With this information as background, we can understand the formula for the actual estimate of the population treatment effects:

$$\hat{\sigma}_A^2 = \frac{(df_A)(MS_A - MS_{S/A})}{a(s)} \quad .$$

(7-2)

(The additional operations specified in equation (7-2) are needed to transform sample data to population estimates, but the underlying logic of the critical operation, the subtraction of $MS_{S/A}$ from MS_A, still remains.)

The other estimates are obtained quite easily from the following formulas:

$$\hat{\sigma}_{S/A}^2 = MS_{S/A} \text{ and}$$

(7-3)

$$\hat{\sigma}_T^2 = \hat{\sigma}_A^2 + \hat{\sigma}_{S/A}^2 \quad .$$

(7-4)

A Numerical Example. As a numerical example, we return to the results of the statistical analysis summarized in Table 4-6 (p. 80). An inspection of equation (7-2) and equation (7-3) indicates that we will need the following information: $MS_A = 180.00$, $MS_{S/A} = 2.67$, $a = 2$, and $s = 10$. Substituting these values in equation (7-2), we obtain

$$\hat{\sigma}_A^2 = \frac{(a - 1)(MS_A - MS_{S/A})}{a(s)}$$

$$= \frac{(2 - 1)(180.00 - 2.67)}{2(10)}$$

$$= \frac{(1)(177.33)}{20} = 8.87 \quad .$$

From equation (7-3), we obtain

$$\hat{\sigma}_{S/A}^2 = MS_{S/A}$$

$$= 2.67 \quad .$$

Finally, we can substitute these two variance estimates in equation (7-1) to obtain an estimate of the magnitude of the treatment effects. That is,

$$\hat{\omega}_A^2 = \frac{\hat{\sigma}_A^2}{\hat{\sigma}_A^2 + \hat{\sigma}_{S/A}^2}$$

$$= \frac{8.87}{8.87 + 2.67}$$

$$= \frac{8.87}{11.54} = .77 \quad .$$

This estimate tells us that 77 percent of the total variance is accounted for by the experimental treatments. Thus, not only is the difference between the two treatment conditions statistically significant, but this difference represents a very sizable effect. The data in this example were not obtained from an actual experiment, however. Consequently, this magnitude estimate is larger than those in actual experiments, where nature dictates the size of the treatment effects. Ratios generally fall in the 5–35 percent range, rarely higher. The size of omega squared, the magnitude index, is limited by the fact that experimental error is usually quite large in psychology experiments.

The Use of Omega Squared in Research

Omega squared enables us to estimate the relative strength with which an independent variable produces changes in behavior. Together with the F statistic, this index helps to round out the picture of a set of experimental results. Despite its usefulness, however, the index is not widely reported in the literature. Still, use of omega squared is growing, and it is likely that future researchers will calculate the value of this estimate almost automatically after conducting the F test.

Researchers can use this index in a number of ways—for example, in developing systematic research programs by identifying independent variables that strongly affect behavior. The index can also be useful in the decision-making process that follows the completion of an experiment, for instance in educational research, medical research, and industrial research, where the primary goal is often to *apply* the results of experimentation in the "real world." In the realm of applied research, the *size* of the effect may actually take on more importance than the results of the statistical test. Finally, for most of us, the index is a *supplement* to the statistical test. It contributes to our understanding of our experimental results and of the importance of a particular experimental manipulation.

SUMMARY

The methods and techniques for describing the results of an experiment are not always used in the analysis of a piece of research, but they do find frequent application in a variety of different research contexts.

While the analysis of variance is based on means and variances, there are occasions when alternative measures of central tendency and variability serve a useful function. Two alternative measures of central tendency are the mode, the most frequent score in a set of scores, and the median, the score that divides a set of scores in half. The mode is rarely used, while the median is used when an experimenter wants to reduce the influence of extreme scores on the measures of central tendency. Two alternative measures of variability are the range and the semi-interquartile range. The range provides a rough but easy-to-compute estimate of the variability present in a set of scores. The semi-interquartile range is often used in conjunction with the median as a measure of variability.

Tables and graphs are widely used and efficient methods of reporting the outcome of an experiment. The advantages of tables are the precision with which summary statistics can be reported and the ease with which additional measures—especially standard deviations—can be included in the research summary. The advantages of graphs are their visual impact and the ease with which trends resulting from the manipulation of quantitative independent variables can be displayed.

A frequency distribution is an orderly arrangement of a set of scores based on the value of the dependent variable and the frequency with which each value occurs. Although frequency distributions can be reported in tabular form, they are most commonly presented graphically. Frequency distributions enable us to spot subjects with extreme scores and to perceive irregularities from the usual symmetrical shape that distributions of large numbers of scores often take. Investigators concerned with survey data and with data to be used for the construction of psychological tests find frequency distributions indispensible in their research.

The estimate of the magnitude of treatment effects, often called omega squared, is relatively new to psychologists, but is finding a useful place in a researcher's collection of statistical procedures. The F test permits the evaluation of the null hypothesis. Nothing can be said from the F test about the magnitude of a set of treatment effects. Omega squared corrects this limitation of the F test and provides a useful estimate of the importance of a particular manipulation.

TERMS, CONCEPTS, AND SYMBOLS

---

descriptive statistics
sample
statistics
parameter
inferential statistics
estimation of population values
mode
median
range
semi-interquartile range
interquartile range
table
graph
line graph
bar graph
frequency distribution
ungrouped frequency distribution
class interval
grouped frequency distribution

midpoint of an interval
apparent limits
real limits
histogram
frequency polygon
symmetrical distribution
skewed distribution
normal distribution (curve)
bimodal distribution
positive skew
negative skew
sampling distribution
magnitude of treatment effects
omega squared
f
$\hat{\sigma}_A^2$
$\hat{\sigma}_{S/A}^2$
$\hat{\sigma}_T^2$
$\hat{\omega}_A^2$

EXERCISES

---

1. This problem illustrates the effect of a deviant, or "maverick," score on the different measures of central tendency. Calculate the mean, median, and mode for each set and note the influence of changing the second score in set A (64) to 24 in set B.

Set A	Set B
72	72
64	**24**
71	71
65	65
52	52
62	62
70	70
66	66
70	70
59	59
58	58
73	73

2. Using the data from problem 3, Chapter 5 (p. 112), calculate the proportion of variance accounted for by the treatment conditions, that is, $\hat{\omega}_A^2$ (omega squared).

The Single-Factor Within-Subjects Design

8

The simplest type of experimental design is that in which subjects are assigned randomly to the different conditions in the experiment and are given only one of the treatments. As we noted in Chapter 4, this type of design is called a completely randomized design; another term is **between-subjects design.** Both terms emphasize the primary characteristics of this design, namely, that subjects are assigned randomly to the treatment conditions and that treatment effects are associated with the differences between subjects. Frequently, however, researchers use a different type of design, in which the same subject serves in all the treatment conditions rather than just one. This second type of design is called a **repeated-measures design,** or **within-subjects design.** Again, both terms stress the nature of this design: Subjects serve more than once in the experiment, repeated measurements are taken, and treatment effects are associated with differences observed *within* each subject.

The within-subjects design has become the typical design used to study such phenomena as learning, transfer of training, and practice effects of all sorts. In a learning experiment, for example, subjects receive a series of study-test trials and performance is charted as a function of these trials; trial number becomes the independent variable in this type of experiment. But use of this design is not limited to learning studies. Researchers in other fields use the within-subjects design because it is characteristically efficient and sensitive, especially in comparison with an equivalent between-subjects design. Undergraduates are often forced by circumstances to use the within-subjects design for their research projects because the number of subjects available to serve in their experiments is limited. Because this design is so prevalent, you should understand its advantages and disadvantages and be able to analyze data from experiments of this type. Fortunately, the analysis is not difficult and is based on procedures discussed in earlier chapters.[1]

REDUCING ERROR VARIANCE

While one reason for using a within-subjects design is a scarcity of subjects, researchers also use this type of design to minimize the amount of experimental error (error variance) operating in their experiments. Everything else being equal, any reduction in error variance will result in an increase in the size of the F ratio, and consequently an increase in the likelihood that the critical value of F will be surpassed and the null hypothesis rejected. To highlight this important advantage of the within-subjects design, we discuss in this section various ways in which error variance may be reduced in general.

Holding Nuisance Variables Constant

In Chapter 3, we discussed the method of reducing error variance by holding nuisance variables constant. Many environmental variables—for example, temperature, humidity, level of illumination, and background noise—can be

---

[1] The analysis of within-subjects designs can be complicated, however, especially when the underlying assumptions of the analysis are not met. We will ignore these considerations in this book and provide references to more detailed discussions when appropriate. Since our objective is to make this book comprehensible to readers new to statistics, we have simplified some of the theoretical details of the analysis of this type of design. We have not distorted the "truth" in this discussion; complicating details have simply been glossed over. For a thorough discussion of the within-subjects design, see *Design and Analysis* (pp. 401–421).

held constant through the use of regulators and the construction of experimental apparatus, and others can be controlled through the careful administration of conditions, for instance, through standardizing the experimental procedures and testing at certain hours. In most experiments, however, the primary source of error variability is the subjects. Controlling, or at least reducing, the effects of subject variability in an experiment requires special attention.

Using Matched Subjects

Using **matched subjects**—matched on characteristics assumed to be relevant to the behavior under study—is equivalent to using some form of physical control to hold environmental factors constant. Two types of matching exist. The first type consists of the formation of a group of "homogeneous" subjects, subjects who possess roughly the same talents or abilities or characteristics deemed important for the experiment. These subjects are then assigned randomly to the treatment conditions. No attempt is made to match individual subjects. Since differences among subjects are reduced through this procedure, subjects so grouped will not differ as greatly among the treatment conditions as those not matched in this way. This technique can result in a considerable reduction in the size of the $MS_{S/A}$, the estimate of experimental error in the completely randomized design.

A second type of matching is accomplished in small sets, or **blocks,** as the sets are usually called. A block of subjects—usually of a size equal to the number of treatment conditions—consists of a group of subjects matched closely on a relevant characteristic, for example, grade-point average in college. Other blocks are formed in the same way except that different values of the matching variable are used to group subjects in different blocks. Once the blocks are formed, subjects within each block are assigned randomly to a different treatment condition.

This second type of matching is generally preferred, since finding small groups of matched subjects (blocks) is easier than finding a large one (a single homogeneous group). Furthermore, the results of an experiment utilizing matched blocks are assumed to have considerable generality, since they are based on the performance of subjects varying widely on the matching characteristic from block to block. In contrast, the results of an experiment using a *single* group of matched subjects may be of limited generality, since the results may be specifically related to the particular type of subject chosen for the study—say, for example, students with high grade-point averages.

Certain problems are associated with the matching procedure. First, as mentioned, finding a sufficiently large number of matched subjects for a single homogeneous group of subjects is often difficult. Second, identifying characteristics that are relatively easy to obtain and, more important, strongly related to the dependent variable, can also present problems. Unless a close relationship exists between the matching variable and the dependent variable, the reduction in error variance from matching will be slight and the efforts expended to achieve the matching will have been wasted. Unfortunately, a lack of relationship between the matching variable and the independent variable is all too common in psychological research.[2]

Using the Same Subject

The most typical method for reducing error variance is to use the same subject in all the treatment conditions. Under these circumstances, matching is perfect, of course. Some problems are associated with this type of design as well, however. The primary problem is the influence on the subjects' behavior of residual effects from previous conditions combining with the currently administered treatment. In such a case, distinguishing the effects of a particular treatment from those carried over from previous treatments is often impossible.

Frequently, researchers are able to convince themselves that **carryover effects,** as they are called, are not a problem—they either assume that such effects do not exist or that they have been minimized through precautions built into the experimental procedure. One such procedure, for example, is to allow sufficient time to pass between successive treatments to guarantee that the effects of earlier treatments are dissipated. Another procedure, used in operant-conditioning research, is to bring each subject back to a predetermined level of performance before starting the next treatment.

In spite of the need to eliminate or minimize carryover effects, the within-subjects design is widely used both by professional researchers and students. In the following section, we consider the analysis of the data collected in this sort of experiment.

THE ANALYSIS OF THE WITHIN-SUBJECTS DESIGN

The Basic Design

Table 8-1 is a comparison between the within-subjects and the between-subjects designs. While both designs contain the same number of

---

[2] See *Design and Analysis* (pp. 501–511) for an elaboration of this point and for a general consideration of designs with matching, including a discussion of the statistical analysis of data obtained with these types of design.

TABLE 8-1   A Comparison of Within-Subjects and Between-Subjects Designs

	A. Within-Subjects Design				B. Between-Subjects Design		
	a_1	a_2	a_3		a_1	a_2	a_3
	S_1	S_1	S_1		S_1	S_5	S_9
	S_2	S_2	S_2		S_2	S_6	S_{10}
	S_3	S_3	S_3		S_3	S_7	S_{11}
	S_4	S_4	S_4		S_4	S_8	S_{12}

observations—four in each treatment condition—they differ in the number of subjects needed to produce them. The between-subjects design has $a(s) = 3(4) = 12$ subjects in this example. As indicated in the table, each subject in this design (numbered 1–12) receives only one of the treatment conditions. The within-subjects design, on the other hand, has $s = 4$ subjects; each subject receives all the treatment conditions, as the table indicates by listing a single subject in all the treatment cells for any given row. As you will see, this change in the nature of the basic experimental design affects the formal statistical analysis.

Sums of Squares

Notation. The notational system needed to represent quantities critical for the statistical analysis of the within-subjects design is enumerated in Table 8-2. Notice that the notational system corresponds exactly to that used for the between-subjects design (see Table 4-1, p. 64) except for the marginal sums listed for each *row,* namely, S_1, S_2, S_3, and S_4. These sums are simply the *totals* for each subject—the sum of his or her scores under the different conditions. For the first subject, for example,

$$S_1 = AS_{11} + AS_{21} + AS_{31}   .$$

(To designate a subject total without specifying any subject in particular, we use S with a j as a subscript, S_j.) Subject sums were not calculated for the between-subjects design, since they were not defined. We could have summed the scores for each row in that design, but this operation would not have made much sense, since each score came from a different and unrelated subject.

TABLE 8-2   Notational System for the Within-Subjects Design

Subjects	Levels of Factor A			Sum
	a_1	a_2	a_3	
S_1	AS_{11}	AS_{21}	AS_{31}	S_1
S_2	AS_{12}	AS_{22}	AS_{32}	S_2
S_3	AS_{13}	AS_{23}	AS_{33}	S_3
S_4	AS_{14}	AS_{24}	AS_{34}	S_4
Sum	A_1	A_2	A_3	T

The Logic of the Analysis. In the analysis of the between-subjects design, discussed in Chapter 4, two component sums of squares are isolated, namely, SS_A and $SS_{S/A}$. The researcher uses the SS_A to estimate the effects of the different treatment conditions, and the $SS_{S/A}$ to estimate the extent to which experimental error is responsible for the differences observed among the treatment means.

We can isolate the same two sums of squares with the data from a within-subjects design. That is, we can calculate a treatment sum of squares (SS_A) from the column totals in Table 8-2 (the A treatment totals) and a within-treatment sum of squares ($SS_{S/A}$) based on the variation of each set of scores within each treatment condition. However, an important difference exists between the $SS_{S/A}$ obtained from the data of a within-subjects design and that obtained from a between-subjects design. In the analysis of the between-subjects design, the $SS_{S/A}$ is used in the estimate of the degree to which experimental error is responsible for the observed differences among the treatment means, but this sum of squares cannot be used for this purpose in the within-subjects design.

An estimate based on the $SS_{S/A}$ *over*estimates the extent to which experimental error influences the treatment differences observed with the within-subjects design. To understand why, note that chance differences between the treatment conditions stemming from the random assignment of subjects to conditions in the between-subjects design are *absent* in the within-subjects design, since the same subjects serve in all of the treatment conditions. Thus, experimental error is considerably smaller in the within-subjects design, and therefore a smaller error term is needed, one that reflects the fact that the same subject receives all the treatments. We obtain such an error term quite easily by subtracting from the $SS_{S/A}$ a sum of squares that reflects the degree to which subjects are consistent over the treatment conditions. Any remaining variation will serve as a reasonable indication of the extent to which chance factors are responsible for the observed differences among the treatment means in the within-subjects design. This "corrected" sum of squares is then used to calculate an F ratio and evaluate the significance of the null hypothesis.

Computational Formulas. In our discussion of the analysis of the between-subjects design, we explained how the calculation of each sum of squares involved the addition or subtraction of certain basic ratios (see pp. 73–75). These ratios took the following form:

$$\frac{\Sigma \ (\text{score or sum})^2}{\text{divisor}} \ ,$$

and were based on three different quantities: the basic observations (AS), the treatment sums (A), and the grand sum (T). As a reminder,

$$[AS] = \Sigma \ (AS)^2, \quad [A] = \frac{\Sigma \ (A)^2}{s}, \quad \text{and } [T] = \frac{(T)^2}{a(s)} \ .$$

Exactly the same ratios are required for the analysis of the within-subjects design. In addition, one more ratio is needed, which is based on the sum of the scores for each subject—an impossible quantity to compute in the between-subjects design, since each subject produced only a single score. For this analysis, then, the ratio based on the subject sums (S_j) is calculated as follows:

$$[S] = \frac{\Sigma \ (S)^2}{a} \ . \tag{8-1}$$

This value is the sum of all the squared subject totals in the experiment divided by a, the number of treatment conditions.

In the between-subjects design, the total sum of squares was divided into two sums of squares, SS_A and $SS_{S/A}$. As we noted in the last section, the $SS_{S/A}$ overestimates the operation of experimental error in the within-subjects design. We can obtain a more adequate estimate of chance factors present in this type of design by subtracting from the $SS_{S/A}$ a sum of squares that reflects the consistent variability of the subjects serving in all the treatment conditions. This latter sum of squares—the **subject sum of squares,** designated SS_S—is based on the deviation of each subject's average score ($\bar{S}_j$) from the grand mean ($\bar{T}$). As we saw in Chapter 4, the computational formula for a sum of squares can be derived from the deviation scores defining that quantity. In the present case, the deviation is $\bar{S}_j - \bar{T}$, and the computational formula is

$$SS_S = [S] - [T] \ . \tag{8-2}$$

By subtracting this new sum of squares from $SS_{S/A}$, we obtain the value that is sometimes called the **residual sum of squares:**

$$SS_{\text{residual}} = SS_{S/A} - SS_S \quad . \tag{8-3}$$

As a result of the subtraction, this residual sum of squares now reflects the chance factors operating in the within-subjects design. Quite properly, this sum will now be used in the calculation of the denominator term of the F ratio formed to evaluate the significance of the overall treatment effects. (To be consistent with the treatment of the within-subjects design in *Design and Analysis* and other advanced statistics texts, we will also refer to this sum of squares as $SS_{A \times S}$.)

While we could obtain the residual sum of squares by subtracting the two sums of squares indicated in equation (8-3), we will calculate this quantity "directly" by using the basic ratios rather than the sums of squares.[3] By applying some simple algebra to the computational formulas for $SS_{S/A}$ and SS_S, we can transform equation (8-3) into

$$
\begin{aligned}
SS_{\text{residual}} &= SS_{S/A} - SS_S \\
&= ([AS] - [A]) - ([S] - [T]) \\
&= [AS] - [A] - [S] + [T] \quad ,
\end{aligned}
$$

which represents the computational formula for the residual sum of squares expressed entirely in terms of basic ratios. The computational formulas for this and the other sums of squares needed for the analysis are presented in Table 8-3. Except for $[S]$, all the ratios specified in the table are identical to those required for the between-subjects design, and by now calculating them should be familiar operations. All the calculations involved in the analysis are illustrated in a numerical example following the discussion of the analysis of variance.

The Analysis of Variance

Degrees of Freedom. The dfs associated with each source of variance in the analysis of the within-subjects design are presented in the third column of Table 8-3. We explained in Chapter 4 that the number of degrees of freedom associated with any variance estimate is equal to the number of observations on which the variance is based minus the number of population estimates required in the process. For the treatments source (A), which is based on *a*

---

[3] We follow this procedure for two reasons: first, to provide us with a useful check on our arithmetic, and, second, to be consistent with the discussion of within-subjects designs in *Design and Analysis* and other advanced statistics books.

TABLE 8-3 A Summary of the Analysis of Variance for the Within-Subjects Design

Source	Sum of Squares[a]	df	MS	F
Treatments (A)	$[A] - [T]$	$a - 1$	$\dfrac{SS_A}{df_A}$	$\dfrac{MS_A}{MS_{A \times S}}$
Subjects (S)	$[S] - [T]$	$s - 1$	$\dfrac{SS_S}{df_S}$	
Residual (A × S)	$[AS] - [A] - [S] + [T]$	$(a - 1)(s - 1)$	$\dfrac{SS_{A \times S}}{df_{A \times S}}$	
Total (T)	$[AS] - [T]$	$a(s) - 1$		

[a] $[A] = \dfrac{\Sigma \, (A)^2}{s}$, $[T] = \dfrac{(T)^2}{a(s)}$, $[S] = \dfrac{\Sigma \, (S)^2}{a}$, $[AS] = \Sigma \, (AS)^2$.

treatment means, 1 df is lost through the estimate of the overall population mean, and $df_A = a - 1$. For the subjects source (S), which is based on s subject means, 1 df is also lost as a consequence of our estimating the overall population mean, and $df_S = s - 1$. While the logic is not obvious, we obtain the number of degrees of freedom for the residual source (A × S) by multiplying together the degrees of freedom for treatments and subjects. That is,

$$df_{A \times S} = (df_A)(df_S) = (a - 1)(s - 1) \quad . \tag{8-4}$$

Mean Squares and F Ratio. The final steps of the analysis, calculation of the mean squares and the F ratio, are summarized in the last two columns of Table 8-3. We test the omnibus null hypothesis,

$$H_0: \mu_1 = \mu_2 = \mu_3 = \text{etc.,}$$

by calculating

$$F = \frac{MS_A}{MS_{A \times S}} \tag{8-5}$$

and applying the following decision rules:

If the obtained value of F exceeds or equals $F(df_A, df_{A \times S})$, $p = \alpha$, reject the null hypothesis; otherwise, do not reject the null hypothesis.

Assumptions. The assumptions underlying the analysis of the within-subjects design are more complicated than those for the between-subjects design, discussed in Chapter 5. In addition to the assumptions of the between-

TABLE 8-4   A Numerical Example

Subjects	Ordinal Position of the Lists (Factor A)						Sum
	a_1	a_2	a_3	a_4	a_5	a_6	
s_1	7	3	2	2	1	1	16
s_2	4	8	3	8	1	2	26
s_3	7	6	3	1	5	4	26
s_4	8	6	1	0	2	0	17
s_5	7	2	3	0	1	3	16
s_6	6	3	3	1	1	1	15
s_7	4	2	0	0	0	0	6
s_8	6	7	5	1	3	2	24
Sum of Scores	49	37	20	13	14	13	146
Sum of Squared Scores	315	211	66	71	42	35	

subjects design (pp. 96–97), we must add the requirement that the subjects show the same degree of consistency for all possible pairs of treatments. While an elaboration of this assumption is beyond the scope of this book, you should be aware that violations of the homogenity-of-variance assumption and the consistency-of-performance assumption are common in psychological research and that these violations can affect the decision to reject or not reject a null hypothesis. (For a full discussion of this problem, see *Design and Analysis* pp. 462–467.)

A Numerical Example

The data for this example are drawn from an actual experiment.[4] In this study, subjects learned a list of ten pairs of words on one day and recalled the pairs two days later. Following recall, subjects learned a second list of pairs, and, again, recalled these pairs after a two-day delay. This cycle of learning-recall-learning-recall was continued for a number of lists, but we limit our example to the first six. The independent variable was the ordinal position of a particular list, that is, whether the list was first, second, ... , or sixth in the sequence. It was hypothesized that recall would be best on the very first list and would grow progressively worse as laboratory experience increased (that is, with the other five lists). There were $s = 8$ subjects in the experiment. Their recall data for the six lists are presented in Table 8-4.

---

[4] Keppel, Postman, and Zavortink (1968).

To facilitate calculations, we have summed the individual scores within the body of the table along the columns to provide the treatment sums (A's), along the rows to provide the subject sums (S's), and in both directions to provide the grand sum (T). We begin the analysis by forming the four basic ratios used to calculate the needed sums of squares:

$$[A] = \frac{\Sigma\,(A)^2}{s}$$

$$= \frac{(49)^2 + (37)^2 + (20)^2 + (13)^2 + (14)^2 + (13)^2}{8}$$

$$= \frac{2{,}401 + 1{,}369 + 400 + 169 + 196 + 169}{8} = \frac{4{,}704}{8}$$

$$= 588.00 \quad ;$$

$$[T] = \frac{(T)^2}{a(s)}$$

$$= \frac{(146)^2}{6(8)} = \frac{21{,}316}{48}$$

$$= 444.08; \text{ and}$$

$$[S] = \frac{\Sigma\,(S)^2}{a}$$

$$= \frac{(16)^2 + (26)^2 + (26)^2 + (17)^2 + (16)^2 + (15)^2 + (6)^2 + (24)^2}{6}$$

$$= \frac{256 + 676 + 676 + 289 + 256 + 225 + 36 + 576}{6} = \frac{2{,}990}{6}$$

$$= 498.33 \quad .$$

We can obtain final quantity, $[AS]$, either by summing each squared observation listed in the table or by summing the subtotals listed for each treatment condition in Table 8-4. By the first method,

$$[AS] = \Sigma\,(AS)^2$$
$$= (7)^2 + (4)^2 + (7)^2 + \cdots + (1)^2 + (0)^2 + (2)^2$$
$$= 49 + 16 + 49 + \cdots + 1 + 0 + 4$$
$$= 740 \quad ,$$

while by the second method,

$$[AS] = 315 + 211 + 66 + 71 + 42 + 35$$
$$= 740 \quad .$$

TABLE 8-5 Summary of the Analysis

Source	SS	df	MS	F
A	143.92	5	28.78	10.32*
S	54.25	7	7.75	
A × S	97.75	35	2.79	
Total	295.92	47		

*$p < .05$.

These four quantities are used to form the sums of squares specified in Table 8-3. From the formulas listed in the table,

$$SS_A = [A] - [T] = 588.00 - 444.08 = 143.92;$$

$$SS_S = [S] - [T] = 498.33 - 444.08 = 54.25;$$

$$SS_{A\times S} = [AS] - [A] - [S] + [T] = 740 - 588.00 - 498.33 + 444.08$$
$$= 97.75;$$

and

$$SS_T = [AS] - [T] = 740 - 444.08 = 295.92 \quad .$$

We have entered these values in the summary table of the analysis (Table 8-5). As an arithmetical check, we should verify that

$$SS_T = SS_A + SS_S + SS_{A\times S}$$
$$295.92 = 143.92 + 54.25 + 97.75$$
$$= 295.92 \quad .$$

All that remains is substitution in the formulas for degrees of freedom, mean squares, and the F ratio specified in Table 8-3. First, we obtain the degrees of freedom:

$$df_A = a - 1 = 6 - 1 = 5;$$

$$df_S = s - 1 = 8 - 1 = 7;$$

$$df_{A\times S} = (a - 1)(s - 1) = (6 - 1)(8 - 1) = 5(7) = 35; \text{ and}$$

$$df_T = a(s) - 1 = 6(8) - 1 = 48 - 1 = 47 \quad .$$

Next, we perform the arithmetical check on these calculations:

$$df_T = df_A + df_S + df_{A\times S}$$
$$47 = 5 + 7 + 35$$
$$= 47 \quad .$$

And we find the mean squares:

$$MS_A = \frac{SS_A}{df_A} = \frac{143.92}{5} = 28.78 \quad,$$

$$MS_S = \frac{SS_S}{df_S} = \frac{54.25}{7} = 7.75 \quad, \text{and}$$

$$MS_{A\times S} = \frac{SS_{A\times S}}{df_{A\times S}} = \frac{97.75}{35} = 2.79 \quad.$$

Finally, we can calculate the omnibus F ratio:

$$F = \frac{MS_A}{MS_{A\times S}} = \frac{28.78}{2.79} = 10.32 \quad.$$

We look in the F table for the critical value of F at $\alpha = .05$ for $df_A = 5$ and $df_{A\times S} = 35$. Although a value of F for the degrees of freedom for this particular denominator is not listed in the table, we can use an approximate value, either the F at $df = 30$ or one that is halfway between $df = 30$ and $df = 40$. With the first, $F(5, 30) = 2.53$, and with the latter, $F(5, 35) = 2.49$, approximately.[5] Either value in this case allows rejection of the null hypothesis. Using the larger value, for example, the decision rules become:

If the obtained value of F exceeds or equals $F_\alpha = 2.53$, reject the null hypothesis; otherwise, do not reject the null hypothesis.

The value of the obtained F, 10.32, exceeds the critical value of F (F_α) specified in the decision rules. Therefore, we reject the null hypothesis. This experiment shows that memory for lists of verbal material learned in succession is not the same. This rather bland conclusion results from the test of the omnibus null hypothesis. Much more specific statements can be made if the data are subjected to a number of analytical comparisons.

ANALYTICAL COMPARISONS

All the analytical techniques discussed in Chapter 6 for asking meaningful questions in the analysis of a between-subjects design are applicable in the analysis of a within-subjects design. Moreover, the formulas for obtaining this information are identical for the two types of designs. The only change is

---

[5] We obtained the second value by averaging $F(5, 30) = 2.53$ and $F(5, 40) = 2.45$, that is, $(2.53 + 2.45)/2 = 2.49$. An alternative procedure is to find a more detailed table of F or to interpolate between the two values (see footnote 4, p. 92).

in the denominator (or error term) of the F ratio. In the between-subjects design, the within-groups mean square ($MS_{S/A}$) is the error term:

$$F_{comp.} = \frac{MS_{A_{comp.}}}{MS_{S/A}} \quad .$$

In the within-subjects design, the *residual* mean square ($MS_{A \times S}$) is the error term. That is, we simply calculate

$$F_{comp.} = \frac{MS_{A_{comp.}}}{MS_{A \times S}} \tag{8-6}$$

to evaluate the significance of analytical comparisons in the within-subjects design.[6]

As an example, suppose we wanted to determine whether the recall of the first list learned in the laboratory was superior to the average recall of the other five lists. Stated in terms of a null hypothesis, the question becomes

$$H_0: \mu_1 = \frac{\mu_2 + \mu_3 + \mu_4 + \mu_5 + \mu_6}{5} \quad .$$

Following the procedures discussed in Chapter 6 (pp. 123–127) for the construction of a set of coefficients, we obtain the following set:

	a_1	a_2	a_3	a_4	a_5	a_6
coefficients (c_i):	+5	−1	−1	−1	−1	−1

As a preliminary step in the calculations, we arrange the coefficients and the treatment sums in a convenient form, as shown in Table 8-6. The sum of the entries in column 4 provides the sum of the weighted treatment totals, and the sum of the entries in column 5 provides the sum of the squared coefficients. Substituting these quantities in the computational formula for a single-df comparison, equation (6-2), we find

$$\begin{aligned} SS_{A_{comp.}} &= \frac{[\Sigma (c_i)(A_i)]^2}{s[\Sigma (c_i)^2]} \\ &= \frac{(+148)^2}{8(30)} \\ &= \frac{21,904}{240} = 91.27 \quad . \end{aligned}$$

---

[6] We must add, however, that this simple translation of the statistical analysis from one type of design to the other only holds when the assumptions underlying the within-subjects design are reasonably met. While a discussion of these complications is not possible in this book, you should at least know that problems can arise in the analysis of within-subjects designs and that we have simplified the situation considerably. (See *Design and Analysis*, pp. 408–414, for a discussion of this problem.)

TABLE 8-6 Preliminary Steps in the Calculation of $SS_{A_{comp.}}$.

1. Levels (a_i)	2. Treatment Sums (A_i)	3. Coefficients (c_i)	4. Product ($c_i)(A_i$)	5. Squared Coefficients ($c_i)^2$
a_1	49	$+5$	$(+5)(49) = +245$	$(+5)^2 = 25$
a_2	37	-1	$(-1)(37) = -37$	$(-1)^2 = 1$
a_3	20	-1	$(-1)(20) = -20$	$(-1)^2 = 1$
a_4	13	-1	$(-1)(13) = -13$	$(-1)^2 = 1$
a_5	14	-1	$(-1)(14) = -14$	$(-1)^2 = 1$
a_6	13	-1	$(-1)(13) = -13$	$(-1)^2 = 1$
Sum	Not Needed	0	$\Sigma (c_i)(A_i) = +148$	$\Sigma (c_i)^2 = 30$

Since $df = 1$ for the comparison between two treatment means,

$$MS_{A_{comp.}} = SS_{A_{comp.}} = 91.27 \quad ,$$

and the F ratio becomes

$$F_{comp.} = \frac{MS_{A_{comp.}}}{MS_{A \times S}} = \frac{91.27}{2.79} = 32.71 \quad .$$

The critical value of F for a single-df comparison is found in the F table under $df_{num.} = 1$ and $df_{denom.} = df_{A \times S}$ at the appropriate significance level. In this example, the critical value of F at $\alpha = .05$ is $F(1, 30) = 4.17$. (The appropriate $df_{A \times S} = 35$ does not appear in the table, and we have chosen $df = 30$ as a compromise.) The decision rules become these:

If $F_{comp.}$ exceeds or equals $F_\alpha = 4.17$, reject the null hypothesis; otherwise, do not reject the null hypothesis.

The obtained F falls within the rejection region defined by this critical value of F, and consequently we conclude that the memory for the first list is superior to the memory for the lists learned later in the laboratory. While additional questions would probably be asked of these data, this single example is sufficient to illustrate the computational procedures.[7]

---

[7] Since the independent variable can be viewed as a *quantitative* manipulation, most researchers would probably conduct a series of tests to determine the shape of the function relating memory and the ordinal position of the list being recalled (that is, first, second, third, and so on). These tests are called an analysis of *trend*. We will consider trend analysis with these data as an example in Chapter 12 (pp. 310–311).

SOME DETAILS OF EXPERIMENTAL DESIGN

Now that you have seen how the data from a within-subjects design are analyzed, we can identify the serious difficulties that can arise and that must be considered before this design is adopted for use in an actual experiment. Because subjects serve in more than one condition in within-subjects designs, two problems are possible: (1) that practice will affect the subjects' performance on the task, and (2) that past treatment effects will influence subjects being given a new treatment in the testing series.

Controlling the Effects of Practice

Practice effects are of two general sorts: a general improvement in performance that results as subjects acquire skills associated with the task, and a general decline in performance as subjects become weary, fatigued, or bored. If both types of practice effects are present in an experiment, a combination of the positive and negative factors is at work. It is unlikely that the two will balance each other perfectly, however. In most situations, then, the researcher will be faced with practice effects of some sort. A number of techniques exist for controlling practice effects. We consider the most common methods in this section.

The negative effects of practice can be minimized fairly easily. Experimenters can control fatigue, for example, by allowing subjects to rest sufficiently between successive treatment conditions. Instructions to subjects can minimize boredom by serving to intrigue, motivate, and involve the subjects in the experiment; also, incentives—monetary or otherwise—can be offered to elicit a high level of performance. The positive effects of practice, on the other hand, are not so easily dealt with, since the effects of learning are relatively permanent—thank goodness!

One approach is to use subjects who have had so much practice with the task at hand that they can no longer show improvement. This approach is frequently used in animal research (involving operant conditioning especially), psychophysical research (where subjects are highly trained as reliable and unchanging observers), and information-processing research (where the interest is in the processing of information in what is called a "steady state," a condition reached through considerable practice and training). But where time is insufficient, skilled subjects are rare, or the researcher is uncertain that subjects can be trained to the point where improvement is impossible, other methods of controlling practice effects are necessary.

Confounding Practice Effects with Treatment Effects. Imagine an experiment with $a = 3$ treatment conditions in which the three population treatment means are in fact equal. (Obtaining equal treatment means in an actual experiment is extremely unlikely due to the operation of various chance factors, but we pose this circumstance for the sake of discussion.) Suppose further that we used a between-subjects design with these three different treatments. Given the assumptions, we would expect to find no differences among the treatment means. Now, suppose we conduct this same experiment with a within-subjects design. What would you expect to find? The answer depends on the presence or absence of practice effects. If *no practice effects* exist— that is, if subjects neither improve nor worsen with practice over the series of three treatments—the results would be identical with those obtained in the between-subjects design, namely, no differences among the treatment means. On the other hand, where practice effects do exist, the experiment will be ruined unless we take specific steps to counteract them during the administration of the treatments.

Let us look more closely at what happens in this experiment if practice effects are present. Suppose the subjects show marked improvement on the task—improving by 10 points on the second treatment as a result of completing the first treatment, and by 5 more points on the third treatment as a result of completing the second treatment. If the treatments are administered in a fixed order or sequence to all subjects, the three treatment means will be *different*, not because of treatment effects, but because of the presence of these practice effects. To be more specific, suppose treatment 1 was presented first to all subjects, followed by treatment 2 and then by treatment 3. Under these circumstances, the mean for treatment 2 will surpass the mean for treatment 1 by the 10 points due to practice. For the same reason, the mean for treatment 3 will surpass the mean for treatment 2 by 5 points. In comparing the first and last treatments, we would have to take into consideration the combined gain from the two previous treatments, namely, 10 and 5 points or a combined total of 15 points.

In this example, then, practice effects and the treatment manipulation are confounded. The practice effects have produced differences in the treatment means where none should have occurred. That the practice effects are responsible is obvious because we assumed that no treatment effects existed. But where treatment effects *are* present the confounding of practice effects and conditions is less obvious. Under these circumstances, practice effects will combine with the treatment effects, and distinguishing the part of the differences due to practice from the part due to the different treatments is impossible.

As an example, suppose that the means for the three conditions are 10, 5, and 15 for levels a_1, a_2, and a_3, respectively, *before* practice effects are taken into consideration. Adding the assumed practice effects to these means—0 to $\overline{A}_1$ (the first condition tested), 10 to $\overline{A}_2$ (the second condition tested), and 15 to $\overline{A}_3$ (the third condition tested), we would expect to observe the following means in the experiment:

	Treatment Effect	+	Practice Effect	=	Observed Mean
$\overline{A}_1 =$	10	+	0	=	10
$\overline{A}_2 =$	5	+	10	=	15
$\overline{A}_3 =$	15	+	15	=	30

Look at the effect on the observed means when the practice effects are added in: Treatment a_2 surpasses treatment a_1 by 5 points when just the *reverse* should have been observed—a_1 should have surpassed a_2 by 5 points. Treatment a_3 surpasses treatment a_2 by 15 points when a_3 should have surpassed a_2 by only 10 points according to the treatment effects assumed for this example.

Thus, practice effects have distorted the expected outcome of the experiment. We can make this point explicitly because we have assigned numerical values to the treatment effects and the practice effects, and were thus able to compare the effects of the two contributing factors on the results of the experiment. In an actual experiment, of course, the value of neither factor is known, and therefore the results of the experiment where practice effects are uncontrolled are generally useless. The effects of treatments and practice are confounded and cannot be disentangled.

Control by Counterbalancing

Confounding of practice and treatment effects will occur in the within-subjects design whenever the treatments are presented in the same sequence for all subjects. The solution is obvious: Vary the sequence for different subjects. The formal technique by which sequence variation is achieved is called **counterbalancing**. To see how this is accomplished, assume that we have three subjects for an experiment and that each receives the three conditions in a different sequence. These three sequences are presented in Table 8-7A. The three columns represent the three testing sessions in which each subject participates (sessions I, II, and III) and the numbers within the body

TABLE 8-7   Two Examples of Counterbalancing

A.					B.				
	Session					Session			
Subject	I	II	III		Subject	I	II	III
1	1	2	3		4	1	3	2
2	2	3	1		5	2	1	3
3	3	1	2		6	3	2	1

of the table (1, 2, and 3) represent the particular treatment administered to each subject in these sessions. That is, subject 1 receives the treatments in the order 1, 2, 3; subject 2 receives them in the order 2, 3, 1; and subject 3 receives them in the order 3, 1, 2.

Note the characteristics of this particular arrangement of the conditions. Each subject is given each treatment once *and* each condition appears once in each session. That is, for session I, all three conditions are represented once. The same is true for session II and for session III. Therefore, the practice effects will influence all three conditions equally. More specifically, we originally assumed that subjects will improve from session I to session II by 10 points. For the first subject, treatment a_2 will gain 10 points; for the second subject, treatment a_3 will gain by 10 points; and for the third subject, treatment a_1 will gain by 10 points. Each treatment condition benefits equally from the practice effect resulting from the first treatment session. The additional gain of 5 points from session II to session III will be added to each of the treatment conditions also. Thus, when we combine the data from these three subjects, practice effects will not contribute *differentially* to the treatment averages. We eliminate the confounding that is surely present when only one sequence is used by counterbalancing the effects of practice over the treatment conditions equally.

The counterbalancing arrangement in Table 8-7A is one of two that are possible with $a = 3$ treatment conditions. The second is presented in Table 8-7B. Again, in this arrangement each condition is administered once to each subject and is represented once in each of the sessions. By the same rationale that underlies the first arrangement, this counterbalancing scheme eliminates the confounding as well.

In an actual experiment, more than three subjects would be tested. In keeping with the logic governing our simplified examples, an equal number of subjects could be assigned randomly to each of the three sequences of treatments. Thus, the total number of subjects would be some multiple of 3, the number of treatment conditions—that is, the sample size could be 3, 6, 9, and so on. It may have occurred to you that we could also use *both* sets of sequences and include all *six* sequences in an experiment. Under these circumstances, subjects would then be assigned in multiples of 6—sample sizes could be 6, 12, 18, and so on.

When all possible sequences are included in an experiment, counterbalancing is said to be **complete.** When only one of the component arrangements is used, we refer to the counterbalancing as **incomplete,** or more formally, as a **Latin-square** arrangement. While complete counterbalancing is preferred, since it includes all possible sequences, this technique requires that increasingly large numbers of subjects be tested as the number of treatment conditions increases. For instance, when $a = 3$, 6 subjects are needed to complete the counterbalancing; when $a = 4$, 24 subjects are needed to complete counterbalancing; and when $a = 5$, 120 subjects are needed to complete the counterbalancing! Consequently, most researchers use some form of incomplete counterbalancing to hold the number of subjects at a reasonable figure.

Differential Carryover Effects

Even where counterbalancing is successful in spreading general practice effects equally over the treatment conditions, it does not solve the other, very serious problem associated with practice effects: that conditions administered early in the sequence will continue to influence performance while the effects of conditions later in the sequence are being observed. If all of the conditions produce carryover effects of the same magnitude, no problem exists. **General practice effects** are of this sort. That is, practice effects are assumed to be the same for all treatment conditions, and, as we have seen, can be controlled through counterbalancing.

All too frequently, however, this assumption does not hold, and we encounter what are called **differential carryover effects.** Differential carryover effects are present when the treatment conditions are affected differently by the conditions appearing before them in the testing sequence. Consider, for example, an experiment with $a = 3$ conditions. Will two of the conditions—a_1 and a_2—be equally affected by the earlier administration of the third, a_3? If not, we have an instance of differential carryover. Suppose the three treatment conditions vary greatly in difficulty. Will subjects receiving the most difficult condition first behave exactly the same way under the condition of medium difficulty as subjects receiving the easiest condition first? If not, we have an instance of differential carryover effects. As another example, suppose one of the treatment conditions is a control treatment and the other two conditions consist of experimental treatments. Will subjects receiving the control condition first display the same level of performance on one of the experimental treatments as do subjects receiving the other experimental treatment first? Again, differential carryover effects will be present if the two sets of subjects behave differently on the second task.

One way to identify the presence of differential carryover effects is to arrange the data so that the changes taking place within each treatment across the testing sessions are obvious. Three things can happen:

1. If no change occurs from session to session for any of the treatment conditions, no carryover effects whatsoever are present.

2. If a change does take place from session to session but is roughly the same for each of the treatment conditions, general practice effects are present.

3. If changes take place from session to session but are different for the different treatment conditions, differential carryover effects are present.

The first case is rare in psychological research, but where it does occur no confounding of practice effects and treatment conditions takes place, simply because practice effects are completely absent. The second and third cases are more typical. Where general practice effects are present (case 2), counterbalancing effectively eliminates any confounding of practice and treatments by spreading the effects of practice equally over the different treatment conditions. On the other hand, where differential carryover effects are present (case 3), counterbalancing would not eliminate the confounding of practice and treatments.

Consider as an example of differential carryover effects the results of an actual experiment in which subjects were instructed to study twelve pairs of words for a certain period of time.[8] Two retention measures, designed to show how well subjects had learned the material, were then administered. With both measuring techniques, subjects were given one member of a pair and required either to *recall* the other member from memory or to *recognize* the other member in a list containing the words used in the experiment. The independent variable was the type of retention measure (recall or recognition), and the dependent variable was the number of words correctly given on the two tests. A within-subjects design was used, with subjects receiving

---

[8] Keppel (1966).

both measures in a counterbalanced order. (Half the subjects received the tests in the order, recall-recognition, and the other half received them in the reverse.) The results are given below:

Retention Measures	First Test	Second Test
Recall	3.12	4.75
Recognition	7.00	5.00

Each subject provided two scores, a recall score and a recognition score. The average recall and recognition scores in each test are shown in the second and third columns of the table.

As you can see by examining the two means in each row, both retention measures showed changes from the first to the second test, but these changes are not the same. In fact, changes are in the opposite directions! More specifically, the recall measure showed a gain of 1.63 words (from 3.12 to 4.75 words) while the recognition measure showed a loss of 2.00 words (from 7.00 to 5.00 words). Differential carryover effects are clearly present. Another way to look at the data is to consider the first and second tests separately. On the first test, when carryover effects are obviously absent, recognition surpassed recall by 3.88 words. In contrast, the difference between recognition and recall was greatly reduced on the second test, the difference now consisting of .25 words. In short, the presence of differential carryover effects makes questionable any analysis in which the results from the two tests are combined.

The major concern in the planning stage of an experiment is whether the results obtained with a within-subjects design will be roughly equivalent to those obtained with a between-subjects design. If you can expect the results to be basically the same, you would probably choose the within-subjects design because of its sensitivity and convenience. If you do not expect them to be the same, you should choose instead the less efficient, but also less ambiguous, between-subjects design. As we have shown, you can always check the adequacy of a within-subjects design after the experiment is completed by examining the differences among the conditions session by session. If the results shift or change, as in our example, you would probably have to pay primary attention to the first session or test, in which the data obviously are free from carryover effects of any kind. This procedure was followed in the analysis of the data in our example. The second test was included to check on the feasibility of the within-subjects design in this type of research setting. The results clearly challenge the wisdom of using the within-subjects design in experiments of this sort.

On a more positive note, differential carryover effects may themselves lead to some interesting speculations. One might ask just why such effects occur and design new experiments to study them specifically. In any case, problems are associated with the within-subjects design in psychology, and these problems must be accounted for in the choice of an experimental design.

SUMMARY

Minimizing the operation of experimental error is a primary concern in the design stage of any experiment. Between-subjects designs, in which subjects are randomly assigned to a single treatment condition, are particularly vulnerable due to the presence of large differences among subjects who are treated alike. Two types of designs can serve to increase the sensitivity of an experiment by reducing experimental error. One design accomplishes this goal through the use of subjects matched on characteristics assumed to be highly related to scores on the dependent variable. The other, the within-subjects design, achieves the same goal by using the same subjects in each of the treatment conditions. We have considered the within-subjects design, as it is a superior method of controlling variation due to subjects.

The analysis of data from a within-subjects design is quite similar to that of data from the between-subjects design considered in preceding chapters. The primary difference lies in the error term, that is, the denominator term of the F ratio. In the between-subjects design, the error term is based entirely on the pooled variability of subjects treated alike. But in using the within-subjects design, the researcher reduces this estimate of experimental error by subtracting a quantity that reflects the consistent performance of each subject over the different treatment conditions.

While investigators can gain considerable advantages by choosing a within-subjects design over a between-subjects design, some difficulties must be overcome before the former design can be used. First, some research projects are not suited to within-subjects designs. For example, instructional variables (common in social-psychology experiments) are not used in within-subjects designs, since subjects are not likely to conveniently disregard the instructional set (or sets) given previously. Second, practice effects must be controlled. If left unchecked, these effects result in a confounding with the independent variable. Some method of counterbalancing, in which the use of different sequences ensures that all the treatment conditions will appear equally in all of the testing sessions, is usually used to solve this problem. Finally, the within-subjects design generally cannot be used where the possibility exists that differential carryover effects may be operating. The severity of this problem varies from research area to research area, but every within-subjects design should be examined for the presence of differential carryover effects.

TERMS, CONCEPTS, AND SYMBOLS

---

between-subjects design   Latin square
repeated-measures design   general practice effects
within-subjects design   differential carryover effects
matched subjects S_j
blocks $\Sigma\,(S)^2$
carryover effects $[S]$
subject sum of squares SS_S
residual sum of squares $SS_{residual}$
practice effects $SS_{A \times S}$
counterbalancing $df_{A \times S}$
complete counterbalancing $MS_{A \times S}$
incomplete counterbalancing

EXERCISES

---

1. Researchers tested ten subjects to find the effects of different lengths of a task on the number of trials to learn. A counterbalancing procedure was used to produce different sequences of task length for each subject; thus, each task length occurred twice as the first, second, third, fourth, and fifth tests. For our purposes, the five task lengths are labeled a_1, a_2, a_3, a_4, and a_5. The numbers of trials taken by these subjects are given below. Analyze these data as the results of a within-subjects design. (Save your calculations for problem 2 of Chapter 12.)

Subject	a_1	a_2	a_3	a_4	a_5
1	2	3	8	10	14
2	1	8	14	9	16
3	4	6	7	16	13
4	3	7	12	14	19
5	3	9	11	11	17
6	5	10	9	13	19
7	4	7	8	15	18
8	2	5	13	16	20
9	4	8	11	10	15
10	3	7	9	12	16

2. In this hypothetical study, the effects of noise on performance in a perceptual task was tested with six subjects. Subjects practiced the task until they reached a level of performance determined by previous research to be ideal. The number of errors made at the end of the training session was used as the measure of performance. In condition a_1, subjects performed the task in the absence of noise. Noise was presented in the other two conditions, either intermittently, a_2 (as an airplane passing overhead), or constantly, a_3 (a diesel generator in an adjoining room). The following data were obtained:

Subject	a_1	a_2	a_3
1	17	19	24
2	30	26	31
3	22	18	27
4	23	17	29
5	26	20	33
6	19	20	25

  a. Analyze the errors made as a within-subjects design.
  b. Compare the condition without noise (a_1) with the two combined noise conditions (a_2 and a_3).
  c. Compare the two noise conditions (a_2 and a_3).

INTRODUCTION TO FACTORIAL DESIGNS

III

In this section, we consider the design and analysis of factorial experiments, studies in which two (or more) independent variables are manipulated systematically. Factorial designs are economical in the sense that they provide the same information available from two single-factor experiments. However, they also provide information that cannot be derived from single-factor studies, namely, the way in which the independent variables combine to influence behavior. Factorial experiments are much more common in psychology than are single-factor experiments, and for good reason. They permit researchers to study behavior under conditions in which independent variables are varied simultaneously rather than one at a time, as with single-factor experiments. The research setting in factorial experiments is thus more realistic than that in single-factor studies.

In Chapter 9, we introduce the simplest form of the factorial design, in which subjects serve in only one of the treatment conditions to which they have been randomly assigned. The analysis of this design utilizes the material in Part II and will serve as a building block for analyzing more complicated designs. The main new concept introduced in this chapter and which is unique to the factorial design is interaction.

In the next chapter, we indicate how the analysis of the results of a factorial experiment can be used to identify the conditions or combination of conditions responsible for significant differences revealed by the standard analysis presented in Chapter 9. Although the nature of these detailed comparisons are not difficult to understand, the computational formulas are relatively complex. In keeping with the introductory nature of this book, our presentation of these analyses is purely descriptive. We refer individuals whose research requires these analyses to appropriate sections of *Design and Analysis*.

In Chapter 11, we consider a within-subjects version of the factorial design called a mixed factorial design. The mixed factorial requires that subjects receive some but not all of the treatment conditions. Mixed factorial designs are extremely common in psychological research and are frequently chosen by students for their research projects. The analysis of this type of design follows directly from the material in Chapters 8 and 9. Thus, by combining what you have learned about the within-subjects design and the factorial design, you will have available a remarkably useful experimental design.

Introduction to the Analysis of Factorial Experiments

9

The experimental designs we have considered so far share one characteristic: they involve the manipulation of a single independent variable. In the hamster study (Chapter 5), for example, we were concerned with the effects of different cage mates on subsequent sexual activity; in the kangaroo-rat study (Chapter 6), we examined the exploratory behavior of kangaroo rats confronted with odors from other members of the same species; and in the forgetting study (Chapter 8), we observed the effects on memory of material learned at different points in a series. In each of these examples, more than two treatment conditions were studied. This feature, as we saw in Chapter 6, permitted us to answer several research questions within the context of a single experiment. Clearly, single-factor experiments can be designed to provide a great deal of useful information in the analysis of a particular problem.

However, a limit does exist on the amount of information single-factor experiments can provide. Through single-factor experiments we study the effects of independent variables *one at a time*. Therefore, by using this design we can determine a great deal about which independent variables influence the behavior, but not about what happens when two or more of these variables are permitted to vary systematically. Single-factor experiments represent an important first step in the analysis of a problem, but usually researchers turn to experiments that offer a more faithful and comprehensive picture of the behavior under study. **Factorial experiments,** in which two or more independent variables are manipulated systematically, provide the means of determining how those independent variables jointly influence the behavior under study.

Factorial designs are quite common in psychology. We discuss only the simplest form of the factorial design—the two-factor design—in this book, but more complicated designs are reported in the contemporary research literature. A good grounding in the design and analysis of two-factor experiments will help you understand more complex designs. As you will see, the two-variable factorial is built on the single-factor design, and much of the material already covered in this book applies directly to this design. The only new concept is that of interaction, explored in detail in a later section. By the same token, factorial designs with more than two independent variables are built on the two-variable factorial; the only complication is the increase in the number of interactions possible with more independent variables.[1]

---

[1] You may find *Design and Analysis* useful with reference to these more complex designs, since the notational system will be familiar to you, an important consideration when you turn to more comprehensive coverages of the design and analysis of experiments. (See *Design and Analysis,* Chapters 13 and 14 for a discussion of the three-variable factorial design, and Chapter 15 for a discussion of factorial experiments in general.) In addition, you might find the following references useful: Edwards (1972), Kirk (1968), Lee (1975), Lindman (1974), Myers (1979), and Winer (1971).

THE FACTORIAL EXPERIMENT

The Basic Design

In the single-factor design, each treatment condition consists of a different *level* of a single independent variable or factor. In the two-variable factorial design, each treatment condition consists of a different *combination* of the levels of *two* independent variables. Note that we use a new term to refer to the treatment a particular group of subjects receives in the factorial design. Previously, we used the term *treatment conditions* to refer to the distinguishing characteristics of the different levels in a single-factor experiment. In the context of the factorial design, we use the term **treatment combinations** to stress the fact that the distinguishing characteristics of the different treatments result from the combination of two independent variables.

The Factorial Arrangement. Consider the graphic representation of a factorial design in Figure 9-1. One of the independent variables, factor A, consists of $a = 4$ levels (designated a_1, a_2, a_3, and a_4); the other independent variable, factor B, consists of $b = 3$ levels (designated b_1, b_2, and b_3). A factorial design is usually referred to in terms of the numbers of levels of the two independent variables. In this particular example, the design is called a 4×3 factorial design (read "four-by-three"). In general, we refer to the factorial design with two independent variables as an $A \times B$ factorial design (read "A-by-B").

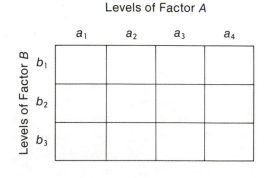

Figure 9-1. An Example of a Factorial Design.

We find the total number of treatment combinations by multiplying the number of levels of one factor by the number of levels of the other. Thus, in the example, $a(b) = 4(3) = 12$ treatment combinations are obtained through the systematic pairing of the levels of the two independent variables.

Factorial designs can be distinguished by the way in which subjects are assigned to the various conditions of an experiment. By far the simplest design is one in which equal numbers of subjects (s) are randomly assigned to each of the $a(b)$ treatment combinations. This type of design, the subject of this chapter, is called the **completely randomized, two-variable factorial design.**

Each cell in Figure 9-1 represents one of the unique treatment combinations a subject might receive. Consider the three treatment cells in the first column. All three cells are associated with the level a_1 treatment, but they differ with regard to the level of factor B with which the a_1 treatment is combined. That is, the top cell represents a treatment resulting from the combination of level a_1 with level b_1; the middle cell, a combination of level a_1 with level b_2; and the bottom cell, a combination of level a_1 with level b_3. As an example, consider an experiment in which subjects are required to solve as many problems as possible in a fixed time interval. Suppose factor A consists of varying amounts of monetary rewards given for solving each problem—none, 10¢, 50¢, and $1—and factor B consists of a variation in problem difficulty—easy, medium, and hard. In the first column, then, the three treatment combinations would consist of the following: a group of subjects receiving no monetary reward (level a_1) for solving the easy problems (level b_1)—the top cell; a group receiving no monetary reward (level a_1) for solving the medium problems (level b_2)—the middle cell; and a group receiving no monetary reward (level a_1) for solving the hard problems (level b_3)—the bottom cell.

We can enumerate the specific treatment combinations represented by the remainder of the figure in the same way. Briefly, the three cells in the second column are all associated with a monetary reward of 10¢ (level a_2). Thus, from top to bottom, a group receives 10¢ for solving easy problems (level b_1), a group receives 10¢ for solving medium problems (level b_2), and a group receives 10¢ for solving hard problems (level b_3). The three cells in the third column are all associated with a reward of 50¢ (level a_3). The top cell represents a group receiving 50¢ for solving easy problems; the middle cell, a group receiving 50¢ for solving medium problems; and the bottom cell, a group receiving 50¢ for solving hard problems. Finally, the three cells in the fourth column are all associated with a reward of $1 (level a_4). The top cell represents a group receiving $1 for solving easy problems; the middle cell, a group receiving $1 for solving medium problems; and the bottom cell, a

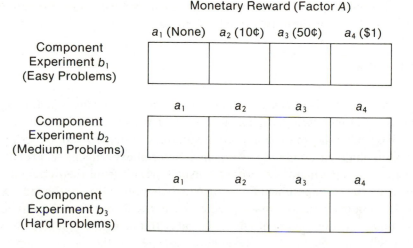

Figure 9-2. The Factorial Design Expressed as Three Component Single-Factor Experiments.

group receiving $1 for solving hard problems. In total, twelve groups represent all possible combinations of the two independent variables. This systematic blending of the two independent variables is the defining characteristic of a factorial design.

Component Single-Factor Experiments. Consider Figure 9-2, which represents the factorial shown in Figure 9-1 as three **component single-factor experiments.** Each experiment consists of the manipulation of the same four levels of factor A (monetary rewards). The experiments differ systematically, each being conducted in conjunction with a different level of factor B (problem difficulty). Thus, component experiment b_1 consists of four treatment conditions differing in the amount of money given for solving problems, but all the subjects in this experiment receive easy problems (level b_1). Component experiment b_2 consists of the same four reward conditions, but in this case all the subjects receive the medium problems (level b_2). Component experiment b_3 also consists of the same four reward conditions, except all the subjects in this experiment receive the hard problems (level b_3).

Each of these experiments represents a perfectly acceptable study and could be conducted by itself as a single-factor design. Such a study would provide useful information about the effects of monetary rewards on problem solving, but would have nothing to say about the role of problem difficulty on this sort of behavior. Only when the three component experiments are conducted simultaneously in a factorial experiment can we study systematically the joint effects of these two independent variables.[2]

Examples

Factorial experiments can be created from almost any single-factor experiment. Sometimes two particular independent variables are chosen because they have been shown to be important variables in single-factor experiments, and studying their combined effects in a factorial experiment seems natural. But just as single-factor experiments usually result from theoretical deductions, factorial experiments are usually theoretically motivated. More specifically, investigators make predictions in the form of research hypotheses about how the treatment effects found with one of the independent variables will be influenced by systematic changes in the other independent variable.

As an example, we will propose three reasonable factorial experiments based on a portion of the kangaroo-rat study originally presented in Chapter 6. You will recall that kangaroo rats tended to avoid investigating the artificial burrow when the odor from a stranger was present, and to avoid investigating the burrow to an even greater degree when the odor was from a rat to whom they had recently lost a territorial fight. The data supporting this statement came from the control, unfamiliar, and familiar-immediate conditions.

This experiment was originally conducted with *male* rats. What would happen if these conditions were administered to *female* rats as well? Would the same general pattern emerge, or would important differences be found? Suppose the males do most of the territorial marking in their natural environment; then females may not be affected to the same degree by these particular manipulations. The design of this experiment is a 3×2 factorial and is presented in Figure 9-3A. Factor A consists of the three smell conditions, while factor B consists of the sex of the tested animals. Specific predictions concerning the differential outcomes of the two component single-factor experiments of which this factorial design is made—one at b_1 for males and one at b_2 for females—would follow directly from whatever theoretical explanations were offered to account for the original set of results obtained with males.

---

[2] We could have made the same argument by ''slicing'' the factorial along the columns rather than the rows of Figure 9-1. In this case, we would obtain four component experiments, each involving a manipulation of problem difficulty (factor B), but each differing in the amount of monetary reward given to the subjects.

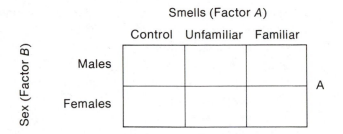

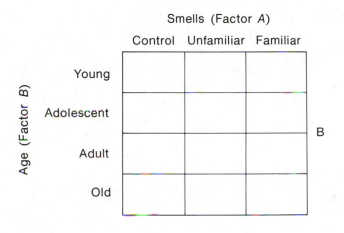

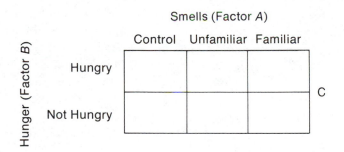

Figure 9-3. Three Examples of Factorial Designs.

As a second example, consider what might happen if the same three smell conditions (factor *A*) were administered to groups of kangaroo rats differing in age. Suppose that the animals in the original example were adults. Would we expect to obtain the same pattern of results using younger kangaroo rats? Perhaps interpreting the meanings of scent markings requires training, experience, or maturation; if so, the results would differ with younger rats. Given this possibility, then, we could certainly justify a factorial experiment in which the three scent conditions (factor A) were conducted with subjects of different ages (factor B). Moreover, if we suspect that a trend will show itself as a function of age, we might consider increasing the number of levels of factor B to include adolescent rats and old rats. The resulting 3×4 factorial is presented in Figure 9-3B.

Finally, we might investigate what would happen if we introduced variations in the hunger drive. Assuming that the rats in the original study had food constantly available and were not hungry, would we obtain the same results using hungry rats? Would hungry rats overcome the tendency to avoid places that smelled of strangers or of "foes"? If so, hungry rats might show little or no difference in the amount of time spent exploring in the three scent conditions. This 3×2 factorial is depicted in Figure 9-3C.

Factorial experiments often seem to evolve from single-factor experiments, where the influence of a particular independent variable is studied in relative isolation. The results of the simpler experiment are incorporated into a theoretical explanation of some sort, and this explanation may suggest additional single-factor experiments that could yield more information on the phenomenon under study. More often than not, however, the development of a theoretical explanation will also suggest factorial manipulations, whereby a second independent variable is expected to change or to duplicate the pattern of results obtained in the original single-factor experiment. The three examples in Figure 9-3 evolved in just this way. We expanded some features of the original kangaroo-rat study,—the sex, age, and degree of hunger of the animals being tested—to provide a second independent variable. Then, without much elaboration, we indicated how each factorial experiment combining these different independent variables with the three smell conditions might change the pattern of results originally observed in the single-factor experiment. Students generally have little difficulty in proposing factorial experiments, especially once they have analyzed and interpreted the results of a single-factor study.

The Advantages of Factorial Designs

Factorial designs have several distinct advantages over their single-factor counterparts. In this section, we discuss each of these advantages in turn.

Economy. Suppose two independent variables, factor A and factor $B,$ are studied in two separate single-factor experiments, and that the same two independent variables are studied in a factorial experiment. Using procedures we will consider in a later section, we can obtain information through the factorial experiment about the effects of *both* factors, generally with fewer subjects than are "consumed" by the two single-factor experiments. Thus, one potential advantage of a factorial experiment is a marked reduction in cost—in terms of number of subjects, time, energy, and money—for essentially the same information obtainable from corresponding single-factor experiments.[3]

Joint Manipulation of Independent Variables. The essence of the factorial design is the joint manipulation of two or more independent variables. Two advantages result from this feature of factorial designs. The first is a relative richness in the experimental setting compared with the environments in which single-factor studies are normally observed. While we should realize that experimentation cannot duplicate the constantly varying patterns of natural events associated with a particular behavior, factorial designs are a better approximation than single-factor designs. Furthermore, the factorial design permits a researcher to disentangle independent variables that are intertwined in the natural environment, and to establish the causal links between each of the variables and the behavior. Thus, factorial experiments have all the virtues of the experiment discussed in Chapter 1, but are less artificial than single-factor studies.

Interaction. A second consequence of the joint manipulation of two independent variables is the opportunity to determine how the two independent variables combine to influence behavior. We have noted that one independent variable can change the pattern of results observed with another independent variable when both variables are included in a factorial design. When such a change occurs, we say that the two independent variables **interact,** or that an **interaction** is present.

Consider again the three examples in Figure 9-3. We suggested that in each case the original pattern of results found with the three smell conditions (control, unfamiliar, and familiar) might change with the manipulation of another independent variable in a factorial arrangement. In the first example, we speculated that female rats would not be affected by the differences in smells as much as male rats are; that is, we hypothesized that male and female rats (factor B) would not show the same pattern of results under the three smell conditions (factor A). In the second example, we suggested that

[3] This point is illustrated by an example in *Design and Analysis* (pp. 171–172). For a discussion of a possible limit to this economy, see *Design and Analysis* (pp. 310–311).

young rats might possibly be unaffected by the different smell conditions while older rats would be affected; again, the hypothesis was that the pattern of results found with factor A would change as the age of the rats is varied (factor B). Finally, we considered the possibility that hungry rats would overcome the inhibiting effects of the smells and investigate the burrow regardless of the smells present; here, too, the effects of factor A were hypothesized to be different for hungry and satiated rats (factor B). All three sets of speculations involve the prediction of an interaction. That is, the pattern of effects observed when factor A is manipulated is expected to be different when the manipulation of factor B is taken into consideration.

The presence of interaction sets qualifiers on any description of the effects of a particular independent variable: We are not able to speak about the influence of one independent variable without also specifying how the second independent variable complicates the results. Information about how independent variables combine to influence behavior—in other words, whether they interact—is simply not attainable from single-factor experiments. Thus, the possibility of determining interaction represents a unique advantage of the factorial design. We discuss this important concept more fully in the following section.

MAIN EFFECTS AND INTERACTION

The means of the different treatment combinations reflect the possible presence of three kinds of treatment effects. As we have noted, one possible effect is interaction, which specifically considers the joint influence of the two independent variables. The other two possible treatment effects, known as the **main effects** of factor A and factor B, disregard this joint influence. Instead, main effects reflect the separate effects of each independent variable *averaged over the levels of the other*. We consider the nature of each of these potential sources of treatment effects in turn.

Main Effects

Consider the results of the hypothetical 3×3 factorial experiment in Table 9-1. The means within the body of the table represent the average score for each of the $a(b) = 3(3) = 9$ treatment combinations, the basic outcome of the experiment. As noted above, the main effect of an independent variable is based on means obtained when we average the results of the experiment over the different levels of the other independent variable. We obtain the

TABLE 9-1   An Example of No Interaction

Levels of Factor B	Levels of Factor A			Mean
	a_1	a_2	a_3	
b_1	6.59	5.92	4.59	5.70
b_2	6.26	5.59	4.26	5.37
b_3	3.26	2.59	1.26	2.37
Mean	5.37	4.70	3.37	4.48

overall means for factor A by summing the three cell means within each level of factor A (the *columns* in Table 9-1) and dividing by the number of means. The overall mean at level a_1, for example, is

$$\overline{A}_1 = \frac{6.59 + 6.26 + 3.26}{3} = \frac{16.11}{3} = 5.37 \quad .$$

This mean represents the average performance of *all* the subjects in the experiment who received the a_1 treatment; the specific condition of factor B is unimportant at this point. We calculate the means for the other two levels in the same way. The overall means for all three levels of factor A are presented in the final row of Table 9-1. These means are called the **column marginal means.**

We obtain the overall means for factor B in a similar manner, namely, by summing the three cell means within each level of factor B (the *rows* in Table 9-1) and dividing by the number of means. The overall mean at level b_3, for example, is

$$\overline{B}_3 = \frac{3.26 + 2.59 + 1.26}{3} = \frac{7.11}{3} = 2.37 \quad .$$

This mean represents the average performance of *all* of the subjects who received the b_3 treatment condition, disregarding the particular condition of factor A these subjects also received. This mean and the other two means of factor B are presented in the final column of Table 9-1. These means are called the **row marginal means.**

Main effects are based on the deviation of the marginal means from the mean of all the subjects in the experiment, that is, the grand mean. These main effects are equivalent to a single-factor experiment involving the *separate manipulation* of either independent variable. For factor A and the column marginal means, for example, 5.37 is the mean of all subjects receiving treatment a_1, 4.70 is the mean for all subjects receiving treatment a_2, and 3.37

is the mean for all subjects receiving treatment a_3. In essence, these three means constitute a single-factor experiment for factor A. The only difference is that here we are creating the single-factor experiment from a factorial experiment by disregarding the treatments associated with factor B. Similarly, the row marginal means (5.70, 5.37, and 2.37) represent a single-factor experiment for factor B. In this case, we create the single-factor experiment by disregarding the treatments associated with factor A. As you will see, the computational formulas for the sums of squares representing the main effects of factor A and factor B are almost identical to those we encounter in the analysis of an actual single-factor experiment.

Interaction

When we determine any given main effect, representing the effects of one independent variable averaged over the levels of the other, we are in a sense ignoring the effects of the second independent variable. Interaction, on the other hand, is specifically concerned with the *joint effects* of the two independent variables. As we have already indicated, interaction is unique to the factorial design; it is not available from single-factor experiments. Interaction is the one new concept introduced by the factorial experiment. Main effects have essentially the same meaning as treatment effects in the single-factor analysis of variance, and they are calculated in an analogous manner. The concept of interaction is important, since it links the two-variable factorial with designs involving three or more independent variables, and it enters into the theoretical thinking on which a great deal of contemporary psychological research is based. In an effort to illustrate this significant concept clearly, we consider two sets of data, the first with no interaction and the second with a clear interaction present.

An Example of No Interaction. It is usually a good idea to plot all the treatment means obtained in a factorial experiment in a figure that permits you to appraise the joint effects of the two independent variables easily. Figure 9-4 is a pictorial representation of the means for the individual treatment combinations listed in Table 9-1. The levels of factor A are designated on the horizontal axis of Figure 9-4, and average values of the response measure (or dependent variable) are represented on the vertical axis. The means for the individual treatment combinations are plotted separately row by row for each level of the other independent variable, factor B.

Let us plot this information step by step. The means from the first row of the table are all associated with level b_1. To plot each mean graphically, we

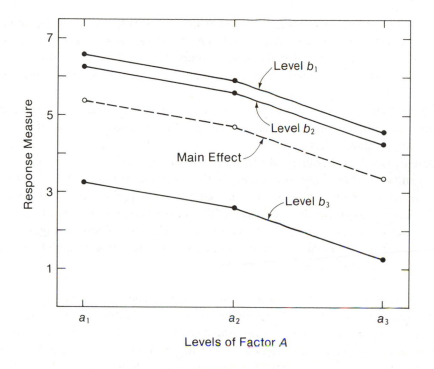

Figure 9-4. An Example of No Interaction (from Table 9-1).

coordinate the appropriate level of factor A (represented by the horizontal axis) with the numerical value of the mean (represented by the vertical axis). As an example, the mean at a_1 is 6.59. We locate it on the graph by moving directly up from a_1 on the horizontal axis to the point directly opposite the value of 6.59 on the vertical axis. We plot the mean at a_2, 5.92, in the same way, directly above the a_2 on the horizontal axis and directly opposite 5.92 on the vertical axis. The mean at a_3, 4.59, is plotted in a similar fashion, but above a_3 on the horizontal axis. We then connect the three points just plotted by straight lines and label them. Next, we plot, connect, and label the three means in the second row of the table (the means at level b_2) in the same manner. Finally, we plot, connect, and label the three means in the third row of the table (the means at level b_3). (For future comparison purposes, we have also plotted the main effect of factor A, obtained from the column marginal means in Table 9-1.)

Each interconnected set of means depicts the results of one component single-factor experiment involving the manipulation of factor A. Three component experiments make up this factorial study, one for each level of factor

B. The results of these component experiments are referred to by the some-times confusing term the **simple main effects** of factor A. Thus, the set of points labeled b_1 are called the simple main effects of factor A at level b_1. Similarly, the set of points labeled b_2 are called the simple main effects of factor A at level b_2; and so on.

Now that we have plotted the data, we can examine the graph for interac-tion. The simplest procedure is to compare the three simple main effects. If the simple main effects show the *same pattern* of results, no interaction is present. On the other hand, if the simple main effects show *different patterns* of results, an interaction is present. In the example in Figure 9-4, the three simple main effects have exactly the same shape. If the individual curves were displaced vertically, they would fall on top of one another. Said another way, the three sets of curves are parallel to each other. Thus, in Figure 9-4, *no interaction* is present. The simple main effects of factor A do not change as a function of variations in factor B.[4]

An Example of Interaction. As a second example, consider a new set of data from the same hypothetical experiment presented in Table 9-2. Note that the marginal means in Table 9-2 are identical to the means in the previous exam-ple (Table 9-1). Thus, the main effects for factor A and factor B are the same in the two examples. There is a big difference, however, in the picture revealed by the means for the treatment conditions presented in the body of the table. The simple main effects for the data in Table 9-2 have been plotted in Figure 9-5 in exactly the same manner as they were in the previous example. That is, the means in the first row of the table have been plotted, connected, and labeled b_1 in the figure, and this set of points represents the simple main effects of factor A at b_1. The means in the other two rows have been plotted in a similar fashion; these two sets of points represent the simple main effects of factor A at b_2 and b_3.

Let us examine the difference between Figures 9-4 and 9-5. In the first example (Figure 9-4), each of the simple main effects showed the same pattern; however, the results of each component experiment show a different pattern in Figure 9-5. This observation is clearly reflected by the fact that the three sets of interconnected points are *not parallel,* as they were in the first example. This is an example of *interaction.*

Clearly, the pictorial representation is extremely useful in inspecting data for the presence of interaction. Interaction is absent when the functions depicting the simple main effects are parallel; an interaction is present

---

[4] We would reach exactly the same conclusion if we marked factor B off on the horizontal axis and plotted in the body of the figure the data from separate "experiments" involving the identical manipulations of factor B but different levels of factor A.

TABLE 9-2 An Example of Interaction

Levels of Factor B	Levels of Factor A			Mean
	a_1	a_2	a_3	
b_1	5.37	6.37	5.37	5.70
b_2	7.37	5.37	3.37	5.37
b_3	3.37	2.37	1.37	2.37
Mean	5.37	4.70	3.37	4.48

when the functions are not parallel. Because of the chance factors that operate in every experiment, we cannot make a definitive statement about interaction until we have conducted the appropriate statistical analysis. Still, the opportunity to spot a potentially significant interaction simply by inspecting a plot of the data is useful.

A Definition of Interaction. Interaction can be defined in various ways. These definitions are not really different; rather, they emphasize different aspects of

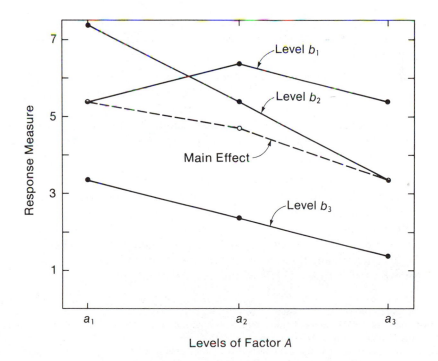

Figure 9-5. An Example of Interaction (from Table 9-2).

the same concept.[5] For example, we can define interaction in terms of the independent variables:

An interaction is present when the effects of one variable on behavior change at different levels of the second variable.

Or, we can define interaction a little more formally in terms of simple main effects:

An interaction is present when the simple main effects of one variable are not the same at different levels of the second variable.

Or, in terms of the main effect, the definition becomes this:

An interaction is present when the main effect of a variable is not representative of the simple main effects of that variable.

The data in Table 9-2, which are plotted in Figure 9-5, illustrate these different definitions. We consider each definition in turn.

1. The behavioral effects of factor A, as indexed by differences among treatment means on the response measure, change at the different levels of factor B.

2. Translated into simple main effects, we would say that an interaction is present because the simple main effects of factor A are not the same at all levels of factor B. We can make either statement because the differences among the A treatment conditions are relatively large at level b_2, relatively small at level b_1, and somewhere in between at level b_3.

3. Finally, in terms of the main effect, we can state that the main effect of factor A, as revealed by the A treatment means plotted in Figure 9-5, is certainly not representative of the corresponding simple main effects.[6] Said another way, any conclusions that are based entirely on the main effects will not fully describe the data. The presence of interaction means that the influence of each of the variables must be interpreted with the levels of the other variable in mind.

---

[5] In addition to the verbal definitions considered here, it is sometimes useful to use numbers to define interaction. One such definition defines interaction in terms of differences between pairs of means (see *Design and Analysis*, pp. 179–181).

[6] In contrast, see how the main effect mirrors the simple main effects in Figure 9-4 where there is no interaction. In this case, the main effect *is* representative of the simple main effects.

SUMS OF SQUARES

Notation

As we consider experimental designs of increasing complexity, we need to expand the notational system denoting the basic observations obtained from an experiment and specifying the sums required for the analysis of variance. In the single-factor design, we designated the basic observation AS to reflect the fact that a score was produced by a particular subject (the S of the designation) in a particular treatment condition (the A of the designation). We used subscripts when it was necessary to specify a particular score in the AS data matrix. We used A to denote the sums of the observations in each treatment condition, and added subscripts to single out a particular treatment sum. We called the sum of all of the observations in the experiment, the grand total, T. These three symbols were all we needed to specify the critical summing operations required to calculate the different sums of squares for the statistical analysis.[7]

Basic Observation. In the factorial design, a second independent variable (factor B) is added to the experimental design. In order to represent the basic observations as well as the different sums and subtotals for the statistical analysis with this design, we must expand the original notational system. The individual score or observation will be represented by ABS, which, as you can see, is derived from its counterpart in the single-factor design (AS) by the addition of the capital letter B. Thus, the combination of three letters indicates that a basic observation was produced by a particular subject (the S in the designation) in a particular treatment combination derived from the factorial arrangement of the two independent variables, factor A (the A in the designation) and factor B (the B in the designation).

Subscripts are added when it becomes necessary to specify a particular subject receiving a particular combination of treatments. Since three pieces of information must be specified—namely, the level of factor A, the level of factor B, and the particular subject in that treatment combination—three subscripts must be specified. For example, the score ABS_{124} refers to the score of the fourth subject receiving the treatment combination formed by pairing level a_1 with level b_2.[8] As with the earlier system, the order of the

---

[7] We introduced an additional symbol, S, with the within-subjects design, where specifying the total sum of scores for each subject became necessary.

[8] Some students have found that numerical subscripts are easier to read and comprehend when commas appear between the three subscripts, as in $ABS_{1,2,4}$.

TABLE 9-3   Notation for the Two-Factor Design

A. ABS Matrix

Treatment Combinations			
ab_{11}	ab_{12}	ab_{21}	ab_{22}
ABS_{111} $+$ ABS_{112}	ABS_{121} $+$ ABS_{122}	ABS_{211} $+$ ABS_{212}	ABS_{221} $+$ ABS_{222}
$\downarrow$	$\downarrow$	$\downarrow$	$\downarrow$
AB_{11}	AB_{12}	AB_{21}	AB_{22}

B. AB Matrix

Levels of Factor B	Levels of Factor A		Marginal Sum
	a_1	a_2	
b_1	AB_{11} $+$	$AB_{21} \longrightarrow$	B_1
	$+$	$+$	$+$
b_2	AB_{12} $+$	$AB_{22} \longrightarrow$	B_2
	$\downarrow$	$\downarrow$	$\downarrow$
Marginal Sum	A_1 $+$	$A_2 \longrightarrow$	T

subscripts is identical to the order of the three capital letters *ABS—A* treatment first, *B* treatment second, and the subject third. If we want to talk about a score without specifying any score in particular, we use the three letters without subscripts, *ABS,* or occasionally with letter subscripts, ABS_{ijk}.

The ABS Matrix. We can illustrate the notational system with a 2×2 factorial design where two levels of factor A ($a = 2$) are combined with two levels of factor B ($b = 2$) to form the following treatment combinations:

$$ab_{11}, ab_{12}, ab_{21}, \text{ and } ab_{22} \quad .$$

To simplify the presentation, we assume that $s = 2$ subjects are randomly assigned to each of these treatment groups. Thus, $a(b)(s) = 2(2)(2) = 8$ subjects, each producing one *ABS* score. These eight scores have been arranged according to treatment group in Table 9-3A in the pattern called an *ABS*

matrix. You can see that two *ABS* scores are listed under each of the four treatment conditions. We arrange the raw data in this way for the eventual statistical summary and analysis of an experiment.

As a preliminary step in the calculations, we add together the *ABS* scores in each group to obtain sums for each of the four treatment combinations. This step is indicated by the plus signs and arrows in the body of the matrix. These totals are designated in this notational system as the **AB sums.** This designation emphasizes the fact that these sums come from treatment conditions formed by a combination of factor *A* (the *A* in the designation) and of factor *B* (the *B* in the designation). One treatment sum is obtained for each of the treatment combinations. The four *AB* sums in this example are specified at the bottom of each column of *ABS* scores. Each sum is identified by means of two subscripts, the first designating the level of factor *A* and the second designating the level of factor *B*. If we wish to refer to these sums in general, we use the two letters either without subscripts, *AB*, or with letter subscripts, AB_{ij}.

The *ABS* matrix is used to list the individual scores and to permit the easy arithmetical processing of the raw data. This arrangement of scores will be used to calculate the sum of squares for the error term.

The AB Matrix. A second matrix is used to arrange the *AB* treatment sums so that the sums of squares can be calculated for the two main effects and the interaction. We call this the **AB matrix,** and it is presented in Table 9-3B. The basic entries within the body of this matrix (often called the cells of the matrix) are the *AB* sums obtained from the *ABS* matrix.

The plus signs and arrows in the *AB* matrix indicate the systematic way in which the *AB* sums are added to produce the additional totals needed for the calculation of the sums of squares. Three sets of sums are produced by these operations. One set consists of the A_i sums, which we obtain by summing across the levels of factor *B*, that is, by adding the *AB* sums in each *column* of the matrix. The two *A* sums—A_1 for level a_1 and A_2 for level a_2—are indicated as column marginal totals in Table 9-3B. A second set of sums consists of the B_j sums which are obtained by summing across the levels of factor *A*, i.e., by adding the *AB* sums in each *row* of the matrix. The two *B* sums, B_1 for level b_1 and B_2 for level b_2, are shown as row marginal totals in the table. The final sum is the grand total (*T*), which we obtain from the *AB* matrix by adding together either set of marginal totals, as indicated in the table. (It is a good idea to sum both sets of marginal totals for a simple check of your arithmetic.)

For purposes of reporting data, we convert the various treatment sums

TABLE 9-4   An Example of the *ABS* and *AB* Matrices

A. *ABS* Matrix

Treatment Combinations			
ab_{11}	ab_{12}	ab_{21}	ab_{22}
2	8	9	3
5	6	6	1
7	14	15	4

B. *AB* Matrix

Factor B	Factor A		Sum
	a_1	a_2	
b_1	7	15	22
b_2	14	4	18
Sum	21	19	40

into means by dividing each sum by the appropriate number of observations. That is,

$$\overline{AB} = \frac{AB}{s} \quad , \quad \overline{A} = \frac{A}{b(s)} \quad ,$$

$$\overline{B} = \frac{B}{a(s)} \quad , \quad \text{and} \quad \overline{T} = \frac{T}{a(b)(s)} \quad .$$

A numerical example is presented in Table 9-4 to illustrate the nature of the quantities appearing in the two matrices. We have kept the calculations simple so that you can determine easily whether you understand the summing operations symbolized by the notational system. You will soon be using these procedures to calculate sums of squares for the analysis of variance. To repeat, the basic *ABS* scores are listed in the appropriate column of the *ABS* matrix. Each set of scores is summed to produce the *AB* sums. These sums are entered in the body of the *AB* matrix according to the treatment combination designated by the subscripts. Marginal totals are obtained by the summing of the *AB* totals separately by columns (the *A* sums) and by rows (the *B* sums). The grand total (*T*) is obtained by the summing of either set of marginal sums.

Basic Deviations

As you have seen in previous chapters, the analysis of variance consists of the systematic subdivision of the total sum of squares—based on the deviation of each basic score from the grand mean—into a number of component sums of squares. The factorial design is more complicated than the single-factor design, and this complexity is reflected in the fact that the total sum of squares is divided into *four* components, rather than the *two* isolated in the single-factor experiment. We can elucidate the logic of this division more easily if we treat it in two steps.

Initial Division. As explained in Chapter 4, the deviation of an AS score from the grand mean (the total deviation) can be divided into two components: the deviation of the treatment means from the grand mean (the between-group deviation) and the deviation of the AS score from its treatment mean (the within-group deviation). We illustrated this relationship with only one AS score, although it holds for all the scores in an experiment. We can state the relationship generally by using letter subscripts as follows:

total deviation = between-group deviation + within-group deviation

$$AS_{ij} - \overline{T} \quad = \quad (\overline{A}_i - \overline{T}) \quad + \quad (AS_{ij} - \overline{A}_i) \ .$$

To begin extracting deviation scores for the factorial experiment, it is convenient to think of the factorial as a single-factor experiment, with the "treatments" consisting of the AB treatment combinations rather than the A treatment conditions. If we do this, we can extend the analysis of deviation scores summarized in the last paragraph to the factorial. That is, we can divide the deviation of each ABS score from the grand mean in the factorial design into a between-group deviation and a within-group deviation. Specifically,

total deviation = between-group deviation + within-group deviation

$$ABS_{ijk} - \overline{T} \quad = \quad (\overline{AB}_{ij} - \overline{T}) \quad + \quad (ABS_{ijk} - \overline{AB}_{ij}) \ .$$

The only difference between the two subdivisions is the addition of B, which is needed to reflect the factorial design.

Applying the logic presented in Chapter 4 for the single-factor experiment, we can say that a sum of squares based on this between-group deviation is influenced by two factors, a "treatment effect" and experimental error, and that a sum of squares based on this within-group deviation is influenced only by experimental error. (The sum of squares based on this latter deviation is designated S/AB to reflect the fact that it represents the variability of subjects within each of the AB treatment combinations.) While the within-group sum of squares ($SS_{S/AB}$) will prove to be useful in the analysis of variance, the between-group sum of squares will not. The reason is that the "treatment effect" is not a meaningful quantity, since it can reflect the presence of three different theoretical quantities, namely, a main effect of factor A, a main effect of factor B, and an interaction of the two factors. To be useful, therefore, the between-group deviation must be divided further into these more meaningful components.

Between-Group Division. To reiterate, the between-group deviation contains three meaningful components, the main effects of factor A and factor B and interaction. The two main effects are easily expressed as deviations from the grand mean:

$$A \text{ main effect} = \overline{A}_i - \overline{T} \quad ;$$
$$B \text{ main effect} = \overline{B}_j - \overline{T} \quad .$$

The interaction effect is a bit more complicated, but involves familiar quantities nevertheless:

$$\text{interaction effect} = \overline{AB}_{ij} - \overline{A}_i - \overline{B}_j + \overline{T} \quad .$$

We simply ask you to accept this definition, although the interaction effect can be derived with the help of a little algebra.[9]

Summary. We can now combine the two steps in the subdivision of the total deviation. More specifically,

$$ABS_{ijk} - \overline{T} = (\overline{A}_i - \overline{T}) + (\overline{B}_j - \overline{T}) + (\overline{AB}_{ij} - \overline{A}_i - \overline{B}_j + \overline{T})$$
$$+ (ABS_{ijk} - \overline{AB}_{ij}) \quad . \tag{9-1}$$

In words, the deviation of a subject from the grand mean can be broken down into four separate components:

1. The main effect at level a_i

2. The main effect at level b_j

3. The interaction effect at the combination of levels a_i and b_j

4. The deviation of the subject from the appropriate treatment mean

---

[9] For the curious, to compute the interaction effect, we start with the following relationship—between-group deviation = A main effect + B main effect + $A \times B$ interaction—and solve for the $A \times B$ interaction by subtracting and substituting deviations for the known quantities. These steps are explained fully in *Design and Analysis* (pp. 190–191).

Let us sum up the procedures so far. We have divided the deviation of any given subject from the grand mean into four components, each of which reflects a different aspect of the results. All that remains is to derive the computational formulas with which these component deviations will be transformed into sums of squares for the analysis of variance.

Computational Formulas

The computational formulas for the necessary sums of squares follow a familiar pattern. We start with basic ratios that perform the same set of operations (squaring, summing, and dividing) on either the raw scores or on sums obtained from the raw scores. We calculate the sums of squares by adding and subtracting these ratios in the patterns indicated by the various sets of deviations specified in equation (9-1).

Basic Ratios. The basic ratios formed in the calculation of sums of squares all have the following form:

$$\frac{\Sigma \,(\text{score or sum})^2}{\text{divisor}} \, . \qquad (9\text{-}2)$$

With reference to Table 9-3, the "scores" specified in equation (9-2) are the *ABS* scores found in the *ABS* matrix, and the "sums" are the different totals and subtotals found in the *AB* matrix. The application of equation (9-2) to each of these quantities is specified systematically in Table 9-5. Since these arithmetical operations should be familiar by now, we comment on them only briefly.

All the calculations begin with the quantities listed in column 1 of Table 9-5, namely, ABS_{ijk}, AB_{ij}, A_i, B_j, and T. In the next three columns, the specific arithmetical operations are performed on each set of scores or sums. As you can see, the same three steps are performed on each of these quantities. That is, each score or sum is first *squared* (column 2), then *summed* if there is more than one squared quantity in the set (column 3), and finally *divided* to form the various basic ratios needed for the calculation of the sums of squares (column 4). The calculations are no more complicated than those performed in the analysis of single-factor experiments. Each ratio is appropriately coded in column 5 to simplify the specification of the computational formulas for the sums of squares.

To illustrate these calculations in as simple a manner as possible, we have performed each step in the calculation of the ratios enumerated in Table 9-5 with the data originally presented in conjunction with the notational system

TABLE 9-5 The Arithmetical Operations Performed on Scores or Sums

1. Basic Score or Sum (from Appropriate Matrix)	2. Squaring	3. Summing (If Relevant)	4. Dividing (If Required)	5. Coding
ABS_{ijk}	$(ABS_{ijk})^2$	$\Sigma(ABS)^2$	$\Sigma(ABS)^2$	$[ABS]$
AB_{ij}	$(AB_{ij})^2$	$\Sigma(AB)^2$	$\dfrac{\Sigma(AB)^2}{s}$	$[AB]$
A_i	$(A_i)^2$	$\Sigma(A)^2$	$\dfrac{\Sigma(A)^2}{b(s)}$	$[A]$
B_j	$(B_j)^2$	$\Sigma(B)^2$	$\dfrac{\Sigma(B)^2}{a(s)}$	$[B]$
T	$(T)^2$	$(T)^2$	$\dfrac{(T)^2}{a(b)(s)}$	$[T]$

(see Table 9-4). This model will assist you in identifying the quantities needed. The results of each calculation are presented in Table 9-6. Farther on in the chapter, we consider a more comprehensive example, but the steps followed there are no more complicated conceptually than those illustrated in Table 9-6. Follow each step in the table until you are certain that you know

TABLE 9-6 An Example of the Calculation of the Basic Ratios

1. Basic Score or Sum	2. Squaring	3. Summing	4. Dividing	5. Coding
ABS_{ijk}: 2 8 9 3 5 6 6 1	4 64 81 9 25 36 36 1	256	256	$[ABS]$
AB_{ij}: 7 15 14 4	49 225 196 16	486	$\dfrac{486}{2} = 243.00$	$[AB]$
A_i: 21 19	441 361	802	$\dfrac{802}{2(2)} = 200.50$	$[A]$
B_j: 22 18	484 324	808	$\dfrac{808}{2(2)} = 202.00$	$[B]$
T: 40	1,600	1,600	$\dfrac{1,600}{2(2)(2)} = 200.00$	$[T]$

TABLE 9-7   The Computational Formulas for the Sums
of Squares

1. Source	2. Basic Deviation	3. Computational Formula[a]
A	$\bar{A}_i - \bar{T}$	$[A] - [T]$
B	$\bar{B}_j - \bar{T}$	$[B] - [T]$
$A \times B$	$\overline{AB}_{ij} - \bar{A}_i - \bar{B}_j + \bar{T}$	$[AB] - [A] - [B] + [T]$
S/AB	$ABS_{ijk} - \overline{AB}_{ij}$	$[ABS] - [AB]$
Total	$ABS_{ijk} - \bar{T}$	$[ABS] - [T]$

[a] $[A] = \dfrac{\Sigma(A)^2}{b(s)}$, $[T] = \dfrac{(T)^2}{a(b)(s)}$, $[B] = \dfrac{\Sigma(B)^2}{a(s)}$, $[AB] = \dfrac{\Sigma(AB)^2}{s}$,   and $[ABS] = \Sigma(ABS)^2$.

where the basic scores and sums come from and how they enter into the determination of the basic ratios used in this particular analysis of variance.

Sums of Squares. The particular patterns in which the basic ratios are combined to produce the sums of squares are indicated by the deviations specified in equation (9-1). Each of these deviations is presented again in column 2 of Table 9-7. The computational formulas for the different sums of squares, which are obviously based on the deviations, are presented in coded form in column 3 of the table. The first four rows of the table designate the component sources of variability normally extracted from this particular factorial design; the last row designates the total amount of variation reflected in the results of an experiment.

We illustrate the use of these computational formulas with the preliminary calculations presented in column 4 of Table 9-6. Specifically,

$$SS_A = [A] - [T]$$
$$= 200.50 - 200.00 = 0.50;$$

$$SS_B = [B] - [T]$$
$$= 202.00 - 200.00 = 2.00;$$

$$SS_{A \times B} = [AB] - [A] - [B] + [T]$$
$$= 243.00 - 200.50 - 202.00 + 200.00 = 40.50;$$

$$SS_{S/AB} = [ABS] - [AB]$$
$$= 256 - 243.00 = 13.00;\text{ and}$$

$$SS_T = [ABS] - [T]$$
$$= 256 - 200.00 = 56.00 \quad .$$

As a check on the calculations, we verify that the component sums of squares equal the total sum of squares. That is,

$$SS_T = SS_A + SS_B + SS_{A \times B} + SS_{S/AB} \qquad (9\text{-}3)$$

$$56.00 = 0.50 + 2.00 + 40.50 + 13.00$$

$$= 56.00 \quad .$$

THE ANALYSIS OF VARIANCE

The final steps in the analysis of variance are summarized in Table 9-8. In these steps, each component sum of squares is transformed into a mean square (a variance), and F ratios are formed. We will discuss each of these operations briefly. (The entire analysis is summarized in Glossary 4, Part IV.)

Degrees of Freedom

The computational formulas specifying the degrees of freedom associated with each source of variance obtained in the analysis of the factorial design are presented under df in Table 9-8. As we have pointed out before, the number of degrees of freedom associated with any mean square is equal to the number of observations on which the mean square is based minus the number of population estimates required in the process. The degrees of

TABLE 9-8   Two-Factor Analysis of Variance

Source	SS^a	df	MS	F
A	SS_A	$a - 1$	$\dfrac{SS_A}{df_A}$	$\dfrac{MS_A}{MS_{S/AB}}$
B	SS_B	$b - 1$	$\dfrac{SS_B}{df_B}$	$\dfrac{MS_B}{MS_{S/AB}}$
$A \times B$	$SS_{A \times B}$	$(a - 1)(b - 1)$	$\dfrac{SS_{A \times B}}{df_{A \times B}}$	$\dfrac{MS_{A \times B}}{MS_{S/AB}}$
S/AB	$SS_{S/AB}$	$a(b)(s - 1)$	$\dfrac{SS_{S/AB}}{df_{S/AB}}$	
Total	SS_T	$a(b)(s) - 1$		

^{a} Computational formulas for the sums of squares are found in Table 9-7.

freedom statements for each of the two main effects (A and B) and for the total source of variability represent straightforward applications of this rule. In addition, the degrees of freedom for the within-group source (S/AB) conform to this rule in the same way as did the within-group source in the single-factor experiment (see p. 78). The degrees of freedom for the interaction source ($A \times B$) are the product of the degrees of freedom associated with the two sources represented in this interaction. That is,

$$df_{A \times B} = (df_A)(df_B) = (a - 1)(b - 1) \quad . \tag{9-4}$$

We will not describe the logic behind the calculation of the degrees of freedom for this particular source, but you can be sure that the general rule for the calculation of degrees of freedom holds in this case even if its application is not immediately obvious. [See *Design and Analysis,* pp. 197–198, for an explanation of equation (9-4)].

Mean Squares and *F* Ratios

The mean squares required for the analysis are designated under *MS* in Table 9-8. All mean squares are calculated by the division of the sum of squares by the appropriate number of degrees of freedom.

Three *F* ratios are obtained from this analysis, one for each of the two main effects and the other for the $A \times B$ interaction. Each ratio is formed by the division of the appropriate mean square by the within-group mean square, $MS_{S/AB}$.

Hypothesis Testing

Statistical Hypotheses. Our evaluation of the significance of each of the three factorial effects—the two main effects and the interaction—follows the same pattern as that of the treatment effects in single-factor designs. First, we form a set of statistical hypotheses. For the main effect of factor A,

$$H_0\text{: All } \mu_i\text{'s are equal;}$$
$$H_1\text{: Not all } \mu_i\text{'s are equal.}$$

The μ_i's refer to the A population treatment means, which are defined by averaging the individual population means over the levels of factor B. We form a similar set of hypotheses for the main effect of factor B:

$$H_0\text{: All } \mu_j\text{'s are equal;}$$
$$H_1\text{: Not all } \mu_j\text{'s are equal.}$$

The μ_j's refer to the B population treatment means, which are defined by averaging the individual population means over the levels of factor A. The statistical hypotheses for the $A \times B$ interaction can be expressed as follows:

H_0: Interaction effects are completely absent;
H_1: Some interaction effects are present.

Evaluation of the Null Hypotheses. Each source of variance in which we are theoretically interested—A, B, and $A \times B$—is assumed to reflect the possible presence of two factors: (1) treatment effects or interaction effects and (2) experimental error. Each of the null hypotheses specifies the complete absence of treatment effects or interaction in the population. When the null hypothesis is true, the first factor will equal zero, leaving only variation due to experimental error. On the other hand, when the null hypothesis is false (and the alternative hypothesis is true), the first factor becomes relevant. In this case, the mean square under consideration is now influenced both by experimental error, which is present no matter which statistical hypothesis is correct, and systematic effects in the form of treatment effects or interaction.

The within-group mean square, $MS_{S/AB}$, is based on the variability of subjects treated alike—in this factorial design, subjects who are given the same treatment combination. Consequently, any variation measured with this mean square represents the degree of experimental error present in the experiment.

The three F ratios specified in Table 9-8 provide the means to test the three null hypotheses. If the null hypothesis is true, the numerator mean square reflects experimental error, as does the denominator mean square, and the value of F is expected to be approximately 1.0. If the null hypothesis is false, the numerator mean square will be systematically larger than the error term, and the value of the F ratio is expected to be greater than 1.0. We will now use information derived from the F distribution to form decision rules specifying the circumstances under which we will reject the null hypothesis.

Decision Rules. We need to form different decision rules for each of the null hypotheses under consideration, but we can obtain them all from the following statement:

If the obtained value of F equals or exceeds $F(df_{\text{effect}}, df_{S/AB})$, reject the null hypothesis; otherwise, do not reject the null hypothesis.

To find the critical value of F for any one of the factorial effects, we substitute the appropriate degrees of freedom for the numerator term (df_{effect}) and

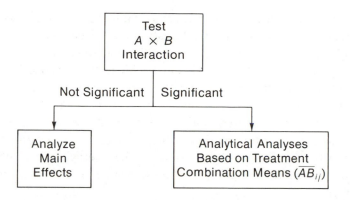

Figure 9-6. The Order of Hypothesis Testing in the Factorial Design.

the denominator term ($df_{S/AB}$), enter the F table, and locate the value of F listed at the particular significance level we have chosen for our research. We illustrate the formulation of the decision rules in the numerical example presented in the last section of this chapter.

Order of Testing Null Hypotheses. Null hypotheses in the factorial design should be tested in a rational sequence. Logically, the first null hypothesis to be evaluated is the $A \times B$ interaction. This test receives priority because its outcome usually determines the researcher's next step. A significant interaction requires the researcher to analyze and interpret the data with respect to the combination of the two independent variables; a nonsignificant interaction indicates that the investigator can treat the factorial experiment as two independent, noninteracting single-factor experiments. These two courses of action, which depend upon the significance or nonsignificance of the test for interaction, are summarized in Figure 9-6.

Starting at the top of the figure, you can see that a significant interaction generally leads a researcher to analyses dealing with the specific treatment means (the $\overline{AB}$s). These analyses, which we will discuss in Chapter 10, help to pinpoint the *locus* of the interaction, that is, to identify the treatments or combinations of treatments responsible for the significant interaction. A nonsignificant interaction, on the other hand, indicates that the results of the experiment can be more appropriately analyzed and interpreted with procedures that disregard the influence of the other independent variable, i.e., procedures based on the marginal means (the $\overline{A}$s or the $\overline{B}$s) rather than on the specific treatment means (the $\overline{AB}$s). In other words, where interaction is nonsignificant, we treat each main effect as if it had come from a single-factor experiment and apply the analytical analyses we discussed in Chapter 6 for that design. We consider the adaptation of these analyses in the next chapter.

Clearly, the test for interaction is most critical. It determines whether the average effects of either independent variable—the main effects—are representative or descriptive of the simple main effects of that variable. If the average effects are *not* representative, we concentrate on the specific treatment means and the interpretation of the significant interaction. If they are representative, we focus our attention on the average effects of the two independent variables and interpret the experimental results in terms of the main effects.

Assumptions. The assumptions held for the single-factor design—concerning the normality of distribution, homogeneity of variance, and independence of the scores in the treatment conditions—apply equally to the factorial design. Violating normality of distribution and homogeneity of variance does not appear to have any practical significance for the statistical analysis of an experiment. The independence assumption is generally met through the random assignment of subjects to conditions.

Magnitude of Factorial Effects

In Chapter 7, we introduced an index that reflects the magnitude or size of the treatment effects in a single-factor experiment. This index, omega squared ($\hat{\omega}_A^2$), is used to provide additional information about the degree to which the total variability among subjects ($\hat{\sigma}_T^2$) can be accounted for by the variability due to the treatment effects ($\hat{\sigma}_A^2$). Estimates of omega squared for factorial effects—for the main effects and interaction—are obtainable from the data of a factorial experiment. Unfortunately, the formulas for obtaining these values are outside the scope of this book. If you need these formulas for a research project, consult either Vaughan and Corballis (1969) or *Design and Analysis* (pp. 552–553).

A NUMERICAL EXAMPLE

The Experiment

We began this chapter by describing three possible experiments involving kangaroo rats. In one experiment, the scent conditions (factor A) were paired with groups of different ages (factor B). We speculated that young rats are not influenced in exactly the same way that older rats are, and that therefore the degree to which kangaroo rats are influenced by the scents from other members of the same species depends on the age of the animals. In this section, we illustrate the statistical analysis of the $A \times B$ factorial with a hypothetical experiment based on these two variables. In order to simplify the example, we have dropped two of the scent conditions, leaving three: the control condition (a_1), the unfamiliar condition (a_2), and the familiar-immediate condition which we will now call the familiar condition (a_3). (For a complete explanation of these particular manipulations, see pp. 117–119.) For the age variable, we are considering only two levels, young (b_1) and adult (b_2). The resulting design is a 3×2 factorial producing a total of $a(b) = 3(2) = 6$ treatment combinations (i.e., control-young, unfamiliar-young, familiar-young, control-adult, unfamiliar-adult, and familiar-adult). Sample size for this example is $s = 7$. Thus, a total of $a(b)(s) = 3(2)(7) = 42$ animals is tested—21 young rats who are assigned randomly to the three scent conditions and 21 adult rats who are assigned randomly to the same conditions.

Preliminary Analysis

The numbers of minutes each rat spent exploring the artificial burrow are entered in the ABS matrix, Table 9-9. The scores for the young rats (level b_1) are shown in the upper half, while the scores for the adult rats (level b_2) are in the lower half. The different scent conditions are shown as columns, and the individual observations (the ABS scores) are listed within each column. The sum of each group of scores (the AB sums) and the sum of the squares of these scores are given at the bottom of each column of numbers.

The treatment totals are entered in the AB matrix in Table 9-10A. The column marginal totals (the A sums) and the row marginal totals (the B sums) and the grand total (T) are also entered in the table. These two matrices provide the components for the calculation of the various sums of squares required in the analysis of variance.

Tabular Summary. A convenient way of studying the outcome of a factorial experiment is through a table of means such as Table 9-10B. In this table, we can examine the main effects (the column and row marginal means) and the simple main effects (in the body of the table) together. Considering the simple main effects first, we can see that the pattern of results observed with the young rats (b_1) is quite different from that observed with the adult rats (b_2). That is, while the adult rats seem to be strongly affected by the different

TABLE 9-9   A Numerical Example: *ABS* Matrix

Young Rats (Level b_1)

	Control a_1	Unfamiliar a_2	Familiar a_3
	46	41	34
	40	44	32
	27	31	51
	34	29	37
	39	47	45
	37	28	48
	26	43	29
Sum of Scores	249	263	276
Sum of Squared Scores	9,167	10,261	11,320

Adult Rats (Level b_2)

	Control a_1	Unfamiliar a_2	Familiar a_3
	33	32	6
	31	19	0
	33	36	0
	38	20	10
	47	20	8
	42	22	12
	37	24	5
Sum of Scores	261	173	41
Sum of Squared Scores	9,925	4,541	369

smell conditions, the young rats seem to be markedly unaffected. Since the two simple main effects are not the same, an interaction appears to be present. To determine whether these differences in patterns are significant, we need to conduct a statistical analysis.

We can also look at the other set of simple main effects, the effects of age (factor *B*) for each of the three scent conditions (levels of factor *A*). For the control condition (a_1), for example, the adult rats appear to do slightly more exploring than the young rats. For the unfamiliar and familiar conditions (a_2 and a_3, respectively), however, the opposite effect is observed: The older rats do less exploring than the younger rats. Thus, the simple main effects of factor *B* are not the same at the different levels of factor *A*. In both ways of viewing the data, in terms of the scent conditions (factor *A*) and the age

TABLE 9-10   A Numerical Example: *AB* Matrix
and Table of Means

A. *AB* Matrix

	a_1	a_2	a_3	Sum
b_1	249	263	276	788
b_2	261	173	41	475
Sum	510	436	317	1,263

B. Table of Means

	a_1	a_2	a_3	Average
(Young) b_1	35.57	37.57	39.43	37.52
(Adult) b_2	37.29	24.71	5.86	22.62
Average	36.43	31.14	22.64	—

conditions (factor B), the simple main effects are not the same; an interaction appears to be present.

Pictorial Representation. It is usually a good idea to plot the means for the treatment combinations for a visual check of the data. To illustrate, we have plotted the means in Figure 9-7, marking off the scent conditions on the horizontal axis and the response measure on the vertical axis.[10] The nature of the interaction—little or no effect of the scent conditions for the young rats and an impressive effect for the adult rats—is obvious at a glance.

What we see with our eyes, either as a set of treatment means in a table or as a plot of these means in a figure, must be assessed statistically. Main effects and interactions must represent variation that cannot be reasonably accounted for by the operation of experimental error.

---

[10] We have spaced the three scent conditions equally on the horizontal axis, and connected the three means within the two age conditions. Technically, this plot of the data is only appropriate for *quantitative* independent variables, where the spacing between successive levels of the variable has a physical or psychological scale of reference. The appropriate way to represent the data is in the form of a *bar graph* (see Chapter 7, pp. 157–159). However, since our intent is to provide a visual check for interaction, and since no one is really confused or misled by the "liberties" taken in this means of plotting the data, we recommend that you use this device in mulling over data. A bar graph simply does not serve this function as well.

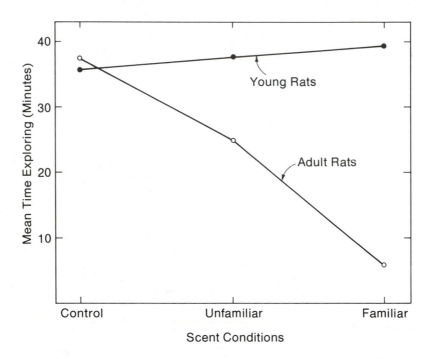

Figure 9-7. Mean Exploration Time as a Function of Scent and Age (from Table 9-10).

Sums of Squares

Basic Ratios. The first step in determining the sums of squares is calculating the basic ratios specified in Table 9-5. By substituting in these formulas the information from the two data matrices, we obtain the following values:

$$[ABS] = \Sigma\,(ABS)^2$$
$$= 9{,}167 + 10{,}261 + 11{,}320 + 9{,}925 + 4{,}541 + 369$$
$$= 45{,}583;$$

$$[AB] = \frac{\Sigma\,(AB)^2}{s}$$

$$= \frac{(249)^2 + (263)^2 + (276)^2 + (261)^2 + (173)^2 + (41)^2}{7}$$

$$= \frac{62{,}001 + 69{,}169 + 76{,}176 + 68{,}121 + 29{,}929 + 1{,}681}{7}$$

$$= \frac{307{,}077}{7} = 43{,}868.14;$$

$$[A] = \frac{\Sigma\,(A)^2}{b(s)}$$

$$= \frac{(510)^2 + (436)^2 + (317)^2}{2(7)}$$

$$= \frac{260,100 + 190,096 + 100,489}{14} = \frac{550,685}{14}$$

$$= 39,334.64;$$

$$[B] = \frac{\Sigma\,(B)^2}{a(s)}$$

$$= \frac{(788)^2 + (475)^2}{3(7)} = \frac{620,944 + 225,625}{21} = \frac{846,569}{21}$$

$$= 40,312.81;\ \text{and}$$

$$[T] = \frac{(T)^2}{a(b)(s)}$$

$$= \frac{(1,263)^2}{3(2)(7)} = \frac{1,595,169}{42}$$

$$= 37,980.21\ .$$

Final Computations. Next, we add and subtract the results of these preliminary calculations in the patterns specified in Table 9-7 to obtain the required sums of squares. Using the values for the basic ratios, we find the following results:

$$SS_A = [A] - [T]$$
$$= 39,334.64 - 37,980.21 = 1,354.43;$$

$$SS_B = [B] - [T]$$
$$= 40,312.81 - 37,980.21 = 2,332.60;$$

$$SS_{A\times B} = [AB] - [A] - [B] + [T]$$
$$= 43,868.14 - 39,334.64 - 40,312.81 + 37,980.21$$
$$= 2,200.90;$$

$$SS_{S/AB} = [ABS] - [AB]$$
$$= 45,583 - 43,868.14 = 1,714.86;\ \text{and}$$

$$SS_T = [ABS] - [T]$$
$$= 45,583 - 37,980.21 = 7,602.79\ .$$

The values for these sums of squares are presented in Table 9-11. As a check on the calculations, we should verify that the component sums of squares

TABLE 9-11   A Summary of the Analysis

Source	SS	df	MS	F
Scent (A)	1,354.43	2	677.22	14.22*
Age (B)	2,332.60	1	2,332.60	48.96*
$A \times B$	2,200.90	2	1,100.45	23.10*
S/AB	1,714.86	36	47.64	
Total	7,602.79	41		

*$p < .05$

add up to the total sum of squares. That is,

$$SS_T = SS_A + SS_B + SS_{A \times B} + SS_{S/AB}$$

$$7,602.79 = 1,354.43 + 2,332.60 + 2,200.90 + 1,714.86$$
$$= 7,602.79 \quad .$$

Final Calculations

Degrees of Freedom. The formulas for determining the degrees of freedom associated with each sum of squares are presented in Table 9-8. Running through these calculations briefly, we find

$$df_A = a - 1$$
$$= 3 - 1 = 2;$$
$$df_B = b - 1$$
$$= 2 - 1 = 1;$$
$$df_{A \times B} = (a - 1)(b - 1)$$
$$= (3 - 1)(2 - 1) = 2(1) = 2;$$
$$df_{S/AB} = a(b)(s - 1)$$
$$= 3(2)(7 - 1) = 3(2)(6) = 36; \text{ and}$$
$$df_T = a(b)(s) - 1$$
$$= 3(2)(7) - 1 = 42 - 1 = 41 \quad .$$

We enter these numbers in Table 9-11. As an arithmetical check, we verify that

$$df_T = df_A + df_B + df_{A \times B} + df_{S/AB}$$
$$41 = 2 + 1 + 2 + 36$$
$$= 41 \quad .$$

Mean Squares and F Ratios. Table 9-8 indicates how the mean squares and F ratios are formed. We calculate the mean squares by dividing a sum of squares by its corresponding degrees of freedom. The results of these calculations are presented in Table 9-11.

We obtain the F ratios by dividing each mean square potentially reflecting systematic variance—namely, MS_A (the main effect of factor A), MS_B (the main effect of factor B), and $MS_{A \times B}$ (the interaction of the two factors)—by the within-group mean square, $MS_{S/AB}$. These results are presented in the final column of the summary table.

Evaluating the Null Hypotheses

As indicated in Figure 9-6, our first significance test consists of the evaluation of the $A \times B$ interaction. To determine the status of the interaction null hypothesis, we first obtain the critical value of F (F_α). The degrees of freedom associated with F_α are

$$df_{A \times B} = 2 \text{ and } df_{S/AB} = 36 \quad .$$

The F table does not list a value for this particular combination of degrees of freedom. We do find that $F(2, 30) = 3.32$ and $F(2, 40) = 3.23$; the value we need, $F(2, 36)$, falls somewhere between the two. Luckily, we do not need a more precise determination, since the obtained F exceeds both critical values. In any case, we will use the larger value of F to illustrate the construction of the decision rules. Specifically,

If the obtained value of F equals or exceeds $F_\alpha = 3.32$, reject the null hypothesis; otherwise, do not reject the null hypothesis.

The obtained value of $F = 23.10$ exceeds the critical value, and we reject the interaction null hypothesis, concluding that significant interaction effects are present in the data.

Because the interaction is significant, we have little interest in the significance of the two main effects. The reasons for this lack of concern were discussed previously. To test your understanding of this point, reexamine the means presented in Table 9-10B. The main effect of factor A (the column marginal averages) does show a difference between each of the three scent conditions, but these differences are not representative of the effects of scent for young kangaroo rats or even for adult kangaroo rats. That is, the young rats show if anything a trend opposite to the effect shown in the marginal averages, while the adult rats show considerably larger differences between the three conditions than are shown in the marginal averages. Thus, we no longer have a compelling theoretical reason to examine the A main effect; this main effect represents an average of two quite different effects, that of scents for young rats and that of scents for adult rats.

A similar argument can be made for the other main effect. The marginal averages of the age variable show that young rats explore the burrow more than the older rats—the difference in time spent is approximately 15 minutes. This average effect comes close to describing the data only for the subjects in the unfamiliar condition, where the means of 37.57 and 24.71 show a difference of approximately 13 minutes. However, the main effect does not describe the opposite trend found in the control condition—that younger rats spend less time exploring the burrow than older ones—and underestimates by an even greater amount the difference found with familiar smells (33.57 minutes).

In any case, we still must illustrate how decision rules are formed for evaluating the two main effects. For the A main effect, we need a critical value of F with 2 df for the numerator and 36 for the denominator. If we take the value appearing in the table at $df_{num.} = 2$ and $df_{denom.} = 30$, the decision rules become these:

> **If the obtained value of F equals or exceeds $F_\alpha = 3.32$, reject the null hypothesis; otherwise, do not reject the null hypothesis.**

For the B main effect, the combination of degrees of freedom is 1 and 36. If we use the value appearing in the table at $df_{num.} = 1$ and $df_{denom.} = 30$, the decision rules become these:

> **If the obtained value of F equals or exceeds $F_\alpha = 4.17$, reject the null hypothesis; otherwise, do not reject the null hypothesis.**

Note that both main effects are significant according to these decision rules. This conclusion does not alter our attitude about the importance of the main effects in the interpretation of the results. The significant interaction more or less precludes further interest, though we do perform the two F tests, since the final steps are so easy. The point is that, because the interaction is significant, we will pay little or no attention to the statistical outcome of the two main effects.

Concluding Comments

We have completed the first stage in the analysis of a factorial experiment, but we are not finished. Since we have found a significant interaction, we must determine which parts of the 3×2 design are responsible for this effect. Figure 9-6 indicates that our next step is to conduct analytical analyses designed to obtain exactly this sort of information. This and other topics are covered in the next chapter.

SUMMARY

In the factorial experiment, two (or more) independent variables are manipulated systematically. Factorial designs are economical in that they provide the information that would be obtained in two single-factor experiments. However, factorial experiments also provide information that cannot be derived from single-factor studies, namely, how the independent variables combine to influence behavior. A concept that specifies the nature of this combination is interaction.

Two new terms are necessary for describing factorial design and interaction: main effects and simple main effects. A main effect consists of the effects of one independent variable averaged over the other. A simple main effect, on the other hand, consists of the effects of one independent variable considered separately for each level of the other independent variable. An interaction exists when the simple main effects of an independent variable are not the same. With interaction present, a researcher's interest generally focuses on an analysis of the individual treatment means in an attempt to pinpoint the locus of the significant interaction. When interaction is absent, a researcher analyzes the main effects, reducing the factorial experiment for analysis purposes to two separate single-factor experiments.

The factorial design is widely used in contemporary psychological research. The design permits investigators to move beyond a single-dimensional view of behavior, the view provided by single-factor experiments, to a richer and more revealing multidimensional view. In this chapter, we have considered only the simplest form of the factorial, two independent variables with independent groups of subjects serving in each of the treatment conditions. Designs become more complicated as subjects serve in more than one treatment condition (some form of within-subjects design) and when additional independent variables are combined to form higher-order factorial experiments. The design considered in this chapter is basic to the analysis of more complex designs. Thus, the two-variable factorial design is an important addition to the research tools a modern-day investigator in psychology must possess in order to contribute effectively to the developing trends of the science.

TERMS, CONCEPTS, AND SYMBOLS

factorial experiments

treatment combinations

completely randomized,
   two-variable factorial design

component single-factor
   experiments

interaction

main effect

column marginal means

row marginal means

simple main effects

ABS matrix

AB sums

AB matrix

magnitude of factorial effects

Notation and Basic Calculations

ABS	$\Sigma\,(ABS)^2$	$[ABS]$	
AB	$\Sigma\,(AB)^2$	$[AB]$	$\overline{AB}$
A	$\Sigma\,(A)^2$	$[A]$	$\overline{A}$
B	$\Sigma\,(B)^2$	$[B]$	$\overline{B}$
T	$(T)^2$	$[T]$	$\overline{T}$

$$a, \quad b, \quad s, \quad a(b), \quad a(b)(s)$$

Terms in the Analysis of Variance

SS_A	df_A	MS_A
SS_B	df_B	MS_B
$SS_{A \times B}$	$df_{A \times B}$	$MS_{A \times B}$
$SS_{S/AB}$	$df_{S/AB}$	$MS_{S/AB}$
SS_T	df_T	

EXERCISES

1. Imagine an experiment in which two kinds of tasks were used, an easy
   task and a difficult task. The time subjects took to perform the task was
   measured (in seconds) under conditions in which the number of distractors was varied at three levels. A 2×3 factorial design resulted in which
   a_1 was the easy task and a_2 was the difficult task. The three levels of
   increasing numbers of distractors are represented by b_1, b_2, and b_3, respectively. The data obtained are given on the next page.

ab_{11}	ab_{12}	ab_{13}	ab_{21}	ab_{22}	ab_{23}
5	5	4	5	9	5
6	4	3	4	5	8
2	3	6	4	3	9
4	4	8	5	7	10
2	5	2	6	3	10
4	5	2	3	8	6
1	6	2	8	5	7
6	7	5	2	8	3
9	5	2	3	6	8
4	7	3	3	8	6
4	4	5	4	9	11
8	3	3	2	6	6
5	4	4	8	6	6

a. Construct the *AB* matrix for the analysis.

b. Write out the *df* statements and calculate the degrees of freedom for each of the terms in the analysis.

c. Perform the necessary steps for the analysis and construct the analysis summary table. Determine whether the obtained *F*s are greater than the critical values. (Since the degrees of freedom for the denominator are unlikely to be found in most tables, use the closest appropriate value.)

2. A major research technique in the field of behavioral genetics is to breed animals selectively on the basis of particular characteristics exhibited by the animals and then to observe the relative performance of the offspring. Suppose an experiment is conducted in which three strains of rats are to be compared. One strain was obtained by selectively breeding rats who performed exceptionally well in a maze-learning task (the "bright" rats); a second strain was obtained by selectively breeding rats who performed quite poorly in the same task (the "dull" rats); and a third strain consisted of rats who were bred without regard for maze-learning performance (the "mixed" rats). One group from each strain was raised under "enriched" conditions, and a second group was raised under "impoverished" conditions. The enriched environment consisted of a large cage containing objects for the animals to play with; the impoverished environment consisted of a similar cage containing nothing except the bare essentials of rat life (food and water dispensers). Following six months of exposure to one of the two environments all of the rats were tested in a standard laboratory maze. There were eight rats randomly assigned to each of the six

groups. The learning scores (trials needed to learn the maze) are presented below:

Environment (Factor *B*)	Strain (Factor *A*)					
	Bright		Mixed		Dull	
Enriched	3	1	4	8	4	9
	4	2	3	9	4	10
	3	3	2	4	6	13
	9	3	6	4	3	10
Impoverished	5	4	4	11	4	13
	10	4	10	9	9	12
	10	3	13	9	16	7
	2	8	12	6	14	14

a. Conduct an analysis of variance on these data, testing for the effects of strain, environment, and their interaction.

b. What conclusions can you draw from this analysis?

Analytical Comparisons in the Factorial Design

10

The analysis covered in the last chapter evaluated the status of three null hypotheses, one for each of the factorial effects normally extracted from the results of a factorial experiment. Each of these null hypotheses specified the complete absence of treatment effects in the population:

1. The null hypothesis for the A main effect stated that all the μ_i's are equal.

2. The null hypothesis for the B main effect stated that all the μ_j's are equal.

3. The null hypothesis for the $A \times B$ interaction stated that no interaction effects are present.

Rejection of any one of these null hypotheses permits the acceptance of an alternative hypothesis, which states that either *some* population means are different or *some* interaction effects are present. Consequently, a significant *F* test in a factorial experiment has exactly the same status as a significant overall *F* test in a single-factor experiment: Knowing that the test is significant is important, but the information is relatively useless by itself. We must turn to other sorts of analyses to obtain more specific information from the data.

Chapter 6 was devoted to a discussion of detailed analyses that serve this purpose for the single-factor experiment. This chapter performs a similar function for the factorial experiment, but with one difference. We have chosen to omit computational formulas from this discussion in order to concentrate on the nature of these specific analyses. The formulas involved are relatively complex and tend to obscure and interfere with a general understanding of these analyses. The purpose of this chapter is to provide you with this general understanding. For those needing the specific details, we cite the specific pages in *Design and Analysis* on which the relevant formulas and calculations are presented and discussed in considerable detail. Also, in the final section of this chapter, we describe the calculations informally, still without presenting computational formulas. This section represents a compromise, but a necessary one given the scope of this book. Rather than omit the topic entirely, which is generally the solution in introductory statistics texts, we use this approach to convey the analytical nature of the factorial experiment and the richness of the information that can be extracted from it.

THE ANALYTICAL ANALYSIS OF MAIN EFFECTS

We begin with a consideration of the detailed analysis of main effects. As shown in the last chapter, the main effects of a factorial experiment come under closer scrutiny when an interaction is absent than when it is present. Under these circumstances—when interaction is nonsignificant—attention is directed to the sets of row and column *marginal means,* which reflect differences due to one of the independent variables averaged over the levels of the other. The analysis of the main effects essentially treats the results of the factorial experiment as deriving from two separate single-factor experiments—the *A* main effect being viewed as a single-factor experiment where factor *A* is manipulated, and the *B* main effect being viewed as a single-factor experiment where factor B is manipulated. No attention is paid to the other independent variable in this analysis.

In Chapter 6, we stated that most independent variables are manipulated to permit more than one meaningful question to be answered through detailed analyses of the data. We called such analyses analytical comparisons. As you have seen, analytical comparisons are possible whenever three or more treatment levels make up the independent variable. If only two treatment levels exist, the analysis can go no further—that is, the overall F test is the only test possible. As the number of treatment levels increases, the number of ways to "slice" the data increases as well. Each "slice" usually represents a different meaningful comparison.

As an example, consider the factorial experiment we analyzed in the last chapter: Young and adult rats (factor B) were tested under three smell conditions (factor A). Assume that the interaction was not significant in this example (even though it was) and that we wish to conduct analytical comparisons on the marginal means of the factorial matrix. The three smell conditions were the control condition (sterile sawdust in the burrow), the unfamiliar condition (sawdust from a stranger), and the familiar condition (sawdust from the winner of a territorial fight). As we saw in Chapter 6, several interesting comparisons can be extracted from this particular manipulation. For example, we can compare the control and unfamiliar conditions (level a_1 versus level a_2) to determine whether kangaroo rats are affected by the odors of strangers. And we can compare the unfamiliar and familiar conditions (level a_2 versus level a_3) to determine whether the rats are especially affected when the odor comes from a "foe" rather than a "stranger." Other meaningful comparisons are also possible—for example, a comparison between the control and familiar conditions (a_1 versus a_3), and a comparison between the control condition and an average of the two smell conditions. Depending on one's research hypotheses, any one of these comparisons might be included in the statistical examination of the differences among the A marginal means.

The other main effect in this example consists of only two treatment levels (young and adult rats) and cannot be subdivided into any analytical comparisons. If additional groups of rats of different ages had been included in the factorial experiment—say, very young or very old rats—then analytical comparisons involving factor B would have been possible as well.

In summary, the detailed analysis of main effects is identical to the analyses of the data from single-factor experiments. The value of the factorial experiment, of course, is that this design makes possible the examination of two main effects—the equivalent of two separate single-factor experiments.[1]

---

[1] For the computational formulas and examples of these sorts of comparisons, see *Design and Analysis* (pp. 208–210).

THE ANALYTICAL ANALYSIS OF INTERACTION

The unique advantage of the factorial design is that it affords us the opportunity to examine the way in which two independent variables combine to influence the behavior under study. When no interaction is present, the combination is simple. When an interaction is present, however, the combination is complex and the researcher must examine the pattern of results associated with one of the independent variables as the other independent variable is changed systematically. The analysis of interaction focuses on the *cell means* in the body of the *AB* matrix rather than the marginal means, used in the analysis of significant main effects. The goal is to pinpoint the specific combinations of the two independent variables responsible for the significant interaction.

In this chapter, we consider two specialized techniques for the detailed analysis of interaction, the analysis of simple main effects and the analysis of factorial comparisons. While each technique is concerned with a different aspect of interaction, both consist of a meaningful "dissection" of the original factorial design into what are in reality smaller and more focused experiments. We discuss the analysis of simple main effects first.

ANALYSIS OF SIMPLE MAIN EFFECTS

In introducing the factorial design in Chapter 9, we pointed out that a factorial experiment is made up of a set of component single-factor experiments. Consider the factorial design presented in Figure 10-1. On the left are two component experiments in which the same factor A is manipulated under two different conditions. In the upper experiment, the three treatment conditions (factor A) are administered in conjunction with a particular setting of factor B (level b_1). In the lower experiment, the same three conditions are administered, but this time in conjunction with a different setting of factor B (level b_2). These two single-factor experiments represent the constituent parts of the factorial design represented on the right side of the figure.

In the context of the factorial design, the means for each component experiment—each row of the AB matrix in Figure 10-1—represent one of the simple main effects of factor A. Interaction, you will recall, can be defined in terms of **simple main effects:** An interaction exists if the simple main effects are different, that is, if the pattern of results for one of the independent variables (factor A in this example) changes at the different levels of the

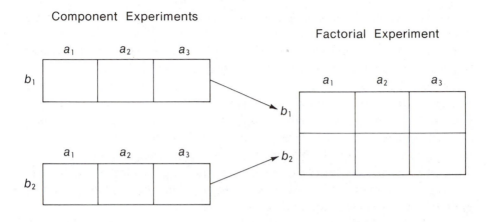

Figure 10-1. The Construction of a Factorial Design.

other variable (factor B). One useful way to analyze interaction is to examine the component experiments individually, row by row (simple main effects of factor A) or column by column (simple main effects of factor B).[2]

Basically, in this method of analyzing interaction separate analyses are made of the individual, component single-factor experiments constituting the original factorial experiment. With reference to the example in Figure 10-1, the analysis would proceed from the factorial design on the right, and presumably a significant interaction, to the analysis of the two separate single-factor experiments on the left.

In all essential respects, these analyses are no different from those described in Chapters 4 and 5, where we began our excursion into the analysis of variance. Simple main effects are in fact treatment effects obtained from single-factor experiments—not just any collection of single-factor experiments, of course, but the *component single-factor experiments* making up the factorial design. We will try to determine which of the component experiments produced significant differences among the treatment means and which did not.

In summary, interaction is defined in terms of different simple main effects, that is, different patterns of results for the component single-factor experiments of the factorial. In analyzing simple main effects, we attempt to supply statistical information concerning the nature of these differences by determining which simple main effects are significant and which are not.

---

[2] In all of our discussions, we will focus only on factor A to illustrate the various analyses. Exactly the same remarks apply where the analyses are conducted on factor B.

With reference to the example in Figure 10-1, the analysis of the simple main effects would consist of two significance tests: one to test the null hypothesis that the three treatment means at level b_1 are equal, and the other to test the null hypothesis that the corresponding treatment means at level b_2 are equal. The main characteristic of this analysis is that it simplifies the original factorial manipulation by focusing on the effects of one of the independent variables while the other is held constant. These separate analyses are quite different from the corresponding analysis of the main effects, where the variation of one of the independent variables is analyzed with data that have been *averaged* over the levels of the other independent variable. The analysis of the main effect obscures the interaction; the analysis of simple main effects illuminates the interaction.

Consider the kangaroo-rat study, analyzed in the last chapter, in which young and adult rats were tested under the three smell conditions. At the time, we predicted that an interaction would be present and that it would be of a particular form—namely, the presence of a smell effect for the adult rats and the absence of a smell effect for the young rats. The theoretical rationale for this prediction consisted of the assumption that some mixture of learning, experience, and maturation is involved in establishing the meaning of the scents for kangaroo rats. Since all these processes involve the passage of time, it was predicted that the manipulation of factor A (the three smell conditions) would have little or no effect with the young animals and a substantial effect with the adult animals. The results of the experiment are presented again in Table 10-1.

As you can see by examining the three means for the young rats (level b_1), the differences among the smell conditions are small. In contrast, the differences among three means for the adult rats (level b_2) are large. The statistical analysis of these data that we performed in the last chapter indicated that the interaction was significant ($p < .05$), but it did not indicate which factors are responsible for the significance. An analysis of the simple main effects of factor A corrects this deficiency by searching for statistical evidence supporting a particular patterning of the treatment means. If we were actually to conduct these additional analyses, we would discover that the differences among the three means for the young rats are not significant ($p > .05$), while the differences among the three means for the adult rats are ($p < .05$).[3] Generally, this latter finding would lead us to make additional analytical comparisons, which would concentrate on meaningful differences between the three smell conditions, but this time for the *adult* rats. Analytical com-

---

[3] For the computational formulas and examples of the analysis of simple main effects, see *Design and Analysis* (pp. 212–221).

TABLE 10-1   Means from the Kangaroo-Rat Data
Presented in Chapter 9

Factor A / Factor B	Control a_1	Unfamiliar a_2	Familiar a_3
Young b_1	35.57	37.57	39.43
Adult b_2	37.29	24.71	5.86

parisons following the discovery of a significant test of simple main effects are discussed in a later section of this chapter.

ANALYTICAL FACTORIAL COMPARISONS

Another type of analysis is useful in examining the data from a factorial experiment. In contrast with an analysis of simple main effects, where the factorial is analyzed as a set of component single-factor experiments, this alternative procedure preserves the factorial nature of the manipulation and concentrates on a number of smaller, component **factorial comparisons.** To demonstrate this procedure, we return to the kangaroo-rat example.

The top portion of Table 10-2 shows the results of the kangaroo-rat study. Below this matrix, we have transformed the original 3 × 2 factorial design into a 2 × 2 factorial experiment by dropping the two familiar groups. This

TABLE 10-2   An Example of a Factorial
Comparison

	Control	Unfamiliar	Familiar
Young	35.57	37.57	39.43
Adult	37.29	24.71	5.86

	Control	Unfamiliar
Young	35.57	37.57
Adult	37.29	24.71

alteration has produced a smaller experiment consisting of two levels of factor A (the control and unfamiliar treatments) crossed with the original factor B (young and adult rats). This new factorial, derived from the larger design, focuses on one particular aspect of the original manipulation of factor A, namely, the influence of the smells from strange rats on exploratory behavior. The interaction of this new design provides specific information about the original interaction of factors A and B, specifically, whether the difference between the control and unfamiliar treatments changes with the age of the rats being tested. The significant $A \times B$ interaction calculated in the last chapter does not give us this particular information. All we know from that analysis is that interaction effects are present—not which ones are present. An examination of the data in the component factorial indicates that an interaction is present: Younger rats are relatively uninfluenced by the smell of strangers while older rats are. If we were to conduct a statistical analysis with the data entering into this factorial comparison, we would find that this component interaction is significant ($p < .05$).

The procedure summarized in Table 10-2 is an example of a factorial comparison. The result is a simple, focused factorial experiment that directs one's attention to a specific component of the overall interaction based on the complete factorial.

Factorial comparisons are made when a specific interaction can provide the researcher with a meaningful interpretation of the outcome of a factorial experiment. That is, if the difference between a selected pair of treatment levels of one independent variable can offer information about the effect of the other independent variable, then a factorial comparison is valuable for interpreting a significant overall (omnibus) interaction. Any of the meaningful comparisons involving factor A we examined in Chapter 6 could be used for a factorial comparison.[4] For instance, one might look at a comparison between the unfamiliar and familiar conditions. A factorial comparison between these two conditions is presented in Table 10-3. This component factorial essentially isolates the two A treatment conditions (levels a_2 and a_3) and concentrates on this more focused design. An inspection of the data in this component factorial indicates that an interaction is present, that is, that small differences with respect to exploratory behavior exist among young rats (level b_1), and that large differences exist among the adult rats (level b_2). The older rats are greatly inhibited in their exploratory behavior when the smell from a rival is present, while the younger rats show no such tendency.

In summary, factorial comparisons analyze interaction within the context

---

[4] Again, our examples will involve only factor A. Exactly the same sorts of analyses are possible if factor B has more than two levels.

TABLE 10-3   Another Example of a
Factorial Comparison

		Unfamiliar	Familiar
Young		37.57	39.43
Adult		24.71	5.86

of the factorial design. Most commonly, a researcher makes such a comparison by rearranging the levels of one of the independent variables to reflect a comparison that would be meaningful in a single-factor experiment. Interactions specified by factorial comparisons help to isolate or to identify the sources contributing to a significant overall $A \times B$ interaction.[5]

THE ANALYSIS OF SIMPLE COMPARISONS

The final step in the analysis of interaction is to follow significant simple main effects or significant factorial comparisons with even more detailed statistical tests. These tests are easy to conceptualize because they usually consist of a comparison between two means appearing either in the same row or the same column of the AB matrix. Again, to illustrate we return to the kangaroo-rat example. The analytic steps are summarized in Table 10-4.

Comparisons Based on Significant Simple Main Effects

On the left side of Table 10-4 is the AB matrix of treatment means. On the basis of the analysis of the complete factorial design in Chapter 9, we found the $A \times B$ interaction significant ($p < .05$). This information is given below the AB matrix. As we suggested earlier, analyzing the simple main effects of factor A—that is, testing the significance of the three smell means separately for each age group—makes theoretical sense. The actual statistical analysis (which we have not presented) reveals no significant differences among the smell conditions for the young rats ($p > .05$) and significant differences for

---

[5] For the computational formulas required to conduct this sort of analysis, see *Design and Analysis* (pp. 235–239).

TABLE 10-4 Analysis of a Simple Comparison Following Analysis of a Significant Simple Main Effect

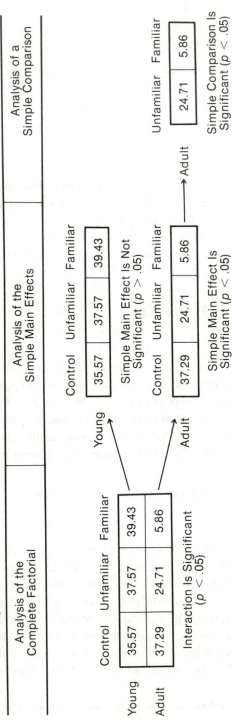

	Analysis of the Complete Factorial		Analysis of the Simple Main Effects			Analysis of a Simple Comparison

Analysis of the Complete Factorial

	Control	Unfamiliar	Familiar
Young	35.57	37.57	39.43
Adult	37.29	24.71	5.86

Interaction Is Significant
($p < .05$)

Analysis of the Simple Main Effects

Young

Control	Unfamiliar	Familiar
35.57	37.57	39.43

Simple Main Effect Is Not
Significant ($p > .05$)

Adult

Control	Unfamiliar	Familiar
37.29	24.71	5.86

Simple Main Effect Is
Significant ($p < .05$)

Analysis of a Simple Comparison

Adult

Unfamiliar	Familiar
24.71	5.86

Simple Comparison Is
Significant ($p < .05$)

the adult rats ($p < .05$). The results of this analysis are indicated in the middle portion of the table.

Should we stop now? Have we extracted all possible information from the data? Shouldn't we analyze the significant simple main effects for the adult rats? If this had been a single-factor experiment in which adult rats were given the different treatment conditions, additional comparisons would certainly be justified and desirable. The same reasoning applies in the present situation. That is, the significant statistical test for the adult rats indicates only that some of the treatment means are different, not which ones differ. To identify the sources of this significant analysis, we must analyze the data further.

A solution to this problem is to perform meaningful comparisons on the data obtained from the adult rats, the means at level b_2. Several such comparisons are possible. One possibility is represented on the right side of Table 10-4, namely, a comparison between the unfamiliar and familiar treatment conditions. An actual statistical analysis shows the difference between these two means to be significant ($p < .05$). The analysis of comparisons contributing to a significant simple main effect is called an analysis of **simple comparisons.** (The word *simple* refers to the fact that the analysis is conducted on a simple main effect, and the word *comparison* refers to the fact that an analytical comparison is involved.)

Other meaningful simple comparisons could be conducted in addition to that represented in the table. For example, we could look at a comparison between the control and unfamiliar conditions, or between the control and the familiar conditions, or even between the control and an average of the unfamiliar and familiar conditions. In short, we can conduct a comparison to extract meaningful information from the set of means residing in any row that produces a significant simple main effect.

Comparisons Based on Significant Factorial Comparisons

The analysis of simple comparisons can also be suggested by a significant factorial comparison. We illustrate this point by considering the factorial comparison in Table 10-3. This factorial comparison, which is presented again in the middle portion of Table 10-5, is formed when the unfamiliar and familiar conditions are crossed with factor B to create a component 2×2 factorial. The statistical analysis of these data indicates that the interaction for the factorial comparison is significant ($p < .05$). What next? An examination of the 2×2 matrix indicates that the interaction is a result of a large

TABLE 10-5 Analysis of Simple Comparisons Following a Significant Factorial Comparison

Analysis of the Complete Factorial

	Control	Unfamiliar	Familiar
Young	35.57	37.57	39.43
Adult	37.29	24.71	5.86

Interaction Is Significant ($p < .05$)

Analysis of a Factorial Comparison

	Unfamiliar	Familiar
Young	37.57	39.43
Adult	24.71	5.86

Interaction Is Significant ($p < .05$)

Analysis of Simple Comparisons

Young

Unfamiliar	Familiar
37.57	39.43

Comparison Is Not Significant ($p > .05$)

Adult

Unfamiliar	Familiar
24.71	5.86

Comparison Is Significant ($p < .05$)

difference between the two smell conditions for the adult rats and a small difference between these conditions for the young rats. Testing the significance of these two sets of differences is the logical next step. The two comparisons are shown on the right side of the table. The comparison for the young rats is not significant ($p > .05$), and the comparison for the adult rats is significant ($p < .05$).

Convergence of the Two Approaches

Note that the conclusion we reached by logically extending the analysis of the factorial comparison in this example (depicted in Table 10-5) is identical to that reached when we examined a significant simple main effect more closely (in Table 10-4). Both methods converged on the same fundamental simple comparisons within the body of the AB matrix of means. This convergence may not always occur, but the circumstance is worth illustrating. In any case, the analysis of simple comparisons is more or less a natural extension of the two techniques available for analyzing interaction: the analysis of simple main effects and of factorial comparisons. Using either technique, we often end up conducting meaningful comparisons between pairs of treatment means, that is, simple comparisons.[6]

AN OVERALL PLAN OF ANALYSIS

Figure 10-2 is an analysis plan for a comprehensive analysis of a factorial experiment. As we stated in Chapter 9, the first step in the analysis of a factorial should be a test of the significance of the overall $A \times B$ interaction. (See pp. 231–232 for an explanation of this point.) Depending on the significance of the interaction effect, two different courses of action are open to us. If the $A \times B$ interaction is significant, we proceed with the analysis of simple main effects and of factorial comparisons. The choice of which technique to use—and one can certainly choose to use both—will depend on the nature of the theoretical questions that can reasonably be asked about the outcome of the experiment. Again, depending on the particular analyses that are significant as a result of these examinations, the researcher might undertake simple comparisons to pinpoint even more precisely the source (or sources) of the significant $A \times B$ interaction. These various steps are specified on the right side of Figure 10-2.

---

[6] For the computational formulas for the evaluation of simple comparisons, see *Design and Analysis* (pp. 233–234).

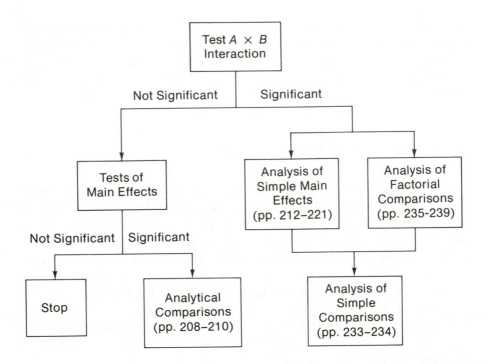

Figure 10-2. A Summary of the Analytical Analysis of a Factorial Experiment. Page References are to *Design and Analysis.*

If the $A \times B$ interaction is not significant, a researcher will generally turn to a statistical analysis of the two main effects. At this point, the analysis will resemble closely the analysis of a single-factor experiment. If a main effect is significant, analytical comparisons of the sort described in Chapter 6 will be conducted on the marginal treatment sums of the AB matrix. These steps are specified on the left side of the figure.

No analysis plan is ever as rigid as the one outlined in Figure 10-2. We offer this particular plan more as a summary than a mandatory course of action. Specific research hypotheses and questions—that is, planned comparisons—will still be assessed statistically regardless of the status of the overall $A \times B$ interaction or the two overall main effects. You should use this plan to guide your thinking in the planning stages of an experiment to remind you of the possible ways in which a factorial experiment can be analyzed. Above all, the figure illustrates that a researcher involved in such an analysis proceeds logically, exploring each significant effect until it is necessary to stop.

SIMPLIFIED COMPUTATIONAL PROCEDURES[7]

As noted earlier, because their level of complexity in some cases exceeds the introductory nature of this book, we chose not to introduce the computational formulas involved in these analyses. However, it is possible to conduct these analyses in a simplified manner by using information covered in earlier chapters. We have modified the procedures involved by simplifying the experimental contexts within which these analyses are conducted and by using these familiar computational formulas, with minor adjustments, to extract the desired information. We begin by considering the form that the F ratio takes in the statistical evaluation of these analyses. Problem 3 of the exercises provides a numerical example of these analyses.

The F Ratio

The F ratio for all the analyses covered in this chapter is constructed as follows:

$$F_{comp.} = \frac{MS_{comp.}}{MS_{S/AB}} \quad . \quad (10\text{-}1)$$

In this equation, $MS_{comp.}$ is the mean square obtained for the analytical comparison of interest, and $MS_{S/AB}$ is the within-groups mean square from the statistical analysis of the original factorial design. The degrees of freedom for the numerator are equal to whatever is appropriate for the analysis under consideration. The degrees of freedom for the denominator are those associated with $MS_{S/AB}$. In all other respects, the analyses proceed as described in the earlier chapters.

Main Effects

The formulas for analytical comparisons involving main effects are functionally equivalent to those presented in Chapter 6 for the single-factor design. A simplified way of conducting these analyses is to think of the marginal treatment sums (A) as coming from a *single-factor experiment* rather than from a factorial design. You can then use the computational formulas for single-df comparisons presented in Chapter 6 to calculate the quantities needed for the analysis. Remember that sample size (s) in these formulas has to be adjusted

---

[7] This section can be omitted without seriously affecting the purpose of this chapter.

for the number of subjects contributing to the marginal sums in the factorial, for example, $b(s)$ for the A treatment sums and $a(s)$ for the B treatment sums.

Simple Main Effects

An easy way of analyzing simple main effects is to think of the treatment sums in a component experiment as coming from an actual *single-factor experiment* consisting of a different groups and containing s subjects per group. That is, you simply isolate the particular row (or column) of data you wish to analyze and perform exactly the same set of operations on these sums as you would in the analysis of a single-factor experiment. If it helps, you might call each AB sum "A" and the overall sum of the treatment totals for the *component* experiment "T"; you can then use the formulas in Chapter 4 to calculate MS_A, which in this analysis is actually the mean square for a simple main effect.

Factorial Comparisons

An alternative way of conducting a factorial comparison is to perform a standard analysis of variance on those cells involved in the factorial comparison. Tables 10-2 and 10-3 illustrate two such factorial comparisons. In both cases, you would transform the original 3×2 factorial design into the 2×2 factorials indicated in the two tables. You would then perform an analysis of variance with these modified AB matrices, defining the levels of the two independent variables and the marginal totals appropriately. For example, the modified design in Table 10-2 is a 2×2 factorial consisting of two levels of factor A (control and unfamiliar) paired with two levels of factor B (young and adult). The AB treatment sums come from the original AB matrix. The marginal treatment sums are based on the sums appearing in this *new* matrix, not the original one. In essence, the component factorial design, which represents the factorial comparison of interest, is being treated as a factorial design in its own right, in disregard of the calculations performed in the original analysis. The interaction mean square for the factorial comparison is of primary concern in this analysis.

Simple Comparisons

A modified way of conducting the analysis of simple comparisons is, again, to think of a simple comparison as part of a *single-factor experiment,* just as we suggested for the analysis of simple main effects. You can then apply the computational procedures presented in Chapter 6 to the treatment sums of a component single-factor experiment (calling the AB treatment sums "A" if necessary) to extract the desired sum of squares for a simple comparison.

SUMMARY

We saw that a significant $A \times B$ interaction in the overall analysis of variance indicates that interaction effects are present, but does not specify which aspects of interaction are critical. Two techniques permit the localization of interaction—an analysis of simple main effects and an analysis of factorial comparisons.

An analysis of simple main effects treats the factorial as a set of single-factor experiments. Such an analysis is most useful when theory specifies the presence of a simple main effect at one level of the other independent variable and the absence of a simple main effect at another level. Such theoretical expectations can be statistically assessed through an analysis of simple main effects. Frequently, a significant simple main effect is further analyzable through the use of simple comparisons, a technique that is quite similar to those discussed in Chapter 6 for the detailed analysis of single-factor experiments.

An analysis of factorial comparisons represents a different way of analyzing the overall $A \times B$ interaction. Rather than treating the factorial as a set of single-factor experiments, the investigator conducts an analysis of factorial comparisons within the context of the factorial design. Most commonly, the levels of one of the independent variables are rearranged to reflect meaningful manipulations and then are combined with the other independent variable to form factorial comparisons—component factorial designs. Interactions specified by factorial comparisons are used in isolating or identifying the sources contributing to a significant overall $A \times B$ interaction. Simple comparisons might be conducted to identify these sources further.

The complete analysis of a factorial experiment is summarized in Figure 10-2. When the $A \times B$ interaction is significant, a researcher will proceed to a more detailed analysis of this effect and to analyze simple main effects and factorial comparisons. When the $A \times B$ interaction is nonsignificant, the researcher's attention shifts to the two main effects and the analytical analysis of these effects if they in turn prove to be significant. These analyses can be conducted with information drawn from earlier chapters.

TERMS, CONCEPTS, AND SYMBOLS

simple main effect $\qquad$ $F_{comp.}$

factorial comparison $\qquad$ $MS_{comp.}$

simple comparison $\qquad$ $MS_{S/AB}$

EXERCISES

1. In problem 2 in the exercises for Chapter 9, we described an experiment in which three different strains of rats (bright, mixed, and dull) were raised in two different environments (enriched and impoverished) for six months and then tested on a standard laboratory maze so that learning performance could be assessed. Consider the outcome of that particular example. For convenience, the treatment means are provided below:

Environment (Factor B)	Strain (Factor A)		
	Bright	Mixed	Dull
Enriched	3.50	5.00	7.38
Impoverished	5.75	9.25	11.13

Since the interaction of the two variables was not significant, our attention is directed to the main effects, both of which are significant. How would you analyze these significant effects?

2. Consider a different outcome of the same experiment described in problem 1:

Environment	Strain (Factor *A*)		
(Factor *B*)	Bright	Mixed	Dull
Enriched	3.50	4.00	7.50
Impoverished	3.75	7.75	11.00

Assume that the statistical analysis indicates that the interaction is significant, leading us to concentrate on the individual treatment means rather than the marginal means. To answer the following questions, identify the specific means to be compared for each analysis and the total number of scores involved in each test. (There are $s = 8$ subjects in each treatment combination.) Indicate also whether the test is a simple main effect, a factorial comparison, or a simple comparison.

a. Do the three groups of rats differ in learning performance when they have been reared in the enriched environment?

b. Do the bright and mixed strains reared in the enriched environment differ in learning performance?

c. What are the effects of the different environments on each of the three strains of rats?

d. Are bright and mixed rats affected equally by the two different environments?

e. Are the effects of the two environments the same for the bright and dull rats?

f. How would you summarize the outcome of this experiment?

3. This problem is for the adventurous. The last section of this chapter indicates how you might conduct detailed analyses of a factorial experiment using formulas presented in earlier chapters. This problem consists of two parts. First, construct the computational formulas for these analyses; second, actually perform the analyses. We suggest that you verify your formulas with the ones presented in Appendix B before proceeding with your calculations. We will use the data from the kangaroo-rat study analyzed in Chapter 9 and discussed in this chapter. For convenience, the *AB* matrix of the sums is provided on the next page. Note that $s = 7$.

Age (Factor B)	Scent Conditions (Factor A)			Sum
	Control (a_1)	Unfamiliar (a_2)	Familiar (a_3)	
Young (b_1)	249	263	276	788
Adult (b_2)	261	173	41	475
Sum	510	436	317	1,263

The error term for all the analyses you will conduct is obtained from the overall factorial analysis of variance. For these data,

$$MS_{S/AB} = 47.64; \ df_{S/AB} = 36 \ .$$

a. Conduct a test of the simple main effects of the scent conditions (factor A) for both the young rats (b_1) and the adult rats (b_2). The means involved are specified in Table 10-1.

b. Conduct a test of the factorial comparison involving the control and the unfamiliar conditions and the young and adult rats. The appropriate means are given in Table 10-2.

c. Test the simple comparison of the unfamiliar versus the familiar conditions for the adult rats. The appropriate means are given in the lower right-hand portion of Table 10-4.

Within-Subjects Factorial Designs

11

Contemporary research in psychology is characterized by two features. First, the experiments employed are primarily factorial in design, and generally two or more independent variables are manipulated in the same experiment. As we noted in Chapter 9, factorial designs are attractive because they are economical, extract information on interaction, and provide a more representative view of factors responsible for behavior outside the laboratory than single-factor designs. The second feature of modern psychological research is a growing tendency to introduce repeated measures—that is, to introduce within-subjects designs in which subjects serve in more than one treatment combination. As we mentioned in Chapter 8, the primary advantage of within-subjects designs is their sensitivity. Research can benefit from both of these characteristics when factorial designs include a certain degree of multiple testing—a representation of the same subject in more than one of the same treatment conditions. We call such designs **within-subjects factorial designs.**

A COMPARISON OF FACTORIAL DESIGNS

Repeated measures are introduced into factorial designs in two basic ways, either partially or completely. Both types of designs are depicted in Table 11-1, along with a completely randomized factorial design for purposes of comparison. In each design the same basic 2×3 factorial arrangement is employed, and each design contains the same total number of observations: $a(b)(s) = 2(3)(3) = 18$.

Design A is an example of a complete within-subjects factorial. By *complete* we mean that each of the $s = 3$ subjects receives all the $a(b) = 2(3) = 6$ treatment combinations in some counterbalanced order.[1]

Design B is an example of a partial within-subjects factorial. Here the same six treatment combinations are present, but any given subject serves in only three of them. Moreover, the particular set of three is explicitly specified, namely, one set of subjects ($s_1, s_2,$ and s_3) serves in all three levels of factor B, but only in combination with the a_1 level of factor A, while a different set of subjects ($s_4, s_5,$ and s_6) receives the three levels of factor B in combination with the a_2 level of factor A. This design combines features of both between-subjects and within-subjects designs. That is, each level of factor A contains a different set of randomly assigned subjects. Consequently, this independent variable can be described as being manipulated in a between-subjects design. On the other hand, each level of factor B at any given level of factor A contains the *same* subjects; this independent variable can therefore be said to be manipulated in a within-subjects design. We refer to this particular type of within-subjects factorial design as a **mixed factorial design,** "mixed" in the sense that it contains elements of both between-subjects and within-subjects designs.[2]

The final design in Table 11-1 is a "pure" between-subjects factorial experiment. A different set of $s = 3$ subjects is randomly assigned to each of

---

[1] We discussed counterbalancing techniques in Chapter 8 (see pp. 191–193). Also, an actual experiment would probably contain $s = 6$ subjects (or some multiple of 6) in order to permit the proper counterbalancing of the treatment combinations. We have used $s = 3$ subjects to simplify the presentation.

[2] Occasionally, you will see this type of design referred to in the literature as a "3×2 factorial design with factor A represented as a between-subjects variable and factor B as a within-subjects variable."

TABLE 11-1 A Comparison of Factorial Designs

A. Complete Within-Subjects Factorial

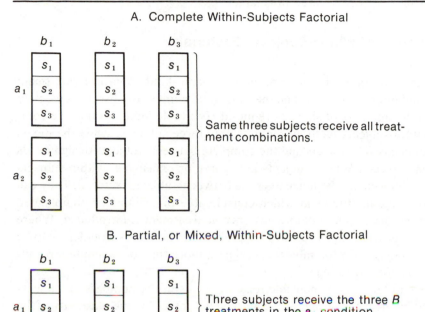

Same three subjects receive all treatment combinations.

B. Partial, or Mixed, Within-Subjects Factorial

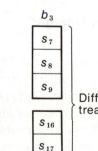

Three subjects receive the three *B* treatments in the a_1 condition.

Three other subjects receive the three *B* treatments in the a_2 condition.

C. Completely Randomized Between-Subjects Factorial

Different subjects in each of the $a(b)$ treatment combinations.

the treatment conditions. This design, the **completely randomized between-subjects design,** was covered in Chapter 9.

Advantages of Within-Subjects Factorials

Although these three designs produce the same kind of information (main effects and interaction) based on the same total number of observations, they differ in the numbers of subjects required. The table indicates that the complete within-subjects factorial requires only three subjects, while the mixed factorial needs six subjects and the complete between-subjects design needs eighteen subjects. Where subjects are scarce or expensive, within-subjects designs offer a clear advantage over the between-subjects factorial. They can also save time in studies in which considerable pretraining or complicated instructions are required before any specific treatment is introduced. Where a within-subjects design is used, such preliminary activities would have to be performed only once for subjects serving in more than one condition resulting in a significant savings.

A second factor is responsible for differences in the numbers of subjects required by the three designs—the marked differences in the **sensitivity** of the three designs. As we have defined it, sensitivity means the relative ability to detect differences when they are present in the population. (We have also referred to design sensitivity in terms of *power*.) Within-subjects designs usually require fewer *total observations* than the complete between-subjects factorial to achieve the same degree of sensitivity or statistical power. To create a between-subjects factorial as sensitive as either version of the within-subjects factorial, a researcher would have to make considerably more observations (and thus use that many more subjects).

Advantages of the Mixed Factorial Design

Complete within-subjects designs frequently raise difficulties of carryover effects and large time demands on a single subject. For these reasons, the complete within-subjects design is not as common in psychological research as the mixed factorial design. Consequently, we do not discuss the statistical analysis of the former in this book, but refer you to advanced statistics books for that information.[3] The mixed factorial design, however, is frequently and widely represented in the contemporary research literature, and therefore we concentrate on the analysis of this design in this chapter. Good reasons

---

[3] See, for example, *Design and Analysis* (pp. 425–433).

account for the popularity of the mixed factorial design. We consider two of them.

First, in contrast with the complete within-subjects factorial, the mixed factorial reduces the number of treatments each subject receives, and this consideration is often important to a researcher. Carryover effects of the sort discussed in Chapter 8 are usually not as much of a problem in the mixed factorial design. In the 2×3 factorial shown in Table 11-1, the mixed factorial requires that subjects serve in three conditions, while the complete within-subjects factorial requires six. The more treatments administered to any given subject the greater are the chances that specific and nonspecific carryover effects will occur. Consequently, the mixed factorial often serves to reduce this potential problem, which is associated with all within-subjects designs.

Second, the mixed factorial is the design of choice when a researcher is studying learning and the processes that influence the speed with which learning takes place. Investigators can easily transform single-factor between-subjects designs, where factor A is represented with independent groups of subjects, into mixed factorial designs by testing the subject more than once under the same A treatment condition. If, for example, factor A consists of a number of different drug conditions, the experimenter might test subjects repeatedly to see whether they acquire the task at the same or at different rates. In this example, factor B—a within-subjects factor—consists of *trials,* and the levels are the trial numbers (b_1 is the first trial, b_2 is the second trial, and so on).

An experimenter could choose to stay with the single-factor experiment, of course, and determine the effects of drugs (factor A) on a single trial, if only one trial is to be given, or over the total learning period if more than one trial is to be given. In the latter case, the researcher would disregard the fact that several trials were given and analyze only the total learning scores. But either approach is a potential waste given the additional information available were the basic experiment expanded into a mixed factorial. In this case, the drug groups could be compared on the first trial (or on any trial, for that matter) and on rates of acquisition as well as on total learning performance.

For just such reasons, students often turn to mixed factorial experiments for individual class projects. A single-factor experiment with independent groups of subjects easily becomes a mixed factorial experiment in which the variable of training trials becomes the second, but within-subjects, factor. The information provided by the mixed factorial is usually worth the time administering the additional trials takes. The possibility of discovering an interaction—that the between-subjects independent variable affects rate of learning—is sufficient justification for using this design in most cases. Discovering the presence of interaction is simply not possible with the single-factor between-subjects experiment.

IDENTIFYING AND CALCULATING SOURCES OF VARIATION

Although the mixed factorial design is simply a combination of designs we have already studied, distinguishing between scores derived from the same subject and scores obtained from different subjects is still necessary. The distinction must be indicated in the notation and identification of variation resulting from between-subjects and within-subjects sources. Similarly, the sums of squares will be calculated so as to preserve the separate contribution of these sources in the mixed factorial design.

Design and Notation

The arrangement of the treatment conditions in the mixed design corre-sponds to that in the standard factorial design with two independent vari-ables, first considered in Chapter 9. The distinguishing feature of the mixed design is the representation of the *subjects* in the treatment conditions. We made this point earlier in connection with Table 11-1. To amplify, subjects are assigned randomly to the block of conditions associated with the different levels of factor A.[4] There are s subjects assigned to each level. This portion of the experimental design corresponds to a typical single-factor between-subjects design. Subjects in each block receive all the treatment combina-tions created in the pairing of the levels of factor B with the corresponding level of factor A. If factor B consists of four levels, the subjects assigned to level a_1 will receive a total of four treatment combinations, namely,

$$ab_{11}, ab_{12}, ab_{13}, \text{ and } ab_{14} \quad ;$$

the subjects assigned to level a_2 will receive another block of four treatment combinations,

$$ab_{21}, ab_{22}, ab_{23}, \text{ and } ab_{24} \quad ;$$

---

[4] The assignment of the letters A and B to independent variables is arbitrary. Here factor A is designated the between-subjects variable and factor B, the within-subjects variable. We could have chosen to reverse the designations. Such a reversal would have no effect, except that the specific notation would have to be changed.

TABLE 11-2   Notational System

ABS Matrix

a_1

Subject	b_1	b_2	b_3	Sum
S_1	ABS_{111}	ABS_{121}	ABS_{131}	AS_{11}
S_2	ABS_{112}	ABS_{122}	ABS_{132}	AS_{12}
S_3	ABS_{113}	ABS_{123}	ABS_{133}	AS_{13}
Sum	AB_{11}	AB_{12}	AB_{13}	A_1

a_2

Subject	b_1	b_2	b_3	Sum
S_4	ABS_{214}	ABS_{224}	ABS_{234}	AS_{24}
S_5	ABS_{215}	ABS_{225}	ABS_{235}	AS_{25}
S_6	ABS_{216}	ABS_{226}	ABS_{236}	AS_{26}
Sum	AB_{21}	AB_{22}	AB_{23}	A_2

AB Matrix

Level	b_1	b_2	b_3	Sum
a_1	AB_{11}	AB_{12}	AB_{13}	A_1
a_2	AB_{21}	AB_{22}	AB_{23}	A_2
Sum	B_1	B_2	B_3	T

and so on. The order in which the treatment conditions are administered to subjects within any given block is usually counterbalanced in some fashion to neutralize practice effects, unless factor B consists of a fixed series of training trials where practice effects themselves are the object of study.

The notational system is nearly identical to that for the between-subjects factorial design (see Table 9-3, p. 220), and it operates in the same way. For convenience, we have presented the notational system again in Table 11-2. The AB matrices for the two designs are the same, reflecting the fact that both designs produce the same sort of information. The two ABS matrices differ in a small, but important way: the ABS scores are segregated according to the levels of factor A, and therefore row marginal sums are introduced for the sets of submatrices. These row sums consist of the total score for each subject and are obtained when the set of observations each subject produces is summed. The total score for each subject is designated AS_{ik} to indicate that it is a sum for a particular subject, s_k, in a particular A treatment group, a_i. In all other respects, the two notational systems are equivalent. (To brush up on the notational system, return to the detailed explanation in Chapter 9, pp. 219–222.)

The Logic of the Analysis

Experimental Design and Error Terms. The arrangement of the treatment conditions in any experiment dictates the nature of the treatment effects to be isolated and evaluated in a statistical analysis, for example, the main effects, interaction, and analytical comparisons permitted by the specific characteristics of the different treatment conditions and the experimental design. The method of representing subjects in the treatment conditions, on the other hand, dictates the nature of the *error term* used to test the significance of the treatment effects justified by the specific experimental design.

Consider for a moment the single-factor designs discussed in Part II. We described two possible arrangements of subjects, one in which subjects are randomly assigned to only one of the treatment conditions (the between-subjects design) and the other in which subjects serve in all the treatment conditions (the within-subjects design). As we saw in Chapters 4 and 8, different error terms are used in evaluating exactly the same treatment effects extracted from the two designs. In the between-subjects design, the error term is based on the variability of different subjects treated alike ($MS_{S/A}$), while in the within-subjects design, the error term is a residual mean square, which represents the inconsistency of subjects from condition to condition ($MS_{A\times S}$).

Specifying error terms for factorial designs with repeated measures can be quite complicated, and a comprehensive presentation of the topic is not feasible in an introductory book. Our coverage of this topic is simplified. The mixed factorial design represents a blending of the between-subjects and the within-subjects designs and, as a result, possesses certain characteristics unique to each, including the difference in error terms. Consequently, the mixed factorial design requires the use of *two* error terms: one for the evaluation of factorial effects based on between-subjects differences, the **between-subjects error term,** and the other for the evaluation of factorial effects based on within-subjects differences, the **within-subjects error term.**

We start with the error term appropriate for the completely randomized factorial design. As indicated in Chapter 9, this quantity is based on the variability of subjects within each treatment condition, the $SS_{S/AB}$. Next, we subdivide this sum of squares into two component sums of squares: one to be used to obtain the error term for the between-subjects portion of the data, and the other to obtain the error term for the within-subjects portion of the data. In symbols,

$$SS_{S/AB} = \text{(between-subjects } SS_{\text{error}}) + \text{(within-subjects } SS_{\text{error}}) \quad . \quad (11\text{-}1)$$

Let us consider the nature of these two component sources of variation and the fundamental logic governing their use.

Between-Subjects Error Term. We begin with the source that is easiest to understand, the sum of squares used to form the between-subjects error term. Suppose we transformed the mixed factorial design into a completely randomized single-factor design by combining the set of scores produced by each subject to form a single composite score. Consider the *ABS* matrix in Table 11-2. Three observations are listed for the first subject in the a_1 treatment group, one for each combination of level a_1 with the *B* treatments:

$$ABS_{111}, ABS_{121}, \text{ and } ABS_{131} \quad .$$

The sum of these three scores eliminates factor *B* to produce a sum (AS_{11}) for that particular subject. That is,

$$AS_{11} = ABS_{111} + ABS_{121} + ABS_{131} \quad .$$

Each subject at level a_1 produces one of these *AS* sums. Similarly, the subjects at the other levels of factor *A* produce sets of *AS* sums.

In effect, this summation removes factor *B*—and the within-subjects component as a consequence—from the analysis. The value of such an undertaking is to create a set of data we can analyze using familiar procedures, namely, a single-factor experiment with independent groups of subjects. To be more specific, each subject has been randomly assigned to the *A* treatments and produces for analysis purposes a single composite score (*AS*); the only difference between this score and that from an actual single-factor design is that the latter represents a single observation rather than a composite score. As we know from Chapter 4, the analysis of this particular design isolates two sums of squares, the SS_A and the $SS_{S/A}$, the former reflecting experimental error and possible treatment effects in the population and the latter reflecting only experimental error. It was this consideration that justified the use of the *F* ratio to evaluate the null hypothesis.

Essentially the same sort of logic can be applied to the evaluation of the *A* *main effect* in the mixed factorial design, where the variability observed is due entirely to differences among subjects—that is, where no repeated measures are involved. Thus, while it may seem strange to extract an error term appropriate for a single-factor experiment from a two-factor experiment, the basic idea makes sense. In short, the error term for the between-subjects portion of the mixed factorial design will be based on a familiar quantity, namely, the $SS_{S/A}$.

Within-Subjects Error Term. Once we have identified the sum of squares needed for the between-subjects error term, $SS_{S/A}$, we can easily subtract to find the sum of squares needed for the within-subjects error term. We begin with equation (11-1):

$$SS_{S/AB} = (\text{between-subjects } SS_{\text{error}}) + (\text{within-subjects } SS_{\text{error}}) \quad .$$

We then solve for the within-subjects component by subtracting the between-subjects component from $SS_{S/AB}$. Specifically,

$$\text{within-subjects } SS_{\text{error}} = SS_{S/AB} - (\text{between-subjects } SS_{\text{error}}) \quad .$$

Since we have indicated that the between-subjects component is $SS_{S/A}$, we can specify the within-subjects component with reasonably familiar quantities:

$$\text{within-subjects } SS_{\text{error}} = SS_{S/AB} - SS_{S/A} \quad . \tag{11-2}$$

We will use this component sum of squares to obtain an error term that reflects the magnitude of experimental error present in the within-subjects portion of the data, that is, to evaluate the significance of the *B main effect* and the *A × B interaction*. We refer to this error term as $MS_{B \times S/A}$ to be consistent with the terminology used in *Design and Analysis* and other advanced statistics books.[5] With this terminology, equation (11-2) becomes

$$SS_{B \times S/A} = SS_{S/AB} - SS_{S/A} \quad . \tag{11-3}$$

Computational Formulas

The computational formulas for the main effects and for interaction are identical to those required for the between-subjects factorial design; consequently, they need not be discussed again. The only new quantities we need to specify for the analysis of the mixed factorial design are the computational formulas for the two error terms covered in the last section. We start by

---

[5] The error term for the within-subjects portion of the mixed factorial and for the single-factor within-subjects design can be understood in terms of an interaction involving subjects and the independent variable with which repeated measurements are taken. This is why we referred to the error term for the single-factor within-subjects design as $MS_{A \times S}$ and to the error term for the mixed factorial design as $MS_{B \times S/A}$. For a more detailed discussion of these error terms, see *Design and Analysis* (pp. 407–408 and pp. 439–442).

considering the formulas for the basic ratios with which the two error term sums of squares are calculated.

Basic Ratios. The total analysis will utilize only one new basic ratio in addition to those specified for the analysis of the completely randomized factorial design in Chapter 9. For convenience, these ratios have been presented again in the footnote to Table 11-3. The new ratio involves the only new quantity appearing in the summary matrices, the AS totals. We calculate these totals by summing the ABS scores obtained from each subject—one for each of the treatment conditions in which a subject serves. Then we simply follow the arithmetical operations specified by the general formula for a basic ratio, namely,

$$\frac{\Sigma \, (\text{sum})^2}{\text{divisor}} \quad .$$

Applied to the composite scores (the AS totals), the ratio becomes

$$[AS] = \frac{\Sigma \, (AS)^2}{b} \quad . \tag{11-4}$$

We square the AS totals, add them up, and divide by b, the number of observations contributing to each sum.

Sums of Squares. We have two new sums of squares to consider in the analysis of the mixed factorial design: one for the between-subjects error term ($SS_{S/A}$) and the other for the within-subjects error term ($SS_{B \times S/A}$). We will discuss the calculation of $SS_{S/A}$ first.

As we indicated in an earlier section, the between-subjects portion of the mixed factorial is functionally equivalent to a completely randomized single-factor experiment. The deviations on which this sum of squares are based are the average scores for each subject, $\overline{AS}$, from the relevant A treatment mean ($\overline{A}$). We have seen in earlier chapters that the basic deviations indicate which basic ratios are involved and how they are combined in the calculation of the required sum of squares. In this case, the deviations have the form $\overline{AS} - \overline{A}$ and the computational formula has the same form:

$$SS_{S/A} = [AS] - [A] \quad . \tag{11-5}$$

The basic ratios required to complete the calculations are presented in the footnote to Table 11-3. A comparison of this computational formula with the one specified for the single-factor experiment reveals their similarity. That is, for the single-factor experiment,

$$SS_{S/A} = \Sigma \, (AS)^2 - \frac{\Sigma \, (A)^2}{s} \quad ,$$

TABLE 11-3 Computational Formulas for the Analysis of Variance

Source	Sum of Squares[a]	df	MS	F
A	$[A] - [T]$	$a - 1$	$\dfrac{SS_A}{df_A}$	$\dfrac{MS_A}{MS_{S/A}}$
S/A	$[AS] - [A]$	$a(s - 1)$	$\dfrac{SS_{S/A}}{df_{S/A}}$	
B	$[B] - [T]$	$b - 1$	$\dfrac{SS_B}{df_B}$	$\dfrac{MS_B}{MS_{B \times S/A}}$
A × B	$[AB] - [A] - [B] + [T]$	$(a - 1)(b - 1)$	$\dfrac{SS_{A \times B}}{df_{A \times B}}$	$\dfrac{MS_{A \times B}}{MS_{B \times S/A}}$
B × S/A	$[ABS] - [AB] - [AS] + [A]$	$a(b - 1)(s - 1)$	$\dfrac{SS_{B \times S/A}}{df_{B \times S/A}}$	
Total	$[ABS] - [T]$	$a(b)(s) - 1$		

[a] $[A] = \dfrac{\Sigma (A)^2}{b(s)}$, $[T] = \dfrac{(T)^2}{a(b)(s)}$, $[AS] = \dfrac{\Sigma (AS)^2}{b}$, $[B] = \dfrac{\Sigma (B)^2}{a(s)}$, $[AB] = \dfrac{\Sigma (AB)^2}{s}$, and $[ABS] = \Sigma (ABS)^2$.

while for the mixed factorial,

$$SS_{S/A} = \frac{\Sigma (AS)^2}{b} - \frac{\Sigma (A)^2}{b(s)} \quad .$$

The only difference between the two computational formulas is the addition of b to the denominator of each basic ratio for the second formula. This value is needed to adjust for the fact that the sum of squares is based on quantities obtained from a factorial design rather than a single-factor design, in which factor B obviously would not be present.

We could obtain the sum of squares for the within-subjects error term from equation (11-3) by subtracting the two sums of squares:

$$SS_{B \times S/A} = SS_{S/AB} - SS_{S/A} \quad .$$

Instead, however, we prefer to transform this equation into a formula specifying basic ratios rather than sums of squares. To do this, we substitute computational expressions for the two terms on the right and simplify the expression. The computational formula for the first term is given in Table 9-7 and for the second term is given by equation (11-5). Specifically,

$$SS_{S/AB} = [ABS] - [AB] \text{ and } SS_{S/A} = [AS] - [A] \quad .$$

Substituting in equation (11-3), we obtain

$$SS_{B \times S/A} = SS_{S/AB} - SS_{S/A}$$
$$= ([ABS] - [AB]) - ([AS] - [A])$$
$$= [ABS] - [AB] - [AS] + [A] \quad . \tag{11-6}$$

THE ANALYSIS OF VARIANCE

Degrees of Freedom

The degrees of freedom associated with each sum of squares are listed in Table 11-3. The degrees of freedom for the factorial effects were discussed in Chapter 9. To obtain the degrees of freedom for $SS_{S/A}$, the sum of squares for the between-subjects error term, we apply the same logic used to determine this quantity in the single-factor experiment. That is, the sum of squares is based on the deviation of each subject's composite mean $(\overline{AS})$ from the appropriate treatment mean $(\overline{A})$. Since $1\,df$ is lost as a result of estimating the population treatment mean,

$$df = s - 1$$

for any *one* of the treatment groups. Since there are a such groups, each with $s - 1$ degrees of freedom,

$$df_{S/A} = (s - 1) + (s - 1) + (s - 1) + \text{etc.}$$
$$= a(s - 1) \quad .$$

The formula for the degrees of freedom for $SS_{B \times S/A}$, the sum of squares for the within-subjects error term, may be obtained by subtraction. Since any relationship established for sums of squares holds for corresponding degrees of freedom,

$$df_{B \times S/A} = df_{S/AB} - df_{S/A} \quad . \tag{11-7}$$

By substituting known quantities for the terms on the right and performing some simple algebra, not outlined here, one can arrive at the compact df statement in Table 11-3, namely,

$$df_{B \times S/A} = a(b - 1)(s - 1) \quad .$$

Mean Squares and F Ratios

We obtain the mean squares, as usual, by dividing a sum of squares by the appropriate number of degrees of freedom. This step is specified in Table 11-3.

The final stage of the calculations is the formation of the three F ratios. It is here that the two different error terms come into play. In the mixed factorial, the between-subjects error term ($MS_{S/A}$) is used to assess the significance of the A main effect, while the within-subjects error term ($MS_{B \times S/A}$) is used to test the significance of the B main effect and the $A \times B$ interaction. These F ratios are indicated in the final column of Table 11-3. Note that the arrangement of the sources of variance in Table 11-3 emphasizes the between-subjects and within-subjects portions of the analysis. The A main effect and its error term are listed first and are based on differences between subjects. The remaining factorial effects and their error term are listed next and are based on the repeated measurements taken from the same subjects, that is, differences within subjects.

The statistical hypotheses are the same as those specified in Chapter 9 for the completely randomized factorial experiment (pp. 229–230). The decision rules follow the same form as those presented in previous chapters. We determine the critical value of F by entering the F table for a specified significance level (α) and combination of numerator and denominator degrees of freedom.

Assumptions underlying the analysis of variance are the same as those for the between-subjects and within-subjects designs (see pp. 96–97 and pp. 182–183, respectively). Researchers tend to be unconcerned with moderate violations of these assumptions, although violations of these assumptions are more serious for the within-subjects portion than for the between-subjects portion of the statistical analysis. For our purposes, however, we will assume that violations have little effect on any conclusions we draw from the statistical evaluation of the data resulting from a mixed factorial experiment.[6]

A NUMERICAL EXAMPLE

As a numerical example, we will analyze data obtained from a ficticious wine-tasting experiment. The primary question under consideration is whether wines benefit from being opened a half hour or so before being poured. One of the sacred beliefs of wine buffs is that wines require a ''breathing period'' to taste their best. A nontechnical justification for this widespread practice is that the early opening allows unpleasant gases and

---

[6] See *Design and Analysis* for a discussion of the specific assumptions (pp. 462–464) and for procedures to follow in the presence of clear violations (pp. 464–467).

aromas to dissipate and permits a measure of oxidation to occur in the wine. Wine connoisseurs (and most waiters) report that wines definitely improve during the course of a meal or a tasting session. Unfortunately, such evidence is usually contaminated by the fact that the wine taster changes during the same period, and therefore any improvement in the taste of the wine might as well be attributed to the judge as to the effects of a breathing period. Obviously, a well-controlled experiment is required to answer this "important" question.

Experimental Design

The primary independent variable is the time elapsed between the opening of a bottle of wine and the moment at which the judgment is made. We will consider three treatment conditions: a wine judged immediately after being opened (level b_1), a wine judged 30 minutes after being opened (level b_2), and a wine judged 60 minutes after being opened (level b_3). We could use a completely randomized design, assigning subjects randomly to the different treatment conditions, but we suspect that the judgments of individual wine tasters differ greatly, and that these differences would result in an unacceptably large amount of experimental error. An obvious solution is to choose a within-subjects design and to have the same subjects judge the wine under all three breathing conditions.

As we saw in Chapter 8, we must account for the possibility of practice effects, usually controlled by counterbalancing. In wine tasting this is generally not a problem since tasters continually switch back and forth from wine to wine to heighten their appreciation of each one. In addition, we must start with three bottles of the same wine and decide randomly which bottle is to represent which condition. In fact, because the same wine varies from bottle to bottle, we would use several sets of three wines to prevent inherent differences in the bottles from confounding the three treatment conditions. Finally, we must open the wines the appropriate number of minutes before the formal tasting to guarantee that the wine in all three bottles is ready for tasting at the same time. The wine is then presented without identification and the taster judges the three samples.

A second independent variable that might be of interest is the type of wine—white or red. Lore has it that red wines benefit more from early opening than white wines. The reasoning is that red wines contain a number of chemical substances that need time to combine with the air to develop fully. We will assume that this independent variable is represented by two levels—white (level a_1) and red (level a_2)—and that the two types of wines are judged by different groups of subjects. Thus, type of wine represents a between-subjects manipulation. The complete design is a 2×3 mixed factorial, with factor A consisting of two types of wine and factor B consisting of the three breathing conditions.

A final consideration in the selection of this particular experimental design deserves mention. The within-subjects manipulation should be assigned to the independent variable of primary interest or to the independent variable that the researcher assumes will produce the smallest effect. Our reason for recommending this precaution is that the error term used in evaluating within-subjects differences is generally much smaller than the error term used in evaluating between-subjects differences, and the smaller error term results in an increased sensitivity where it is most appropriate.[7]

Preliminary Calculations

Summary Matrices. The results of this hypothetical experiment are presented in Table 11-4. There are $s = 5$ subjects randomly assigned to each of the A treatments (types of wine). The response measure consists of each subject's rating on a 10-point scale (1 poor, 10 excellent) of the three wines offered for judgment. The ABS matrix contains the basic observations, the separate ratings for all subjects, and row and column marginal sums for the two levels of factor A. The row sums are the overall sums based on a subject's combined rating of the three wines, and the column sums are the treatment sums (AB) for the different treatment combinations. These latter sums are entered within the body of the AB matrix, Table 11-4B.

Table 11-4C presents the means for the treatment conditions as well as the column and row marginal means on which the main effects are based. The means within the body of the factorial matrix indicate that, contrary to expectations, neither wine showed improvement with breathing; in fact, both showed a deterioration in judged quality. Moreover, an interaction of the two independent variables appears to be present such that the observed deterioration is much smaller for the white wine than for the red one.[8]

---

[7] The experiment could have been designed as a complete within-subjects factorial, with the same subjects judging all *six* wines represented in the 2×3 factorial. One might worry about later judgments being adversely affected by the consumption of wine during the earlier judgments. (Only professional wine tasters spit out the wine during tastings!) Another potential problem is that subjects might be overwhelmed by the differences between the two kinds of wine (factor A) and not be able to discern the smaller and subtler differences due to differential breathing time (factor B).

[8] These findings are ficticious, but they are based on the results of an actual series of experiments reported in *New York Magazine* (1977) by Alexis Bespaloff.

TABLE 11-4   A Numerical Example

A. *ABS* Matrix

a_1

Subject	b_1	b_2	b_3	Sum
s_1	3	4	2	9
s_2	7	5	7	19
s_3	4	3	4	11
s_4	6	4	4	14
s_5	6	6	3	15
Sum of Scores	26	22	20	68
Sum of Squared Scores	146	102	94	

a_2

Subject	b_1	b_2	b_3	Sum
s_6	10	8	5	23
s_7	10	9	7	26
s_8	8	6	3	17
s_9	7	8	6	21
s_{10}	10	7	4	21
Sum of Scores	45	38	25	108
Sum of Squared Scores	413	294	135	

B. *AB* Matrix

Level	(Imm.) b_1	(30 Min) b_2	(60 Min) b_3	Sum
a_1 (White)	26	22	20	68
a_2 (Red)	45	38	25	108
Sum	71	60	45	176

C. Table of Means

Level	(Imm.) b_1	(30 Min) b_2	(60 Min) b_2	Average
a_1 (White)	5.20	4.40	4.00	4.53
a_2 (Red)	9.00	7.60	5.00	7.20
Average	7.10	6.00	4.50	5.87

Basic Ratios. The entries in the two summary matrices are used in computing the set of basic ratios required in the calculation of the various sums of squares (see Table 11-3). Starting with the *ABS* matrix, we can obtain the sum of the squared *ABS* scores by adding together the subtotals listed below each column sum. That is,

$$[ABS] = \Sigma\,(ABS)^2$$
$$= 146 + 102 + 94 + 413 + 294 + 135$$
$$= 1{,}184 \quad .$$

Also from the ABS matrix, we calculate

$$[AS] = \frac{\Sigma \, (AS)^2}{b}$$

$$= \frac{(9)^2 + (19)^2 + (11)^2 + \cdots + (17)^2 + (21)^2 + (21)^2}{3}$$

$$= \frac{81 + 361 + 121 + \cdots + 289 + 441 + 441}{3} = \frac{3,360}{3}$$

$$= 1,120.00 \quad .$$

All the remaining basic ratios can be calculated with the information appearing in the AB matrix. Specifically,

$$[AB] = \frac{\Sigma \, (AB)^2}{s}$$

$$= \frac{(26)^2 + (22)^2 + (20)^2 + (45)^2 + (38)^2 + (25)^2}{5}$$

$$= \frac{676 + 484 + 400 + 2,025 + 1,444 + 625}{5} = \frac{5,654}{5}$$

$$= 1,130.80;$$

$$[A] = \frac{\Sigma \, (A)^2}{b(s)}$$

$$= \frac{(68)^2 + (108)^2}{3(5)} = \frac{4,624 + 11,664}{15} = \frac{16,288}{15}$$

$$= 1,085.87;$$

$$[B] = \frac{\Sigma \, (B)^2}{a(s)}$$

$$= \frac{(71)^2 + (60)^2 + (45)^2}{2(5)}$$

$$= \frac{5,041 + 3,600 + 2,025}{10} = \frac{10,666}{10}$$

$$= 1,066.60; \text{ and}$$

$$[T] = \frac{(T)^2}{a(b)(s)}$$

$$= \frac{(176)^2}{2(3)(5)} = \frac{30,976}{30}$$

$$= 1,032.53 \quad .$$

Sums of Squares. The sums of squares needed for the analysis of variance are specified in Table 11-3. We calculate these values by adding and subtracting the basic ratios in the patterns of combination indicated in the table. To illustrate,

$$SS_A = [A] - [T]$$
$$= 1,085.87 - 1,032.53 = 53.34;$$

$$SS_{S/A} = [AS] - [A]$$
$$= 1,120.00 - 1,085.87 = 34.13;$$

$$SS_B = [B] - [T]$$
$$= 1,066.60 - 1,032.53 = 34.07;$$

$$SS_{A \times B} = [AB] - [A] - [B] + [T]$$
$$= 1,130.80 - 1,085.87 - 1,066.60 + 1,032.53 = 10.86;$$

$$SS_{B \times S/A} = [ABS] - [AB] - [AS] + [A]$$
$$= 1,184 - 1,130.80 - 1,120.00 + 1,085.87 = 19.07; \text{ and}$$

$$SS_T = [ABS] - [T]$$
$$= 1,184 - 1,032.53 = 151.47 \quad .$$

These sums of squares are entered in Table 11-5, the analysis of variance summary table. As an arithmetical check, we should verify that the sum of the component sums of squares equals the total sum of squares. That is,

$$SS_T = SS_A + SS_{S/A} + SS_B + SS_{A \times B} + SS_{B \times S/A}$$

$$151.47 = 53.34 + 34.13 + 34.07 + 10.86 + 19.07$$

$$= 151.47 \quad .$$

The Analysis of Variance

The degrees of freedom for the different sums of squares are calculated by means of the formulas presented in Table 11-3. To illustrate,

$$df_A = a - 1$$
$$= 2 - 1 = 1;$$

$$df_{S/A} = a(s - 1)$$
$$= 2(5 - 1) = 2(4) = 8;$$

$$df_B = b - 1$$
$$= 3 - 1 = 2;$$

$$df_{A \times B} = (a - 1)(b - 1)$$
$$= (2 - 1)(3 - 1) = 1(2) = 2;$$

$$df_{B \times S/A} = a(b - 1)(s - 1)$$
$$= 2(3 - 1)(5 - 1) = 2(2)(4) = 16; \text{ and}$$

$$df_T = a(b)(s) - 1$$
$$= 2(3)(5) - 1 = 30 - 1 = 29 \quad .$$

As an arithmetical check,

$$df_T = df_A + df_{S/A} + df_B + df_{A \times B} + df_{B \times S/A}$$
$$29 = 1 + 8 + 2 + 2 + 16$$
$$= 29 \quad .$$

We calculate the mean squares for each of the component sources of variance by dividing each sum of squares by the appropriate number of degrees of freedom. The results of these divisions are presented in Table 11-5. The final step in the calculations is finding the F ratios. For the main effect of factor A, which is based on the between-subjects portion of the statistical analysis,

$$F = \frac{MS_A}{MS_{S/A}}$$

$$= \frac{53.34}{4.27} = 12.49 \quad .$$

The critical value of this F, for which $df_{num.} = 1$ and $df_{denom.} = 8$, is 5.32 at the 5 percent level of significance. Since the obtained F of 12.49 exceeds this critical value, application of the decision rules results in the rejection of the null hypothesis.

The other two sources of variance are based on the within-subjects portion of the statistical analysis and thus are assessed by the residual error term, $MS_{B \times S/A}$. Specifically,

$$F = \frac{MS_B}{MS_{B \times S/A}}$$

$$= \frac{17.04}{1.19} = 14.32, \text{ and}$$

$$F = \frac{MS_{A \times B}}{MS_{B \times S/A}}$$

$$= \frac{5.43}{1.19} = 4.56 \quad .$$

Since both Fs are associated with the same numbers of degrees of freedom—$df_{num.} = 2$, and $df_{denom.} = 16$—both are compared with the same critical value. At $\alpha = .05$, the critical value of $F(2, 16) = 3.63$. Both Fs

TABLE 11-5   Summary of the Analysis of Variance

Source	SS	df	MS	F
A	53.34	1	53.34	12.49*
S/A	34.13	8	4.27	
B	34.07	2	17.04	14.32*
A × B	10.86	2	5.43	4.56*
B × S/A	19.07	16	1.19	
Total	151.47	29		

*$p < .05$

exceed this value. Thus, application of the decision rules results in the rejection of the null hypothesis in both cases.

Because significant interaction is present, we are more interested in the nature of the interaction than in the nature of the two significant main effects. The means in Table 11-4C indicate that while a general negative trend exists in the preferences—the longer the bottles remain open the less the tasters like the wine in both cases—this effect is more pronounced with respect to the red wine (level a_2). Analytical comparisons applied to the cell means are called for to add statistical support to this observation.

Though a significant interaction is present, the main effects are not completely without interest. Our interest in main effects is dependent on a number of factors, including the consistency with which a particular manipulation is observed in an experiment. For example, consider the variable of wine type (factor A). The main effect is significant; that is, the tasters generally seem to prefer the red wine to the white wine (see Table 11-4C). This preference is consistent in that the red wine received higher average preference scores than the white wine in each of the three breathing conditions. Thus, the data suggest that the red wine is generally preferred in spite of the complication introduced by the presence of interaction. Whether this difference is significant after a 60-minute breathing period—when the difference between the two wines is the smallest (5.00 versus 4.00)—would have to be determined by subsequent statistical analyses. The important point here is that significant main effects should not be totally disregarded in the assimilation and interpretation of a set of results when an interaction is significant. You should always try to extract as much information from an experiment that is reasonable in light of the outcome of the statistical analyses and the particular patterning of the treatment means.

The increased sensitivity provided by the mixed factorial design is demonstrable through a comparison of the two error terms, 4.27 for the between-subjects portion of the analysis and 1.19 for the within-subjects portion. Although the data for this example are ficticious, differences in the relative sizes of the two error terms are usually of this order of magnitude (or even larger). A smaller error term increases the sensitivity of a statistical test by increasing the chances that the null hypothesis will be rejected. This added sensitivity is the primary reason why within-subjects designs are so frequently seen in the psychological research literature and why they can be an advantage when the expected effects are small.

ANALYTICAL COMPARISONS

As we noted in Chapter 10, an analysis of the main effects and of interaction usually represents only the first stage in the detailed analysis of a factorial experiment. Different sorts of analytical comparisons are contemplated according to the significance or nonsignificance of the $A \times B$ interaction (and the logic guiding the manipulations that define the levels of the two independent variables). Generally, if the interaction is significant, the investigator searches for the locus of interaction through the use of such statistical techniques as analyses of simple main effects, factorial comparisons, and simple comparisons. On the other hand, if the interaction is not significant, the researcher focuses instead on the main effects and analytical comparisons involving the means of one independent variable obtained by averaging over the levels of the other independent variable. Examples of these different analyses were presented and discussed in Chapter 10.

All these analyses are available for use with the mixed factorial experiment. The most obvious ones with the present example would be a statistical assessment of the two simple main effects of factor B. That is, while the significant interaction tells us that the two wines lose their appeal with increased breathing time at differential rates—in other words, white wine (a_1) does not drop as quickly as does the red wine (a_2)—an analysis of this drop for each of the two wines considered separately would tell us whether either wine on its own would show a significant decline as the wine is permitted to breathe.

The actual statistical analysis of analytical comparisons is more complicated with the mixed factorial than it is with the completely randomized factorial. The complications are due to the different error terms required for assessing the significance of different analytical comparisons. If you have reached this point in our discussion with your own data in hand and need to conduct these analyses, we suggest that you review the general discussion of analytical analyses offered in Chapter 10 and then turn to *Design and Analysis* (pp. 442–454) for information concerning the problem of error terms in the mixed factorial experiment.[9]

SUMMARY

Our general discussion of factorial experiments is concluded with this chapter. Our concern here has been the design and analysis of factorial experiments that include the multiple testing of the same subjects. We concentrated on one such experiment—a mixed factorial design, in which subjects receive all the treatment conditions associated with one of the independent variables (factor B) in combination with only one level of the other independent variable (factor A).

Mixed factorial designs are extremely common in psychological research. Researchers often choose them in order to conduct a sensitive test when only a small number of subjects is available. In addition, they can easily expand a basic single-factor experiment with independent groups of subjects into a mixed factorial simply by administering a series of learning trials to each of the subjects in the original design. In this case, the variable of trials (a within-subjects factor) becomes a second independent variable in the experiment.

The statistical analysis of the mixed factorial is identical to that required of the completely randomized factorial experiment, except for the error terms. Most of the chapter was devoted to an explanation of these complications. In brief, a general principle emerged: One error term is used to evaluate the main effect of factor A, which is based on between-subjects differences; this mean square ($MS_{S/A}$) is functionally equivalent to the error term used in the analysis of a completely randomized single-factor experiment. A second error term ($MS_{B \times S/A}$) is used to evaluate differences based on repeated measures; this mean square is usually considerably smaller than the between-subjects error term, accounting for the increased sensitivity associated with this type of experimental design.

---

[9] You might also want to examine the more comprehensive discussion of analytical comparisons possible with factorial designs covered in Chapters 11 and 12 of *Design and Analysis*.

TERMS, CONCEPTS, AND SYMBOLS

within-subjects factorial designs
mixed factorial design
completely randomized between-subjects design
sensitivity
between-subjects error term
within-subjects error term

AS_{ik} $\Sigma (AS)^2$ $[AS]$ $\overline{AS}$

$SS_{S/A}$ $df_{S/A}$ $MS_{S/A}$

$SS_{B \times S/A}$ $df_{B \times S/A}$ $MS_{B \times S/A}$

EXERCISES

1. An investigator was interested in the effects of the loudness of an auditory
   message on a person's ability to process the messages at different speeds
   (rates) of presentation. Previous research indicated that subjects could be
   tested on messages presented at different rates without any apparent
   problems of contamination from one rate to another. Thus, the researcher
   decided to test each subject at each of the three rates, slow (b_1), medium
   (b_2), and fast (b_3). However, subjects were tested with only one loudness
   level, thus, three different groups of subjects were given either soft (a_1),
   moderate (a_2), or loud (a_3) auditory messages. The result, of course, was
   a mixed design with loudness as a between-subjects variable and rate as a
   within-subjects variable. Rate was completely counterbalanced, which
   required six subjects in each loudness level. The response measure was
   the number of messages correctly detected. The data for the eighteen
   subjects are given in the table on the next page.

	a_1 (Soft)		
Subject	b_1	b_2	b_3
s_1	9	6	5
s_2	11	9	6
s_3	11	8	5
s_4	12	10	10
s_5	12	12	9
s_6	11	11	7

	a_2 (Moderate)		
Subject	b_1	b_2	b_3
s_7	15	10	8
s_8	15	9	7
s_9	14	6	4
s_{10}	17	13	11
s_{11}	11	7	5
s_{12}	16	10	8

	a_3 (Loud)		
Subject	b_1	b_2	b_3
s_{13}	12	9	7
s_{14}	15	11	7
s_{15}	15	12	8
s_{16}	16	14	12
s_{17}	17	14	11
s_{18}	15	13	10

Perform an analysis of variance on these data. To understand the results, construct a graph of the treatment means. How would you summarize the outcome of the experiment?

2. In this experiment, twelve subjects (small, nonhuman mammals) were randomly assigned to one of three treatment conditions. Condition a_1 was a control group that was prepared for surgery, given anesthetic, but not operated upon. Condition a_2 consisted of a group of subjects who were operated upon and had an area of the brain critical to the interest of the researcher removed. Condition a_3 consisted of a group of subjects who were also operated upon but had an area of the brain removed that was thought to be unrelated to the behavior under study. The second factor in the experiment was a battery of four different tests. We will not be concerned with the exact nature of the tests except to note that they were relevant to the research. Each of the subjects was tested on the four tests, but due to the limited number of subjects available a form of incomplete counterbalancing was used. The data from this experiment are presented on the next page.

a_1 (Control)

Subjects	b_1	b_2	b_3	b_4
s_1	3	5	9	7
s_2	6	9	13	9
s_3	10	15	15	14
s_4	10	12	18	15

a_2 (Critical Area)

Subjects	b_1	b_2	b_3	b_4
s_5	4	5	3	1
s_6	7	11	8	4
s_7	12	14	13	9
s_8	11	12	11	7

a_3 (Noncritical Area)

Subjects	b_1	b_2	b_3	b_4
s_9	8	5	9	7
s_{10}	9	8	11	12
s_{11}	12	13	12	9
s_{12}	4	13	10	8

Analyze these data with a mixed-design analysis of variance. What conclusions would you draw from this experiment?

LINEAR REGRESSION AND CORRELATION

IV

One important purpose of science is establishing relationships between variables. Throughout this book, we have concerned ourselves with the analysis of *experimental data,* that is, with relationships between independent (or manipulated) variables and behavior. These analyses provide us with evidence we can use in drawing causal inferences about the effect of one variable on another.

As mentioned in Chapter 1, another major type of research consists of the discovery of relationships between different aspects of behavior. This type of research is made up of correlational methods, which are used to establish associations between two *dependent variables.* Using these methods, researchers do not vary the antecedent conditions as they do in experimental research; rather, they measure the joint occurrence of different aspects of behavior as revealed in their natural environment or under carefully controlled conditions. As a consequence of the methodology, the correlational approach usually does not permit investigators to clearly infer causality. On the other hand, correlational relationships serve an important and useful function in the development of psychology and in the real world, where future behavior is predicted on the basis of past performance. In addition, knowing that a relationship between two variables exists is important in itself. As we pointed out earlier, this information can open up new avenues of experimental research designed to determine the causal bases underlying observed relationships.

The next three chapters are concerned with a particular type of relationship between two variables, which can best be described by a straight line (or linear function, as it is called). We begin this discussion in Chapter 12 with a consideration of experimental data in which one of the variables is manipulated by the experimenter and the other consists of what the subject provides us—performance on some response measure. In Chapter 13, we examine the data obtained from correlational studies, in which both variables consist of dependent variables, and see how the establishment of a linear relationship between two response measures can be used for prediction purposes. Finally, in Chapter 14, we discuss linear correlation, which provides information on the degree to which a linear relationship is present between two variables.

Linear Regression: Experimental Data

12

A straight line depicting the relationship between two variables is called a **regression line.** In earlier chapters, we discussed the outcomes of experiments in which quantitative independent variables were manipulated and could reasonably be summarized by means of a straight line linking the independent variable with the dependent variable. Consider, for instance, the data from the kangaroo-rat study in Chapter 6. You will recall that there were three conditions in which rats were subjected to the smells of animals with whom they had unsuccessful territorial battles (the familiar conditions); the differences among three conditions lay in the time that elapsed following the encounter (immediately afterwards, two weeks later, and four weeks later). The data from this study are presented again in Figure 12-1A. While not perfect, you will note that the relationship among the three conditions

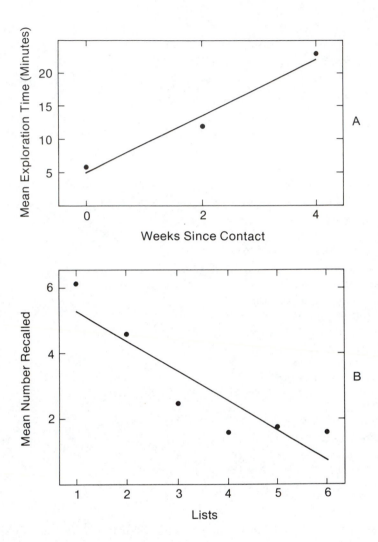

Figure 12-1. Two Examples of Linear Trends.

can be very well expressed by a rising regression line drawn among the three means. The procedures by which a regression line can be used to describe the outcome of an experiment make up one of the topics of this chapter.

A second example of a linear trend comes from Chapter 8. In this experiment, subjects were asked to recall a list of verbal material two days after learning it; each subject learned and recalled a series of six different lists. Recall performance as a function of the order in which the lists were learned is presented in Figure 12-1B. The function relating recall and the ordinal position of the list can also be reasonably expressed by a regression line, although one that falls rather than rises.

In both cases, a straight line can be used to represent the relationship between the independent and dependent variables. In the first case, the approximation is quite close—that is, the three data points do not deviate greatly from the straight line. In the second case, the approximation is less impressive, with relatively more space between the regression line and the six data points.

When the independent variable is quantitative, researchers usually attempt to see how well a straight line describes (or fits) a set of data, since a straight line is the simplest means of representing mathematically the relationship between two variables. More complicated relationships are possible, of course, and these take the form of curves with one or more "humps," or changes of direction. We will consider only linear relationships in this chapter, but you should be aware that techniques are available for analyzing and assessing more complicated relationships.

THE PROPERTIES OF A STRAIGHT LINE

Characteristics

We begin by considering two numerical quantities that are used in the writing of a formula that describes the straight line.

Slope. A straight line is completely defined by two characteristics, its **slope** and its **intercept.** Slope refers to the angle of a line's tilt relative to one of the axes. Consider the straight line in Figure 12-2. By convention, the horizontal axis is designated the X variable (or X axis) and the vertical axis is designated the Y variable (or Y axis). This line can be used to describe changes in the Y variable associated with changes in the X variable. Used in this way, the line is often called "Y on X"; more descriptively, the line might be called "Y predicted from X." Formally, slope is defined in this way:

$$\text{slope} = \frac{\text{rate of change in } Y}{\text{rate of change in } X} \quad .$$

To determine the slope of any line, we must first define "change in X." Since the slope is constant for the entire length of the line, we are free to

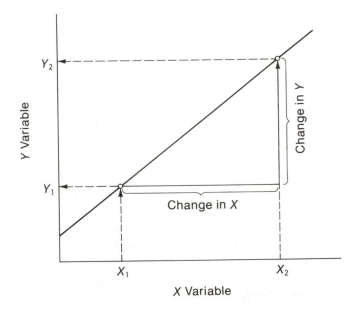

Figure 12-2. An Illustration of the Two Factors Entering into the Determination of the Slope of a Straight Line Specifying the Relationship Between Two Variables (X and Y).

select any two convenient points on the X axis to serve this purpose. We call these two points X_1 and X_2. The numerical difference between these two values of X literally defines the change in X. That is,

$$\text{change in } X = X_2 - X_1 \quad .$$

To determine change in Y, we extend perpendicular lines upward from X_1 and X_2 until the two intersect the straight line (the dashed lines from the X axis in Figure 12-2). We find the values of Y associated with these two points on the line by extending lines from these points, parallel to the X axis, until they intersect the Y axis. This intersection occurs at Y_1 and Y_2, the points of intersection on the Y axis associated with X_1 and X_2, respectively. (These two lines are the dashed lines to the Y axis in the figure.) Expressed in numerical terms, the difference between Y_1 and Y_2 defines the change in Y associated with the corresponding change in X. In symbols,

$$\text{change in } Y = Y_2 - Y_1 \quad .$$

We calculate the slope by dividing the change in Y by the change in X. For this diagram,

$$\text{slope} = \frac{Y_2 - Y_1}{X_2 - X_1} \quad .$$

The numerical value of the slope tells us something about the rate at which the Y variable changes as the X variable is varied. For example, a slope of 1.0 means that for every change of 1 unit in the X variable, a 1 unit change occurs in the Y variable. A decimal slope means that Y changes more slowly than X. A slope of .5, for instance, indicates that for every unit change in the X variable a half-unit change occurs in Y. On the other hand, slopes greater than 1 (disregarding sign) indicate that Y changes faster than X. For example, a slope of 2.0 means that for every unit change in the X variable, a 2-unit change occurs in the Y variable.

The sign of a slope provides additional information. A **positive slope** indicates that the Y variable changes in the *same* direction as X; in other words, when X increases, Y increases; or when X decreases, Y decreases. The linear function representing the kangaroo-rat data in Figure 12-1A has a positive slope. A **negative slope** indicates that the Y variable changes in the direction *opposite* to X; that is, when X increases, Y decreases; or when X decreases, Y increases. The linear function relating recall to list number in Figure 12-1B has a negative slope.

Intercept. The intercept of a straight line refers to the point at which the line crosses the Y axis. This point is called the Y **intercept.** It is the point at which $X = 0$. Suppose a line has a particular slope. A very large number of lines exists with this particular slope; individual lines differ only in the point at which they intersect the vertical axis. A few linear functions with the same slope are depicted graphically in Figure 12-3. The Y intercept can be either positive or negative, depending on whether the line intersects the Y axis above the 0 point (positive) or below it (negative).

The Formula for a Straight Line

It should be obvious that once the slope and the intercept of a straight line are specified, the line is completely defined. Only one possible straight line can be drawn to those specifications. Stated as a mathematical rule, the formula for a straight line is

$$Y = a_Y + (b_Y)(X) \quad . \tag{12-1}$$

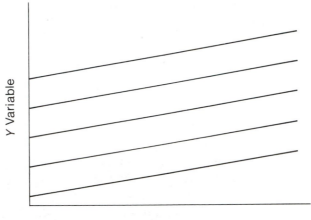

Figure 12-3. Each line has the same slope but different Y intercepts.

In this formula,

Y = the dependent variable (or the variable on the vertical axis)

X = the independent variable (or the variable on the horizontal axis)

a_Y = the intercept (or point at which the line crosses the Y axis)

b_Y = the slope of the line[1]

Once this line is specified, we can enter values of X (levels of the independent variable) and calculate the corresponding values of Y specified by the formula.

THE BEST-FIT STRAIGHT LINE

We would not expect "real" data to be perfectly fit or perfectly described by a straight line. Even under the best of circumstances, we would expect some of the data points to fall above the line and some to fall below. The idea

---

[1] The Y subscript indicates that the intercept and slope refer to the straight line relating Y to variations in the X variable.

behind finding the **best-fit straight line** is to find a line that minimizes the amount of variation from the line as much as possible.[2]

The Formula for the Best-Fit Straight Line

At this point we need to make a small change in our formula for a straight line. Remember that we are interested in *estimates* from the data under the assumption that a linear function underlies the relationship between the independent and dependent variables. That is, we are interested in predicting Y values from a knowledge of the X values. If we designate the estimated Y values as Y', the formula becomes

$$Y' = a_Y + (b_Y)(X) \quad . \tag{12-2}$$

In the following sections, we consider formulas that provide values for the slope (b_Y) and the intercept (a_Y). This information will enable us to draw the best-fit straight line through a set of data points.

Estimating Slope

An Overview. Recall that the slope of a straight line is defined in terms of the change in the Y variable associated with a given change in the X variable. When working with data from which the slope is to be estimated, we use a different definition. More specifically, we obtain the estimate of the slope from this formula:

$$b_Y = \frac{\text{covariation of } X \text{ and } Y}{\text{variation of } X} \quad .$$

The numerator term is a quantity we have not discussed before, while the denominator term should at least be familiar. **Covariation of X and Y** refers to the degree to which the two variables *covary,* that is, *vary together.* This term represents the variation in Y associated with the variation in X. In essence, this value is the change in Y associated with a change in X. The denominator term is simply a measure of the variability of the X values, an index of the change in X represented in the manipulation of the independent variable.

---

[2] The concept behind the procedure is one of reducing the sum of the squared deviations from the line to the smallest amount. This method of line-fitting is called *the method of least squares;* the values of the slope and intercept obtained by these procedures are called *least-square estimates.* A complete explanation of the rationale and derivation of the formulas used to calculate a line of best fit is beyond the scope of our interests here. See Hays (1973, pp. 622–624) for a discussion of this method as applied to regression analysis.

Let's examine these two quantities a bit more closely. Variation of X can be expressed in terms of the *variance* of the X values. That is,

$$\text{variance } (X) = \frac{\Sigma (X - \bar{X})^2}{df} = \frac{SS_X}{df} \quad .$$

This is the familiar formula for the variance of a set of scores. Although not needed for the present calculations, a variance may be calculated from the set of Y values as well:

$$\text{variance } (Y) = \frac{\Sigma (Y - \bar{Y})^2}{df} = \frac{SS_Y}{df} \quad .$$

The covariation of X and Y can be expressed in terms of a quantity called **covariance,** which represents a blending of the deviations of X values from their mean $(X - \bar{X})$ with the corresponding deviations of Y values from their mean $(Y - \bar{Y})$. In symbols,

$$\text{covariance } (X,Y) = \frac{\Sigma (X - \bar{X})(Y - \bar{Y})}{df} \quad .$$

We refer to the numerator term as the sum of products of corresponding deviations on the X and Y variables, or more simply, as the **sum of products,** abbreviated as SP_{XY}. Thus,

$$\text{covariance } (X,Y) = \frac{SP_{XY}}{df} \quad .$$

Since covariance is a new quantity, an explanation of the logic of this measure is called for. *Variance* is a measure that accounts for the deviation of a numerical quantity from the mean. In linear regression, two variances are involved, the variance of the X variable and the variance of the Y variable. *Covariance* measures the degree to which these two sets of deviations vary together. If the deviations on the X variable tend to be of the same magnitude as the corresponding deviations on the Y variable, the covariance will be large. That is, covariance will be large when large deviations on X are associated with the large deviations on Y, medium deviations on X are associated with medium deviations on Y, and small deviations on X are associated with small deviations on Y. On the other hand, if this relationship is inconsistent, and the large deviations on X are associated with deviations of *various* magnitudes on Y, then covariance will be small in value. Where the relationship between the two sets of deviations is completely absent, covariance will be 0.

Covariance can be either positive or negative. Covariance is positive when the signs of the pairs of deviations on X and Y tend to be the *same* (that is, +, + or −, −) and negative when the signs tend to be different (+, − or

TABLE 12-1 Notation for Linear
Regression and Correlation

Values of X	Values of Y	Products of X and Y
X_1	Y_1	$(X_1)(Y_1)$
X_2	Y_2	$(X_2)(Y_2)$
X_3	Y_3	$(X_3)(Y_3)$
ΣX^a	ΣY	$\Sigma (X)(Y)$
$\Sigma (X)^2$	$\Sigma (Y)^2$	

$^a \Sigma X = X_1 + X_2 + X_3$;
$\Sigma (X)^2 = (X_1)^2 + (X_2)^2 + (X_3)^2$;
$\Sigma Y = Y_1 + Y_2 + Y_3$;
$\Sigma (Y)^2 = (Y_1)^2 + (Y_2)^2 + (Y_3)^2$; and
$\Sigma (X)(Y) = (X_1)(Y_1) + (X_2)(Y_2) + (X_3)(Y_3)$.

$-,+$). The sign of the covariance term determines the sign or direction of the slope of the regression line. That is, if covariance is positive, the slope will be positive; and if covariance is negative, the slope will be negative. Similarly, the sign of the covariance term controls the sign of the correlation coefficient, an index representing the degree of relationship between two variables. (Correlation is discussed in Chapter 14.)

It will be clear soon that all the quantities needed for calculating the straight line are easily obtained by means of computational formulas and a systematic layout of the values of X and of Y. At this point, however, it is sufficient to state the formula for the slope in a more convenient form:

$$b_Y = \frac{\text{covariance}\,(X,Y)}{\text{variance}\,(X)} = \frac{SP_{XY}/df}{SS_X/df} \quad .$$

The formula can be simplified because the degrees of freedom for both numerator and denominator terms are the same and cancel. Thus,

$$b_Y = \frac{SP_{XY}}{SS_X} \quad . \tag{12-3}$$

Data Layout and Preliminary Calculations. We begin by arranging the X and Y values in two columns; each value of X is paired with the appropriate value of Y. These values are symbolized in the first two columns of Table 12-1. The subscripts are used to identify members of each pair of values, namely, the X and Y values. That is, X_1 and Y_1 constitute the first pair of values, X_2 and Y_2

constitute the second pair of values, and so on. From the X values, we obtain their sum, ΣX, and the sum of their squared values, $\Sigma (X)^2$. These two sums are designated at the bottom of the X column. As a reminder, the meaning of these notational symbols is made explicit in the footnote to the table. The same set of operations is performed on the Y values as well—the sum of the scores, ΣY, and the sum of the squared scores, $\Sigma (Y)^2$. These two sets of sums are used in the calculation of the means and the sums of squares for X and Y.[3]

The third column consists of *products* obtained by the multiplication of each X value by its corresponding Y value. The sum of these quantities is symbolized at the bottom of the column as $\Sigma (X)(Y)$. This sum, the only new operation required, is used in calculating the sum of products (SP_{XY}).

Computational Formulas. We use the preliminary calculations specified in Table 12-1 in convenient computational formulas to obtain the quantities required for determining the slope of the best-fitting straight line. As specified in equation (12-3), we need two quantities for calculating the slope of the regression line. One quantity is the sum of squares for the X variable, defined by

$$SS_X = \Sigma (X - \bar{X})^2 = \Sigma (X)^2 - \frac{(\Sigma X)^2}{s} , \tag{12-4}$$

where s in this case refers to the number of data points, that is, the number of paired values of X and Y. The computational formula for the other quantity, SP_{XY}, results from a blending of the X and Y variables:

$$SP_{XY} = \Sigma (X - \bar{X})(Y - \bar{Y}) = \Sigma (X)(Y) - \frac{(\Sigma X)(\Sigma Y)}{s} . \tag{12-5}$$

Each of these calculations will be illustrated shortly.

Estimating the Y Intercept

In addition to slope, we need to know the Y intercept in order to specify a straight line completely. The intercept, as you will recall, is the point at which the line cuts across the Y axis; this occurs when $X = 0$. The computational formula for the intercept is

$$a_Y = \bar{Y} - (b_Y)(\bar{X}) , \tag{12-6}$$

---

[3] You may have noticed that we have returned to the standard notation we used originally in Chapter 2. We will use standard notation in Part IV, since it is well-suited to our needs in expressing the arithmetical operations required in linear regression and correlation.

TABLE 12-2 A Numerical Example of Linear Regression

Independent Variable: Number of Items (X)	Dependent Variable: Mean Exposures (Y)	Products of X and Y (X)(Y)
2	1	(2)(1) = 2
4	2	(4)(2) = 8
6	5	(6)(5) = 30
8	9	(8)(9) = 72
10	12	(10)(12) = 120
12	14	(12)(14) = 168
14	15	(14)(15) = 210
16	18	(16)(18) = 288
$\Sigma X = 72$	$\Sigma Y = 76$	$\Sigma (X)(Y) = 898$
$\Sigma (X)^2 = 816$	$\Sigma (Y)^2 = 1,000$	
$\bar{X} = 9.00$	$\bar{Y} = 9.50$	

where $\bar{Y}$ and $\bar{X}$ are means based on the sets of the Y and X values, respectively, and b_Y is the slope as obtained in the last section. We are now ready for a numerical example.

A Numerical Example

As an example, consider a hypothetical experiment in which different groups of subjects are asked to learn lists consisting of different numbers of items (ranging in number from 2 to 16). Each group is assigned a list of different length. There are eight treatment conditions, each of which is specified in the first column of Table 12-2. Number of items, then, is the independent variable, designated X. The dependent variable, or response measure, consists of the average number of exposures required by subjects to master the list. These means, designated Y, are given in the second column of Table 12-2.[4] For example, subjects required an average of 1 exposure to learn 2 items, 2 exposures to learn 4 items, 5 exposures to learn 6 items, and so on. These data have been plotted in Figure 12-4, where the relationship between list length and the number of exposures required clearly can be reasonably de-

---

[4] It may seem strange to refer to the means of an experiment as Y. We adopted this new terminology in order to make our treatment of the topic consistent with our discussions of analyses performed with correlational data and with similar discussions in other statistics texts.

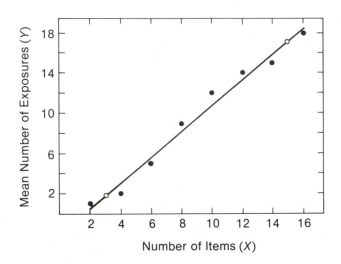

Figure 12-4. The Relationship Between the Number of Items Studied (the Independent Variable) and the Mean Number of Exposures Required to Learn (the Dependent Variable.)

scribed by a linear function with a positive slope, that is, Y increases as X increases. The line drawn through the data points is the best-fit straight line, which we will now calculate for ourselves.

Preliminary Calculations. The first two columns of Table 12-2 contain the eight X,Y pairs representing the results of the experiment. The products obtained by multiplying the X and Y members of each pair are given in the third column of the table. The preliminary calculations needed for obtaining the slope and the intercept are given at the bottom of the three columns. We are assuming that you are using a calculator that permits the summing of a set of numbers *and* the set of these numbers squared all in the same operation. If you do not have this type of calculator, you might find it useful to add two columns to Table 12-2 where you can record the two sets of *squared* numbers, $(X)^2$ and $(Y)^2$, in order to be systematic in your calculations and handling of the data. For this particular problem, however, it is not necessary to calculate $\Sigma (Y)^2$, since it does not enter into the calculations.

Calculation of the Slope. We have indicated that to calculate the slope we need the sum of squares for the X variable (SS_X) and the sum of products

(SP_{XY}). From equation (12-4) and the preliminary calculations summarized in Table 12-2, we find that

$$SS_X = \Sigma (X)^2 - \frac{(\Sigma X)^2}{s}$$

$$= 816 - \frac{(72)^2}{8}$$

$$= 816 - \frac{5,184}{8} = 816 - 648.00 = 168.00 \quad .$$

We obtain the sum of products by substituting the relevant preliminary calculations from Table 12-2 in equation (12-5) as follows:

$$SP_{XY} = \Sigma (X)(Y) - \frac{(\Sigma X)(\Sigma Y)}{s}$$

$$= 898 - \frac{(72)(76)}{8}$$

$$= 898 - \frac{5,472}{8} = 898 - 684.00 = 214.00 \quad .$$

While a sum of squares can never be negative (unless a mistake has been made in calculation), the sign of the sum of products can be either positive or negative. If this term is positive, as it is here, the *slope* will be *positive,* indicating that the line rises from left to right on the graph. If it is negative, the slope will be negative also, indicating that the line decreases from left to right.

Entering these two quantities in equation (12-3), we find

$$b_Y = \frac{SP_{XY}}{SS_X}$$

$$= \frac{214.00}{168.00} = +1.27 \quad .$$

A slope of $b_Y = +1.27$ indicates that for a change of 1 unit in the independent variable—for example, from 2 to 3 items or from 15 to 16 items—subjects require an increase of 1.27 exposures to learn the longer list.

Calculating the Intercept. The Y intercept is calculated from equation (12-6):

$$a_Y = \bar{Y} - (b_Y)(\bar{X}) \quad .$$

We have already obtained the slope in the last section. The two means are easily calculated with the summary data provided in Table 12-2. That is,

$$\bar{X} = \frac{\Sigma X}{s} = \frac{72}{8} = 9.00, \text{ and}$$

$$\bar{Y} = \frac{\Sigma Y}{s} = \frac{76}{8} = 9.50 \quad.$$

With this information, we find that the intercept is equal to

$$a_Y = 9.50 - (1.27)(9.00)$$
$$= 9.50 - 11.43 = -1.93 \quad.$$

The intercept, $a_Y = -1.93$, is the point at which the best-fit straight line intersects the Y axis. The intercept seldom makes psychological sense, although instances do occur where the intercept has theoretical importance. Here, if one were to describe the intercept in terms of the variables used, it would indicate that 0 items ($X = 0$) would take *minus* 1.93 exposures to learn! The real value of the intercept, however, lies in its use in the construction of the best-fit straight line relating the independent and dependent variables.

The Equation for the Best-Fit Straight Line. By substituting the calculated values for a_Y and b_Y in equation (12-2), we can express the best-fit straight line as a formula. Specifically,

$$Y' = a_Y + (b_Y)(X)$$
$$= -1.93 + (1.27)(X) \quad.$$

We can now use this equation to locate points on a graph so that a straight line can be drawn between them. We need a minimum of two points to accomplish this task. It is usually a good idea to choose two points that are widely spaced so the regression line can be placed on the graph with reasonable accuracy. Arbitrarily, in this example we use $X = 3$ and $X = 15$. By substituting $X = 3$ in the formula for Y', we find

$$Y' = -1.93 + (1.27)(3)$$
$$= -1.93 + 3.81 = 1.88 \quad.$$

Substituting $X = 15$,

$$Y' = -1.93 + (1.27)(15)$$
$$= -1.93 + 19.05 = 17.12 \quad.$$

Refer back to Figure 12-4, where the eight data points and the best-fit straight line are plotted. The two points we used in drawing the linear function ($X = 3$, $Y' = 1.88$; $X = 15$, $Y' = 17.12$) are indicated by open circles on the line. As a further check on placing a line you are drawing, make sure the line passes through the point representing the means of the two variables $(X = \bar{X} = 9.00; Y' = \bar{Y} = 9.50)$. This will always be the case for the line of best fit.[5]

THE STATISTICAL TEST OF THE SLOPE

The procedures outlined in the last section can be used in the drawing of best-fit lines through means obtained from experiments or pairs of scores obtained from correlational studies. The statistical assessment of how well the regression line actually describes, or fits, the data involves different procedures for the two kinds of data. In this section, we present the procedures appropriate for the analysis of *experimental data,* where the X variable refers to the treatment levels and the Y variable to the treatment means. We consider the statistical assessment of the goodness of fit with correlational data in Chapter 13.

We estimate the slope of the best-fit straight line from the data of an experiment. Because of experimental error, it is entirely possible that the observed slope of the line is not statistically different from 0, a slope that represents the *absence* of a linear relationship between the X and Y variables. Several procedures are available for testing the hypothesis that the slope of the linear function in the population is 0. When the data come from an experiment—as these do—the hypothesis of 0 slope can easily be evaluated with procedures known collectively as **trend analysis.**

As we have mentioned several times in previous chapters, the results from experiments in which a quantitative independent variable has been manipulated are analyzed with an eye towards the overall shape of the function relating the independent and dependent variables. Usually, a straight line is considered first, followed by the examination (if necessary) of more complicated functions, which are referred to as **higher-order trends.** We will concentrate on the statistical analysis of linear trend for the sake of simplicity and clarity, but you should realize that higher-order trends can be analyzed as well.[6]

---

[5] You can verify this fact by substituting $\bar{X}$ into the linear equation and solving for Y'. That is,

$$Y' = -1.93 + (1.27)(9.00)$$
$$= -1.93 + 11.43 = 9.50 = \bar{Y} \ .$$

[6] If you are interested in a more thorough treatment of trend analysis, see *Design and Analysis* (pp. 113–132).

Computational Formulas

The statistical assessment of trend is accomplished by means of the same methods and procedures we used to analyze single-df comparisons involving *qualitative* manipulations. As you will recall from Chapter 6, where these comparisons were originally discussed, the heart of these analyses is the set of coefficients constructed for extracting specific information from the treatment means. Coefficients will be used here, but it will not be necessary to construct specialized coefficients—this has been done by your friendly statistician and the coefficients are generally available in tables. Because much of the material involved in trend analysis duplicates that in Chapter 6, however, we will cover the procedures only briefly. We suggest that you review the relevant portions of Chapter 6 if necessary to fill in the details.

Linear Coefficients. **Linear coefficients,** c_i, describe a perfectly straight line. If there are $a = 3$ treatment conditions, for example, a set of linear coefficients consists of

$$
\begin{array}{cccc}
 & a_1 & a_2 & a_3 \\
c_i: & -1 & 0 & +1
\end{array} \quad .
$$

Note that the coefficients sum to 0, a necessary requirement of coefficients in general; also, they must reflect a straight line.[7] Any set of numbers may be used as long as these two requirements are met. Examples of acceptable sets when $a = 3$ are $(-2, 0, +2)$, $(-1/2, 0, +1/2)$, and $(+1, 0, -1)$. The last set is different from the others, since it reflects a straight line with a *negative* slope while the others reflect straight lines with *positive* slopes. Happily, slopes of either direction will extract the same information from the data because of a squaring operation in the computational formula for the sum of squares. The critical aspect of the coefficients is the linear relationship reflected in the coefficients themselves. Some examples of linear coefficients for larger numbers of treatment conditions are these:

$$
\begin{aligned}
&\text{for } a = 4, (-3, -1, +1, +3); \\
&\text{for } a = 5, (-2, -1, 0, +1, +2); \text{ and} \\
&\text{for } a = 6, (-5, -3, -1, +1, +3, +5) \quad .
\end{aligned}
$$

Note that each set of coefficients sums to 0 and if plotted describes a straight line.

---

[7] You can demonstrate this quality by plotting the coefficients on graph paper, spacing the levels of factor A equally on the horizontal axis, and placing the values of the coefficients on the vertical axis.

Linear coefficients for experiments up to $a = 10$ treatment conditions are listed in Table 3 of Appendix A.[8] Also listed are coefficients for higher-order trends, but these are not of interest to us in this discussion. For the analysis of linear trend, we simply use the coefficients designated "linear" for the appropriate number of treatment conditions.

Sum of Squares. The sum of squares associated with linear trend is obtained by means of the general formula for single-df comparisons. From Chapter 6,

$$SS_{A_{\text{linear}}} = \frac{[\Sigma \ (c_i)(A_i)]^2}{s \, [\Sigma \ (c_i)^2]} \quad , \tag{12-7}$$

where c_i represents the linear coefficients, A_i the treatment sums associated with each coefficient, and s the number of observations in each treatment condition.[9]

Analysis of Variance. We evaluate the linear effect in exactly the same manner we would evaluate any other comparison. First, we transform the sum of squares into a mean square. More specifically,

$$MS_{A_{\text{linear}}} = \frac{SS_{A_{\text{linear}}}}{df_{A_{\text{linear}}}} \quad , \tag{12-8}$$

where $SS_{A_{\text{linear}}}$ is given by equation (12-7) and $df_{A_{\text{linear}}} = 1$. We form the F ratio by dividing the linear mean square by the appropriate error term:

$$F_{\text{linear}} = \frac{MS_{A_{\text{linear}}}}{MS_{\text{error}}} \quad . \tag{12-9}$$

The MS_{error} is the error term appropriate for evaluating the overall treatment effect (MS_A). For the single-factor between-subjects design,

$$MS_{\text{error}} = MS_{S/A} \quad ,$$

while for the corresponding within-subjects design,

$$MS_{\text{error}} = MS_{A \times S} \quad .$$

---

[8] These coefficients assume that the treatment levels are equally spaced, for example, retention intervals of 1, 2, and 3 days; exposure intervals of 50, 250, and 450 milliseconds; and noise levels of 20, 50, and 80 decibels. If the intervals are not equal (for example 1, 2, and 4 days; 50, 200, and 500 milliseconds; and 20, 40, and 80 decibels), you will have to construct a set of coefficients for this particular situation. The procedure for calculating linear coefficients is described in *Design and Analysis* (pp. 581–588). Intervals do not have to be equally spaced to enable you to calculate the equation for the line of best fit, however, because the formulas we discussed for calculating the regression line account for the spacing of the levels of the independent variable. The complication only arises in the statistical analysis of trend.

[9] Note that we have reverted back to the notation we originally used to designate required quantities in the analysis of single-factor designs. We did so to make this discussion consistent with the discussion of the analysis of comparisons in Chapter 6.

The statistical hypotheses tested by this analysis are these:

H_0: No linear relationship exists among the treatment population means;
H_1: A linear relationship is present.

The decision rules for deciding between these two hypotheses are formed in the usual manner. That is,

If the obtained value of F exceeds or equals $F(1, df_{error})$, reject the null hypothesis; otherwise, do not reject the null hypothesis.

We find the critical value of F by setting α at the desired level of significance and finding the appropriate value of F in the F table.

A Numerical Example

As an example, consider the data originally presented in Table 8-4 (p. 183) and depicted graphically in Figure 12-1B (p. 294). In this experiment, subjects learned and recalled a series of six lists separated by two-day intervals. In this case, list number (1, 2, 3, and so on) is the independent variable. An examination of the outcome of this experiment clearly suggests a downward linear trend. All the information we need for calculating the linear sum of squares is presented in Table 12-3. We are now ready to conduct an analysis of linear trend.

We have arranged Table 12-3 to facilitate the preliminary calculations required for substitution in the computational formula for the linear sum of squares. The treatment sums, which are based on $s = 8$ subjects, are listed in column 2. The linear coefficients for $a = 6$ treatment conditions, obtained from Table 3 of Appendix A, are given in column 3. The products resulting from the multiplication of each treatment sum by its corresponding linear coefficient are given in column 4. The squares of each coefficient are indicated in column 5. The sums of columns 4 and 5 are two of the values we substitute in equation (12-7); the remaining quantity is the number of subjects ($s = 8$). Performing the indicated operations on these three values, we obtain

$$SS_{A_{linear}} = \frac{[\Sigma (c_i)(A_i)]^2}{s[\Sigma (c_i)^2]}$$

$$= \frac{(-256)^2}{8(70)} = \frac{65,536}{560} = 117.03 \quad .$$

This final quantity is entered in the analysis of variance summary table presented in Table 12-4.

TABLE 12-3   Preliminary Calculations for the Analysis of Linear Trend

1. Levels (a_i)	2. Treatment Sums (A_i)	3. Coefficients (c_i)	4. (Coefficient) × (Sum) $(c_i)(A_i)$	5. Squared Coefficients $(c_i)^2$
a_1	49	-5	$(-5)(49) = -245$	$(-5)^2 = 25$
a_2	37	-3	$(-3)(37) = -111$	$(-3)^2 = 9$
a_3	20	-1	$(-1)(20) = -20$	$(-1)^2 = 1$
a_4	13	$+1$	$(+1)(13) = +13$	$(+1)^2 = 1$
a_5	14	$+3$	$(+3)(14) = +42$	$(+3)^2 = 9$
a_6	13	$+5$	$(+5)(13) = +65$	$(+5)^2 = \underline{25}$
Sum	Not Needed	0	$\Sigma(c_i)(A_i) = -256$	$\Sigma(c_i)^2 = 70$

The sum of squares for the error term, which was calculated in Chapter 8 (see Table 8-5, p. 185), is also presented in the summary table. There is 1 degree of freedom for the linear sum of squares and 35 degrees of freedom for the error sum of squares. The mean squares are obtained by dividing each sum of squares by the appropriate number of degrees of freedom. The F ratio becomes

$$F_{\text{linear}} = \frac{117.03}{2.79} = 41.95 \quad .$$

We find the critical value of F at $\alpha = .05$ by entering the F table for $df_{num.} = 1$ and $df_{denom.} = 35$. This value is approximately $F_\alpha = 4.17$. (Since the actual F_α is not listed in the table, we use a compromise F_α for $df_{denom.} = 30$.) The decision rules can now be stated as follows:

If the obtained value of F exceeds or is equal to $F_\alpha = 4.17$, reject the null hypothesis; otherwise, do not reject the null hypothesis.

Since the obtained F ratio exceeds this critical value, we reject the null hypothesis and conclude that linear trend is present in these data.

TABLE 12-4   A Summary of the Linear Trend Analysis

Source	SS	df	MS	F
Linear	117.03	1	117.03	41.95*
$A \times S$	97.75	35	2.79	

*$p < .05$

The Best-Fit Straight Line

Since we have found a significant linear trend in these data, we are interested
in calculating the line of best fit and placing it on a graph along with the actual
treatment means. To calculate the linear regression line, we will need to
arrange the data in pairs consisting of the values of the independent variable
associated with each treatment condition (the X variable) and the corresponding treatment means (the Y variable). For this example, the X scores
are the numbers of the lists—1 through 6—and the Y scores are the treatment
means, which we can calculate from the treatment sums in Table 8-4. All the
information we need for obtaining the linear regression line is given in Table
12-5.

The slope of the best-fit straight line is given by equation 12-3 and requires
the calculation of SP_{XY} and SS_X. We find SP_{XY} from equation 12-5 as
follows:[10]

$$SP_{XY} = \Sigma (X)(Y) - \frac{(\Sigma X)(\Sigma Y)}{s}$$

$$= 47.94 - \frac{(21)(18.27)}{6}$$

$$= 47.94 - \frac{383.67}{6} = 47.94 - 63.95 = -16.01 \quad .$$

From equation 12-4,

$$SS_X = \Sigma (X)^2 - \frac{(\Sigma X)^2}{s}$$

$$= 91 - \frac{(21)^2}{6}$$

$$= 91 - \frac{441}{6} = 91 - 73.50 = 17.50 \quad .$$

We now calculate the slope:

$$b_Y = \frac{SP_{XY}}{SS_X}$$

$$= \frac{-16.01}{17.50} = -.91 \quad .$$

---

[10] Keep in mind the changed meaning of s in these calculations. In the statistical analysis of
linear trend, covered in the last section, s referred to the number of scores in each treatment
condition—in that case, $s = 8$. In the calculation of the regression line, s refers to the number of
paired X and Y values. In this case, there are six pairs of treatment conditions and treatment
means, and $s = 6$.

TABLE 12-5 The Preliminary Calculations for Determining the Linear Regression Line

List Number (X)	Mean Recall (Y)	Products of X and Y (X)(Y)
1	6.13	6.13
2	4.63	9.26
3	2.50	7.50
4	1.63	6.52
5	1.75	8.75
6	1.63	9.78
$\Sigma X = 21$	$\Sigma Y = 18.27$	$\Sigma (X)(Y) = 47.94$
$\Sigma (X)^2 = 91$	$\Sigma (Y)^2 = 73.65$	
$\bar{X} = 3.50$	$\bar{Y} = 3.05$	

The intercept, a_Y, is calculated from equation 12-6:

$$a_Y = \bar{Y} - (b_Y)(\bar{X})$$
$$= 3.05 - (-.91)(3.50)$$
$$= 3.05 - (-3.19) = 3.05 + 3.19 = 6.24 \quad .$$

From equation 12-2, we find the best-fit straight line to be

$$Y' = a_Y + (b_Y)(X)$$
$$= 6.24 + (-.91)(X) \quad .$$

This line is drawn through the treatment means in Figure 12-1B.

The Proportion of Treatment Variation Due to Linear Trend

We can obtain a simple index that supplements the test of significance of linear trend by determining the **proportion of variation due to linear trend** of the treatment means associated with the best-fit straight line. Specifically,

$$\text{proportion variation} = \frac{SS_{A_{\text{linear}}}}{SS_A} \quad . \tag{12-10}$$

From Table 12-4 (for $SS_{A_{\text{linear}}}$) and from Table 8-5, p. 185 (for SS_A), we determine

$$\frac{117.03}{143.92} = .81 \quad .$$

This index indicates that approximately 81 percent of the variation observed among the six treatment means is attributed to the linear function.

Higher-Order Trends

You may have noticed in addition to the pronounced linear trend that a tendency also exists for the means to stop dropping and to begin to level off for the last three lists. The presence of a "bend" in the data suggests a second trend, or factor, one that specifies this particular aspect of the data. The statistical analysis of this and other trends follows the same steps as in the analysis of linear trend—the only quantity that changes is the set of coefficients, and these are available in such tables as Table 3 of Appendix A. As with the linear function, curves of best fit corresponding to higher-order trends can be constructed. In addition, trend components can be combined to provide a better fit of the data than that provided by any one trend considered separately.

If you are curious about these higher-order trends, refer to *Design and Analysis* (pp. 113–123). A researcher is usually interested in these trends when the theory underlying the interpretation of the results specifies that they might be present. Where no such theory applies, a researcher might want to analyze the data further anyway, especially when the discrepancy between the treatment means and the regression line is fairly large. In our example, the discrepancy is relatively small (only 19 percent of the variation among the treatment means is not accounted for by the linear function). Determining whether this discrepancy from the regression line is due to the presence of higher-order trends or merely reflects experimental error requires an additional statistical test, found in *Design and Analysis* (pp. 126–128).

Limitations of Trend Analysis

It is important to remember that trend analysis and linear regression are based on only those points on the manipulated continuum that were actually included in the study. If several points are represented and they are not too widely separated along the assumed continuum, then one can safely assume that any trend detected in the data would be corroborated if additional levels of factor *A* were included that fall between those already chosen. On the other hand, we should always be cautious concerning any inferences drawn about the shape of the function *beyond* or outside the extreme points included in the study.

Consider, for instance, the present example. Clearly a linear trend is present in these data. But would you be willing to predict performance on list 7 or on list 8 on the basis of the linear trend observed for the first six lists? We hope not, because eventually the downward sloping straight line would predict zero recall and then *negative* recall values thereafter. In fact, the regression equation based on these data points predicts a recall of *minus* .13 responses on list 7! The negative value is not possible logically.

The data we have analyzed were taken from a much larger experiment in which subjects received a total of *thirty-six* lists, thirty more than the first six with which we have been concerned. The data from these additional lists (increasing levels of the independent variable) show no further change either upward or downward, with recall performance stabilizing around 1.0 for lists 7 through 36. Thus, while the linear function was descriptive of the *first six levels* of the independent variable (lists 1–6), the suggestion of leveling off was in fact a more accurate statement of the outcome of the experiment when the manipulation was extended beyond six lists.

Despite these limitations, however, analysis of linear trend (and higher-order trends as well) occupies an important place in the analysis of experiments in which the manipulation is a quantitative variable. We are simply urging you to be aware of potential problems that may arise if you use this analysis too zealously and without sufficient thought!

SUMMARY

A straight line can be used to describe or summarize a set of data obtained from an experiment in which a quantitative independent variable was manipulated. Specific procedures permit the drawing of the line of best fit—the linear regression line—through the data points, and the formal specification of the linear function in terms of an equation for that line.

A straight line can be drawn through any set of data produced by a quantitative manipulation. The critical question, however, concerns the actual degree to which the regression line fits or describes the data. We presented a statistical analysis that provides one answer to this important question. The analysis of linear trend determines whether the linear trend exhibited by the data can be reasonably attributed to experimental error. The analysis uses a set of specialized coefficients designed for trend analysis in conjunction with the general formula for analytical comparisons that we considered originally in Chapter 6. A second answer to the question is provided by an index that indicates the proportion of treatment variation associated with the linear trend. This information, together with the results of the statistical analysis, indicates just how well a linear function accounts for the treatment variation observed in the experiment.

The use of a straight line to describe the results of an experiment does have certain limitations. The approach is totally dependent on the specific levels of the independent variable included in the experiment. If the number of treatment conditions is sufficiently large to enable the researcher to feel safe in drawing a straight line through potential levels falling between those chosen, it is probable that no danger exists. On the other hand, it is dangerous to extend the linear function (or any higher-order function, for that matter) *beyond* the range of values of the independent variable actually appearing in the experiment. Despite this potential limitation, however, the use of a linear function to describe a set of data represents an important technique in the analysis of experimental results where a quantitative independent variable has been manipulated.

TERMS, CONCEPTS, AND SYMBOLS

---

regression line
slope
intercept
Y on X
positive slope
negative slope
Y intercept
best-fit straight line

covariation of X and Y
covariance
sum of products
trend analysis
higher-order trends
linear coefficients
proportion of variation due
  to linear trend

Notation and Basic Calculations

X	ΣX	$\Sigma (X)^2$	$\bar{X}$
Y	ΣY	$\Sigma (Y)^2$	$\bar{Y}$
	$(X)(Y)$	$\Sigma (X)(Y)$	

Other Symbols

a_Y

b_Y

Y'

variance (X)

SS_X

variance (Y)

SS_Y

covariance (X, Y)

SP_{XY}

c_i

$SS_{A_{linear}}$

$df_{A_{linear}}$

$MS_{A_{linear}}$

F_{linear}

MS_{error}

EXERCISES

---

1. A researcher was interested in the effect of increasing a cart's load on the distance subjects would pull the cart. The load was varied in kilograms and the distance was measured in meters. The mean number of meters pulled was calculated for each load and the results are given on p. 318.

Load (Kilograms)	Mean Number of Meters Pulled
1	19
2	21
3	18
4	14
5	6
6	4
7	3

With the information provided, determine the formula for the best-fit straight line.

2. Take the data from problem 1 of Chapter 8 (p. 199) and test the statistical significance of linear trend. Assume that the different task lengths are equally spaced on the length dimension, that is, lengths of 5, 10, 15, 20, and 25. Since there is significant linear trend present in these data, calculate the linear regression line.

Linear Regression: Correlational Data

13

A primary characteristic of correlational research is the absence of a manipulated independent variable. A group of individuals is studied and scores on two response measures are obtained, or, alternatively, responses are taken on these individuals at two different points in time. Whatever differences are observed on the X variable or on the Y variable are due entirely to the whims and designs of nature; essentially none of the observed variations is the result of the intervention of the researcher. This fact greatly limits the researcher's ability to infer causality from correlational studies, but the results of such studies are indispensible to researchers in all fields of psychology.

An important value of correlational research is that it can establish the *possibility* of a causal relationship between two variables. The first causal links between smoking and cancer were correlational, for example. Subse-

quent experiments with direct manipulations in the laboratory were necessary, however, to help establish the causal connection. Correlational studies
can often be conducted where experimental manipulation is either infeasible
or unethical.

Second, correlational data can form the basis for the prediction of future
performance. Proficiency and aptitude tests are frequently used in the selection of job applicants. In this regard, earlier research that presumably established a relationship between scores on the test and actual job success is used
to predict the future success of job applicants. Analogously, academic
achievement tests are used to predict performance in college and graduate
school. The actuarial tables used by insurance companies provide correlational information between various human characteristics—for example,
age, weight, level of education, socioeconomic level, and so on—and longev-
ity. These cheerful statistics are then used in the preparation of rate tables
for insurance policies.

Finally, correlational research serves a useful theoretical function. Such
fields of psychology as personality, clinical, social, and developmental are
dependent on the analysis of correlational data for the creation and development of theories of human functioning. Even in research fields consisting
almost exclusively of experimentation, the argument can be made that correlational analyses have a critical impact on theories based entirely on experimental data. This point is considered more fully at the end of Chapter 14.

SCATTERPLOT

Correlational data consist of pairs of *observations*. In the most common way
of examining and digesting the results of a correlational study, the data are
entered in what is called a **scatterplot.** In a scatterplot, each individual (the
usual observational unit) is plotted according to the two scores that make up
the pair of observations; one of the variables is arranged along the horizontal
axis (the X variable) and the other is represented on the vertical axis (the Y
variable).

To obtain maximum usefulness from a scatterplot, researchers should
follow a number of simple construction rules. First, a scatterplot should be
roughly square in shape—that is, both axes should be approximately the
same length. Second, one should try to arrange the scales so that each one
begins in the lower left-hand corner with a convenient number a little smaller
than the lowest score in the data set and ends with a convenient number a

little larger than the highest score in the set. This arrangement guarantees that most of the scatterplot will be used to represent the pairs of data points.

Examples

Two examples of scatterplots based on actual data are presented in Figure 13-1. Figure 13-1A depicts the relationship between the scores on a test of quantitative skills (represented by the X axis) taken by students on the first day of a statistics course (a great way to begin a stat course!) and their combined scores on two midterm examinations (represented by the Y axis). Be sure you understand how each pair of scores is charted in the scatterplot. One student, for example, obtained a score of 11 on the quantitative test and a combined score of 128 on the two midterms. We charted that person's scores in the scatterplot by finding 11 on the X axis and then moving upward vertically on a line drawn through $X = 11$ until we reached 128 on the Y scale, where a dot was placed on the graph. The remaining students were plotted in a similar manner. Note that we shortened both axes to create a square scatterplot just large enough to "capture" all the data points.

What information can you derive from Figure 13-1A? First, a generally positive linear relationship exists between the two variables; that is, students with high scores on the quantitative test tended to receive high midterm scores and students with low scores on the quantitative test tended to receive low midterm scores. This relationship is represented by a best-fit straight line, also plotted in the figure. Using this line, we could predict a student's probable performance in this course simply by knowing his or her quantitative score. However, a discrepancy exists between these predicted scores—represented by the straight line—and the actual scores observed in this class—the data points. The line *is* the line of best fit, but it does not fit the data too well. The discrepancy between the predicted score and the actual score is referred to as the **error of prediction,** and is used in the evaluation of the significance of the trend found with these data. We will be concerned with this problem later in this chapter.[1]

Figure 13-1B presents additional data obtained from this statistics course, namely, the relationship between a student's performance on the first midterm (represented by the X axis) and his or her performance on the second

---

[1] You may have noticed that the students tend to "bunch" together with the higher scores on the quantitative test. This sort of bunching at the extreme values of either variable can cause some problems in the interpretation of the data. If you ever obtain data like this, you should probably seek advice from someone familiar with the statistical interpretation of correlational data.

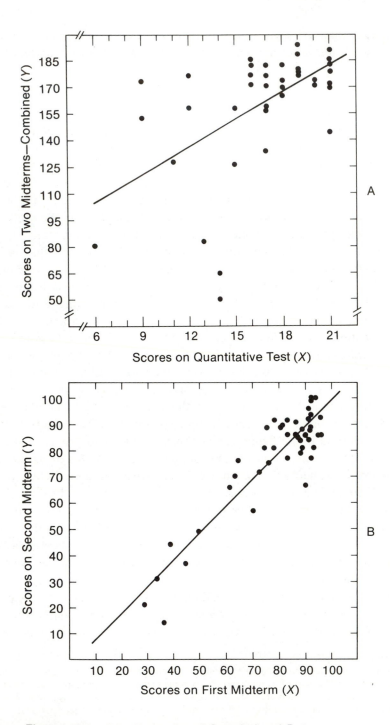

Figure 13-1. Two Examples of Correlational Data.

midterm (represented by the Y axis). In contrast with the previous example, this relationship is more well-defined and consistent. Fewer students deviate greatly from the regression line.

Designation of Variables

For regression problems with experimental data, the manipulated variable is designated as the X variable and the dependent variable is designated as the Y variable. With correlational data, where both variables are response measures, the designation is often arbitrary, although there are situations in which certain rules are followed. We will consider three.

If one of the variables is to be used to predict a subject's performance on the other, then X will refer to the variable used to predict and Y to the variable to be predicted. Figure 13-1A is such an example, where we could use the scores on the quantitative test to predict scores on the midterms. Predicting success on a job (Y variable) on the basis of an aptitude test (X variable) is another example.

If two variables are separated in time, then the X designation is used for the earlier measure. This is why in the scatterplot of Figure 13-1B we placed the scores on the first midterm on the horizontal axis (X) and the scores on the second midterm on the vertical axis (Y). Finally, if one of the variables is thought to be the ''cause'' of the other behavior, then the ''causal'' variable is designated X and the ''dependent'' variable is designated Y. An example would be the number of cigarettes smoked daily (X variable) and blood pressure (Y variable). Any decision concerning causality based entirely on correlational data is, of course, always difficult to defend.

LINEAR REGRESSION

We will now describe the procedure for calculating the formula for the best-fit straight line.

Computational Formulas

The procedures for constructing the best-fit straight line with correlational data are nearly identical to those for use with experimental data covered in Chapter 12. The only difference is the meaning of the X and Y scores. In Chapter 12, the data were from experiments; X referred to the values of the

TABLE 13-1   The Heights and Weights of Fifteen Males (Ages 17–19)

Subject	Height (cm) (X)	Weight (kg) (Y)	Product (X)(Y)
1	150	56	(150)(56) = 8,400
2	154	54	(154)(54) = 8,316
3	168	55	(168)(55) = 9,240
4	162	58	(162)(58) = 9,396
5	152	49	(152)(49) = 7,448
6	155	64	(155)(64) = 9,920
7	178	71	(178)(71) = 12,638
8	163	62	(163)(62) = 10,106
9	173	57	(173)(57) = 9,861
10	179	75	(179)(75) = 13,425
11	174	80	(174)(80) = 13,920
12	165	60	(165)(60) = 9,900
13	182	75	(182)(75) = 13,650
14	183	70	(183)(70) = 12,810
15	160	60	(160)(60) = 9,600
	$\Sigma X = 2,498$	$\Sigma Y = 946$	$\Sigma (X)(Y) = 158,630$
	$\Sigma (X)^2 = 417,750$	$\Sigma (Y)^2 = 60,822$	
	$\bar{X} = 166.53$	$\bar{Y} = 63.07$	
	$\hat{\sigma}_X^2 = 124.98^a$	$\hat{\sigma}_Y^2 = 82.92$	
	$\hat{\sigma}_X = 11.18$	$\hat{\sigma}_Y = 9.11$	

[a] $\hat{\sigma}^2$ is the symbol for estimating variance ($df = s - 1$) and $\hat{\sigma}$ is the symbol for the corresponding standard deviation. (See Chapter 16.)

independent variable and Y referred to the treatment means. In this chapter, the data consist of pairs of scores obtained from a sample of subjects—no manipulated variable is involved. Thus, X refers to the scores of one set (the X variable) and Y refers to the scores of the other set (the Y variable). We will consider the formulas presented in Chapter 12 again without elaboration in the context of a numerical example.

A Numerical Example

Suppose we were interested in the relationship between two relatively innocuous characteristics, height and weight. Table 13-1 contains pairs of scores for fifteen males between 17 and 19 years of age. Arbitrarily, a sub-

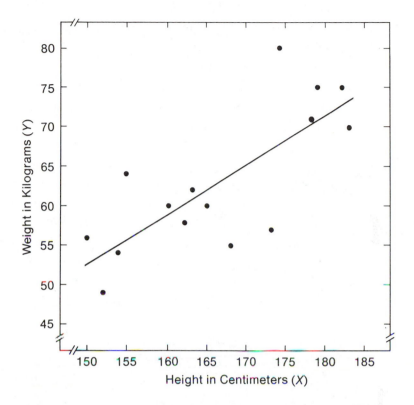

Figure 13-2. The Linear Relationship Between Height (*X* Variable) and Weight (*Y* Variable).

ject's height (measured in centimeters) is designated as X and his corresponding weight (measured in kilograms) is designated as Y. As we already noted, the relationship between X and Y (height and weight) is most easily revealed when each subject is charted in a scatterplot. A scatterplot of these data is presented in Figure 13-2. Remember, we chart the first subject (height = 150 centimeters, and weight = 56 kilograms) in the scatterplot by moving along the horizontal axis to $X = 150$ centimeters and then upward vertically to $Y = 56$ kilograms, where we place a dot. We plot each of the remaining subjects on the graph in the same way. The completed scatterplot contains a total of fifteen points (one point for each subject listed in Table 13-1).

The first step in constructing the regression line is to complete the preliminary calculations. These calculations are listed in the bottom rows of Table 13-1. Next, we substitute data in the relevant computational formulas. We will go through these procedures step by step.

We calculate the slope of the best-fit straight line first, using the quantities specified in equation (12-3):

$$b_Y = \frac{SP_{XY}}{SS_X} \quad .$$

From the preliminary calculations summarized in Table 13-1, we find

$$SP_{XY} = \Sigma (X)(Y) - \frac{(\Sigma X)(\Sigma Y)}{s}$$

$$= 158,630 - \frac{(2,498)(946)}{15}$$

$$= 158,630 - \frac{2,363,108}{15} = 158,630 - 157,540.53$$

$$= 1,089.47; \text{ and}$$

$$SS_X = \Sigma (X)^2 - \frac{(\Sigma X)^2}{s}$$

$$= 417,750 - \frac{(2,498)^2}{15}$$

$$= 417,750 - \frac{6,240,004}{15} = 417,750 - 416,000.27$$

$$= 1,749.73 \quad .$$

Bringing these two quantities together, we obtain

$$b_Y = \frac{1,089.47}{1,749.73} = .62 \quad .$$

Next, using equation (12-6), we obtain the Y intercept:

$$a_Y = \bar{Y} - (b_Y)(\bar{X})$$
$$= 63.07 - (.62)(166.53)$$
$$= 63.07 - 103.25 = -40.18 \quad .$$

Substituting the estimates of the slope and intercept into equation (12-2), we obtain the equation for the regression line relating weight to height for this sample of young males. That is,

$$Y' = a_Y + (b_Y)(X)$$
$$= -40.18 + (.62)(X) \quad .$$

In order to draw this regression line, we just choose two convenient values of X (height) and substitute them in the formula for the best-fit straight line. For example, if a person's height is 150 centimeters ($X = 150$), his weight is predicted to be

$$Y' = -40.18 + (.62)(150) = -40.18 + 93.00 = 52.82 \text{ kilograms};$$

and if his height is 180 centimeters ($X = 180$), his weight is predicted to be

$$Y' = -40.18 + (.62)(180) = -40.18 + 111.60 = 71.42 \text{ kilograms} \quad .$$

Marking these two points on the scatterplot permits us to draw the regression line and to examine visually how well it fits. The regression line calculated above is indicated in Figure 13-2. It appears that a straight line provides a reasonable summary of the relationship between height and weight, but that this particular relationship is far from perfect.

As part of the descriptive phase of a regression (or correlational) analysis, variances (or standard deviations) of the two sets of scores are usually calculated and reported along with the two means and the regression information we have just obtained. The means, variances, and standard deviations for the data in this example are presented at the bottom of Table 13-1.

A VARIANCE INTERPRETATION OF LINEAR REGRESSION[2]

You have seen how we can use the same general procedures to calculate the best-fit straight line with both experimental and correlational data. At some point in dealing with correlational data, you will also need to evaluate the significance of the slope of the regression line, that is, to determine whether the slope constant, b_Y, differs from 0. (Recall that a slope of $b_Y = 0$ indicates that no linear relationship exists between the two variables.) At this stage the statistical procedures for experimental and correlational data diverge and require different formulas and calculations. In Chapter 12, we showed that the significance of the slope is evaluated in exactly the same manner we have tested the significance of single-df comparisons in the past. However, this procedure cannot be used with correlational data.

This section has two purposes. One is to show how the sum of squares of the Y scores can be divided into components with linear regression. The other is to describe a statistical test by which we determine whether b_Y is significantly different from 0. The calculations involved in this test use quantities we have already discussed at some length, namely, SS_X, SS_Y, and SP_{XY}. What is new is the logic of the operations and the ways in which these quantities are combined.

---

[2] This section contains some complicated arguments and may be omitted without seriously affecting the main purpose of this chapter. The statistical test of the hypothesis that the slope of the linear regression line is 0, which is described in this section, can be performed with an equivalent and simpler test involving the correlation coefficient, which we discuss in Chapter 14.

We use the regression line to predict Y from a knowledge of X. Without this knowledge, our best estimate of a subject's score is the mean of the sample, $\overline{Y}$. The deviation of the Y scores from this mean reflects the magnitude of the prediction error when we have absolutely no other information on which to base our predictions. A knowledge of a subject's X score and the linear relationship between the X and Y variables permits us to predict with more accuracy.

Component Sums of Squares Based on the Y Scores

Basic Deviations. The total variation under scrutiny is the variability of the Y scores. We want to determine the portion of this variability that is attributable to linear regression—predictable from a knowledge of a subject's X score—and the portion that is not. Once we make that determination, we can ask whether the portion attributed to linear regression is significantly different from that expected if chance factors alone were operating. As with the analysis of variance, the key factors in this line of reasoning are basic deviation scores. If we let

$$Y_i = \text{a subject's score on the } Y \text{ measure,}$$
$$\overline{Y} = \text{the mean of the } Y \text{ scores, and}$$
$$Y_i' = \text{the subject's } predicted \text{ } Y \text{ score based on}$$
$$\text{the linear regression line,}$$

we are able to express the following important relationship:

$$Y_i - \overline{Y} = (Y_i' - \overline{Y}) + (Y_i - Y_i') \quad . \tag{13-1}$$

In words, the deviation of a Y score from the mean $(Y_i - \overline{Y})$ is made up of two component deviations:

1. The deviation of the predicted Y score from the mean $(Y_i' - \overline{Y})$

2. The deviation of the Y score from the predicted value $(Y_i - Y_i')$

The first component represents the degree to which linear regression accounts for variation among the Y scores, while the second component represents the degree to which it does not.

The relationship expressed in equation (13-1) is represented geometrically in Figure 13-3. Notice first the location of one of the pairs of scores, X_i, Y_i. This pair is located at the intersection of two lines, one extending perpendicularly from X_i on the X axis (the unbroken vertical line in the figure) and

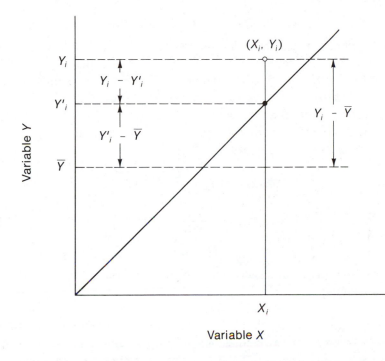

Figure 13-3. A Geometric Representation of Equation (13-1).

the other extending perpendicularly from Y_i on the Y axis (the uppermost dashed horizontal line in the figure). The point of intersection is labeled (X_i, Y_i) and is indicated by an unfilled circle. Next, notice the point at which the vertical line drawn from X_i intersects with the regression line. This point is indicated by a filled circle. The dashed line extending from the point of intersection meets the vertical axis at Y' and represents the Y score predicted from X_i and the regression line. Finally, the bottommost dashed line indicates the position of the mean of the Y scores ($\overline{Y}$) on the vertical axis. An examination of the vertical distances between the three dashed lines clearly reveals the meaning of equation (13-1). Specifically, the distance between the top and bottom dashed lines represents the deviation of Y_i from $\overline{Y}$ and is obviously made up of two component parts, the distance between the middle and bottom dashed lines ($Y'_i - \overline{Y}$) and the distance between the top and middle dashed lines ($Y_i - Y'_i$).

Computational Formulas. The relationship expressed in equation (13-1) for individual Y scores can be extended to sums of squares. That is,

$$SS_Y = SS_{\text{lin. regr.}} + SS_{\text{residual}} \quad , \tag{13-2}$$

where SS_Y refers to the sum of the squared deviations of the Y scores from their mean, $SS_{\text{lin. regr.}}$ refers to the sum of squares reflecting variability accounted for by linear regression, and SS_{residual} refers to the sum of squares *not* accounted for by linear regression—the **residual sum of squares.** (This last sum of squares reflects the magnitude of the error involved in predicting Y from X on the basis of the regression function.) The computational formulas for the three sums of squares are as follows:

$$SS_Y = \Sigma\,(Y)^2 - \frac{(\Sigma\,Y)^2}{s} \quad , \tag{13-3}$$

$$SS_{\text{lin. regr.}} = \frac{(SP_{XY})^2}{SS_X} \quad , \text{ and} \tag{13-4}$$

$$SS_{\text{residual}} = SS_Y - SS_{\text{lin. regr.}} \quad . \tag{13-5}$$

As we promised, the formulas contain familiar quantities. We are ready for a numerical example.

A Numerical Example. An inspection of the three computational formulas indicates the need for the two sums of squares (SS_X and SS_Y) and the sum of products (SP_{XY}). We continue to use the height-weight example, since we have calculated two of these quantities already. The one quantity we have not yet obtained from the data presented in Table 13-1 (p. 324) is the SS_Y. Substituting in equation (13-3), we find

$$SS_Y = \Sigma\,(Y)^2 - \frac{(\Sigma\,Y)^2}{s}$$

$$= 60{,}822 - \frac{(946)^2}{15}$$

$$= 60{,}822 - \frac{894{,}916}{15} = 60{,}822 - 59{,}661.07$$

$$= 1{,}160.93 \quad .$$

The other two quantities have been calculated previously (p. 326):

$$SS_X = 1{,}749.73 \text{ and } SP_{XY} = 1{,}089.47 \quad .$$

All that remains is to substitute these quantities in the appropriate computational formulas.

Having calculated the SS_Y, we next determine the sum of squares associated with linear regression. That is,

$$SS_{\text{lin. regr.}} = \frac{(SP_{XY})^2}{SS_X}$$

$$= \frac{(1,089.47)^2}{1,749.73}$$

$$= \frac{1,186,944.88}{1,749.73} = 678.36 \quad .$$

Finally, we are able to calculate the error sum of squares:

$$SS_{\text{residual}} = SS_Y - SS_{\text{lin. regr.}}$$

$$= 1,160.93 - 678.36 = 482.57 \quad .$$

These three sums of squares are entered in the second column of Table 13-2.

The Analysis of Variance

We will now use the two component sums of squares to test the hypothesis that the slope of the linear regression line is 0. This hypothesis is equivalent to stating that the two variables are unrelated or uncorrelated. (We consider correlation in Chapter 14 and present a simpler but equivalent procedure to test the hypothesis.)

Degrees of Freedom. The degrees of freedom associated with SS_Y are 1 less than the number of Y scores, that is,

$$df_Y = s - 1 \quad . \tag{13-6}$$

Without attempting to explain the reason, we will simply state that 1 degree of freedom is associated with linear regression, or

$$df_{\text{lin. regr.}} = 1 \quad . \tag{13-7}$$

TABLE 13-2   A Summary of the Test for Zero Slope

Source	SS	df	MS	F
Linear Regression	678.36	1	678.36	18.27*
Residual	482.57	13	37.12	
Total (Y)	1,160.93	14		

*$p < .05$

By subtraction, the degrees of freedom for the residual sum of squares are found to be

$$df_{residual} = df_Y - df_{lin.\ regr.}$$
$$= (s - 1) - 1$$
$$= s - 2 \quad . \tag{13-8}$$

In the present example,

$$df_Y = 15 - 1 = 14 \quad ,$$
$$df_{lin.\ regr.} = 1, \text{ and}$$
$$df_{residual} = 15 - 2 = 13 \quad .$$

These numbers are entered in the third column of the summary table.

Mean Squares. In general, we transform sums of squares into variances (or mean squares) simply by dividing each sum of squares by the appropriate number of degrees of freedom. To illustrate,

$$MS_{lin.\ regr.} = \frac{SS_{lin.\ regr.}}{df_{lin.\ regr.}}$$
$$= \frac{678.36}{1} = 678.36; \text{ and}$$

$$MS_{residual} = \frac{SS_{residual}}{df_{residual}}$$
$$= \frac{482.57}{13} = 37.12 \quad .$$

The values for these two mean squares are entered in the fourth column of the table.

The F Ratio. The statistical hypotheses are these:

H_0: The population slope is zero;
H_1: The population slope is not zero.

To evaluate the reasonableness of this null hypothesis, we test the significance of the following F ratio:

$$F = \frac{MS_{lin.\ regr.}}{MS_{residual}} \quad . \tag{13-9}$$

If H_0 is true, both mean squares reflect the operation of chance factors, and the F is expected to be approximately 1.0. On the other hand, if H_1 is true, the $MS_{\text{lin. regr.}}$ will be influenced by an additional source of variability—linear regression—and the F is expected to be greater than 1.0. (You will recall a similar line of reasoning when we discussed the use of the F ratio in the analysis of data from experiments. If this reasoning seems hazy, you might want to review the discussions of these general procedures in Chapter 3, pp. 52–54, and in Chapter 5, pp. 86–90.)

From the information in Table 13-2, we obtain

$$F = \frac{678.36}{37.12} = 18.27 \quad .$$

We evaluate the significance of this F ratio in the usual way. We obtain the critical value of F from Table 2 in Appendix A by choosing some value for α and locating the F value at the appropriate numerator and denominator degrees of freedom. In this example, $df = 1$ and 13, respectively. At $\alpha = .05$, the critical value of F is 4.67. With this information, we can form the decision rules and take the appropriate action. First, we complete the decision rules:

If the obtained value of F equals or exceeds $F_\alpha = 4.67$, reject the null hypothesis; otherwise, do not reject the null hypothesis.

Since the observed value of F does exceed the critical value, we reject the null hypothesis and conclude that a significant linear relationship is present between height and weight.

In reporting the slope of the best-fit straight line and the results of the statistical test, researchers usually include the square root of the residual mean square, called the **standard error of estimate.** Here,

$$\text{standard error of estimate} = \sqrt{MS_{\text{residual}}} \quad (13\text{-}10)$$

$$= \sqrt{37.12} = 6.09 \quad .$$

The standard error of estimate is analagous to the standard deviation of a set of scores. Both statistics are based on the deviation of scores from some reference point, the mean in the case of the standard deviation and the regression line in the case of the standard error of estimate. The standard error of estimate serves a number of useful functions in regression and correlation, one of which is to estimate the degree of error involved in predicting a Y score from an X score and a regression equation.[3]

---

[3] See Kirk (1978, pp. 136–140) for an elaboration of this particular function of the standard error of estimate.

The Variation Accounted for by Linear Regression

The deviation of the predicted Y scores from the mean of the Y scores is the source of variance accounted for by the regression line. Let's pause for a moment and think about this source of variability. As the predicted scores approach the actual Y scores, the sum of squares based on the regression line ($SS_{\text{lin. regr.}}$) approaches the sum of squares based on the actual Y scores (SS_Y). With this in mind, we can calculate a very simple index that reflects the proportion of variation accounted for by the linear relationship between the X and Y variables. The index consists of

$$\text{explained variability} = \frac{SS_{\text{lin. regr.}}}{SS_Y} \quad . \tag{13-11}$$

Theoretically, this index ranges from 0 when no linear relationship exists between X and Y (when $SS_{\text{lin. regr.}}$ is equal to 0) to 1.00 when a perfect linear relationship exists (when $SS_{\text{lin. regr.}}$ and SS_Y are equal). Using the data from the numerical example, we find that

$$\frac{SS_{\text{lin. regr.}}}{SS_Y} = \frac{678.36}{1,160.93} = .58 \quad ,$$

that is, 58 percent of the variability reflected among the fifteen weights (the Y scores) is accounted for by the linear relationship between height and weight.[4]

It is important to remember that the presence of a significant linear relationship and a sizable proportion of explained variability do not establish a *causal link* between height and weight. This fact represents a limitation usually associated with correlational data, although procedures have been developed to attempt to deal with this problem (see footnote 7, p. 354). On the other hand, the knowledge that a significant linear relationship exists between two variables can be useful in many applied settings and even in the evaluation of theories based largely on data obtained from experiments (see pp. 356–357).

A SECOND REGRESSION LINE

So far we have concerned ourselves with the linear function relating the Y variable to changes in the X variable. This relationship is represented in the

---

[4] This index is algebraically equivalent to the square of the correlation coefficient (r^2), which we consider in Chapter 14.

scatterplot by the regression line and is specified formally by the regression equation. But a *second* regression line is possible with correlational data, namely, a line relating the X variable to changes in the Y variable.[5] This second regression line is useful when one is interested in establishing an empirical prediction in either direction, that is, Y from X and X from Y. The need to make such predictions is quite common in applied research. In addition, the second regression line is often introduced as an aid to understanding correlation and the relationship between linear regression and correlation. While we do not develop this particular approach when we consider correlation in the next chapter, it is interesting to note that correlation can be defined in terms of the slopes of the two regression lines. (This relationship is specified in footnote 3, p. 348.)

Again, we illustrate the second regression line with the example of height and weight. In a previous section, we saw how a person's weight is related to and can be predicted from a knowledge of his height. One could easily have been concerned with the reverse relationship, namely, the function relating height to weight. We will cover this example briefly, since no new ideas or principles are involved.

Regression of X on Y

We begin with a formula expressing the linear relationship in a form that permits the prediction of height from weight. Although we could use the formulas of the last section and simply reverse the designations, calling weight X and height Y, this technique is usually avoided, since it can be confusing, and since researchers often have some interest in examining the two regression lines on the same scatterplot. For these reasons, then, we will keep the same designations for height (variable X) and weight (variable Y); under these circumstances, the second regression line has this form:

$$X' = a_X + (b_X)(Y) \quad . \tag{13-12}$$

Note that several changes have been made in the formula for the best-fit straight line. First, the formula is expressed in terms of variable Y. That is, we are predicting scores on variable X (designated as X') by entering values on variable Y. Second, the slope and intercept have X subscripts instead of Y subscripts. This change is made to distinguish between the values of the

---

[5] The only time the two lines actually coincide is when the linear relationship is *perfect,* a phenomenon rarely encountered in the empirical world.

intercept and slope required to express the **linear regression of X on Y** from those required to express the linear regression of Y on X.

Computational Formulas

The formulas for the slope and the intercept for the second regression line are quite similar to those for the first and involve the same sorts of information. The formula for the slope is given by

$$b_X = \frac{SP_{XY}}{SS_Y} \quad . \tag{13-13}$$

If you compare this formula with equation (12-3) on p. 301, you will see the critical difference, namely, that SP_{XY} is divided by SS_Y rather than by SS_X. This change is appropriate because the slope we are now interested in relates the covariation of X and Y (represented by SP_{XY}) to variation in Y (represented by SS_Y). The intercept is the value of X when Y equals 0 (often called the X intercept). It is given by the following formula:

$$a_X = \bar{X} - (b_X)(\bar{Y}) \quad . \tag{13-14}$$

We are now ready for a numerical example.

A Numerical Example

We will calculate the regression line of X on Y with the data presented in Table 13-1 (p. 324). The equation for the slope requires the sum of products and the sum of squares for variable Y. We have already determined both quantities in previous calculations:

$$SP_{XY} = 1,089.47, \text{ and } SS_Y = 1,160.93 \quad .$$

From equation (13-13),

$$b_X = \frac{SP_{XY}}{SS_Y}$$

$$= \frac{1,089.47}{1,160.93} = .94 \quad .$$

Next, we calculate the X intercept from equation (13-14):

$$a_X = \bar{X} - (b_X)(\bar{Y})$$

$$= 166.53 - (.94)(63.07)$$

$$= 166.53 - 59.29 = 107.24 \quad .$$

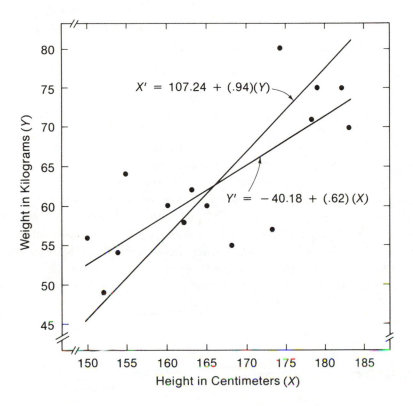

Figure 13-4. Two Regression Lines Relating Height (X Variable) and Weight (Y Variable).

Substitution in equation (13-12) gives us the equation for the regression line:

$$X' = a_X + (b_X)(Y)$$
$$= 107.24 + (.94)(Y) \quad .$$

In order to draw this regression line on the scatterplot, we need to calculate two points on the line. For convenience, we have chosen $Y = 50$ and 80. Entering these values of Y in the regression equation, we obtain

$X' = 107.24 + (.94)(50) = 107.24 + 47.00 = 154.24$ centimeters; and
$X' = 107.24 + (.94)(80) = 107.24 + 75.20 = 182.44$ centimeters   .

Using these two points, we can draw the regression line on the scatterplot. This we have done in Figure 13-4, where the original regression line has also been drawn for purposes of comparison.

As you can see, the two regression lines are different, though still fairly close to each other. The two lines intersect[6] at the point where

$$X = \bar{X} \ (166.53), \text{ and}$$
$$Y = \bar{Y} \ (63.07) \quad .$$

You may have noticed that the second regression line we calculated (predicting X from Y) is not as convenient to use as the first (predicting Y from X). With the first regression line, one uses the graph in the normal manner, locating the predictor value of X on the horizontal axis, extending a vertical line to the regression line from this point, and reading the predicted value of Y represented by this intersection off the vertical axis. This is the way we usually read and interpret graphs. With the second regression line, however, we begin with the *vertical* axis (the Y variable), find the predictor value of Y, and read the value of X predicted from the second regression line off the *horizontal* axis. This technique can easily become confusing. To avoid this confusion and to obtain an accurate estimate—from either regression line— use the regression *equation* and arithmetic rather than the regression line and the eye.

SUMMARY

A best-fit straight line can be constructed to describe correlational data where the relationship of interest is between two dependent variables. The formulas presented in the last chapter, which were applied to the data from experiments, are applicable here as well.

One can test the significance of the slope of the regression line by calculating two mean squares, one assumed to reflect the presence of a linear relationship between the two variables and experimental error ($MS_{\text{lin. regr.}}$) and one assumed to reflect experimental error alone (MS_{residual}). The isolation of these sources of variability also permits the calculation of an index relating the amount of variation due to linear regression to the total amount of variation among the scores. A large percentage indicates a strong linear relationship between the two variables.

A second regression line is present with any set of correlational data. Although most researchers are only interested in one of the regression lines, investigators often obtain the second line to provide a more complete description of the relationship between the two variables.

---

[6] You will recall that a best-fit straight line always goes through the center of the scatterplot, which is defined by the point ($\bar{X}$, $\bar{Y}$). This is true for both regression lines.

TERMS, CONCEPTS, AND SYMBOLS

---

scatterplot	$Y_i - \overline{Y}$	$df_{\text{lin. regr.}}$
error of prediction	$Y_i' - \overline{Y}$	df_{residual}
residual sum of squares	$Y_i - Y_i'$	$MS_{\text{lin. regr.}}$
standard error of estimate	SS_Y	MS_{residual}
explained variability	$SS_{\text{lin. regr.}}$	X'
linear regression of X on Y	SS_{residual}	b_X
	df_Y	a_X

EXERCISES

---

1. A student tested sixteen subjects in an experiment in which subjects were required to learn a list of eleven word pairs. The student noticed that subjects needed an unusually long time to master the entire list and wondered whether the number correct on the first trial could be used to predict the number of trials necessary to learn the eleven pairs. Using the data given on p. 340, find the regression line and test whether such a prediction is possible—that is, test the significance of the slope of the regression line.

Subject	Number Correct on Trial 1 (X)	Number of Trials to Learn (Y)
1	4	13
2	1	31
3	3	17
4	3	42
5	7	18
6	3	12
7	2	17
8	3	33
9	7	54
10	1	32
11	8	5
12	3	33
13	8	44
14	7	16
15	3	29
16	7	13

2. This problem illustrates the meaning of the residual sum of squares (SS_{residual}). The SS_{residual} represents the variation *not* accounted for by linear regression. Computationally, we obtain this sum of squares by subtraction: $SS_Y - SS_{\text{lin. regr.}}$ (see p. 330). A more laborious way of calculating the SS_{residual} is to determine for each subject the difference between the actual score (Y_i) and that predicted by linear regression (Y_i'), to square these differences, and then to sum them. In symbols, $SS_{\text{residual}} = \Sigma (Y_i - Y_i')^2$. With the data presented in Table 13-1 (p. 324) and the regression line obtained from these pairs of points (p. 326), calculate the SS_{residual} with this alternative formula. The final answer will equal the value obtained from the simpler computational formula (see p. 331) except for a small amount of rounding error. To get you started, we have set up a worksheet and filled in a few numbers.

Sub-ject	Observed Height (X)	Observed Weight (Y)	Predicted Weight (Y')	Dif-ference (Y − Y')	(Y − Y')²
1	150	56	52.82	+3.18	10.11
2	154	54	55.30	−1.30	1.69
3	168	55	_____	_____	_____
4	162	58	_____	_____	_____
5	152	49	_____	_____	_____
6	155	64	_____	_____	_____
7	178	71	_____	_____	_____
8	163	62	_____	_____	_____
9	173	57	_____	_____	_____
10	179	75	_____	_____	_____
11	174	80	_____	_____	_____
12	165	60	_____	_____	_____
13	182	75	_____	_____	_____
14	183	70	_____	_____	_____
15	160	60	_____	_____	_____

3. Additional practice in calculating regression lines is provided in problem 1 of Chapter 14 (p. 361).

Correlation

14

Many individuals are more familiar with correlation than with linear regression, although the two concepts are closely related. A regression line specifies the linear relationship that can be used to predict individual scores on one variable from a knowledge of the other. Although we can test the statistical significance of the slope of a linear regression line, neither the results of this test nor the value of the slope in the regression equation give any direct clue as to the degree to which the two variables are interrelated or to the degree of association present between the two variables.

In contrast, the correlation measure provides this information directly. More specifically, the correlation index has theoretical maximum values for a perfect linear relationship between two variables ($+1.0$ for a perfect positive relationship and -1.0 for a perfect negative relationship) and a theoretical minimum value for the absence of a linear relationship between two variables (0). In addition, the square of the correlation index (or coefficient, as it is usually called) conveys directly the proportion of total variability of either variable (X or Y) accounted for by the linear relationship with the other. On the other hand, the correlation coefficient does not permit the direct prediction of Y from X (or X from Y), as the regression equation does.

Thus, both statistical indices serve useful but different functions: The regression equation is used for prediction and the correlation coefficient is used as an index of the degree of association. While it is possible to write equations relating linear regression and correlation algebraically, this is not our purpose here. We want to make sure that you understand this additional index of the association between two variables and how to calculate its value. As you will see, the latter is not a difficult task, since the correlation coefficient requires exactly the same ingredients as the linear regression equation.

SCATTERPLOT

The scatterplot is a convenient visual display of the degree of linear association between two variables. We have already noted this use of the scatterplot by indicating that the degree of precision attainable in predicting one variable from another is reflected by the deviation of observed data points from the linear regression line. These deviations are called **residual deviations,** and we can square and sum these values to obtain an index of the *failure* of linear association to predict the actual scores observed on the predicted variable. In Chapter 13, we referred to this index as the residual sum of squares.

One can learn to estimate the degree of correlation by studying the scatterplot of the data. A complete lack of correlation is reflected by a circular spread around the "center" of the scatterplot, the point $(\overline{X}, \overline{Y})$. As the linear association between the two variables increases, the circle begins to flatten to form an ellipse (a football shape), which is tilted either upward from left to right when a positive relationship is present or downward from left to right when a negative relationship is present. This envelope of data points continues to flatten as the degree of association increases until it becomes perfectly flat—that is, a straight line—which happens when the correlation is perfect.

Another way to estimate the degree of correlation is to examine the two regression lines (Y on X and X on Y), discussed in the last chapter. When no correlation is present, the two regression lines are perpendicular to one another: Y on X is parallel to the horizontal, or X, axis; and X on Y is parallel to the vertical, or Y, axis. As the degree of correlation increases, the two lines begin to approach each other. They completely converge to form a single straight line when a perfect correlation exists.

Look back at the two sets of correlational data in Figure 13-1 (p. 322). In that figure, two relationships were plotted, that between scores on a diagnostic test and performance on two midterms (upper graph) and that between scores on the two midterms (lower graph). For the first scatterplot, the correlation between the two variables is +.52, while for the second scatterplot, it is +.91. At this point do not try to make much out of the numerical value of the coefficient; just notice that the index seems to reflect the magnitude of the discrepancies of data points from the regression line. The magnitude is perceived visually in the "tightness" of an envelope drawn around the scores. The second case represents a much "tighter" fit by the straight line—a skinnier envelope—than does the first.

As a contrast, consider the relationship between a student's midterm performance and the order in which he or she turned in the examination paper. These data are presented in the form of a scatterplot in Figure 14-1. (These data were obtained from a different class than the one producing the relationships presented in Figure 13-1.) The correlation between these two variables is approximately 0 (−.04). The regression line predicting Y from X (not shown) is parallel to the X axis—that is, it has essentially zero slope. The data points are scattered about the graph in a haphazard pattern. Clearly, they do not reflect a linear relationship between the two variables.

THE COMPUTATIONAL FORMULA

The index of correlation we consider in this chapter is termed the **product-moment correlation coefficient** and is symbolized by r.[1] The coefficient may be defined as the ratio of the joint variation of X and Y relative to the variation of X and Y considered separately. As you might suspect, joint variation is

---

[1] The index is also known as the *Pearson product-moment correlation* or, more simply, the Pearson r.

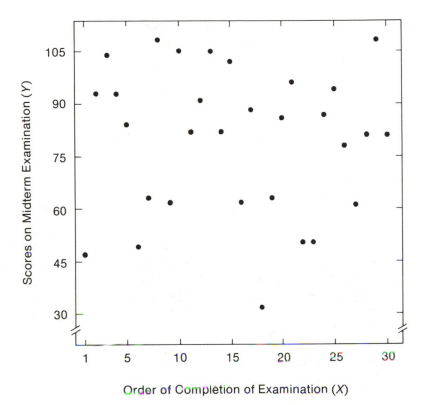

Figure 14-1. The Relationship Between the Order of Completion (*X* Variable) and Scores on a Midterm Examination (*Y* Variable).

measured in terms of covariance and the independent variation is measured in terms of variance. Both variance and covariance are based on deviations of individual subjects from the mean. Variance, as you know, is essentially an average of the squared deviations. In regression and correlation there are two variances, each reflecting the separate variability of the individual sets of scores. Covariance, on the other hand, relates subjects' deviations on *X* to their corresponding deviations on *Y*. Covariance is an average also, but in this case an average of the products obtained in the multipication of a deviation on *X* by a deviation on *Y*. With this preamble, we can define the product-moment correlation coefficient as

$$r = \frac{\text{covariance } (X, Y)}{\sqrt{[\text{variance } (X)][\text{variance } (Y)]}} \; . \tag{14-1}$$

The computational formula for r is expressed in terms of sums of squares and products. While all these sums have been presented in previous chapters, we repeat them here for the sake of convenience. Thus,

$$r = \frac{SP_{XY}}{\sqrt{(SS_X)(SS_Y)}} \quad , \text{ where} \qquad (14\text{-}2)$$

$$SP_{XY} = \Sigma\ (X)(Y) - \frac{(\Sigma\ X)(\Sigma\ Y)}{s} \quad ,$$

$$SS_X = \Sigma\ (X)^2 - \frac{(\Sigma\ X)^2}{s} \quad , \text{ and}$$

$$SS_Y = \Sigma\ (Y)^2 - \frac{(\Sigma\ Y)^2}{s} \quad .$$

If you examine these equations, you will quickly see that they use the sums obtained in the initial preparation of the data for linear regression. That is, for both the X and the Y scores, we obtain the sum of the scores and the sum of the squared scores; in addition, we multiply each pair of scores and sum these products.

A Numerical Example

In this section we calculate the correlation coefficient using the height-weight data we worked with in Chapter 13. From Table 13-1 (p. 324), we find the following values:

$$\Sigma\ X = 2{,}498, \qquad\qquad \Sigma\ Y = 946,$$
$$\Sigma\ (X)^2 = 417{,}750, \qquad\qquad \Sigma\ (Y)^2 = 60{,}822,$$
$$\Sigma\ (X)(Y) = 158{,}630 \quad .$$

Since we have already calculated the sums of squares and products from these summary data, we can simply set the formulas up and indicate the answers:

$$SP_{XY} = 158{,}630 - \frac{(2{,}498)(946)}{15} = 1{,}089.47;$$

$$SS_X = 417{,}750 - \frac{(2{,}498)^2}{15} = 1{,}749.73; \text{ and}$$

$$SS_Y = 60{,}822 - \frac{(946)^2}{15} = 1{,}160.93 \quad .$$

Substituting these calculations in equation (14-2), we find

$$r = \frac{1,089.47}{\sqrt{(1,749.73)(1,160.93)}}$$

$$= \frac{1,089.47}{\sqrt{2,031,314.05}} = \frac{1,089.47}{1,425.24}$$

$$= .76 \quad .$$

THE STRENGTH OF CORRELATION

The **strength of linear correlation**—that is, the degree to which two variables are linearly related—is defined as the proportion of variance in either variable X or variable Y that is linearly associated with the other. Due to a fortunate circumstance that we will not develop here, this proportion of variance is given by the square of the correlation coefficient. That is,

$$\text{proportion variance} = r^2 \quad . \tag{14-3}$$

In our example,

$$r^2 = (.76)^2 = .58 \quad .$$

This means that the linear correlation between height and weight accounts for approximately 58 percent of the variance of either variable considered separately. Note carefully that we index the proportion of overlap between the two variables by *squaring* the coefficient, not by using the coefficient itself. Thus, a correlation of $r = .5$ does not mean that half the variance of X or Y is accounted for by linear correlation, but rather that $r^2 = (.5)^2 = .25$, or 25 percent, is the correct value. The proportion of variation *not* accounted for, or not held in common between the two variables, can also be found easily:

$$1 - r^2 \quad . \tag{14-4}$$

In our example, it is $1 - (.76)^2 = 1 - .58 = .42$.[2]

Interestingly, equation (14-3) gives exactly the same estimate of variance explained by linear correlation as equation (13-11), which we considered in the context of linear regression (see p. 334). By means of that formula, we found that 58 percent of the variance observed among the Y scores was predictable from a knowledge of X, exactly the value we found using equa-

---

[2] These two indices are frequently referred to as the *coefficient of determination* (r^2) and the *coefficient of nondetermination* or *alienation* ($1 - r^2$).

tion (14-3). It is at this point that linear regression and correlation involve equivalent mathematical operations.[3]

THE STATISTICAL TEST OF THE CORRELATION COEFFICIENT

Since the correlation coefficient is obtained from data, in order to make any inference concerning the existence in the population of a correlation, we must employ a statistical test. In this case, the statistical hypotheses are these:

H_0: The population correlation is zero;

H_1: The population correlation is not zero   .

While this null hypothesis can be tested in several different ways, including analysis of variance, we will describe only one, which simply requires the comparison of r with a critical value listed in a statistical table. To find the critical value of r, we choose a value for α (usually $\alpha = .05$) and enter Table 4 of Appendix A for the appropriate number of degrees of freedom associated with the correlation coefficient. This number is

$$df_r = s - 2   ,$$
(14-5)

where s equals the number of data pairs in the sample.

In our example, $df_r = 15 - 2 = 13$. For $\alpha = .05$, the critical value of r (r_α) listed in the table is .51. With this information, the decision rules can be stated thus:

If the obtained value of r is equal to or exceeds $r_\alpha = .51$, reject the null hypothesis; otherwise, do not reject the null hypothesis.

Our correlation of $r = .76$ exceeds the tabled value, and we conclude that the two variables are linearly related in the population.

This statistical test is equivalent to the one we described for evaluating the significance of the slope of the regression line (see pp. 327–333). This is because the slope of the regression line and the correlation coefficient are interrelated mathematically. Thus, either statistical test—evaluation of the

---

[3] A simple way to express the relationship between regression and correlation is by a formula relating r to the slopes of the two regression lines relating X and Y. Specifically, $r = \sqrt{(b_Y)(b_X)}$. From our calculations in Chapter 13, we found $b_Y = .62$ and $b_X = .94$. From this information, we find that $r = \sqrt{(.62)(.94)} = \sqrt{.58} = .76$, which equals the value of r we obtained with equation (14-2).

significance of the slope of the regression line or evaluation of the significance of the correlation coefficient—can be substituted for the other. Obviously, the present version involves considerably less work than its alternative, although it is not as understandable. Which version one uses depends on the primary purpose of the data collection. If the goal is prediction, the focus becomes the regression line. Analyzing the data in terms of the analysis of variance then seems appropriate, since this procedure results in the test of the significance of the slope and estimates of the magnitude of prediction error and of the variance accounted for by linear regression. On the other hand, if the goal is to establish an association between the variables rather than to predict, the focus becomes the correlation coefficient. Under these circumstances, the best choice would be to assess the significance of r.

ASSUMPTIONS UNDERLYING THE STATISTICAL TESTS

The statistical justification for the statistical tests of slope and correlation depends on a set of assumptions about the data:

1. That the true relationship between the variables is linear
2. That each pair of scores is based on individuals who are independent of each other
3. That the variables are continuous
4. That the joint distribution is normal[4]

You will recall that the analysis of variance is relatively insensitive to violations of the statistical assumptions underlying the mathematical development of the test. Apparently, the tests of significance we discussed for regression and correlation exhibit a similar insensitivity (see Havlicek and Peterson, 1977).

ADDITIONAL POINTS TO CONSIDER

Next, we consider a number of points that pertain to the use of correlation in research.

---

[4] The normal joint distribution is referred to as *bivariate normal*. It pertains to the joint distribution of the two variables and is not the same as the distribution of each variable separately.

Sample Size

Table 4 in Appendix A, which lists critical values of r for different numbers of degrees of freedom, indicates that one's ability to detect a significant correlation varies directly with increases in sample size. A correlational study with a large sample size is more powerful than one with a small sample size. This same relationship between power and sample size was demonstrated with respect to the analysis of variance.

One should be extremely cautious in accepting large correlations when small sample sizes are involved. The presence of an individual who is extreme on the two variables can have a dramatic influence on the size of r. For example, it could easily be the case that the correlation is significant when the deviant subject is included and not significant when the subject is excluded. A scatterplot of the data points would reveal the presence of this sort of situation.

Restriction of Range

The range of scores for each variable can affect the size of r. We have been interested in the correlation between height and weight. Suppose we enlarge our study to include a much wider age range of subjects, for example, males ages 10–19 rather than 17–19, as was the case in our example. The broader sample of ages would permit considerably shorter males to be included. The correlation between height and weight in the broader sample (ages 10–19) will be larger than the correlation in the original sample. Of course, the ages included depend on the interest of the researcher. If the restricted population *is* the population of interest, the correlation will be taken as an estimate of the correlation of these two variables in this population. On the other hand, if the population of interest is broader than this, the restricted sample will generally result in an *underestimate* of the magnitude of the population correlation.

Information Provided by the Means and Standard Deviations

No correlational analysis is complete unless the means and the standard deviations of the two variables are examined. The means are particularly useful in the interpretation of the relationship between two response measures obtained at different times. Consider the relationship between the two midterm examinations presented in Chapter 13 (see Figure 13-1B, p. 322). The correlation between the two examinations ($r = +.91$), a strong relationship, tells us nothing about average performance on the two tests. That is, students on the average might have scored higher on the second test or lower on the second test—we cannot tell from the correlation coefficient. (In actuality, the mean on the first test was slightly higher than the mean on the second, 79.20 and 77.32, respectively.) Thus, the means can provide important information about the relationship between the two variables that is not reflected in the index of correlation.

The standard deviations are useful in the interpretation of a nonsignificant, or low, correlation. As noted earlier, the correlation coefficient depends in part on the range or variability of the two variables. An extremely small standard deviation for one of the variables might imply that a restriction of range is having an adverse effect on the size of the correlation coefficient.

Nonlinear Relationships Between Two Variables

The emphasis in Chapters 13 and 14 has been on the linear relationship between two variables. While there are numerous examples of linear relationships in psychology, higher-order relationships, or **nonlinear relationships,** are occasionally reported in the literature. A common nonlinear relationship is one in which a U-shaped function relates the two variables. That is, instead of the Y variable increasing steadily as X increases (a linear relationship), Y first increases and then decreases. In a scatterplot, the data points look like an inverted U. (A nonlinear relationship is also possible in which Y first decreases and then increases as X increases; in this case, the scatterplot looks like a normal U.) Nonlinear relationships are commonly found between age and various psychomotor skills, for example, since children and elderly persons do not perform as well on tasks requiring these skills as individuals from the middle range of ages.

While a nonlinear relationship will produce a small correlation coefficient, a low correlation could also mean that no relationship exists between X and Y. By arranging the data in a scatterplot, a researcher can easily see whether a nonlinear relationship is present and thus distinguish between these two different explanations of a low correlation.

OTHER CORRELATIONAL PROCEDURES

The concepts of linear regression and correlation are topics with which psychology majors must at least be familiar. You should realize, however, that in actual correlational research more complicated and sophisticated procedures are used than the ones we have discussed here. Unfortunately, these topics are simply beyond the scope of this book. We mention briefly a few of these procedures in the following sections so you will be familiar with their names. We assume that you will turn to more advanced treatments of correlation when you have become seriously involved in a research area or project that requires a detailed analysis of correlational data.

Special Features of the Data

In all the examples considered in this chapter, the X and Y variables were *continuous* in nature—that is, they could take on many values and were measured in what are assumed to be equal units. Occasionally, correlational data do not have this form, but reflect the use of less precise scales. For example, two variables can take the form of *ranks,* with each subject in the sample being given a rank indicating his or her relative position on the two variables. This procedure is often employed when the characteristics to be ranked are complex and difficult to measure, for example, the leadership skills of executives or the creativity of student art work. Under these circumstances, researchers usually compute a **rank-order correlation coefficient.**[5] In fields of psychological testing or in public-opinion surveys, one of the variables may be continuous in nature—say, grade-point average or annual income—while the other is dichotomous (has only two values), such as pass or fail, agree or disagree, yes or no. Investigators can analyze data of this sort by calculating a **point biserial correlation coefficient,** which approximates what r would be if *both* distributions were continuous. When both variables are dichotomous in nature, a **phi coefficient** is appropriate.

The range of values possible with the rank-order coefficient is the same as r, namely, -1.0 to $+1.0$ for a perfect negative or positive correlation, respectively, and 0 for the absence of a correlation. The range of values possible with the point biserial and the phi coefficients is complicated and not closely

---

[5] The procedure is referred to in many statistics texts as the *Spearman rank-order correlation coefficient*. Data expressed as ranks can be used in the calculation of a product-moment correlation coefficient, although this approach does involve more computational effort than use of the rank-order coefficient.

related to the product-moment coefficient. Edwards (1976, Chapter 7) offers a useful presentation and discussion of these three alternative measures of correlation. Kirk (1978, p. 120) provides a table in which he summarizes the most common correlation coefficients and gives page references to extended treatments of these indices in other statistics books.

Multiple Correlation

More than two response measures can be included in a correlational study. Under these circumstances, a different set of procedures—**multiple regression** and **multiple correlation**—becomes appropriate. The intercorrelations between the several variables are used to achieve a level of prediction (and correlation) that is not possible if variables are correlated one pair at a time. Most psychological screening devices utilize multiple-regression procedures and techniques. Personality theory is built on the combination of a large number of tests and assessment devices that individually are poorly correlated with some behavior of interest, but collectively can be combined in appropriate proportions to raise prediction to quite acceptable and useful levels. Edwards (1976, Chapter 14) provides an informative introduction to this topic.

Factor Analysis

An extremely useful multiple-correlational technique is **factor analysis.** In this research, an investigator starts by examining the performance of a group of subjects on a large number of tests and other observational measures. By means of some fairly complicated procedures, he or she then segregates the sets of scores to form distinct patterns, or factors, of scores. A factor consists of a set of scores on two or more tests that are highly correlated among themselves but poorly correlated with others. With this procedure, the results of a mammoth testing program—say a battery of fifty tests given to a large sample of individuals—can be summarized in terms of a limited number of factors. These factors might then be used in a multiple-regression equation to predict future behavior or to form hypothetical constructs concerning the nature of the intellect or personality.[6]

---

[6] Neale and Liebert (1973, pp. 113–119) present a nontechnical discussion of multiple correlation and factor analysis. Kerlinger (1973, pp. 603–692) offers a more demanding but still comprehensible discussion of these various procedures.

CAUSATION AND CORRELATION

It seems to be our nature to seek out functional relationships that permit us to say, "This is the cause of that!" On occasion, the temptation to interpret a significant correlation as somehow imparting *causality* is almost overwhelming. Two factors seem to lead to this temptation, one having to do with the variables themselves and the other with characteristics of the statistics.

Consider the following example. Suppose we were to find that among children a strong negative correlation existed between the numbers of hours per day spent watching television and reading proficiency. That is, the more time a child spent watching television, the lower was his or her reading proficiency. Most of us would be almost irresistably tempted to impute causation and thus to conclude that television watching *causes* reading ability to be poor.

In this example, one variable, television watching, occurs prior to the development of the other variable, reading ability. Just knowing that the number of hours spent watching television accounted for substantial variance in reading proficiency would be of considerable importance. However, neither correlation nor firmly held predispositions justify the inference of causality. Without an experimentally imposed and manipulated variable, we lack control over potentially large numbers of confounded variables. In our example, it might be that difficulty in developing the skills for reading leads children to compensate by watching television for a large number of hours. In this case, a third variable—difficulty in developing skills—would be responsible for the relationship and not the actual watching of television.

The language used to describe the various statistics associated with correlation might also encourage us to make causal inferences from correlational data. When we use r^2, we speak of *variance explained*. It is easy to translate this expression as *producing* or *causing,* even though all that has been established is a statistical *association* between two naturally occurring variables.

However, procedures are available to assist researchers in drawing tentative causal inferences from correlational data. These procedures, which involve the analysis of the patterns taken by a set of correlations, are too complicated to be included in an introductory discussion of correlation.[7] In any case, we must always be skeptical when advertisers, governmental officials, and even social scientists claim that a certain factor is the *cause* of a particular behavior until we are able to determine the nature of the reported

---

[7] One type of procedure is known as *cross-lagged panel correlations* (see Neale and Liebert, 1973, pp. 99–104). Another approach is *path analysis* (see, for example, Kerlinger and Pedhazur, 1973, pp. 305–330).

data. If the data come from experiments, causal inference is at least possible. But if the data are correlational, any causal statement offered is suspect; in such a case, we must look for other sorts of evidence, either more sophisticated correlational procedures or experimental data, with which to substantiate the conclusion.

THE USE OF CORRELATION IN EXPERIMENTATION

This book has focused on the analysis of experiments where independent variables are manipulated and dependent variables are observed. We introduced the analysis of correlational data because it is used in many fields of psychology. You might wonder whether the collection of correlational data in the context of an experiment serves any useful purpose. We will discuss this question briefly.

The Analysis of Covariance

In completely randomized designs where subjects are assigned at random to the different treatment conditions, the largest source of experimental error is attributed to differences among subjects. As you will recall, the magnitude of experimental error influences the sensitivity of an experiment: The smaller the experimental error, the more sensitive the experiment. In Chapter 8, we discussed a number of ways in which experimental error can be reduced through the choice of experimental design, for example, the use of homogeneous subjects, matched groups, and repeated measures. Experimental error can also be reduced *statistically* by means of a procedure known as the **analysis of covariance.**

In order to use this method, one needs to have some information about the subjects before the start of the experiment. This information, called the **control variable,** must be linearly related to the behavior under study, that is, the dependent variable. In a perception experiment, the control variable might be scores on a visual-acuity test; in a learning experiment, the control variable might be an IQ score or a score on a pretest administered to all subjects before the start of the experiment. Briefly, the correlation between the control variable and the dependent variable is used for two purposes: to adjust the treatment means for chance differences due to the random assignment of subjects to conditions, and to reduce the size of the error term by an amount related to the degree of correlation between the control and dependent variables. The procedure is complicated and involves considerably more computational effort than the analysis of variance, but occasionally the time and the energy are worth it. (For a detailed discussion of the analysis of covariance, see *Design and Analysis,* Chapter 22.)

Multiple Response Measures

Most investigators include more than one response measure in an experiment. A researcher interested in the speed with which a subject learns a set of material might also plan to record the nature and number of overt errors made during learning, the speed with which a subject gives a correct response, a subject's confidence in being right or wrong on any given recall attempt, and so on. Data of this sort can be used in several different ways. First, the researcher might determine which measures are highly correlated with the primary response measure—for example, speed of learning—and which are not. These correlated variables might give suggestions as to the nature of the processes involved in the behavior under study.

Second, correlational procedures might be used in a comparison of response measures across the different treatment conditions. One possibility is to examine the different correlations between *two* dependent variables (one being the dependent variable of primary interest) over the different treatment conditions. Procedures not covered here are available that permit the comparison of correlations obtained for different treatment conditions (see for example, Edwards, 1976, pp. 89–92). Another possiblity is using these measures to determine how all the response measures are affected by the treatment conditions. In this case, the researcher would look for patterns of responses changing from condition to condition.[8]

Use In Theory

We have had little to say about theory in this book except with respect to the necessary connection between theory and experimentation—namely, that deductions from theory lead to particular experimental tests and the results of experiments dictate subsequent changes in theory. In psychology, theorizing often takes the form of inferences about internal processes, on the one hand influenced by experimental manipulations, and on the other responsible for the observed differences in behavior. Typically, the manipulations are

---

[8] These procedures are quite complicated and completing them usually requires the use of a computer. The general method of analysis is called the *multivariate analysis of variance*.

carried out on different groups of subjects, but the changes in the inferred processes are assumed to occur *within* individuals. For example, suppose one found that lists of words were better recalled when they were of high imagery value than when they were of low imagery value. This sort of finding would immediately suggest a theoretical interpretation in which the nature of imagery could be inferred as a memory process.

Underwood (1975) has offered an argument that all such *process theories* should be subjected to test through an analysis of *individual differences,* which, as we will see, means the collection of correlational data relevant to the theoretical argument. To continue with this example, it would be desirable to find some way to show that subjects who differ in *imagery ability* also differ in *memory ability*. Such a demonstration would allow a theory that was developed on the basis of treatment conditions presumed to affect the degree of visual imagery in subjects to be applied to individuals thought to differ in their use of visual imagery. The presence of a positive correlation between imagery ability and memory would serve as evidence to confirm the theory. It is Underwood's point that it is *negative* findings—that is, failures to find confirmatory correlational data—that are devastating for theory. The theory proposes the operation of a particular process within individuals, and this basic postulate is invalidated by the lack of correlation between imagery ability and memory.

Underwood contends that any theory inferring processes from experimental manipulations should be immediately assessed by a relevant correlational analysis. That is, the investigator should seek some quality or ability of individuals that reflects the process under question and correlate this ability with the behavior under investigation—memory in these examples we have considered. Underwood quickly points out that establishing correlations as expected by theory does not *validate* the theory—the problems of causation and correlational data are still lurking about. These problems must be overcome by additional experiments, in which variation of the X variable is under the control of the experimenter. But the *failure* to find expected correlations, should immediately bring the theoretical interpretation into question. It is in this sense that correlational data can serve a critical function in the construction of theories.

A Summary of Procedures

Our approach in the chapters on linear trend, linear regression, and correlation has been consistent with that taken throughout the text. Our emphasis has been on variance and on distinguishing among the various sources of

TABLE 14-1   Analyses Performed on Two Types of Data

Type of Data	Regression Line	Significance of Slope	Strength of Relationship
Experimental	$Y' = a_Y + (b_Y)(X)$	$F = \dfrac{MS_{A_{\text{linear}}}}{MS_{\text{error}}}$	$\dfrac{SS_{A_{\text{linear}}}}{SS_A}$
Correlational	$Y' = a_Y + (b_Y)(X)$ $X' = a_X + (b_X)(Y)$	$F^a = \dfrac{MS_{\text{lin. regr.}}}{MS_{\text{residual}}}$	r^2

^{a} This test is equivalent to the test of the hypothesis that $r = 0$ discussed in this chapter.

identifiable variation such as total variation, explained or predicted variation, and unexplained or residual variation. You may have some difficulty determining when to use these different procedures. In this section, we summarize this material and supplement it where necessary.

In the context of these topics, we are concerned with data that come in *pairs*. If the data come from an *experiment*, the pairs consist of the numbers used to represent the treatment levels of the independent variable and the average performance by the subjects receiving that particular level of the independent variable. Procedures of linear regression are used to find the best-fitting line linking the independent variable (the X variable) with average performance on the dependent variable (the Y variable). The first row of Table 14-1 is a summary of the various procedures involved in the analysis of linear trend conducted on experimental data. The second column gives the formal statement of the regression line. Values for the Y intercept (a_Y) and the slope (b_Y) are calculated from the data. Analysis of variance provides a statistical test of the hypothesis that the slope of the regression line is 0; the appropriate F ratio is specified in the third column. Finally, it is possible to estimate the degree to which X and Y are linearly related. This value is calculated by means of the formula in the fourth column of the table. The larger the proportion, the more confident we can be that the variation observed among the treatment means is attributable to the linear function. Assuming that the slope of the line is statistically different from 0, this proportion provides a useful index of the goodness with which a straight line can be used to describe the functional relationship observed with a set of data. The analysis of a linear relationship between a manipulated variable and a dependent variable, called a linear trend analysis, was discussed in Chapter 12.

If the data are *nonexperimental* in nature—that is, correlational—the pairs of scores are both measured characteristics of the subjects or units under observation. (The word *unit* includes those cases where one might use a classroom, a city, an organization, or a similar entity to provide the paired scores.) Procedures of linear regression are also used to link the two sets of scores with a straight line. As indicated in the second row of Table 14-1, two regression lines can be constructed to permit the prediction of scores on one variable from a knowledge of the scores on the other variable. As in the trend analysis, the intercepts and slopes of the two lines are also calculated from the sets of paired scores. We can determine whether the slope of either line is statistically different from 0 either by means of the F ratio listed in the third column (discussed in Chapter 13) or the corresponding correlation coefficient (discussed in this chapter). Finally, we can obtain a measure of the strength of the linear relationship between the X and Y variables either by squaring the correlation coefficient (as listed in the fourth column) or by substituting in equation (13-11) the variances obtained from an analysis of linear regression.

The goal with either type of data is to determine whether a straight line provides a reasonably good description of the data at hand. Of course, the straight line represents only a guess, since some other, naturally more complex and difficult to understand relationship may offer a better fit. Still, we try to "fit" a straight line through the plot of the data points because it is easy to work with and to understand relative to the meaning of the data.

Table 14-1 indicates that the same sorts of information can be derived from experimental and correlational data. Both types of data can be used in drawing regression lines, testing the significance of slopes, and measuring the strength of linear relationships. The only real difference lies in the form of these different operations. The estimates of slope and intercept involve different sorts of quantities, treatment levels and treatment means for experimental data and two sets of scores for correlational data. The statistical tests of the significance of the linear relationship—that is, of whether the slope of the regression line is 0—are different as well. That is, we follow the same procedures used for evaluating any single-df comparison when the regression line is based on the data of an experiment and different procedures when the line is based on the data of a correlational study. The estimation of the amount of variability accounted for by the linear relationship is also different for the two types of data. These differences are not arbitrary, but reflect the differences in the nature of experimental and correlational data and the statistical models developed to deal with them.

SUMMARY

Correlation and linear regression are closely related topics, the former providing an index of the strength of a linear relationship between two dependent variables, and the latter providing a best-fit straight line linking the two variables. The most common index of correlation is the product-moment correlation coefficient, r, which equals 0 when the two variables are uncorrelated and -1.0 or $+1.0$ when the two variables are perfectly correlated. (The sign of the coefficient indicates the direction of the relationship, that is, the slope of the regression line.)

The correlation coefficient is calculated with the quantities we originally needed for linear regression. The index is defined as a ratio of the joint variation of X and Y (covariance) relative to the variation of X and Y considered separately (variance). The significance of a correlation coefficient is easily assessed by the use of a specialized table listing critical values of r for varying numbers of degrees of freedom. The square of the correlation coefficient specifies the proportion of variability of either dependent variable accounted for by the linear relationship between the two variables.

Correlational techniques and procedures are important research tools in the behavioral sciences. Researchers primarily concerned with correlational data, either for descriptive-theoretical purposes or for prediction, must master a number of complicated analytical techniques, briefly mentioned in this chapter. Researchers primarily concerned with the analysis of data from experiments have much to gain from the study and use of correlational procedures as well.

TERMS, CONCEPTS, AND SYMBOLS

residual deviation

product-moment correlation coefficient

strength of linear correlation

proportion of variance due to linear regression

restriction of range

nonlinear relationships

rank-order correlation coefficient

point biserial correlation coefficient

phi coefficient

multiple correlation

multiple regression

factor analysis

analysis of covariance

control variable

multiple response measures

r

r^2

$1 - r^2$

df_r

r_α

EXERCISES

1. A student in a statistics course believed that little or no correlation existed between scores on a take-home test requiring calculating skills and an in-class test requiring memory for concepts. The student took a sample of the class scores and the scores are given on the next page.

Student	Take-Home	In-Class
1	73	83
2	68	72
3	66	72
4	56	56
5	66	68
6	78	86
7	57	49
8	56	64
9	64	69
10	56	52
11	61	55
12	51	50
13	68	49
14	79	66
15	59	64

a. Calculate the correlation coefficient, r, and determine whether it is statistically significant. (Save your calculations for problem 1 of Chapter 16, p. 412.)

b. Calculate the variance accounted for by the linear relationship between the two tests.

c. Calculate the variance not explained by the linear relationship.

d. Calculate the formula for each of the two regression lines.

ADDITIONAL STATISTICAL PROCEDURES

V

In this final section, we consider a number of statistical procedures that fit better here than in earlier sections. In Chapter 15, we present statistical techniques appropriate for use with data that consist of response categories rather than scores obtained from continuous measures. An example of a category measure is the division of subjects into two groups: those who learned a given task and those who did not. Each subject in any given treatment condition would be classified simply as a learner or a nonlearner. The summary data would consist of the frequency or proportion of subjects appearing in the two categories for the different treatment conditions. In all the analyses discussed in previous chapters, we assumed that a subject's performance was indexed by a number that referred to a location on some continuous scale. Fortunately, we are able to conduct similar sorts of analyses when the dependent variable is in the form of response categories as well. In this chapter, we consider the statistical analysis of public opinion or preference polls, the analysis of a single-factor experiment, and the statistical determination of a correlation between two dependent measures where the data consist of frequency counts rather than continuous measures.

Chapter 16 covers two topics not frequently encountered by researchers concerned with data extracted from experiments but quite important in applied fields of the behavioral sciences. The first topic consists of a discussion of standard scores, a useful measure that reflects the relative position of a particular score in a set of ordered scores. Standard scores are commonly found in educational and personality testing. The second topic comprises the methods and procedures used to estimate population characteristics on the basis of information obtained from a sample drawn randomly from a population. Government agencies use estimation procedures widely to obtain demographic and other descriptive information in public opinion polls and in voter preference surveys. These two topics, though generally not central to the design and analysis of experiments, serve to round out this introduction to the statistical and quantitative aspects of psychological research.

The Analysis of Categorical Data

15

Most experiments in psychology are designed to measure behavior on a more or less continuous scale of measurement. Behavior varies in degree or in amount, and we try to "capture" this variation through the assignment of numbers that reasonably reflect the extent of the behavior observed. At times, however, the behavior under study cannot be measured precisely. For instance, it may only be possible to characterize the behavior in terms of a small number of categories, each representing either relatively gross performance on the experimental task—for instance, success-failure, completed-incompleted, type of errors—or an attitude towards an issue or policy—agree-disagree-uncertain, like-dislike, or approve-disapprove. Field research, survey research, and consumer studies often consist of such measurements. Occasionally, however, this sort of response measure is also found in an experiment.

Suppose, for example, that we were studying the social behavior of chimpanzees under a number of different treatment conditions. Assuming that we possessed an acceptable measuring scale of social behavior, we would assign numbers to each animal observed in the experiment that reflected the degree of social behavior displayed. Several animals would be randomly assigned to each treatment condition, the means would be calculated, and the groups would be compared by means of the analysis of variance.

But suppose we did not have a measurement scale available and could only classify the observed behavior of each chimpanzee either as social or as antisocial. The basic data for any given treatment contition would thus consist of a tabulation of the number of subjects displaying social behavior and the number of subjects displaying antisocial behavior. These numbers would be called *frequencies;* each being the frequency with which one form of behavior was observed in each condition.

To compare the different treatment conditions under these circumstances, we could examine changes in the patterns of frequencies across the different groups. That is, we would examine whether the number (or frequency) of animals showing social behavior as opposed to antisocial behavior differed from condition to condition.[1] If social behavior were affected by the independent variable, we would expect to find changes in the frequency patterns, just as we would with averages if a continuous measure were used.

In short, we can ask the same sort of questions in an experiment where the basic data consist of a two-category classification as we can where scores are on a continuous dependent variable. Unfortunately, however, the procedures for the statistical analysis of frequency data are different from those we have already considered and discussed. This chapter is concerned with the analyses appropriate for data of this sort.

THE SIMPLE CLASSIFICATION OF OBSERVATIONS

We begin our discussion with a very common use of categorical data, namely, the simple classification of observations. This type of categorical data is used in public opinion surveys. For example, a random sample of voters is contacted, and the voters are asked to indicate their attitudes towards a particular policy currently endorsed by the federal government.

---

[1] This kind of data is often reported in percentages or proportions, especially when the different treatment conditions contain unequal numbers of subjects.

Each individual is asked for an opinion, which, more often than not, is reduced to one of two **response categories,** for example, *yes* and *no,* or *agree* and *disagree*. The results are tabulated—say, 53 percent yes, and 47 percent no—and the two percentages are compared. The research question is whether voters agree or disagree with a governmental policy. Stated as a null hypothesis, the question becomes:

$$H_0: \text{percent yes} = \text{percent no} \quad .$$

If the null hypothesis is rejected (by means of the statistical procedure discussed below), we conclude that a majority of voters is in favor of the current policy.

Stated more generally, each subject is placed in one of several categories according to the nature of his or her response or behavior. The basic descriptive index reported is usually a proportion or percentage relating the number of subjects in each of the categories to the total number of subjects represented in the sample. Proportions or percentages are used to permit comparions across samples with different numbers of subjects in the different studies. Statistical analysis is usually based on the *frequency* or *number* of subjects in each of the categories, although formulas are easily modified to accept proportions as well.

Expected Frequencies

The statistical evaluation of the null hypothesis is based on an index that compares the **observed frequency** with which a given type of response is given with the **expected frequency** of that response assuming that the null hypothesis is true. In the survey example, the null hypothesis states that *no differences* exist between those in favor of the policy and those opposed. Another way of stating the null hypothesis is that a 50-50 percentage split in opinion will be observed. Thus, if 200 voters were surveyed, the expected frequencies would be 100 yes responses and 100 no responses. Translating the sample percentages reported above into frequencies, we find that the 53 percent in favor becomes $.53 \times 200 = 106$ voters, and the 47 percent opposed becomes $.47 \times 200 = 94$ voters. In the statistical analysis, we compare these obtained frequencies (106 and 94) with those expected if the null hypothesis is true (100 and 100).

As another example, consider the typical preference, or choice, study conducted to determine subjects' preferences (if any) for one product over another. For example, subjects might be presented with a number of foods to sample or several advertising layouts to view and then asked to pick the one that is most pleasing. In both cases, the null hypothesis states that each food or each layout will be selected by an equal number of subjects. If 75 individuals are asked to select a favorite from three alternatives, the expected number of subjects choosing each alternative is 25. In the statistical analysis, the three observed frequencies—the number of subjects actually choosing each alternative—are compared with the expected frequencies, which in this example are equal (25). If the observed frequencies are found to deviate significantly from the expected frequencies, the researcher will conclude that subjects have definite preferences for the three foods or for the three advertising layouts.

The Chi Square Statistic

Computational Formula. Null hypotheses dealing with frequency data are usually evaluated by means of the **chi square** statistic (pronounced "kye"). Chi square, symbolized χ^2, is based on the differences between observed and expected frequencies for each response category. In fact, these two sets of frequencies are the *only* quantities in the computational formula; they are designated f_O (the *observed* frequency for a given response category) and f_E (the *expected* frequency for the same response category). We start with an $f_O - f_E$ difference for each class of response. These differences are squared and divided by the appropriate *expected frequency* (f_E). The chi square statistic simply consists of the sum of these quantities. In symbols,

$$\chi^2 = \sum \frac{(f_O - f_E)^2}{f_E} \quad . \tag{15-1}$$

Evaluation of the Null Hypothesis. Just as with the analysis of variance, a set of statistical hypotheses is formed in the analysis of categorical data. The null hypothesis (H_0) is evaluated with the chi square statistic, and the alternative hypothesis (H_1) is accepted if the null hypothesis is rejected. To be more specific.

H_0: $f_O - f_E$ differences are zero for all categories;
H_1: Not all $f_O - f_E$ differences are zero   .

Under the assumption that the null hypothesis is true, the investigator uses the sampling distribution of the chi square statistic to select a critical value of χ^2 (χ^2_α) to define the regions of rejection and nonrejection at a selected significance level (α). Like the F statistic, the specific distribution of χ^2 depends on the degrees of freedom (df). For this type of problem,

$$df = c - 1 \quad , \tag{15-2}$$

TABLE 15-1   An Example of Simple Response Classification

Display	1. Observed (f_0)	2. Expected (f_E)	3. $f_0 - f_E$	4. $(f_0 - f_E)^2$	5. $\dfrac{(f_0 - f_E)^2}{f_E}$
1	50	40	$50 - 40 = +10$	$(+10)^2 = 100$	$\dfrac{100}{40} = 2.50$
2	33	40	$33 - 40 = -7$	$(-7)^2 = 49$	$\dfrac{49}{40} = 1.23$
3	37	40	$37 - 40 = -3$	$(-3)^2 = 9$	$\dfrac{9}{40} = .23$
Total	120	120	$\Sigma (f_0 - f_E) = 0$	Not Needed	$\chi^2 = 3.96$

where c refers to the number of response categories. Critical values of χ^2 for $\alpha = .05$ and .01 are listed in Table 5 of Appendix A. With this information, the investigator forms a set of decision rules:

If the obtained value of χ^2 equals or exceeds $\chi_\alpha^2 = $ _____ , reject the null hypothesis; otherwise, do not reject the null hypothesis.

Now we are ready for a numerical example.

Numerical Example. Suppose an industrial psychologist is interested in determining whether any one of three advertising displays is preferred over the others by potential customers. The researcher selects a group of 120 subjects, each of whom examines the displays and indicates which one he or she prefers. The number of subjects selecting each of the three displays is indicated in column 1 of Table 15-1.

If the null hypothesis is true and no preference differences are shown for the displays, we would expect one-third of the subjects to choose each of the three displays. Since there are 120 subjects, the expected frequency for each of the displays is $1/3 \times 120 = 40$. These frequencies are listed in column 2 of the table. A comparison of the observed and expected frequencies indicates that display 1 was preferred over the other two, but as we well know, the critical question is whether these differences could have reasonably occurred through the operation of chance factors.

To answer this question, we calculate the chi square statistic with the data appearing in Table 15-1. The first step is to obtain differences between observed and expected frequencies; these appear in column 3. The second step is to square each of these differences (column 4). The third step is to divide each squared difference by the appropriate expected frequency, shown in column 5. The final step is to sum each of these quantities to obtain χ^2. Specifically,

$$\chi^2 = \sum \frac{(f_O - f_E)^2}{f_E}$$
$$= 2.50 + 1.23 + .23$$
$$= 3.96 \quad .$$

For this example, $df = c - 1 = 3 - 1 = 2$. From Table 5 in Appendix A, we find that $\chi^2_\alpha = 5.99$ at the 5 percent level of significance. With this information, we can state the decision rules as follows:

If the obtained value of χ^2 equals or exceeds $\chi^2_\alpha = 5.99$, reject the null hypothesis; otherwise, do not reject the null hypothesis.

The obtained value is 3.96. Thus, we do not reject the null hypothesis and conclude that the experimental evidence is not sufficiently compelling to single out any one of the displays over the others.

Other Applications. The research problem in the example belongs to a general class of problems concerned with distribution of responses in a sample of individuals. In the numerical example, it was hypothesized that the three displays were *equally preferred* in the population; the observed distribution of choices in the study—that is, the numbers of subjects choosing each of the three displays—was compared to the expected distribution of choices in the population. The chi square statistic was then used to evaluate the discrepancies between the observed and the expected response distributions.

Application of chi square to comparisons between observed and expected response distributions can take other forms as well as the sort described. These may be distinguished on the basis of the *source* of the expected frequencies. One source stems from the assumption that no differences exist among the frequencies associated with the different categories in the population. The numerical example and the opinion survey we considered are both instances of this type of problem.

A second source of expected frequencies comes from *theory;* that is, specific predictions concerning relative frequencies of behavior are deduced from the inner workings of a theory. A prediction from genetics theory that offspring of a particular set of pairings will occur in a particular ratio is one example. Predictions based on probability theory—for example, expected probabilities of poker hands or rolls of a die—constitute another example.

A third source of expected frequencies is *empirical;* that is, the frequencies are based on the availability of previously collected data. For example, a researcher might be interested in changes in attitudes toward sex education in elementary school that may have occurred over a ten-year period. To make this comparison, the researcher would have to obtain information concerning the nature of the attitudes ten years earlier. This distribution, based on previously collected data, would be used to define the *expected* frequencies associated with the different attitudes. The investigator would compare the distribution of attitudes from the new sample with the earlier one to detect shifts or changes in the two distributions of frequencies. As another example, suppose a governmental agency wished to determine whether the hiring pattern of a large public utility reflected the present distribution of individuals according to ethnic origins in a particular city. A recent census might be used to establish the distribution of employable adults by ethnicity; the census would provide the information necessary for determining expected frequencies of new hirings. The observed frequencies of new hirings by the utility would then be compared with the expected frequencies to answer this research question.

All three types of research problems can be analyzed by means of the chi square statistic. The computational procedures are identical to those we illustrated with the numerical example. The only potential difficulty is in the translation of the expected response distribution into frequencies that are relevant to the sample data. This translation was no problem in the numerical example, since we simply divided the total number of subjects in the sample (120) equally among the three displays in order to obtain the expected frequencies. When expected frequencies are based on theory or surveys, however, this information must usually be converted into proportions which are then multiplied by the total number of subjects in the sample to yield the expected frequencies necessary for completing the statistical analysis. This conversion is necessary because the total number of expected frequencies must equal the total number of observed frequencies for the formula to work.[2]

THE ANALYSIS OF SINGLE-FACTOR EXPERIMENTS

We are now ready to consider how chi square is used to analyze the results of an experiment in which the response measure consists of a limited number of

---

[2] Alternative formulas are available that permit working with proportions directly rather than converting to frequencies.

categories. The most common examples are **dichotomous classifications** (two categories)—for example, yes-no, pass-fail, solve-not solve—although more than two response categories are certainly possible—say, degree of agreement or degree of success.

An Experiment

As an example, consider a hypothetical problem-solving experiment in which subjects are required to use a common object (a screwdriver) in an uncommon way (as the weight for a penduluum). Subjects are given a fixed amount of time to solve the problem. Ninety subjects are assigned randomly and in equal numbers to $a = 3$ instructional conditions. One group (a_1) is given no special instructions other than those required to describe the problem; a second group (a_2) is asked to list ten common uses to which a screwdriver can be put; and the third group (a_3) is asked to list ten uncommon uses for a screwdriver.

It is hypothesized that subjects who are asked to think of a screwdriver in its usual function will have difficulty in using that object in an unusual way to solve the problem. On the other hand, subjects who are asked to think of the screwdriver in an unusual way will be primed for the unusual use of the object in the experimental task. The uninstructed group serves as a baseline for performance in the absence of special instructions.

The subjects are given ten minutes to solve the problem. Since not all the subjects are able to give the correct solution within the ten-minute period, it is possible to divide the subjects in each group into two response categories, those who solve the problem (solvers) and those who do not (nonsolvers).[3] The results of the experiment are entered in Table 15-2, a two-dimensional matrix called a **contingency table,** with the treatment conditions (factor A) defining one dimension in the table and the response categories defining the other.

The performance of each subject is entered within the body of the matrix. All we know is whether or not a subject solved the problem within the time limit; the number of subjects solving the problem is entered in the first row and the number of subjects not solving the problem is entered in the second row. Column and row totals are also obtained. The column totals provide us with a check to see that we have accounted for all the $s = 30$ subjects in each of the treatment conditions, and the row totals indicate the overall results of

---

[3] If all subjects solved the problem, it might be possible to use a time measure (solution time) as the response measure and the analysis of variance to assess the differences.

TABLE 15-2   Solvers and Nonsolvers in a Problem-Solving Task

Response Category	No Instruction a_1	Common Uses a_2	Unique Uses a_3	Row Total
Solve	9	17	22	48
Not Solve	21	13	8	42
Column Total	30	30	30	90

the experiment. We will use this information to calculate the expected frequencies for the statistical analysis.

Expected Frequencies

The expected frequencies against which the observed frequencies will be compared are derived from the assumption that the distribution of solvers and nonsolvers will not differ from condition to condition. The first step is to estimate the distribution of solvers and nonsolvers if this hypothesis were in fact true. We can obtain this information by using the row totals to calculate two proportions, one reflecting the proportion of solvers in the *total* sample—disregarding group affiliation—and the other reflecting the proportion of nonsolvers, also disregarding group affiliation. With the data in Table 15-2, we find the overall proportion of solvers to be

$$\frac{48}{90} = .53$$

and the overall proportion of nonsolvers to be

$$\frac{42}{90} = .47 \quad .$$

If the independent variable had no effect on problem-solving performance, we would expect to find 53 percent solvers and 47 percent nonsolvers in *each* of the treatment conditions. We will now use these two proportions to calculate the necessary expected frequencies (f_E). We obtain the f_E's by multiplying the two overall proportions by the number of subjects in each treatment condition. That is,

$$f_E = (\text{overall proportion}) \times (\text{number of subjects}) \quad . \qquad (15\text{-}3)$$

In order to minimize rounding errors, it is usually better to use the alternative formula,

$$f_E = \frac{(\text{row total})(\text{column total})}{\text{grand total}} \quad , \tag{15-3a}$$

where the "row total" refers to the total number of subjects giving a particular response, the "grand total" refers to the total number of subjects in the experiment, and the "column total" refers to the number of subjects in a given treatment condition.

Since equal numbers of subjects were assigned to each of the conditions, we need only perform these calculations once.[4] From equation (15-3a), the expected number of solvers for each treatment group is

$$f_{E_{\text{solve}}} = \frac{(48)(30)}{90} = \frac{1,440}{90} = 16.00 \quad ,$$

and the expected number of nonsolvers for each treatment group is

$$f_{E_{\text{not solve}}} = \frac{(42)(30)}{90} = \frac{1,260}{90} = 14.00 \quad .$$

These expected frequencies are entered in column 2 of Table 15-3, the expected frequency of solvers for the three treatment conditions in the upper half of the table and the expected frequency of nonsolvers in the lower half.

Statistical Analysis

The steps involved in calculating the chi square statistic are enumerated in Table 15-3. Columns 1 and 2 specify the observed and expected frequencies, respectively. Column 3 indicates the differences between the observed and expected frequencies for each cell of the contingency table; column 4 lists the squares of these differences. From column 5, where each squared difference is divided by the corresponding expected frequency, we can obtain the values needed for chi square, namely,

$$\chi^2 = \sum \frac{(f_O - f_E)^2}{f_E}$$
$$= 3.06 + .06 + 2.25 + 3.50 + .07 + 2.57$$
$$= 11.51 \quad .$$

The degrees of freedom for a chi square calculated from a contingency table is given by

$$df = (a - 1)(c - 1) \quad , \tag{15-4}$$

---

[4] Of course, if the number of subjects were different for each condition, expected frequencies would have to be calculated separately for each condition.

TABLE 15-3   The Analysis of a Single-Factor Design

Conditions	1. Observed (f_O)	2. Expected (f_E)	3. $f_O - f_E$	4. $(f_O - f_E)^2$	5. $\dfrac{(f_O - f_E)^2}{f_E}$
			Solvers		
a_1	9	16	$9 - 16 = -7$	$(-7)^2 = 49$	$\dfrac{49}{16} = 3.06$
a_2	17	16	$17 - 16 = +1$	$(+1)^2 = 1$	$\dfrac{1}{16} = .06$
a_3	22	16	$22 - 16 = +6$	$(+6)^2 = 36$	$\dfrac{36}{16} = 2.25$
			Nonsolvers		
a_1	21	14	$21 - 14 = +7$	$(+7)^2 = 49$	$\dfrac{49}{14} = 3.50$
a_2	13	14	$13 - 14 = -1$	$(-1)^2 = 1$	$\dfrac{1}{14} = .07$
a_3	8	14	$8 - 14 = -6$	$(-6)^2 = 36$	$\dfrac{36}{14} = 2.57$
Total	90	90	$\Sigma (f_O - f_E) = 0$	Not Needed	$\chi^2 = 11.51$

where a is the number of treatment conditions and c is the number of response categories. For this example,

$$df = (3 - 1)(2 - 1) = 2(1) = 2 \quad .$$

The statistical hypotheses can be stated in terms of the frequencies with which the different classes of responses occur in the several treatment conditions. We refer to these sets of frequencies as **response distributions.** The statistical hypotheses can be stated as follows:

> H_0: All treatment response distributions are equal;
> H_1: Not all treatment response distributions are equal.

Where the response distribution consists of only *two* categories, the statistical hypotheses can be stated in terms of proportions, that is, a ratio of the frequency of one class of response (for instance, the frequency of solvers) to the total number of subjects in a treatment condition. In the present example,

> H_0: Proportions of solvers for the treatment conditions are equal;
> H_1: Not all of these proportions are equal.

We determine the critical value of χ^2 by entering Table 5 of Appendix A at the appropriate number of degrees of freedom and the desired significance level (α). In the example, $df = 2$; at $\alpha = .05$, the critical value of χ^2 is 5.99. With this information, we can state the decision rules as follows:

If the obtained value of χ^2 equals or exceeds $\chi^2_\alpha = 5.99$, reject the null hypothesis; otherwise, do not reject the null hypothesis.

The obtained value of χ^2 is 11.51. Consequently, the null hypothesis is rejected.

ANALYTICAL COMPARISONS

As was true with the single-factor analysis of variance, rejection of the overall null hypothesis does not provide an unambiguous assessment of the results. In the present example, we would like to know a number of things, for example, whether the special instructions had an effect (a_1 versus $a_2 + a_3$) and whether the two instructional conditions differ (a_2 versus a_3). As suggested in Chapter 6, we would hope that such questions would be asked during the planning stage of the experiment and thus qualify as planned comparisons. As you will recall, planned comparisons are conducted directly, without reference to the significance or nonsignificance of the overall statistical test. We will work through two examples of analytical comparisons conducted on the data of the problem-solving experiment.

Two Comparisons

First Comparison. Analytical comparisons consist of small **component contingency tables** created when the investigator singles out two treatment conditions for comparison or combines conditions for comparison with another treatment condition or combination of treatment conditions. Suppose we wanted to test the hypothesis that the two instructional conditions together surpassed the noninstructional baseline condition. In the analysis of variance, we could use the coefficients ($+2, -1, -1$) in order to obtain the sum of squares associated with this comparison. With frequency data, we simply combine the conditions with like signs, positive and negative, and arrange the resulting frequencies in a new contingency table. In the present example, the following table results:

Response Category	Treatment Conditions		Total
	a_1	$a_2 + a_3$	
Solve	9	39	48
Not Solve	21	21	42
Total	30	60	90

We obtain the frequencies in the combined instructional category by adding the appropriate frequencies for levels a_2 and a_3. For the first response category, $17 + 22 = 39$; for the second category, $13 + 8 = 21$.

The computational formula for analytical comparisons is a little more complicated than the usual formula in that it requires the use of *two* expected frequencies for each ratio, one based on the marginal totals of the *component* contingency table and the other based on the marginal totals of the *original* contingency table. The new formula is

$$\chi^2_{comp.} = \sum \frac{(f_O - f_E)^2}{F_E} \quad , \tag{15-5}$$

where f_O is the observed frequency in any given cell of the comparison contingency table, f_E is the expected frequency for that cell based on the marginal totals of the comparison contingency table, and F_E is the expected frequency for that cell obtained from the original contingency table.[5] Let's see how this works out in practice.

We obtain the expected frequencies based on the comparison contingency table (f_E) by applying equation (15-3a) to each combination of row and column totals taken from the comparison table. For example, the expected frequency of solvers for the control condition (a_1) is

$$f_E = \frac{\text{(row total)(column total)}}{\text{grand total}}$$

$$= \frac{(48)(30)}{90} = \frac{1,440}{90} = 16.00 \quad ;$$

and the expected frequency of solvers for the combined instruction conditions is

$$f_E = \frac{(48)(60)}{90} = \frac{2,880}{90} = 32.00 \quad .$$

---

[5] See Bresnahan and Shapiro (1966) for a detailed illustration of this formula and Castellan (1965, pp. 337–338) for a discussion of the reasons for its use.

TABLE 15-4   A Comparison Between Control and Combined
Instructional Conditions

Con-ditions	1. f_o[a]	2. f_E	3. $f_o - f_E$	4. $(f_o - f_E)^2$	5. F_E	6. $\dfrac{(f_o - f_E)^2}{F_E}$
			Solvers			
a_1	9	16	$9 - 16 = -7$	$(-7)^2 = 49$	16	$\dfrac{49}{16} = 3.06$
$a_2 + a_3$	39	32	$39 - 32 = +7$	$(+7)^2 = 49$	32	$\dfrac{49}{32} = 1.53$
			Nonsolvers			
a_1	21	14	$21 - 14 = +7$	$(+7)^2 = 49$	14	$\dfrac{49}{14} = 3.50$
$a_2 + a_3$	21	28	$21 - 28 = -7$	$(-7)^2 = 49$	28	$\dfrac{49}{28} = 1.75$
Total	90	90	$\Sigma (f_o - f_E) = 0$	Not Needed	90	$\chi^2_{comp.} = 9.84$

[a] f_o = observed frequency
f_E = expected frequency based on the comparison contingency table
F_E = expected frequency based on the original contingency table (Table 15-3)

The other two expected frequencies are obtained in an identical fashion. All four of the expected frequencies derived from the comparison contingency table are listed in column 2 of Table 15-4.

The set of expected frequencies based on the original contingency table (F_E) is most conveniently obtained from the original analysis. From Table 15-3, we find the following expected frequencies:

Response Category	Treatment Conditions	
	a_1	$a_2 + a_3$
Solve	16	$16 + 16 = 32$
Not Solve	14	$14 + 14 = 28$

These frequencies are entered in column 5 of Table 15-4. You will note that the two sets of expected frequencies are identical for this analysis. This will not always be the case, as you will see in the comparison we consider next.

The steps in the analysis are summarized in the various columns of Table 15-4. We obtain the value for chi square by adding the quantities appearing in column 6 of the table. Specifically,

$$\chi^2_{comp.} = 3.06 + 1.53 + 3.50 + 1.75 = 9.84 \quad .$$

The degrees of freedom for this comparison are obtained from equation (15-4):

$$df = (a - 1)(c - 1)$$
$$= (2 - 1)(2 - 1) = 1(1) = 1 \quad .$$

(In this case, a is defined as the number of treatment *categories* rather than treatment conditions.) The table of χ^2 in the appendix indicates that a value of 3.84 is required for the 5 percent level of significance. The χ^2 associated with this comparison exceeds this critical value, and the null hypothesis is rejected. We can conclude that the instructed subjects in general were more successful with the problem-solving task than were the baseline control subjects.

Second Comparison. As a second example, we will compare the two instructional conditions. We obtain the contingency table for this comparison directly from the original data matrix (Table 15-2, p. 373):

Response Category	Treatment Conditions		Total
	a_2	a_3	
Solve	17	22	39
Not Solve	13	8	21
Total	30	30	60

The expected frequencies based on the comparison contingency table (f_E), which we calculate by substituting in equation (15-3a), are presented in column 2 of Table 15-5. The other set of expected frequencies (F_E) are obtained from the original analysis (Table 15-3 p. 375), and are listed in column 5. Note in this example that the two sets of expected frequencies are different.

The step-by-step calculations of chi square are enumerated in the remaining columns of the table. From column 6,

$$\chi^2_{comp.} = .39 + .39 + .45 + .45 = 1.68 \quad .$$

TABLE 15-5   A Comparison Between the Instructional Conditions

Con-ditions	1. $f_O{}^a$	2. f_E	3. $f_O - f_E$	4. $(f_O - f_E)^2$	5. F_E	6. $\dfrac{(f_O - f_E)^2}{F_E}$
			Solvers			
a_2	17	19.5	$17 - 19.5 = -2.5$	$(-2.5)^2 = 6.25$	16	$\dfrac{6.25}{16} = .39$
a_3	22	19.5	$22 - 19.5 = +2.5$	$(+2.5)^2 = 6.25$	16	$\dfrac{6.25}{16} = .39$
			Nonsolvers			
a_2	13	10.5	$13 - 10.5 = +2.5$	$(+2.5)^2 = 6.25$	14	$\dfrac{6.25}{14} = .45$
a_3	8	10.5	$8 - 10.5 = -2.5$	$(-2.5)^2 = 6.25$	14	$\dfrac{6.25}{14} = .45$
Total	60	60	$\Sigma (f_O - f_E) = 0$	Not Needed	60	$\chi^2_{comp.} = 1.68$

^{a} f_O = observed frequency
f_E = expected frequency based on the comparison contingency table
F_E = expected frequency based on the original contingency table (Table 15-3)

This comparison also has $df = 1$ and, thus, the same critical value of χ^2 as in the last comparison, $\chi^2_\alpha = 3.84$. Since the obtained value of 1.68 does not exceed the critical value, the null hypothesis is not rejected. We conclude that the evidence is not sufficiently strong to indicate that the instructions produced differential effects.

Some Comments

It is instructive to consider the nature of the conclusions permitted by these comparisons. Taken together, the two comparisons suggest that while the special instructions have a facilitating effect on the solution of this particular problem (the first comparison), the uniqueness of the uses listed by the subjects seems not to be important (the second comparison). Any investigator posing a theory predicting that special instructions will produce a differential effect would now have to account for this negative finding. Perhaps the theory is correct but the experimental test insufficient. The data do contain a nonsignificant "hint" that subjects were more successful in solving the problem after they listed ten unusual uses. Maybe if subjects listed *more* uses, the difference between the two conditions would widen. On the other hand, maybe subjects listing common uses of a screwdriver ran out of common ones quickly and shifted to more unusual ones in order to complete their lists of ten. If this latter possibility were true, then a new experiment requiring only *five* uses might produce results more favorable to the theory. Of course, one might also speculate that the results show that *any kind* of cognitive activity will have a beneficial effect on problem solving. This conclusion could be examined in a different series of experiments designed to determine the nature of the facilitating effect.

Whatever the conclusion, it is this sort of speculation that sharpens theory, improves experimental designs, and leads to new and potentially more revealing experiments. But note that the conclusions and speculations do *not* stem from the overall statistical analysis, from which one can only conclude that the three treatment conditions do not all have the same effect, but from the *analytical comparisons* that identify the specific manipulations responsible for the significant overall chi square. As in Chapter 6, we can see the value of analytical comparisons in both the design and the analysis of experiments. Whether the behavior under study is measured on a continuous scale or in terms of a number of discrete response categories is not critical. All that is required is that an experiment be designed in such a way that these pointed and analytical questions can be examined by the procedures outlined in this section.

THE ASSUMPTIONS AND RESTRICTIONS OF CHI SQUARE

The chi square statistical test is not without its own assumptions and restrictions. We summarize these briefly in the following sections.

Independence

It is assumed that each observation is independent of all the other observations in the experiment. Generally, the researcher meets this assumption by obtaining *one* response from each subject. A common mistake in the use of chi square consists of obtaining two or more responses from subjects and entering these frequencies in a contingency table. Such a procedure violates the independence assumption. One check on this assumption is to verify that the total number of observations (the grand total) equals the total number of subjects in the experiment. If observations exceed subjects, either an arithmetical mistake has been made or the independence assumption has been violated, that is, subjects have been counted more than once.

Frequency Data

Chi square is designed to deal with data where each response in any particular category counts as 1. The frequencies appearing in the contingency table reflect the number of subjects falling into each of the cells of the matrix. The check described for verifying independence is also applicable to this assumption. That is, the grand total of the matrix must equal the total number of subjects.

Expected Frequencies

From a statistical point of view, the information provided in the χ^2 table (Table 5 of Appendix A) is not entirely accurate for all the applications discussed in this chapter. The accuracy is best when the total number of observations is large, for example, more than a hundred. The accuracy of the table decreases systematically as the sample size decreases in number.

Over the years, a number of rules of thumb have been developed to cope with this problem. They are usually stated in terms of the size of the *expected* frequencies appearing in the data analysis. It appears that the problem is not very serious if 2 or more degrees of freedom are associated with the chi square statistic. Under these circumstances, the use of the values in Table 5 become questionable only when any of the expected frequencies in the analysis is smaller than 5. The problem is more acute with 1 degree of freedom, however, and researchers must pay close attention to the size of the expected frequencies and to the "remedial" steps recommended for restoring the accuracy of the statistical test. The following are the rules that apply and the generally recommended courses of action when $df = 1$:

1. The expected frequencies for all cells must be equal to or greater than 10 for the chi square tests as we have described them to be reasonably accurate.

2. If any expected frequencies are smaller than 10 but greater than or equal to 5, it is necessary to apply a **correction for continuity**, known as the **Yates's Correction.**[6] The correction for continuity should also be applied if the total number of subjects is equal to 40 or less.

3. If one or more of the expected frequencies are smaller than 5, the **Fisher Exact Test** must be performed. (This is also recommended if

---

[6] This correction is applied by disregarding the sign of the differences between observed and expected frequencies and subtracting .5 from each difference *before* squaring in the calculation of the chi square statistic.

the total number of subjects is 20 or less.) We will not discuss this test, but it can be found in a number of statistics books.[7]

THE TEST OF INDEPENDENCE

Chi square is very frequently applied in psychology to determine whether two dependent variables are correlated. Investigators often present public opinion surveys, for example, by listing the distribution of attitudes as a function of some meaningful classification of the respondents. This sort of research is used to answer questions as, "How are individuals from different parts of the country going to vote in a presidential election?" or, "What are the attitudes towards abortion for individuals of different religious beliefs?" Both of these questions involve correlational data, and both concern the relationship between the subjects' characteristics on the one hand and certain attitudes or beliefs on the other. The data in these surveys are typically frequency counts—the number of individuals of a certain type offering a particular opinion or belief. The frequencies may be reported as proportions or percentages, but they represent categorical data nevertheless.

In essence, the data are set up as a contingency table with two sets of subject characteristics (dependent variables), each of which consists of a number of categories. Consider the voter-preference example. The contingency table for this survey might consist of the following arrangement:

Presidential Candidates	Geographical Location			
	East	Midwest	West	South
A				
B				
C				

Subjects would be classified or placed in this contingency table according to the appropriate column and row characteristics: geographical region (col-

[7] See, for example, Siegel (1956, pp. 96–104) or Hays (1973, pp. 737–740) for a discussion and illustration of the procedures involved in the Fisher Exact Test. It is interesting to note that this test does not produce a chi square statistic, but rather, a probability, which, if less than α, indicates that the null hypothesis may be rejected.

umns) and voting preference (rows). Neither of these variables is *manipulated* by an experimenter. The researcher does not randomly assign subjects to different geographical areas and then ask them for voting preferences, nor does the researcher tell individuals how to vote and then observe where they subsequently choose to live. Of course not! The researcher simply attempts to determine whether one characteristic of individuals—place of residence—is related to (in other words, is correlated with) how they say they will vote.

This sort of contingency table is commonly used in studies of sex differences. In the problem-solving example, for instance, we could have tested a number of subjects on the same problem, treating them all exactly the same way, and have noted the sex of each subject. The original response classification of those who solve and those who do not would remain, but the other classification would consist of male or female. The resulting contingency table is given below:

Response Category	Sex of Subject		Total
	Male	Female	
Solve			
Not Solve			
Total			

After testing, each subject would be placed in one of the cells of the contingency table depending on his or her sex and whether he or she solved the problem. The research question is concerned with the relationship, if any, between a person's biological sex and success with the problem.

Once we enter numbers in the contingency table, we can calculate the chi square statistic exactly as described and illustrated in the analysis of a single-factor experiment. For this reason, we do not work through a numerical example of these calculations in this section.

An important difference exists between the nature of the information afforded when chi square is used with experimental data, where one classification consists of treatments and the other different response categories, and that used with correlational data, where both classifications consist of subject characteristics. With experimental data, conclusions permit the inference of cause and effect. To illustrate, in the example from the previous section, we were able to conclude that the instructions given to the subjects had differential effects on problem-solving behavior. On the other hand, when both sets of classifications are based on classifications of subjects, all that can be concluded with a significant chi square is that a relationship exists between the two variables. The chi square test with correlational data is often referred to as a **test of independence,** or a **test of association.**[8]

SUMMARY

While a great deal of data collected in psychological experimentation reflects behavior that has been measured on a continuous scale, a scale that reflects variations in amount, there are many instances reported in the literature in which measurement occurs at a less precise level. In this chapter, we consider statistical procedures appropriate for experiments in which the dependent variable consists of a number of mutually exclusive classes or categories. Under these circumstances, an observation is placed in one of these classifications with all other observations that satisfy the definition of that response category. The basic data consist of frequencies, that is, the number of individuals displaying each of the different sorts of behaviors or possessing a particular type of descriptive characteristic.

The chi square statistic was designed to deal with these sorts of data. We saw how the results of an experiment may be expressed in terms of frequencies—for example, the number of subjects solving or not solving a particular problem—and how this information can be used in the evaluation of research hypotheses concerning the effects of independent variables on the behavior under investigation. The actual calculations are relatively simple, and the procedures are easily adapted to permit the statistical assessment of analytical comparisons.

Chi square is also used in contexts other than that of an experiment. For example, chi square is used frequently in the analysis of results obtained from field observations and from survey research. The analysis of simple response classifications, for example, voter preference or attitudes on policies and issues, is one common application of chi square. Another use of chi square is to establish the presence of correlations between two different sets of subject characteristics.

---

[8] The information from a contingency matrix can be used in obtaining a measure of the *degree* of relationship between two subject variables. The index of correlation appropriate for two dichotomous variables—for example, sex and problem solution—is called the phi coefficient. (See Edwards, 1976, pp. 68–72, for example, for a discussion of the phi coefficient.)

TERMS, CONCEPTS, AND SYMBOLS

---

response categories   test of independence
observed frequency   test of association
expected frequency χ^2
chi square statistic f_O
dichotomous classification f_E
response distribution χ^2_α
contingency table c
component contingency table $c - 1$
correction for continuity $\chi^2_{comp.}$
Yates's Correction F_E
Fisher Exact Test

EXERCISES

---

1. Suppose an experiment is conducted in a large mental institution comparing the effectiveness of three different types of therapy—psychotherapy,
   chemotherapy, and shock therapy—in treating depressed patients. Eighty
   patients are randomly assigned in equal numbers to one of four
   conditions—the three therapy conditions and a control condition of no
   treatment. After two months of treatment (or no treatment), the patients
   are classified as either "improved" or "not improved." The numbers of
   patients falling into these two categories for each group are given below:

Outcome	Psychotherapy	Chemotherapy	Shock Therapy	No Therapy
Improved	14	11	12	5
Not Improved	6	9	8	15

   a. Do the four conditions differ in effectiveness?
   b. Are the three therapy conditions differentially effective in treating
      depressed patients?

c. If we combine the three therapy conditions, does a significant difference exist between this group of subjects and that in the no-therapy control condition?

2. A researcher conducted two studies concerned with visual perception. The first experiment required two hours of participation and the second required five hours. Thirty subjects were included in each experiment by the time it was completed, but the investigator was somewhat concerned over the loss of subjects in the second experiment. Since the two experiments were part of a series, the researcher wanted the results of each to be comparable and decided to use chi square to determine whether the subject loss was reliably different in the two experiments. The numbers of subjects completing or not completing the two experiments are given in the table below. Apply a chi square test to determine if the subject loss is different for the two experiments.

Status of Subject	Two-Hour Experiment	Five-Hour Experiment
Completing	15	9
Not Completing	15	21

3. A student was convinced that certain memory techniques play a role in how well a person remembers material in a simple memory task. After administering the test, the student asked subjects whether they used visual imagery to remember or used any of a variety of other methods. Subjects were classified as fast or slow memorizers based upon their performance on the previous test. The numbers of subjects reporting the use of visual imagery or other methods grouped according to subject performance are given below.

Method	Fast	Slow
Visual	18	9
Other	7	16

Use the chi square statistic to determine whether the fast and slow memorizers differed in the type of memory reported.

Standard Scores and Estimation Procedures

16

The two topics covered in this chapter are of considerable importance to psychologists. The first topic is concerned with measures designed to reflect relative position in an ordered set of observations. The second topic comprises procedures that permit an investigator to estimate population characteristics from a sample drawn randomly from that population. Both sets of procedures are used more frequently in such applied fields as educational testing and survey research than in experimental research projects. Nevertheless, undergraduates majoring in psychology will encounter these topics in their studies and should therefore become sufficiently familiar with them to understand how they function in a behavioral science.

STANDARD SCORES

The value of a particular score tells us very little about what the score means or signifies. What does the fact that a student scored 50 on a test tell us about his or her performance? Nothing, except that 50 is higher than 49 and lower than 51! If we were also told that the mean on the test was 40, we would be a little better able to judge the student's performance—at least we would know that the score was in the upper part of the distribution. The meaning of the 10-point difference between the score and the mean, however, is dependent on the variability present in the total set of scores. For example, a deviation of 10 points above the mean would be considerably less impressive if the range of scores were 10–90 than if it were 35–55. When the meaning of individual scores is of interest, one can overcome these problems by transforming each score into what is known as a **standard score,** which expresses a score in terms of the mean and the variability.

Definition

A standard score, also referred to as a z **score,** is defined as follows:

$$z = \frac{\text{deviation}}{\text{standard deviation}} = \frac{X - \bar{X}}{SD} \; , \tag{16-1}$$

where $X - \bar{X}$ is the deviation of a score above or below the mean, and SD is the standard deviation of the scores.[1] For this particular formula, the definition of standard deviation is different from that elsewhere in this book. In this context,

$$SD = \sqrt{\frac{SS}{s}} \; . \tag{16-2}$$

You will notice that the denominator of equation (16-2) is the number of scores (s) rather than the value we have used before, the degrees of freedom ($df = s - 1$). The particular definition one should use depends on the ultimate use of the statistic. If the measure is intended to *describe* the variability of a single set of scores, the only set of interest to the researcher, then equation (16-2) is appropriate. If, on the other hand, the measure will be used in problems of *statistical inference*—estimation or hypothesis testing— then the alternative definition is appropriate. The reason for this relatively minor difference lies in statistical theory: The latter definition of the variance

---

[1] We have reverted to standard notation to be consistent with other statistics texts.

(SS/df) provides an unbiased estimate of the variance in the population, while the former definition (SS/s) does not.[2]

Standard-Score Scales

Standard scores use the standard deviation of the distribution as a kind of measuring stick, expressing deviation from the mean in what are called **standard-deviation units.** A standard score of a particular value—say, −1.64—means that the raw score from which the standard score was derived is 1.64 standard-deviation units *below* the mean of the distribution. A score from any other distribution that results in a standard score of −1.64 means exactly the same thing, regardless of the value of the mean or the standard deviation of the other distribution. It is this property of standard scores that makes them attractive to test constructors and educators, since it enables them to compare scores obtained from a number of different tests. The z score "locates" the relative position of a score on a scale that can be universally applied to any test.

Suppose an instructor wants to combine the scores on three examinations and to weight them equally in determining the final grades in a course. One's first impulse would be simply to add the three scores for each individual and to examine the final composite distribution. But suppose the three tests resulted in the following outcomes:

Test	Mean	Standard Deviation
1	55.3	5.0
2	54.5	2.5
3	55.0	22.5

When the raw scores for each student are combined, they are not weighted equally; greater weight is given to the more variable test (test 3). This test has more larger and smaller scores than the other two tests, and the deviant scores would therefore be emphasized in the final determination of the grades.

Standard scores neutralize the problems associated with the presence of unequal variability for sets of scores to be combined. As you will see below,

---

[2] The concept of bias in statistics is difficult to explain. However, you should note that the use of *df* in the denominator gives a slightly larger value for the variance and standard deviation than the use of *s*, and this difference is sufficient to eliminate the bias associated with equation (16-2).

TABLE 16-1   Calculation of a Set of z Scores

X_i	$X_i - \bar{X}$	z_i
5	$5 - 4 = +1$	$+1/1.41 = +0.71$
3	$3 - 4 = -1$	$-1/1.41 = -0.71$
4	$4 - 4 = 0$	$0/1.41 = 0.00$
4	$4 - 4 = 0$	$0/1.41 = 0.00$
6	$6 - 4 = +2$	$+2/1.41 = +1.42$
1	$1 - 4 = -3$	$-3/1.41 = -2.13$
3	$3 - 4 = -1$	$-1/1.41 = -0.71$
4	$4 - 4 = 0$	$0/1.41 = 0.00$
6	$6 - 4 = +2$	$+2/1.41 = +1.42$
4	$4 - 4 = 0$	$0/1.41 = 0.00$
$\Sigma X = 40$	$\Sigma (X_i - \bar{X}) = 0$	$\Sigma z = 0.00$
$\Sigma (X)^2 = 180$		$\Sigma (z)^2 = 10.08$

a set of standard scores has a mean of 0 and a standard deviation of 1. It is this property that makes it possible to weight the three tests equally. Each set of transformed test scores will have exactly the same mean (0) and standard deviation (1).

Calculating Standard Scores. We will convert the set of raw scores appearing in Table 16-1 into standard scores. The first step is to calculate the mean and the standard deviation from the raw scores (X_i) using the summary data provided at the bottom of the table. For the mean,

$$\bar{X} = \frac{\Sigma X}{s}$$

$$= \frac{40}{10} = 4.00 \quad .$$

The standard deviation is calculated next. First, we obtain the sum of squares:

$$SS = \Sigma (X)^2 - \frac{(\Sigma X)^2}{s}$$

$$= 180 - \frac{(40)^2}{10}$$

$$= 180 - \frac{1,600}{10} = 180 - 160.00 = 20.00 \quad .$$

Second, we substitute in equation (16-2):

$$SD = \sqrt{\frac{SS}{s}}$$

$$= \sqrt{\frac{20.00}{10}} = \sqrt{2.00} = 1.41 \quad .$$

The next step is to calculate the deviation of each raw score from the mean. These calculations are indicated in the second column of Table 16-1. (A useful check at this point is to verify that the sum of the deviation scores equals 0.) The final step is to calculate the z scores by dividing each deviation by the standard deviation. This step is enumerated in the third column of the table.

The point to note from this illustration is that the mean of the z scores is 0 and the standard deviation is 1.0. From the summary information in the last column of Table 16-1, we find

$$\bar{X}_z = \frac{\Sigma z}{s}$$

$$= \frac{0.00}{10} = 0.00;$$

$$SS_z = \Sigma (z)^2 - \frac{(\Sigma z)^2}{s}$$

$$= 10.08 - \frac{(0.00)^2}{10}$$

$$= 10.08 - 0.00 = 10.08; \text{ and}$$

$$SD_z = \sqrt{\frac{SS_z}{s}}$$

$$= \sqrt{\frac{10.08}{10}} = \sqrt{1.01} = 1.00 \quad .$$

Except for small rounding errors, this sort of result will be found with any set of raw scores transformed to standard scores.

Inferring Relative Position

In your studies, you will find references made to the relative position of a score in a distribution of scores. When the number of scores involved is small, the actual ordinal position is usually specified, for example, first, second, third, and so on. When the number of scores is relatively large, however, **percentile ranks** (percentiles for short) usually replace rank order as a measure of relative position. A percentile is a point in a distribution below which a certain percentage of the scores lie. A score with a percentile

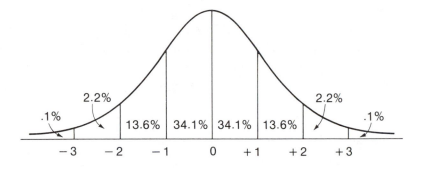

Figure 16-1. Example of a Standard Normal Distribution.

of 37, for example, indicates that 37 percent of the distribution consists of scores that are smaller than that particular value.[3] You will also see relative position expressed in terms of standard or z scores. This latter measure requires a bit of explanation.

Using the z Distribution. If a score is assumed to come from a distribution that is approximately normal in form, and if the mean and the standard deviation of the distribution are known, we can determine the percentile rank of that score by using what is known about normal distributions. Let's assume that the distribution of scores in a population is normal—a reasonable assumption, as we have pointed out in Chapter 7. If all the scores are transformed into z scores, the resulting distribution will also be normal, with a mean of 0 and a standard deviation of 1.0. This particular normal distribution is called the **standard normal distribution,** or the z **distribution.** A picture of a standardized normal distribution is presented in Figure 16-1.

Figure 16-1 exhibits several features of interest. First, the horizontal axis is marked off in standard-deviation units, ranging from -3 to $+3$ from the mean of 0. Second, the curve extends in both directions to extremely small and large values without ever touching the baseline, although most of the curve is contained between -3 and $+3$ standard deviations from the mean. Third, the vertical axis is not given, since the height of various parts of the curve, although necessary for drawing the curve, is not our interest. We are, however, interested in the areas under the curve, because the area between two points on the baseline can be expressed in terms of the proportion of cases in the total distribution that falls between these two points.

---

[3] You may have noticed that the median is located at the 50th percentile of a distribution, since the median is defined as the score below which 50 percent of the cases fall.

Suppose we arbitrarily set the total area under the normal curve—that is, all the cases in the distribution—equal to 1.0. From statistical tables, it is possible to determine the proportion of area between any two points on the baseline. Consider the proportion of the total area occurring between lines drawn at successive standard deviations in Figure 16-1. As you can see,

34.1 percent of the area occurs between -1 and 0 and between 0 and $+1$

13.6 percent of the area occurs between -2 and -1 and between $+1$ and $+2$

2.2 percent of the area occurs between -3 and -2 and between $+2$ and $+3$

.1 percent of the area occurs from -3 downward and from $+3$ upward

Note that the sum of these individual portions of the area equals 100 percent. Specifically, summing from left to right,

$$.1 + 2.2 + 13.6 + 34.1 + 34.1 + 13.6 + 2.2 + .1 = 100 \text{ percent} \quad .$$

To calculate percentiles based on the normal distribution, we simply transform a raw score into a z score and add up the proportion of area under the normal curve occurring *below* that particular point. As an illustration, we will determine the percentile rank of a z score of -1.0. In Figure 16-1, the percentage of the area under the normal curve falling below a vertical line drawn at $z = -1.0$ is equal to the sum of the percentages for each segment occurring to the left of that point. That is, for $z = -1.0$, the cumulative percentage is

$$.1 + 2.2 + 13.6 = 15.9 \text{ percent} \quad .$$

Thus, the percentile rank of a score with a z score of -1.0 is 15.9. Percentile ranks for any of the other z scores listed in Figure 16-1 can be calculated in the same way. The percentiles for each of the z scores are calculated as follows:

z Score	Percentage of Area Below the z Score
-3.0	.1 percent
-2.0	$.1 + 2.2 = 2.3$ percent
-1.0	$.1 + 2.2 + 13.6 = 15.9$ percent
0.0	$.1 + 2.2 + 13.6 + 34.1 = 50.0$ percent
$+1.0$	$.1 + 2.2 + 13.6 + 34.1 + 34.1 = 84.1$ percent
$+2.0$	$.1 + 2.2 + 13.6 + 34.1 + 34.1 + 13.6 = 97.7$ percent
$+3.0$	$.1 + 2.2 + 13.6 + 34.1 + 34.1 + 13.6 + 2.2 = 99.9$ percent

Table 6 of Appendix A is designed to permit the easy determination of percentile ranks for z scores.[4] To find a particular z score between -3.09 and $+3.09$, which are the limits of the table, simply locate the score to the nearest *tenth* first (the entires for each row on the left-hand side of the table) and then to the nearest *hundredth* (the entries listed for each column at the top of the table). The values within the body of the table are the proportions of area under the normal curve occurring to the left of the entered z score. Multiplying by 100 will give the corresponding percentage area and percentile rank. From Table 6, for example,

if $z = +0.16$, the area below that point is .5636

if $z = -1.30$, the area below that point is .0968

if $z = +2.79$, the area below that point is .9974

if $z = -2.00$, the area below that point is .0228

To obtain percentile ranks for these z scores, we transform the proportions to percentages. (Percentile ranks are 56.4, 9.7, 99.7, and 2.3, respectively.)

Standard scores and the normal curve are often used to indicate the *uniqueness* of an individual. If it is reasonable to assume that a particular trait or characteristic—for instance, intelligence scores, grade-point averages, height-weight, or personality traits—is distributed normally in the population under consideration, then z-score transformations of raw scores indicate the relative standing of individuals in the population. A person with a z score of $+3.00$, for example, is a unique individual in the sense that he or she surpasses approximately 99.9 percent of the total population.

For many, the presence of positive and negative numbers makes the z scale seem awkward and confusing. Consequently, most test constructors transform z scores into a more convenient scale—one that eliminates negative values and decimal numbers and centers the scores around a reasonably comprehensible mean. The Wechsler IQ Scale, for instance, is a standard-score scale with a mean of 100 and a standard deviation of 15. The scales used for the College Entrance Examination Board Test (CEEB) and the Graduate Records Examination (GRE) have a mean of 500 and a standard deviation of 100. By knowing the mean and the standard deviation of any particular standard-score scale, you can easily transform a standardized test score into the z score. An IQ score of 124 on the Wechsler scale is trans-

---

[4] Alternative ways exist for listing the area under the normal curve. This particular format facilitates the calculation of percentiles. Other formats are designed for use in different aspects of statistical inference; percentiles can be obtained from these tables, but the process is more complicated and often confusing to beginning students.

formed into a z through subtracting the arbitrary mean (100) and dividing by the arbitrary standard deviation (15). Specifically,

$$z = \frac{124 - 100}{15} = \frac{24}{15} = +1.60 \quad .$$

A GRE score of 750, for which the arbitrary mean is 500 and the arbitrary standard deviation is 100, is equivalent to

$$z = \frac{750 - 500}{100} = \frac{250}{100} = +2.50 \quad .$$

Once you have calculated the z score, you can obtain the percentile rank by referring to Table 6 of Appendix A.

Using Standard Scores in Experiments

While standard scores find widespread application in evaluative and predictive testing, they are of limited usefulness in the analysis of experiments. In experimentation, we treat subjects in the various treatment conditions differently in order to produce systematic *differences* among the treatment means. Suppose we transformed the scores within each treatment condition into z scores, using the means and the standard deviations of the appropriate treatment conditions. Since the mean of a set of z scores is 0, a z-score transformation will produce treatment conditions with the *same* means (that is, 0)—hardly the state of affairs desired by a researcher! Occasionally, one finds z scores used in the detailed analysis of an experiment where an investigator does want to focus on relative position of scores independent of their absolute levels. These applications of standard scores are fairly technical, however, and fall outside the range of this brief overview.

ESTIMATING POPULATION CHARACTERISTICS

The second major topic of this chapter is an introduction to procedures that permit us to estimate population characteristics from information derived from a sample drawn from a population. Estimation is primarily used in the survey-research areas of the behavioral sciences. Public opinion surveys and consumer marketing research are the most common examples. In these endeavors, the motivation is to estimate characteristics of large populations of individuals—for example, all eligible voters or all potential consumers—

from information derived from small samples of individuals drawn from these populations. Estimation procedures are used in these situations because examining all members of the population—say, all eligible U.S. voters—is either infeasible or undesirable. Survey techniques have become very sophisticated and extremely accurate. The effectiveness of these procedures is displayed during every major election, when computers analyze data from a tiny sample of the overall voters to predict final outcomes with deadly accuracy.

In turning from survey research to the arena of experimentation, we find relatively few examples of estimation reported in the literature. Instead, the emphasis is on hypothesis testing. We discuss the use of estimation in experimental research later in this chapter. First, however, we examine estimation procedures in the context of survey research. This presentation is not lengthy or overly technical, since a detailed discussion of these procedures is beyond the scope of this book. We limit our coverage of estimation to one population characteristic, the mean, but you should realize that obtaining estimates of other characteristics is possible as well.[5]

RANDOM SAMPLING

Accurate estimates of population characteristics are critically dependent on the way in which a sample is selected. Strictly speaking, a sample must be drawn *randomly* from the population if the statistical procedures of estimation are to work properly. *Random,* in this case, refers to a selection process that guarantees that each member of the population has an equally likely chance of being included in the sample. Such a procedure has been called **simple random sampling.** With all the estimation procedures discussed, it is assumed that simple random sampling has taken place. Professional survey researchers employ a modified and more complicated set of sampling procedures, since various problems are associated with simple random sampling from extremely large populations. But even with these procedures—for example, multistage cluster sampling—random sampling still enters into the selection process.[6]

---

[5] Hays (1973) is an excellent source of information concerning the estimation of variances, proportions, and correlational measures.

[6] See Freedman, Pisani, and Purves (1978) for an excellent discussion of this form of sampling (pp. 307–310) and for a description of the Current Population Survey conducted monthly by the Census Bureau for the Bureau of Labor Statistics, which is noted for its accuracy and efficiency (Chapter 22).

In simple random sampling, each member of the population is given a unique number code, and a table of random numbers or some other random device is used in the selection of numbers for the sample on the basis of these identification codes. Survey research employs a form of random sampling called **sampling without replacement,** in which individuals are *not* returned to the population once they have been selected for inclusion in the sample. It would make little sense to study an individual more than once in a survey. Another form of random sampling—**sampling with replacement**—returns scores to the population as soon as they are selected for the sample. This latter form of random sampling is usually employed by statisticians in the development of statistical models and theory.

TYPES OF ESTIMATION

Point Estimation

The simplest form of estimation is one in which a single value is offered as an estimate of a parameter. This value is called a **point estimate.** The point estimate of the population mean is easy to obtain; it is simply the mean calculated from the random sample.[7] In symbols,

$$\hat{\mu} = \bar{X} \quad , \tag{16-3}$$

where $\hat{\mu}$ designates an estimate of the population mean (μ) and $\bar{X}$ refers to the sample mean. (The caret over the μ is generally used to designate the estimated population characteristic, which, in this case, is the population mean.)

Interval Estimation

Estimation of a parameter from a random sample is not expected to hit the population value exactly. As a result of the sampling process, where chance factors determine which members of the population will be selected, a single sample mean will probably underestimate or overestimate the population mean by some finite amount. Since any single estimate is influenced by this

---

[7] Statisticians judge the accuracy of estimators on a number of clearly defined criteria. On these, the sample mean is viewed as the single best estimate of the population mean. (See Hays, 1973, pp. 268–277, for a detailed discussion of these criteria.)

chance error, or **sampling error,** a point estimate is of little value by itself. An estimate that specifies the *degree of accuracy* involved in the estimate is preferred. An **interval estimate,** as this sort of estimate is called, takes the form of a range of values within which the population parameter is said to be "contained" (or "covered") with a certain degree of confidence.

INTERVAL ESTIMATION OF THE POPULATION MEAN

We now examine the method for obtaining interval estimates of the mean from the data of a single random sample. The first step is to describe the way sample means are distributed.

The Sampling Distribution of the Mean

Suppose we have available a population of scores from which we draw an extremely large number of random samples, replacing each sample of scores once they have been recorded. We compute the mean for each of these samples and make a frequency distribution such as the one in Figure 16-2. This distribution represents all possible sample means that might be obtained from this population and the relative frequency with which different values will occur through repeated random sampling. This particular frequency distribution is referred to as the **sampling distribution of the mean.**[8]

As an aside, we should mention that the statistical justification for any statements we make about the sampling distribution of the mean is known as the **Central Limit Theorem.** This theorem states that the sampling distribution of the mean approaches the normal distribution in shape as the size of the random sample on which the means are based is increased. The statement holds true even though the distribution from which the scores are obtained is not itself normal in form. While not readily apparent, the Central Limit Theorem is extremely important to researchers concerned with the statistical analysis of data; it provides the basis for the various theoretical arguments needed to justify nearly all the statistical procedures in this book.

The sampling distribution of the mean specifies pictorially the nature of the sampling error present in our hypothetical example. The mean of the

---

[8] As we noted in Chapter 7, any frequency distribution of a statistic calculated from many samples drawn randomly from a population is called the sampling distribution of that statistic.

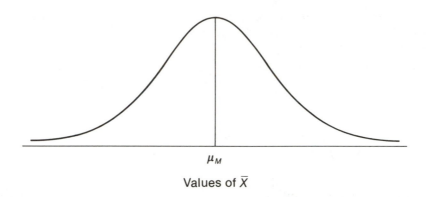

μ_M

Values of $\overline{X}$

Figure 16-2. The Sampling Distribution of the Mean.

sampling distribution (μ_M) is equal to the mean of the population of the scores (μ), that is,

$$\mu_M = \mu \quad .$$

The variance of this sampling distribution—a variance based on the sample means—provides a measure of the extent or size of the sampling error. We will designate this quantity by the symbol σ_M^2. The *standard deviation* of this distribution is more useful than the variance in interval estimation and is given a special name, the **standard error of the mean.** That is,

$$\text{standard error of the mean } (\sigma_M) = \sqrt{\sigma_M^2} \quad .$$

In words, the standard error of the mean is the standard deviation of the sampling distribution of the mean.

Consider the problem before us. The mere existence of a sampling distribution of the mean indicates that a point estimate based on a single random sample will most likely be in *error* no matter how careful we are in our sampling procedures. The reason for this statement is the improbability that any given sample mean will actually equal the population mean. Thus, we turn to an interval estimate to offer a range of values in the hope that the population mean will be included within the range.

Confidence Intervals

It is acknowledged that estimation involves a certain degree of risk. The only way to construct an interval to eliminate the risk entirely would be to make the interval *infinitely wide*. Such an interval would be of no use to a researcher, however; one could specify an infinitely wide interval without ever collecting a random sample! Obviously, this maximum interval must be narrowed to serve as a useful interval estimate. But the narrower the interval the greater is the possibility that the interval estimate will not include the population mean. In short, we must decide on a compromise in which the size of the interval will be narrowed but the number of erroneous estimates kept at a reasonably low level.

Interval estimates that are formed in consideration of the degree of risk are called **confidence intervals.** The degree of confidence is given by the expression

$$\text{confidence} = 100(1 - \alpha) \text{ percent} \quad .$$

If we let the proportion of erroneous interval estimates we may ever conceivably make be $\alpha = .05$, our interval estimates are referred to as

$$100(1 - .05) = 100(.95) = 95 \text{ percent confidence intervals} \quad .$$

The Logic. To explain how a confidence interval works, we begin with the theoretical sampling distribution of the mean and assume we know the value of the population mean and the standard deviation of the sampling distribution (the standard error). Suppose we locate an interval that extends an equal distance above and below the mean and includes 95 percent of the total possible sample means. As an example, let's say that the population mean (μ) is 10 and that the required interval extends 3 points above the mean and 3 points below the mean. That is, 95 percent of all sample means drawn from this population have values that lie between

$$10 - 3 = 7 \text{ and}$$
$$10 + 3 = 13 \quad .$$

Suppose we now draw a random sample from this population, calculate the mean, and use the interval obtained from the sampling distribution (3 units above the mean and 3 units below the mean) to produce a range of values based on the *sample mean* ($\bar{X}$). If the sample mean were 12, for example, the range of values would be

$$12 - 3 = 9 \text{ and}$$
$$12 + 3 = 15 \quad .$$

Will this particular interval include the population mean? We can see that it does, because the assumed value of the population mean, $\mu = 10$, is included within the interval, that is, between 9 and 15. What about means from additional random samples? If the mean were one of the samples included *within* the interval marked off on the sampling distribution—that is, between 7 and 13—then an interval centered on the sample mean would in fact include the population mean. On the other hand, if the mean came from *outside* of these boundaries, the confidence interval would not include the population mean.

Let's consider some examples to see that this conclusion is true. We have already shown that a sample mean of $\overline{X} = 12$ will produce an interval that includes $\mu = 10$. What about other sample means between 7 and 13?

For $\overline{X} = 7$, the interval is between 4 and 10;
for $\overline{X} = 8$, the interval is between 5 and 11;
for $\overline{X} = 9$, the interval is between 6 and 12;
for $\overline{X} = 10$, the interval is between 7 and 13;
for $\overline{X} = 11$, the interval is between 8 and 14; and
for $\overline{X} = 13$, the interval is between 10 and 16 .

Each of these intervals, including the means on the boundaries of the original interval (7 and 13), encompasses the population mean, $\mu = 10$. What about sample means outside of this interval?

For $\overline{X} = 6$, the interval is between 3 and 9;
for $\overline{X} = 5$, the interval is between 2 and 8;
for $\overline{X} = 14$, the interval is between 11 and 17; and
for $\overline{X} = 15$, the interval is between 12 and 18 .

Each of these intervals *fails* to include $\mu = 10$.

Thus, there are two classes of sample means, namely, those that come from the central portion of the sampling distribution and those that come from the extremes of the sampling distribution. The "central" means will produce intervals that include the population mean, while the "extreme" means will produce intervals that do not. Since we have defined the original interval as one that includes 95 percent of the sample means, we can attach probabilities to these two sets of interval estimates. More specifically, 95 percent of the means of random samples will come from the central portion of the sampling distribution, and the remaining 5 percent of the sample means will come from the two extremes of the sampling distribution. Therefore, repeated random sampling from this population will result in confidence intervals that include the population mean 95 percent of the time and confidence intervals that do not include the population mean 5 percent of the time.

In an actual situation, we will have only a single random sample. We will not know the value of the population mean (obviously) or the exact shape of the sampling distribution of the mean. Certain quantities can be estimated, however, and information recorded in statistical tables used to locate the deviation on the sampling distribution that will then permit the construction of confidence intervals.

Calculating Confidence Intervals

A confidence interval for the mean is based on information derived from the sample of data available and from properties of the sampling distribution of the mean. We start with the mean of the random sample. This value will be the center of the confidence interval. The width of the interval above and below this point is obtained by multiplying two quantities, the standard error of the mean estimated from the sample data and a value found in a statistical table provided in Appendix A. Let's see how we accomplish these steps.

Calculating the Standard Error of the Mean. The first measure we need after finding the mean is an estimate of variability for the distribution to which the mean "belongs." This measure is the standard error of the mean (the standard deviation of a sampling distribution of means). We can estimate the standard error from sample data by using the simple formula

$$\hat{\sigma}_M = \frac{\hat{\sigma}}{\sqrt{s}} \quad . \qquad (16\text{-}4)$$

The numerator of this formula is the estimate of the standard deviation obtained from the sample data,

$$\hat{\sigma} = \sqrt{\frac{SS}{df}} \quad . \qquad (16\text{-}5)$$

The denominator is the square root of the sample size, s. The size of the standard error reflects the amount of sampling error present in a random sample and consequently influences directly the width of the confidence interval of the mean.

The Width of the Confidence Interval. The mathematical properties of the sampling distribution of the mean are known to statisticians. If the sample size is reasonably large, the distribution is nearly normal (the z distribution). In most situations, the sample size is relatively small and a related distribution is used, the ***t* distribution.**[9] Although the t distribution is similar

---

[9] The formula for t is $t = (\bar{X} - \mu)/\hat{\sigma}_M$, and was developed by W. S. Gossett, who published under the pseudonym "Student." The development of t represented a major step in the evolution of statistics and is discussed in many statistics texts.

to the z (or normal) distribution, it changes as the degrees of freedom change. The procedure for calculating confidence intervals is the same for both very large (using z) or small (using t) sample sizes. Here we demonstrate confidence intervals for small samples and so use the values of t to locate a point above and a point below the mean of the sampling distribution.

The Computational Formula. Three values are used to calculate confidence intervals: the estimated sample mean ($\hat{\mu}$), the value of t determined by the level of confidence chosen and the degrees of freedom, and the estimated standard error of the mean ($\hat{\sigma}_M$). The value of t must be multiplied by $\hat{\sigma}_M$, that is,

$$(t)(\hat{\sigma}_M) \quad ,$$

in order to give us the number of standard error units above and below the estimated population mean that mark the boundaries of the confidence interval.[10]

We are now ready to fit together the several pieces of information necessary to construct a confidence interval. The confidence interval is centered around $\hat{\mu}$ and extends above and below this point by an amount equal to the product of t and $\hat{\sigma}_M$. Theoretically, this product, $(t)(\hat{\sigma}_M)$, is used to define a range of values on the sampling distribution of the mean that encompasses 95 or 99 percent of the sample means that in principle could be drawn from the population under consideration. In practical terms, we calculate the lower limit of the confidence interval by subtracting this product from $\hat{\mu}$, and we calculate the upper limit of the confidence interval by adding this product to $\hat{\mu}$. In symbols,

the lower limit is equal to $\hat{\mu} - (t)(\hat{\sigma}_M)$, and
the upper limit is equal to $\hat{\mu} + (t)(\hat{\sigma}_M)$.

We can express the formula for the confidence interval more succinctly as follows:

$$\text{confidence interval} = \hat{\mu} \pm (t)(\hat{\sigma}_M) \quad , \tag{16-6}$$

where $\pm$ indicates that the product, $(t)(\hat{\sigma}_M)$, is both subtracted from and added to $\hat{\mu}$ in the determination of the lower and upper limits of the confi-

---

[10] A simple analogy demonstrates what is achieved by the adjustment $(t)(\hat{\sigma}_M)$. When buying a commodity in the grocery store, we find the unit cost, say 50¢, and if we are buying 1.5 units, we determine the total price by multiplying $1.5 \times .50$ to arrive at 75¢. The operations are analogous: t is the number of units and $\hat{\sigma}_M$ is the degree of variability (that is, the "cost").

TABLE 16-2 Scores on a
Quantitative Exam

17	18	18	6
20	11	18	19
10	8	13	18
15	18	16	16
17	17	11	18
10	15	8	17

$$\Sigma X = 354$$
$$\Sigma (X)^2 = 5{,}598$$

dence interval respectively.[11] In the following section, we work through an example of interval estimation, indicating how the value of t is found and how equation (16-6) works.

A Numerical Example

To illustrate interval estimation, we use a set of hypothetical data assumed to have been obtained randomly from a large number of students preparing to enroll in a statistics class. The random sample contains twenty-four students, and the data of interest are their scores on a quantitative aptitude test given during the registration period. The scores for these students are presented in Table 16-2. The preliminary calculations needed for computing the confidence interval are also indicated in the table.

An inspection of equation (16-6) indicates that we need three quantities to calculate the confidence interval: $\hat{\mu}$, $\hat{\sigma}_M$, and t. The first quantity, $\hat{\mu}$, is the point estimate of the mean. From equation (16-3) and the data from Table 16-2,[12]

$$\hat{\mu} = \overline{X}$$
$$= \frac{\Sigma X}{s}$$
$$= \frac{354}{24} = 14.75 \quad .$$

---

[11] Equation (16-6) is often written in the alternative form $\hat{\mu} - (t)(\hat{\sigma}_M) \leq \mu \leq \hat{\mu} + (t)(\hat{\sigma}_M)$, which states that the population mean (μ) lies within an interval greater than or equal to $\hat{\mu} - (t)(\hat{\sigma}_M)$ and smaller than or equal to $\hat{\mu} + (t)(\hat{\sigma}_M)$.

[12] Again, we will be using standard notation to present calculations because it is convenient and consistent with the notation found in other texts.

The next quantity, $\hat{\sigma}_M$, is the estimate of the standard error of the mean. We calculate this value by substituting in equation (16-4):

$$\hat{\sigma}_M = \frac{\hat{\sigma}}{\sqrt{s}} \quad .$$

From the sample data, we first calculate the standard deviation of the sample ($\hat{\sigma}$) given by equation (16-5),

$$\hat{\sigma} = \sqrt{\frac{SS}{df}} \quad .$$

The data needed in obtaining the sum of squares are provided in Table 16-2. Substituting in the usual formula for the sum of squares, we find

$$SS = \Sigma \, (X)^2 - \frac{(\Sigma \, X)^2}{s}$$

$$= 5{,}598 - \frac{(354)^2}{24}$$

$$= 5{,}598 - \frac{125{,}316}{24} = 5{,}598 - 5{,}221.50$$

$$= 376.50 \quad .$$

The degrees of freedom associated with these data are equal to

$$df = s - 1$$
$$= 24 - 1 = 23 \quad .$$

Substituting in equation (16-5), we find the estimated standard deviation of the population to be

$$\hat{\sigma} = \sqrt{\frac{SS}{df}}$$

$$= \sqrt{\frac{376.50}{23}} = \sqrt{16.37}$$

$$= 4.05 \quad .$$

We are now ready to calculate the estimate of the standard error of the mean from equation (16-4):

$$\hat{\sigma}_M = \frac{\hat{\sigma}}{\sqrt{s}}$$

$$= \frac{4.05}{\sqrt{24}} = \frac{4.05}{4.90}$$

$$= 0.83 \quad .$$

The value for t is found in Table 7 of Appendix A. You will notice that the table consists of two columns of numbers, one for $\alpha = .05$ and the other for $\alpha = .01$. The values of t given under the heading of $\alpha = .05$ permit the calculation of a 95 percent confidence interval; the values of t given under the heading of $\alpha = .01$ permit the calculation of a 99 percent confidence interval.[13]

In order to find the value of t required for a particular interval estimate, we need to know the degrees of freedom associated with the standard error. This number is given by

$$df_M = s - 1 \quad . \tag{16-7}$$

In this example,

$$df_M = 24 - 1 = 23 \quad .$$

If we had decided to construct a 95 percent confidence interval, we would look up the value of t in the table under $df_M = 23$ and $\alpha = .05$; in this case, $t = 2.07$.

We now have the various ingredients required in equation (16-6) and can calculate the 95 percent confidence interval. For the lower limit,

$$\begin{aligned}
\hat{\mu} - (t)(\hat{\sigma}_M) &= 14.75 - (2.07)(0.83) \\
&= 14.75 - 1.72 \\
&= 13.03 \quad .
\end{aligned}$$

For the upper limit,

$$\begin{aligned}
\hat{\mu} + (t)(\hat{\sigma}_M) &= 14.75 + (2.07)(0.83) \\
&= 14.75 + 1.72 \\
&= 16.47 \quad .
\end{aligned}$$

The 95 percent confidence interval is specified by a set of values ranging from 13.03 to 16.47.

For purposes of illustration, we will calculate the 99 percent confidence interval with the same data. An inspection of the t table indicates that $t = 2.81$ at $\alpha = .01$. For the two limits,

$$\begin{aligned}
\hat{\mu} \pm (t)(\hat{\sigma}_M) &= 14.75 \pm (2.81)(0.83) \\
&= 14.75 \pm 2.33 \quad .
\end{aligned}$$

The value for the lower limit is

$$14.75 - 2.33 = 12.42 \quad ,$$

and the value for the upper limit is

$$14.75 + 2.33 = 17.08 \quad .$$

---

[13] More extensive tables of t are available that permit the choice of additional confidence levels. However, the 95 percent and 99 percent confidence intervals are the ones most commonly encountered in the literature.

Note that the 99 percent confidence interval is larger than the 95 percent confidence interval (a range of 4.66 versus a range of 3.44). This is just as it should be, of course, since a larger interval is more likely to include the population mean within its limits than a smaller one.

Comments

A Clarification. Interval estimates take the form of confidence intervals. A confidence interval consists of a specification of a range of values within which we say, with a certain degree of confidence, that the population mean occurs. The population mean itself does not shift around, but it is difficult to locate because our *estimates* of it will vary. That is, means from samples randomly chosen from the same population are not expected to be the same, and, consequently, neither will be the confidence intervals that are based on them. In effect, we are saying that out of a large number of intervals determined in the same way, 95 percent (or any other degree of confidence) of them will include the population mean.[14]

Sharpening Interval Estimates. We can reduce the width of any chosen confidence interval—that is, sharpen the interval estimate—simply by increasing the number of scores on which the interval is based. Increasing the sample size (s) has two effects. First, the estimate of the standard error of the mean becomes smaller. An inspection of equation (16-4),

$$\hat{\sigma}_M = \frac{\hat{\sigma}}{\sqrt{s}} \quad ,$$

indicates that $\hat{\sigma}_M$ decreases as sample size increases. From equation (16-6),

$$\text{confidence interval} = \hat{\mu} \pm (t)(\hat{\sigma}_M) \quad ,$$

we can see that the confidence interval will become smaller as $\hat{\sigma}_M$ becomes smaller. Second, the t value from the table becomes smaller as the df_M increases. Since $df_M = s - 1$, the t value will decrease as sample size is increased. Again from equation (16-6), we can see that a smaller value for t will result in a smaller interval estimate.

---

[14] Be careful not to confuse **confidence level,** which is associated with interval estimation, with **significance level,** which is associated with hypothesis testing. The two concepts are different. Confidence level refers to the proportion of times confidence intervals constructed in the same way will include the population parameter (usually the mean); significance level refers to the probability with which an experimenter is willing to reject the null hypothesis when in fact it is correct.

Using Interval Estimation in Experimentation

The validity of estimation procedures is critically dependent on random sampling. If we consider for a moment experimental research rather than survey research, where estimation is the primary goal, we find that random *sampling* is rarely used.[15] Every investigator employs some form of random *assignment* of subjects to treatment conditions in order to remove systematic biases that might otherwise be present, but typically the subjects themselves are not selected randomly from a larger population of subjects. Think about how you might obtain subjects for a class project. You would probably take whomever you could coax or beg to serve in the experiment. You would *not* obtain a random sample from your friends or from the people you live with or from your psychology class. Your sample of subjects, like the samples of most researchers, would be a sample of *convenience*—not a sample of subjects chosen randomly from a well-identified population. Because of your failure to sample randomly from a known population, you would not be justified *statistically* in extending your results beyond the bounds of the experiment itself.

Given that the results of an experiment usually cannot be generalized to a larger population of potential subjects, how is it possible ever to establish findings that *are* generalizable to a meaningful population of organisms? The answer is that past research in a number of laboratories with subjects chosen from different sources (for example, different breeding stocks, different suppliers of laboratory animals, human subjects from different schools in different sections of the country, and so on) have shown that these differences are relatively unimportant in the study of various phenomena. Knowing this, an investigator working in that field may feel safe in generalizing his or her results beyond the single experiment.

We are referring here to **nonstatistical generalization** as opposed to **statistical generalization.** As we have stated, statistical generalization is dependent on random sampling. Nonstatistical generalization, on the other hand, is dependent on one's knowledge of a particular research area. Thus, most experimenters are willing to extend a set of findings to a broader class of subjects when in the past such generalizations have proved to be appropriate in a particular field of research.

---

[15] When we developed the rationale for hypothesis testing, we assumed that the subjects in an experiment represented a random sample drawn from different treatment populations. In that case, the assumption of random sampling was part of statistical theory and not a realistic or accurate statement of how subjects were obtained for an experiment.

Confidence intervals can be easily constructed around the treatment means of an experiment. The formulas for the calculation of such confidence intervals are identical to those presented in this chapter. We simply treat the data from a treatment condition exactly as we would treat the data from a single random sample. No new procedures are involved.

We have not emphasized confidence intervals in this text, since they are rarely reported in psychological research reports. Confidence intervals are used primarily in survey research, although the argument has been made in a variety of sources that interval estimation procedures can serve a valuable function in the analysis and interpretation of experimental data. In this regard, we should note that confidence intervals reflect the degree to which chance factors are operating in each treatment condition. While a standard deviation indicates the variability of the scores within a given condition, a confidence interval also accounts for the number of scores in the condition. Both factors, variability and sample size, directly affect the degree of precision operating in a given experiment. In this sense, confidence intervals provide more information than do standard deviations and, for this reason, should be reported more frequently than they currently are.

In addition to confidence intervals, other forms of estimation are useful to researchers dealing with the data from experiments. One example, discussed in Chapter 7, is the estimation of the size, or magnitude, of treatment effects (omega squared), an index that provides useful information in the interpretation of experimental results. A second example is the estimation of power following the completion of a statistical analysis. Power, you will recall, refers to the sensitivity of a statistical test in detecting differences present in the population. A final example is the estimation of sample size during the planning stage of an experiment. Power and the determination of sample size are fairly complicated and technical topics and are beyond the scope of an introductory book.[16]

SUMMARY

The two topics covered here, standard scores and estimation procedures, supplement the material on the analysis of experiments. Although these topics are not frequently encountered by a researcher concerned with experimental data, they are vital to researchers in the applied fields of psychology and in the areas of survey research.

---

[16] Cohen (1969) offers a thorough discussion of these topics. For a less comprehensive presentation, see *Design and Analysis* (pp. 525–541).

We calculate a standard score by subtracting the mean from a score and dividing by the standard deviation. The result of this operation is a set of scores with a mean of 0 and a standard deviation of 1.0. This transformation permits the meaningful comparison between two or more tests given to the same individuals. Standard scores are also used to determine an individual's relative rank in a set of scores. We make this determination by referring standard scores to a table of areas under the normal curve and finding the percentile rank associated with the location of each standard score on the normal curve.

The second topic considered was methods and procedures employed to estimate population characteristics from the data of a random sample. Although obtaining point estimates of population characteristics is possible, interval estimates are more satisfactory. In the latter, the mean and standard deviation of a sample are combined with tabled statistical information to form an interval that can be said with a certain level of confidence to contain the population mean. Confidence refers to the probability with which confidence intervals constructed in the same manner would actually contain the population mean. As with hypothesis testing, interval estimation is never completely free from the uncertainties caused by chance factors operating during the process of data collection. On the other hand, through certain statistical methods and procedures we can control and estimate the extent of these uncertainties to prevent them from retarding unduly the growth and development of science.

TERMS, CONCEPTS, AND SYMBOLS

---

standard score	interval estimate	z
z score	sampling distribution of the mean	$X - \overline{X}$
standard-deviation units		SD
percentile (rank)	Central Limit Theorem	$\overline{X}_z$
standard normal distribution	standard error of the mean	SS_z
z distribution	confidence interval	SD_z
simple random sampling	width of the confidence interval	μ and $\hat{\mu}$
sampling without replacement		μ_M and $\hat{\mu}_M$
	t distribution	σ_M and $\hat{\sigma}_M$
sampling with replacement	confidence level	$\hat{\sigma}$
point estimate	significance level	t
sampling error	nonstatistical generalization	df_M
	statistical generalization	

EXERCISES

---

1. For this problem use the in-class test scores from problem 1, Chapter 14 (p. 362). Calculate z scores for the following individual test scores: 69, 50, 86, and 64. Assuming that the underlying distribution is normal, determine the percentile ranks for each of these scores.

2. Calculate $\hat{\sigma}_M$ for the estimates given below:

s	$\hat{\sigma}$
6	12.25
36	12.25
10	4.38
18	1.41

3. Using the data in problem 1 above, calculate the confidence interval (95 percent) for the in-class test scores.

4. Calculate the confidence interval (95 percent) for the take-home test scores (see problem 1, Chapter 14, p. 362).

APPENDICES

APPENDIX A. Statistical Tables

APPENDIX B. Answers to the Chapter Exercises

Appendix A

Statistical Tables

TABLE 1.   Table of Random Numbers

Instructions for Use: This table contains 2,500 digits generated by a random process. To obtain a random string of digits, enter the table at a point chosen randomly by some reasonable process and record the digits as they are listed in the table. If you need random strings of two-digit numbers, record the numbers two at a time. You may move in any direction in the table as long as your path through the table is determined before you select your starting point. See pp. 43–46 for a discussion of how this table can be used to neutralize the operation of nuisance variables in an experiment.

63 73 35 20 05	02 78 59 68 21	39 90 76 98 19	24 61 74 15 34	36 58 68 02 24
66 09 89 21 81	50 03 16 23 18	41 30 54 76 53	89 77 39 66 91	58 57 52 01 19
55 78 43 34 24	78 06 18 87 41	06 85 73 71 64	62 68 43 33 38	23 83 83 38 88
57 55 44 74 82	65 61 17 55 86	12 96 65 07 83	77 97 76 75 71	67 60 86 47 86
41 91 16 20 30	67 34 38 20 14	21 02 57 07 97	20 94 63 58 64	76 11 62 04 62
90 00 04 40 80	22 39 05 26 63	16 44 29 19 62	62 89 68 37 28	45 98 07 34 06
73 14 66 97 68	88 66 44 73 13	15 54 24 48 11	80 79 07 37 71	81 40 94 77 67
28 38 38 62 37	46 07 30 11 56	16 96 51 36 35	84 63 04 81 61	59 32 58 85 74
20 80 06 18 32	13 95 59 62 08	95 01 01 76 88	74 00 36 70 13	10 15 14 46 89
04 85 32 97 44	50 01 32 70 85	39 66 64 10 59	97 39 41 13 46	82 41 43 17 58
28 29 27 01 57	86 38 39 63 24	90 94 51 70 91	08 07 58 60 08	67 44 35 98 47
53 48 24 92 94	03 53 96 15 42	84 31 07 16 79	04 52 70 07 18	08 61 92 80 60
46 74 13 42 72	45 60 54 47 07	21 90 18 87 32	51 35 85 47 53	51 44 15 57 35
37 52 88 74 48	82 74 05 05 44	02 61 38 89 48	17 17 27 36 09	28 89 91 47 96
09 21 40 44 26	72 74 11 36 03	14 56 55 77 99	08 92 37 14 90	40 57 78 32 28
67 27 99 98 71	43 26 00 78 54	90 52 69 02 74	76 00 60 08 95	01 25 80 72 66
42 96 44 70 18	79 50 31 54 30	24 54 11 08 37	27 02 32 43 52	71 33 77 83 28
89 23 14 10 81	61 04 20 46 67	82 82 11 62 83	73 14 90 37 43	46 38 00 29 36
09 92 00 48 30	03 31 43 40 78	20 39 26 11 52	03 38 84 51 49	48 22 16 86 27
06 77 40 12 10	32 79 51 06 80	67 49 41 03 41	56 62 05 70 15	11 95 25 47 48
14 46 74 16 88	24 92 31 78 69	40 38 63 90 22	11 92 17 39 59	23 19 16 86 37
83 04 89 15 47	36 87 12 65 14	84 24 39 69 12	16 17 53 35 18	71 71 30 00 04
81 92 21 06 02	94 80 79 31 77	92 71 95 62 68	23 79 57 66 90	71 10 82 98 90
96 80 87 59 34	72 69 98 19 16	16 73 09 18 96	18 80 37 70 72	78 96 83 48 52
43 36 45 14 47	59 95 71 48 76	73 08 27 30 29	63 27 27 34 67	73 06 91 08 74
19 75 91 02 49	18 39 77 72 60	42 24 74 32 19	27 12 03 69 32	59 80 85 84 83
08 07 97 12 70	57 24 06 76 07	08 49 46 45 20	90 95 16 45 58	99 10 42 65 99
91 77 40 05 08	53 47 42 27 60	43 22 89 44 93	62 00 09 55 40	23 86 21 71 47
37 13 15 48 06	07 29 70 17 41	92 00 24 48 16	19 23 71 40 34	72 84 95 90 29
14 41 39 66 60	77 21 82 55 16	56 85 11 14 16	70 00 58 37 63	59 17 41 11 29
09 60 07 12 47	99 88 01 56 60	22 95 24 70 12	99 02 39 80 61	82 53 25 07 66
75 83 19 60 55	78 09 47 76 67	25 77 23 98 33	60 56 38 19 62	96 75 34 96 52
09 13 61 69 22	06 40 17 46 74	51 36 78 98 93	95 38 28 41 48	59 70 50 13 69
87 77 74 71 19	01 65 44 76 95	55 59 08 50 54	76 56 64 52 18	25 94 57 85 22
08 39 55 85 17	33 41 06 70 83	52 05 65 17 68	59 39 12 94 95	10 22 32 02 84
64 69 65 77 16	58 20 74 03 86	18 23 26 69 95	04 29 42 94 56	65 63 73 30 02
25 07 40 75 96	84 98 07 87 34	75 38 01 54 63	29 37 43 07 94	61 69 56 38 68
43 33 63 15 85	70 74 32 94 52	91 82 97 52 14	56 73 74 51 99	46 70 45 21 05
35 43 23 49 53	44 67 01 03 68	38 17 19 10 03	37 33 60 39 38	49 69 33 25 80
41 39 12 03 50	69 72 63 38 14	65 79 08 31 65	44 37 85 14 41	85 33 20 24 59
15 84 36 85 93	89 46 33 32 99	13 03 76 79 00	16 64 26 37 81	15 70 33 75 18
53 81 43 10 71	69 81 72 54 08	94 63 68 89 73	09 72 81 59 33	79 61 75 66 86
94 38 20 81 52	45 89 88 71 36	93 93 87 42 44	96 24 52 49 21	27 58 72 54 88
35 88 06 84 31	58 53 91 72 14	49 72 45 10 50	15 52 77 10 87	31 61 84 51 06
93 88 13 29 99	44 22 50 26 27	12 12 22 99 49	14 21 27 93 35	40 69 31 23 40
44 25 22 22 89	08 41 64 73 49	32 77 25 49 39	65 19 29 18 15	03 28 74 47 86
15 62 52 72 07	97 73 04 77 87	43 30 41 70 60	79 61 44 42 58	26 75 99 86 38
61 10 24 35 02	65 91 78 89 77	15 60 32 76 58	40 01 90 97 88	57 97 97 99 97
71 84 84 14 98	79 58 48 21 95	49 75 61 18 47	67 61 56 05 36	59 39 59 41 62
04 10 56 90 17	24 37 09 97 30	59 44 61 94 64	60 88 75 60 01	69 03 73 61 29

TABLE 2. Critical Values of the F Distribution

Instructions for Use: To find the critical value of F, locate the cell in the table formed by the intersection of the row containing the degrees of freedom associated with the denominator of the F ratio and the column containing the degrees of freedom associated with the numerator of the F ratio. The numbers listed in **boldface** type are the critical values of F at $\alpha = .05$; the numbers listed in Roman type are the critical values of F at $\alpha = .01$. As an example, suppose we have adopted the 5 percent level of significance and wish to evaluate the significance of an F with $df_{num.} = 2$, and $df_{denom.} = 12$. From the table we find that the critical value of $F(2, 12) = 3.89$ at $\alpha = .05$. If the obtained value of F equals or exceeds this critical value, we will reject the null hypothesis; if the obtained value of F is smaller than this critical value, we will not reject the null hypothesis in evaluating the null hypothesis. See pp. 91–93 for a discussion of the use of the F table in evaluating the null hypothesis.

Degrees of Freedom for Numerator

Denom.	1	2	3	4	5	6	7	8	9	10	12	15	20	24	30	40	60	Infinity
1	**161** 4052	**200** 4999	**216** 5403	**225** 5625	**230** 5764	**234** 5859	**237** 5928	**239** 5981	**241** 6022	**242** 6056	**244** 6106	**246** 6157	**248** 6209	**249** 6235	**250** 6261	**251** 6287	**252** 6313	**254** 6366
2	**18.5** 98.5	**19.0** 99.0	**19.2** 99.2	**19.2** 99.2	**19.3** 99.3	**19.3** 99.3	**19.4** 99.4	**19.4** 99.4	**19.4** 99.4	**19.4** 99.4	**19.4** 99.4	**19.4** 99.4	**19.4** 99.4	**19.4** 99.5	**19.5** 99.5	**19.5** 99.5	**19.5** 99.5	**19.5** 99.5
3	**10.1** 34.1	**9.55** 30.8	**9.28** 29.5	**9.12** 28.7	**9.01** 28.2	**8.94** 27.9	**8.89** 27.7	**8.85** 27.5	**8.81** 27.4	**8.79** 27.2	**8.74** 27.0	**8.70** 26.9	**8.66** 26.7	**8.64** 26.6	**8.62** 26.5	**8.59** 26.4	**8.57** 26.3	**8.53** 26.1
4	**7.71** 21.2	**6.94** 18.0	**6.59** 16.7	**6.39** 16.0	**6.26** 15.5	**6.16** 15.2	**6.09** 15.0	**6.04** 14.8	**6.00** 14.7	**5.96** 14.6	**5.91** 14.4	**5.86** 14.2	**5.80** 14.0	**5.77** 13.9	**5.75** 13.8	**5.72** 13.8	**5.69** 13.6	**5.63** 13.5
5	**6.61** 16.3	**5.79** 13.3	**5.41** 12.1	**5.19** 11.4	**5.05** 11.0	**4.95** 10.7	**4.88** 10.5	**4.82** 10.3	**4.77** 10.2	**4.74** 10.0	**4.68** 9.89	**4.62** 9.72	**4.56** 9.55	**4.53** 9.47	**4.50** 9.38	**4.46** 9.29	**4.43** 9.20	**4.36** 9.02
6	**5.99** 13.8	**5.14** 10.9	**4.76** 9.78	**4.53** 9.15	**4.39** 8.75	**4.28** 8.47	**4.21** 8.26	**4.15** 8.10	**4.10** 7.98	**4.06** 7.87	**4.00** 7.72	**3.94** 7.56	**3.87** 7.40	**3.84** 7.31	**3.81** 7.23	**3.77** 7.14	**3.74** 7.06	**3.67** 6.88
7	**5.59** 12.2	**4.74** 9.55	**4.35** 8.45	**4.12** 7.85	**3.97** 7.46	**3.87** 7.19	**3.79** 6.99	**3.73** 6.84	**3.68** 6.72	**3.64** 6.62	**3.57** 6.47	**3.51** 6.31	**3.44** 6.16	**3.41** 6.07	**3.38** 5.99	**3.34** 5.91	**3.30** 5.82	**3.23** 5.65
8	**5.32** 11.3	**4.46** 8.65	**4.07** 7.59	**3.84** 7.01	**3.69** 6.63	**3.58** 6.37	**3.50** 6.18	**3.44** 6.03	**3.39** 5.91	**3.35** 5.81	**3.28** 5.67	**3.22** 5.52	**3.15** 5.36	**3.12** 5.28	**3.08** 5.20	**3.04** 5.12	**3.01** 5.03	**2.93** 4.86
9	**5.12** 10.6	**4.26** 8.02	**3.86** 6.99	**3.63** 6.42	**3.48** 6.06	**3.37** 5.80	**3.29** 5.61	**3.23** 5.47	**3.18** 5.35	**3.14** 5.26	**3.07** 5.11	**3.01** 4.96	**2.94** 4.81	**2.90** 4.73	**2.86** 4.65	**2.83** 4.57	**2.79** 4.48	**2.71** 4.31
10	**4.96** 10.0	**4.10** 7.56	**3.71** 6.55	**3.48** 5.99	**3.33** 5.64	**3.22** 5.39	**3.14** 5.20	**3.07** 5.06	**3.02** 4.94	**2.98** 4.85	**2.91** 4.71	**2.85** 4.56	**2.77** 4.41	**2.74** 4.33	**2.70** 4.25	**2.66** 4.17	**2.62** 4.08	**2.54** 3.91
11	**4.84** 9.65	**3.98** 7.21	**3.59** 6.22	**3.36** 5.67	**3.20** 5.32	**3.09** 5.07	**3.01** 4.89	**2.95** 4.74	**2.90** 4.63	**2.85** 4.54	**2.79** 4.40	**2.72** 4.25	**2.65** 4.10	**2.61** 4.02	**2.57** 3.94	**2.53** 3.86	**2.49** 3.78	**2.40** 3.60

Degrees of Freedom for Denominator

416

Degrees of Freedom for Denominator

Each cell shows the upper value (bold, $\alpha = 0.05$) and the lower value ($\alpha = 0.01$). Columns are read left‑to‑right as in the printed table.

df																		
12	**2.30** 3.36	**2.38** 3.54	**2.43** 3.62	**2.47** 3.70	**2.51** 3.78	**2.54** 3.86	**2.62** 4.01	**2.69** 4.16	**2.75** 4.30	**2.80** 4.39	**2.85** 4.50	**2.91** 4.64	**3.00** 4.82	**3.11** 5.06	**3.26** 5.41	**3.49** 5.95	**3.89** 6.93	**4.75** 9.33
13	**2.21** 3.17	**2.30** 3.34	**2.34** 3.43	**2.38** 3.51	**2.42** 3.59	**2.46** 3.66	**2.53** 3.82	**2.60** 3.96	**2.67** 4.10	**2.71** 4.19	**2.77** 4.30	**2.83** 4.44	**2.92** 4.62	**3.03** 4.86	**3.18** 5.21	**3.41** 5.74	**3.81** 6.70	**4.67** 9.07
14	**2.13** 3.00	**2.22** 3.18	**2.27** 3.27	**2.31** 3.35	**2.35** 3.43	**2.39** 3.51	**2.46** 3.66	**2.53** 3.80	**2.60** 3.94	**2.65** 4.03	**2.70** 4.14	**2.76** 4.28	**2.85** 4.46	**2.96** 4.69	**3.11** 5.04	**3.34** 5.56	**3.74** 6.51	**4.60** 8.86
15	**2.07** 2.87	**2.16** 3.05	**2.20** 3.13	**2.25** 3.21	**2.29** 3.29	**2.33** 3.37	**2.40** 3.52	**2.48** 3.67	**2.54** 3.80	**2.59** 3.89	**2.64** 4.00	**2.71** 4.14	**2.79** 4.32	**2.90** 4.56	**3.06** 4.89	**3.29** 5.42	**3.68** 6.36	**4.54** 8.68
16	**2.01** 2.75	**2.11** 2.93	**2.15** 3.02	**2.19** 3.10	**2.24** 3.18	**2.28** 3.26	**2.35** 3.41	**2.42** 3.55	**2.49** 3.69	**2.54** 3.78	**2.59** 3.89	**2.66** 4.03	**2.74** 4.20	**2.85** 4.44	**3.01** 4.77	**3.24** 5.29	**3.63** 6.23	**4.49** 8.53
17	**1.96** 2.65	**2.06** 2.83	**2.10** 2.92	**2.15** 3.00	**2.19** 3.08	**2.23** 3.16	**2.31** 3.31	**2.38** 3.46	**2.45** 3.59	**2.49** 3.68	**2.55** 3.79	**2.61** 3.93	**2.70** 4.10	**2.81** 4.34	**2.96** 4.67	**3.20** 5.18	**3.59** 6.11	**4.45** 8.40
18	**1.92** 2.57	**2.02** 2.75	**2.06** 2.84	**2.11** 2.92	**2.15** 3.00	**2.19** 3.08	**2.27** 3.23	**2.34** 3.37	**2.41** 3.51	**2.46** 3.60	**2.51** 3.71	**2.58** 3.84	**2.66** 4.01	**2.77** 4.25	**2.93** 4.58	**3.16** 5.09	**3.55** 6.01	**4.41** 8.29
19	**1.88** 2.49	**1.98** 2.67	**2.03** 2.76	**2.07** 2.84	**2.11** 2.92	**2.16** 3.00	**2.23** 3.15	**2.31** 3.30	**2.38** 3.43	**2.42** 3.52	**2.48** 3.63	**2.54** 3.77	**2.63** 3.94	**2.74** 4.17	**2.90** 4.50	**3.13** 5.01	**3.52** 5.93	**4.38** 8.18
20	**1.84** 2.42	**1.95** 2.61	**1.99** 2.69	**2.04** 2.78	**2.08** 2.86	**2.12** 2.94	**2.20** 3.09	**2.28** 3.23	**2.35** 3.37	**2.39** 3.46	**2.45** 3.56	**2.51** 3.70	**2.60** 3.87	**2.71** 4.10	**2.87** 4.43	**3.10** 4.94	**3.49** 5.85	**4.35** 8.10
22	**1.78** 2.31	**1.89** 2.50	**1.94** 2.58	**1.98** 2.67	**2.03** 2.75	**2.07** 2.83	**2.15** 2.98	**2.23** 3.12	**2.30** 3.26	**2.34** 3.35	**2.40** 3.45	**2.46** 3.59	**2.55** 3.76	**2.66** 3.99	**2.82** 4.31	**3.05** 4.82	**3.44** 5.72	**4.30** 7.95
24	**1.73** 2.21	**1.84** 2.40	**1.89** 2.49	**1.94** 2.58	**1.98** 2.66	**2.03** 2.74	**2.11** 2.89	**2.18** 3.03	**2.25** 3.17	**2.30** 3.26	**2.36** 3.36	**2.42** 3.50	**2.51** 3.67	**2.62** 3.90	**2.78** 4.22	**3.01** 4.72	**3.40** 5.61	**4.26** 7.82
26	**1.69** 2.13	**1.80** 2.33	**1.85** 2.42	**1.90** 2.50	**1.95** 2.58	**1.99** 2.66	**2.07** 2.81	**2.15** 2.96	**2.22** 3.09	**2.27** 3.18	**2.32** 3.29	**2.39** 3.42	**2.47** 3.59	**2.59** 3.82	**2.74** 4.14	**2.98** 4.64	**3.37** 5.53	**4.23** 7.72
28	**1.65** 2.06	**1.77** 2.26	**1.82** 2.35	**1.87** 2.44	**1.91** 2.52	**1.96** 2.60	**2.04** 2.75	**2.12** 2.90	**2.19** 3.03	**2.24** 3.12	**2.29** 3.23	**2.36** 3.36	**2.45** 3.53	**2.56** 3.75	**2.71** 4.07	**2.95** 4.57	**3.34** 5.45	**4.20** 7.64
30	**1.62** 2.01	**1.74** 2.21	**1.79** 2.30	**1.84** 2.39	**1.89** 2.47	**1.93** 2.55	**2.01** 2.70	**2.09** 2.84	**2.16** 2.98	**2.21** 3.07	**2.27** 3.17	**2.33** 3.30	**2.42** 3.47	**2.53** 3.70	**2.69** 4.02	**2.92** 4.51	**3.32** 5.39	**4.17** 7.56
40	**1.51** 1.80	**1.64** 2.02	**1.69** 2.11	**1.74** 2.20	**1.79** 2.29	**1.84** 2.37	**1.92** 2.52	**2.00** 2.66	**2.08** 2.80	**2.12** 2.89	**2.18** 2.99	**2.25** 3.12	**2.34** 3.29	**2.45** 3.51	**2.61** 3.83	**2.84** 4.31	**3.23** 5.18	**4.08** 7.31
60	**1.39** 1.60	**1.53** 1.84	**1.59** 1.94	**1.65** 2.03	**1.70** 2.12	**1.75** 2.20	**1.84** 2.35	**1.92** 2.50	**1.99** 2.63	**2.04** 2.72	**2.10** 2.82	**2.17** 2.95	**2.25** 3.12	**2.37** 3.34	**2.53** 3.65	**2.76** 4.13	**3.15** 4.98	**4.00** 7.08
120	**1.25** 1.38	**1.43** 1.66	**1.50** 1.76	**1.55** 1.86	**1.61** 1.95	**1.66** 2.03	**1.75** 2.19	**1.83** 2.34	**1.91** 2.47	**1.96** 2.56	**2.02** 2.66	**2.09** 2.79	**2.17** 2.96	**2.29** 3.17	**2.45** 3.48	**2.68** 3.95	**3.07** 4.79	**3.92** 6.85
Infinity	**1.00** 1.00	**1.32** 1.47	**1.39** 1.59	**1.46** 1.70	**1.52** 1.79	**1.57** 1.88	**1.67** 2.04	**1.75** 2.18	**1.83** 2.32	**1.88** 2.41	**1.94** 2.51	**2.01** 2.64	**2.10** 2.80	**2.21** 3.02	**2.37** 3.32	**2.60** 3.78	**3.00** 4.61	**3.84** 6.63

This table is abridged from Table 18 in *Biometrika tables for statisticians*, vol. 1 (3rd ed.), New York: Cambridge University Press, 1970, edited by E. S. Pearson and H. O. Hartley, by permission of the *Biometrika* Trustees.

TABLE 3.   Coefficients of Orthogonal Polynomials

Instructions for Use: The coefficients needed for a trend analysis are grouped according to the number of treatment levels entering into the analysis. Different numbers of treatment levels are identified in the left-hand column of the table. Coefficients for assessing the degree of linear trend and certain higher-order trends (quadratic and cubic) are listed in the rows designated in the second column of the table. The underlying assumption in this table is that the levels of the independent variable represent equally spaced points on a quantitative dimension.

Number of Treatment Levels	Nature of Trend	Values of Coefficients									
3	Linear	−1	0	+1							
	Quadratic	+1	−2	+1							
4	Linear	−3	−1	+1	+3						
	Quadratic	+1	−1	−1	+1						
	Cubic	−1	+3	−3	+1						
5	Linear	−2	−1	0	+1	+2					
	Quadratic	+2	−1	−2	−1	+2					
	Cubic	−1	+2	0	−2	+1					
6	Linear	−5	−3	−1	+1	+3	+5				
	Quadratic	+5	−1	−4	−4	−1	+5				
	Cubic	−5	+7	+4	−4	−7	+5				
7	Linear	−3	−2	−1	0	+1	+2	+3			
	Quadratic	+5	0	−3	−4	−3	0	+5			
	Cubic	−1	+1	+1	0	−1	−1	+1			
8	Linear	−7	−5	−3	−1	+1	+3	+5	+7		
	Quadratic	+7	+1	−3	−5	−5	−3	+1	+7		
	Cubic	−7	+5	+7	+3	−3	−7	−5	+7		
9	Linear	−4	−3	−2	−1	0	+1	+2	+3	+4	
	Quadratic	+28	+7	−8	−17	−20	−17	−8	+7	+28	
	Cubic	−14	+7	+13	+9	0	−9	−13	−7	+14	
10	Linear	−9	−7	−5	−3	−1	+1	+3	+5	+7	+9
	Quadratic	+6	+2	−1	−3	−4	−4	−3	−1	+2	+6
	Cubic	−42	+14	+35	+31	+12	−12	−31	−35	−14	+42

This table is abridged from Table 47 in *Biometrika tables for statisticians,* vol. 1 (3rd ed.), New York: Cambridge University Press, 1970, edited by E. S. Pearson and H. O. Hartley, by permission of the *Biometrika* Trustees.

TABLE 4.   Critical Values of the Product-Moment Correlation Coefficient (*r*)

Instructions for Use: To find the critical value of *r*, locate the row in the left-hand column of the table corresponding to the number of degrees of freedom (*df_r*) associated with *r*, and select the value of *r* listed for the desired level of significance (α). See pp. 348–349 for a discussion of the use of this table in determining whether an observed correlation coefficient is significantly different from a hypothetical population correlation coefficient of zero.

$df_r{}^a$	$\alpha = .05$	$\alpha = .01$	$df_r{}^a$	$\alpha = .05$	$\alpha = .01$
1	.997	.9999	16	.47	.59
2	.95	.99	17	.46	.58
3	.88	.96	18	.44	.56
4	.81	.92	19	.43	.55
5	.75	.88	20	.42	.54
6	.71	.83	25	.38	.49
7	.67	.80	30	.35	.45
8	.63	.76	35	.32	.42
9	.60	.74	40	.30	.39
10	.58	.71	45	.29	.37
11	.55	.68	50	.27	.35
12	.53	.66	60	.25	.32
13	.51	.64	70	.23	.30
14	.50	.62	80	.22	.28
15	.48	.61	90	.20	.27
			100	.20	.25

$^a df_r - s - 2$ (where *s* = the number of pairs of scores).

This table is abridged from Table 13 in *Biometrika tables for statisticians,* vol. 1 (3rd ed.), New York: Cambridge University Press, 1970, edited by E. S. Pearson and H. O. Hartley, by permission of the *Biometrika* Trustees.

TABLE 5. Critical Values of the Chi Square (χ^2) Distribution

Instructions for Use: To find the critical value of χ^2, locate the row in the left-hand column of the table corresponding to the number of degrees of freedom (*df*) associated with χ^2, and select the value of χ^2 listed for the desired level of significance (α). See Chapter 15 for different applications of the chi square statistic to research problems.

df	$\alpha = .05$	$\alpha = .01$	df	$\alpha = .05$	$\alpha = .01$
1	3.84	6.63	16	26.30	32.00
2	5.99	9.21	17	27.59	33.41
3	7.81	11.34	18	28.87	34.81
4	9.49	13.28	19	30.14	36.19
5	11.07	15.09	20	31.41	37.57
6	12.59	16.81	21	32.67	38.93
7	14.07	18.48	22	33.92	40.29
8	15.51	20.09	23	35.17	41.64
9	16.92	21.67	24	36.42	42.98
10	18.31	23.21	25	37.65	44.31
11	19.68	24.72	26	38.89	45.64
12	21.03	26.22	27	40.11	46.96
13	22.36	27.69	28	41.34	48.28
14	23.68	29.14	29	42.56	49.59
15	25.00	30.58	30	43.77	50.89

TABLE 6.   Areas Under the Normal Curve (for z scores)

Instructions for Use: To find the proportion of area *below* a particular z score, locate first the row in the left-hand column of the table that matches the z score through the first decimal place. Next, find the column in this row corresponding to the digit in the second decimal place of the z score. The entry in this cell of the table is the proportion of area under the normal curve that falls below an ordinate drawn at this z score (see the diagram). Multiplying this proportion by 100 results in the percentage of area that can be translated directly into a percentile rank. For example, one finds a z score of −2.39 by locating the row designated −2.3 and the column intersecting with this row designated .09; the tabled entry is .0084. One finds a z score of +1.27 by locating the row designated +1.2 and the column intersecting with this row designated .07; the tabled entry is .8980. See pp. 393–395 for a discussion of the use of this table in inferring the relative position of a score in a normal distribution of scores.

Area given in table

TABLE 6.   Areas Under the Normal Curve (for z scores) (*continued*)

z^a	Digit in the Second Decimal Place									
	.00	.01	.02	.03	.04	.05	.06	.07	.08	.09
−0.0	.5000	.4960	.4920	.4880	.4840	.4801	.4761	.4721	.4681	.4641
−0.1	.4602	.4562	.4522	.4483	.4443	.4404	.4364	.4325	.4286	.4247
−0.2	.4207	.4168	.4129	.4090	.4052	.4013	.3974	.3936	.3897	.3859
−0.3	.3821	.3783	.3745	.3707	.3669	.3632	.3594	.3557	.3520	.3483
−0.4	.3446	.3409	.3372	.3336	.3300	.3264	.3228	.3192	.3156	.3121
−0.5	.3085	.3050	.3015	.2981	.2946	.2912	.2877	.2843	.2810	.2776
−0.6	.2743	.2709	.2676	.2643	.2611	.2578	.2546	.2514	.2483	.2451
−0.7	.2420	.2389	.2358	.2327	.2296	.2266	.2236	.2206	.2177	.2148
−0.8	.2119	.2090	.2061	.2033	.2005	.1977	.1949	.1922	.1894	.1867
−0.9	.1841	.1814	.1788	.1762	.1736	.1711	.1685	.1660	.1635	.1611
−1.0	.1587	.1562	.1539	.1515	.1492	.1469	.1446	.1423	.1401	.1379
−1.1	.1357	.1335	.1314	.1292	.1271	.1251	.1230	.1210	.1190	.1170
−1.2	.1151	.1131	.1112	.1093	.1075	.1056	.1038	.1020	.1003	.0985
−1.3	.0968	.0951	.0934	.0918	.0901	.0885	.0869	.0853	.0838	.0823
−1.4	.0808	.0793	.0778	.0764	.0749	.0735	.0721	.0708	.0694	.0681
−1.5	.0668	.0655	.0643	.0630	.0618	.0606	.0594	.0582	.0571	.0559
−1.6	.0548	.0537	.0526	.0516	.0505	.0495	.0485	.0475	.0465	.0455
−1.7	.0446	.0436	.0427	.0418	.0409	.0401	.0392	.0384	.0375	.0367
−1.8	.0359	.0351	.0344	.0336	.0329	.0322	.0314	.0307	.0301	.0294
−1.9	.0287	.0281	.0274	.0268	.0262	.0256	.0250	.0244	.0239	.0233
−2.0	.0228	.0222	.0217	.0212	.0207	.0202	.0197	.0192	.0188	.0183
−2.1	.0179	.0174	.0170	.0166	.0162	.0158	.0154	.0150	.0146	.0143
−2.2	.0139	.0136	.0132	.0129	.0125	.0122	.0119	.0116	.0113	.0110
−2.3	.0107	.0104	.0102	.0099	.0096	.0094	.0091	.0089	.0087	.0084
−2.4	.0082	.0080	.0078	.0075	.0073	.0071	.0069	.0068	.0066	.0064
−2.5	.0062	.0060	.0059	.0057	.0055	.0054	.0052	.0051	.0049	.0048
−2.6	.0047	.0045	.0044	.0043	.0041	.0040	.0039	.0038	.0037	.0036
−2.7	.0035	.0034	.0033	.0032	.0031	.0030	.0029	.0028	.0027	.0026
−2.8	.0026	.0025	.0024	.0023	.0023	.0022	.0021	.0021	.0020	.0019
−2.9	.0019	.0018	.0018	.0017	.0016	.0016	.0015	.0015	.0014	.0014
−3.0	.0013	.0013	.0013	.0012	.0012	.0011	.0011	.0011	.0010	.0010

TABLE 6.   Areas Under the Normal Curve (for z scores) (*continued*)

z^a	Digit in the Second Decimal Place									
	.00	.01	.02	.03	.04	.05	.06	.07	.08	.09
+0.0	.5000	.5040	.5080	.5120	.5160	.5199	.5239	.5279	.5319	.5359
+0.1	.5398	.5438	.5478	.5517	.5557	.5596	.5636	.5675	.5714	.5753
+0.2	.5793	.5832	.5871	.5910	.5948	.5987	.6026	.6064	.6103	.6141
+0.3	.6179	.6217	.6255	.6293	.6331	.6368	.6406	.6443	.6480	.6517
+0.4	.6554	.6591	.6628	.6664	.6700	.6736	.6772	.6808	.6844	.6879
+0.5	.6915	.6950	.6985	.7019	.7054	.7088	.7123	.7157	.7190	.7224
+0.6	.7257	.7291	.7324	.7357	.7389	.7422	.7454	.7486	.7517	.7549
+0.7	.7580	.7611	.7642	.7673	.7704	.7734	.7764	.7794	.7823	.7852
+0.8	.7881	.7910	.7939	.7967	.7995	.8023	.8051	.8078	.8106	.8133
+0.9	.8159	.8186	.8212	.8238	.8264	.8289	.8315	.8340	.8365	.8389
+1.0	.8413	.8438	.8461	.8485	.8508	.8531	.8554	.8577	.8599	.8621
+1.1	.8643	.8665	.8686	.8708	.8729	.8749	.8770	.8790	.8810	.8830
+1.2	.8849	.8869	.8888	.8907	.8925	.8944	.8962	.8980	.8997	.9015
+1.3	.9032	.9049	.9066	.9082	.9099	.9115	.9131	.9147	.9162	.9177
+1.4	.9192	.9207	.9222	.9236	.9251	.9265	.9279	.9292	.9306	.9319
+1.5	.9332	.9345	.9357	.9370	.9382	.9394	.9406	.9418	.9429	.9441
+1.6	.9452	.9463	.9474	.9484	.9495	.9505	.9515	.9525	.9535	.9545
+1.7	.9554	.9564	.9573	.9582	.9591	.9599	.9608	.9616	.9625	.9633
+1.8	.9641	.9649	.9656	.9664	.9671	.9678	.9686	.9693	.9699	.9706
+1.9	.9713	.9719	.9726	.9732	.9738	.9744	.9750	.9756	.9761	.9767
+2.0	.9772	.9778	.9783	.9788	.9793	.9798	.9803	.9808	.9812	.9817
+2.1	.9821	.9826	.9830	.9834	.9838	.9842	.9846	.9850	.9854	.9857
+2.2	.9861	.9864	.9868	.9871	.9875	.9878	.9881	.9884	.9887	.9890
+2.3	.9893	.9896	.9898	.9901	.9904	.9906	.9909	.9911	.9913	.9916
+2.4	.9918	.9920	.9922	.9925	.9927	.9929	.9931	.9932	.9934	.9936
+2.5	.9938	.9940	.9941	.9943	.9945	.9946	.9948	.9949	.9951	.9952
+2.6	.9953	.9955	.9956	.9957	.9959	.9960	.9961	.9962	.9963	.9964
+2.7	.9965	.9966	.9967	.9968	.9969	.9970	.9971	.9972	.9973	.9974
+2.8	.9974	.9975	.9976	.9977	.9977	.9978	.9979	.9979	.9980	.9981
+2.9	.9981	.9982	.9982	.9983	.9984	.9984	.9985	.9985	.9986	.9986
+3.0	.9987	.9987	.9987	.9988	.9988	.9989	.9989	.9989	.9990	.9990

[a] Value of z through the first decimal place.

This table is abridged from Table 1 in *Biometrika tables for statisticians,* vol. 1 (3rd ed.), New York: Cambridge University Press, 1970, edited by E. S. Pearson and H. O. Hartley, by permission of the *Biometrika* Trustees.

TABLE 7.   Selected Values from the t Distribution

Instructions for Use: To find a value of t, locate the row in the left-hand column of the table corresponding to the number of degrees of freedom (df_M) associated with the standard error of the mean, and select the value of t listed for your choice of α. The value given in the column labeled $\alpha = .05$ is used in the calculation of the 95 percent confidence interval, and the value given in the column labeled $\alpha = .01$ is used to calculate the 99 percent confidence interval. See pp. 406–407 for a discussion of the use of this table in the construction of confidence intervals based on sample means.

df_M^a	$\alpha = .05$	$\alpha = .01$	df_M^a	$\alpha = .05$	$\alpha = .01$
1	12.71	63.66	18	2.10	2.88
2	4.30	9.92	19	2.09	2.86
3	3.18	5.84	20	2.09	2.84
4	2.78	4.60	21	2.08	2.83
5	2.57	4.03	22	2.07	2.82
6	2.45	3.71	23	2.07	2.81
7	2.36	3.50	24	2.06	2.80
8	2.31	3.36	25	2.06	2.79
9	2.26	3.25	26	2.06	2.78
10	2.23	3.17	27	2.05	2.77
11	2.20	3.11	28	2.05	2.76
12	2.18	3.06	29	2.04	2.76
13	2.16	3.01	30	2.04	2.75
14	2.14	2.98	40	2.02	2.70
15	2.13	2.95	60	2.00	2.66
16	2.12	2.92	120	1.98	2.62
17	2.11	2.90	Infinity	1.96	2.58

[a] $df_M = s - 1$ (where s = the number of scores in the sample).

This table is abridged from Table 12 in *Biometrika tables for statisticians*, vol. 1 (3rd ed.), New York: Cambridge University Press, 1970, edited by E. S. Pearson and H. O. Hartley, by permission of the *Biometrika* Trustees.

Appendix B

Answers to the Chapter Exercises

Since Chapter 2 may represent your first opportunity to perform the calculations required for statistics, we have made the answers to the problems in this chapter more complete than those in later chapters. Still, where procedures are introduced for the first time, we have made an effort to provide enough information to enable you to check your work for sources of errors.

We encourage you to save the work you do for the exercises both for review purposes and because certain problems appear again in subsequent chapters. As you learn new procedures, you will be able to make additional calculations using the same data and thus be able to analyze the data in the exercises more thoroughly.

Finally, we can not overemphasize the usefulness of examining the results of an analysis and comparing different sets of scores. As you gain in practice, you will become sensitive to patterns in results and possible errors in computations.

CHAPTER 2

1. (a) $\Sigma X = 24$ (b) $\Sigma X = 66$ (c) $\Sigma X = 48$

          $s = 6$ $s = 6$ $s = 6$

         $\bar{X} = 4.00$ $\bar{X} = 11.00$ $\bar{X} = 8.00$

A constant of 7 was added to each score in (a) to give the (b) scores. Each score in (c) is two times larger than the corresponding score in (a). The mean of (b) is 7 more than the mean of (a). The mean of (c) is two times larger than the mean of (a).

2. (a)
$$3 - 4 = -1$$
$$5 - 4 = +1$$
$$2 - 4 = -2$$
$$8 - 4 = +4$$
$$1 - 4 = -3$$
$$5 - 4 = +1$$
$$\Sigma (X - \bar{X}) = \overline{0}$$

(b)
$$10 - 11 = -1$$
$$12 - 11 = +1$$
$$9 - 11 = -2$$
$$15 - 11 = +4$$
$$8 - 11 = -3$$
$$12 - 11 = +1$$
$$\Sigma (X - \bar{X}) = \overline{0}$$

(c)
$$6 - 8 = -2$$
$$10 - 8 = +2$$
$$4 - 8 = -4$$
$$16 - 8 = +8$$
$$2 - 8 = -6$$
$$10 - 8 = +2$$
$$\Sigma (X - \bar{X}) = \overline{0}$$

3.
$$SS = \Sigma (X)^2 - \frac{(\Sigma X)^2}{s} \qquad \text{Equation (2-7)}$$

(a) $SS = 128 - \dfrac{(24)^2}{6} = 128 - 96.00 = 32.00$

(b) $SS = 758 - \dfrac{(66)^2}{6} = 758 - 726.00 = 32.00$

(c) $SS = 512 - \dfrac{(48)^2}{6} = 512 - 384.00 = 128.00$

4.
$$\text{variance} = \frac{SS}{s - 1} \qquad \text{Equation (2-8)}$$

(a) $\text{variance} = \dfrac{32.00}{6 - 1} = 6.40$

(b) $\text{variance} = \dfrac{32.00}{6 - 1} = 6.40$

(c) $\text{variance} = \dfrac{128.00}{6 - 1} = 25.60$

$$\text{standard deviation} = \sqrt{\text{variance}} \qquad \text{Equation (2-10)}$$

(a) $\sqrt{6.40} = 2.53$

(b) $\sqrt{6.40} = 2.53$

(c) $\sqrt{25.60} = 5.06$

CHAPTER 4

1. *Summary of the Preliminary Calculations:*

Calculation	No Additives	Additives
Mean	28.67	32.67
Sum	258	294
Sum of (scores)^2	7,472	9,776
Sum of squares	76.00	172.00
Variance	9.50	21.50
Standard Deviation	3.08	4.64

(a) $[A] = \dfrac{\Sigma\,(A)^2}{s} = \dfrac{153{,}000}{9} = 17{,}000.00$

$[T] = \dfrac{(T)^2}{a(s)} = \dfrac{(552)^2}{2(9)} = \dfrac{304{,}704}{18} = 16{,}928.00$

$[AS] = \Sigma\,(AS)^2 = 17{,}248$

(b) $SS_A = [A] - [T] = 17{,}000.00 - 16{,}928.00 = 72.00$

$SS_{S/A} = [AS] - [A] = 17{,}248 - 17{,}000.00 = 248.00$

$SS_T = [AS] - [T] = 17{,}248 - 16{,}928.00 = 320.00$

(c) $df_A = a - 1 = 2 - 1 = 1$

$df_{S/A} = a(s - 1) = 2(9 - 1) = 2(8) = 16$

$df_T = a(s) - 1 = 2(9) - 1 = 17$

(d) $MS_A = \dfrac{SS_A}{df_A} = \dfrac{72.00}{1} = 72.00$

$MS_{S/A} = \dfrac{SS_{S/A}}{df_{S/A}} = \dfrac{248.00}{16} = 15.50$

(e)

Source	SS	df	MS	F
Additives (A)	72.00	1	72.00	4.65
S/A	248.00	16	15.50	
Total	320.00	17		

2.

Source	SS	df	MS	F
Advertisements (A)	25.81	2	12.91	2.76
S/A	84.00	18	4.67	
Total	109.81	20		

CHAPTER 5

1. For $\alpha = .05$, $df_A = 1$, and $df_{S/A} = 16$, $F_\alpha = 4.49$. Yes.
2. For $\alpha = .05$, $df_A = 2$, and $df_{S/A} = 18$, $F_\alpha = 3.55$. No.

3.

Source	SS	df	MS	F
Rating (A)	267.80	3	89.27	17.71*
S/A	302.56	60	5.04	
Total	570.36	63		

*$p < .05$

4.

Source	SS	df	MS	F
Reinforcement (A)	1,607.82	3	535.94	3.04*
S/A	4,230.29	24	176.26	
Total	5,838.11	27		

*$p < .05$

CHAPTER 6

1. (a)

	Meaning	Word	Sound	Syllable
Comp. 1	+1	−1	+1	−1
Comp. 2	+3	−1	−1	−1
Comp. 3	0	+1	0	−1

(b)

Source	SS	df	MS	F
Comp. 1	83.27	1	83.27	16.52*
Comp. 2	206.26	1	206.26	40.92*
Comp. 3	60.50	1	60.50	12.00*
S/A	302.56	60	5.04	

*$p < .05$

(c) $F_S = (a - 1)F(df_A, df_{S/A}) = (4 - 1)(2.76) = 8.28$. Since all the F's are equal to or greater than F_S, the null hypothesis would have been rejected in each case.

2. (a)

Source	SS	df	MS	F
Comp. 1	2.01	1	2.01	0.01
Comp. 2	1,585.79	1	1,585.79	9.00*
S/A	4,230.29	24	176.26	

*$p < .05$

(b)

Source	SS	df	MS	F
Comp. 3	1,348.67	1	1,348.67	7.65
Comp. 4	391.14	1	391.14	2.22

Since $F_S = (3)(3.01) = 9.03$, Comp. 4 is not statistically significant, but Comp. 3 falls between F_α and F_S, which can be taken as an indication to suspend judgment.

CHAPTER 7

1.

	Set A	Set B
	Mean = 65.17	Mean = 61.83
	Median = 65.50	Median = 65.50
	Mode = 70	Mode = 70

You will note that only the mean was affected by the score change. The median and the mode would be affected only when the change involved the middlemost scores (median) or the most frequent score (mode). It is the relative insensitivity to extreme scores that makes the median preferable to the mean as a descriptive measure of central tendency when a distribution is badly skewed.

2. $MS_A = 89.27$; $MS_{S/A} = 5.04$; $a = 4$; $s = 16$.

$$\hat{\sigma}_A^2 = 3.95; \quad \hat{\omega}_A^2 = 0.44 \quad .$$

Approximately 44 percent of the total variability in the experiment is due to the effects of the independent variable.

CHAPTER 8

1. $[A] = 6,003.00$; $[T] = 4,920.32$; $[S] = 4,980.80$; $[AS] = 6,210.$

Source	SS	df	MS	F
Task Length (A)	1,082.68	4	270.67	66.50*
Subjects (S)	60.48	9	6.72	
A × S	146.52	36	4.07	
Total	1,289.68	49		

*$p < .05$

2. (a) $[A] = 10,288.33$; $[T] = 10,082.00$; $[S] = 10,252.00$; $[AS] = 10,510.$

Source	SS	df	MS	F
Noise (A)	206.33	2	103.17	19.96*
Subjects (S)	170.00	5	34.00	
A × S	51.67	10	5.17	
Total	428.00	17		

*$p < .05$

(b) $SS_{comp. \ 1} = 6.25$; $F = 1.21, p > .05$.
(c) $SS_{comp. \ 2} = 200.08$; $F = 38.70, p < .05$.

CHAPTER 9

1. (a)

	b_1	b_2	b_3	Sum
a_1	60	62	49	171
a_2	57	83	95	235
Sum	117	145	144	406

(b) $df_A = a - 1 = 2 - 1 = 1$
$df_B = b - 1 = 3 - 1 = 2$
$df_{A \times B} = (a - 1)(b - 1) = (2 - 1)(3 - 1) = 2$
$df_{S/AB} = a(b)(s - 1) = 2(3)(13 - 1) = 6(12) = 72$
$df_T = a(b)(s) - 1 = 2(3)(13) - 1 = 78 - 1 = 77$

(c) $[A] = 2,165.79$; $[T] = 2,113.28$; $[B] = 2,132.69$; $[AB] = 2,231.38$;
$[ABS] = 2,514$.

Source	SS	df	MS	F
Type of Task (A)	52.51	1	52.51	13.36*
Number of Distractors (B)	19.41	2	9.71	2.47
$A \times B$	46.18	2	23.09	5.88*
S/AB	282.62	72	3.93	
Total	400.72	77		

*$p < .05$

2. (a) $[A] = 2,523.50$; $[T] = 2,352.00$; $[B] = 2,492.08$; $[AB] = 2,672.25$;
$[ABS] = 3,096$.

Source	SS	df	MS	F
Strain (A)	171.50	2	85.75	8.50*
Environment (B)	140.08	1	140.08	13.88*
$A \times B$	8.67	2	4.34	0.43
S/AB	423.75	42	10.09	
Total	744.00	47		

*$p < .05$

(b) Both independent variables affected speed of learning. The bright rats learned more quickly than the mixed rats, and the mixed rats learned more quickly than the dull rats. Animals raised in the enriched environment learned the maze more quickly than those raised in the impoverished environment. The nonsignificant interaction indicates that the effects of the two environments are the same for all three strains of rats. The two environments do not differentially help or hinder the different types of rats.

CHAPTER 10

1. The main effect of factor A (strain) is an omnibus test involving three treatment means and, consequently, does not indicate which treatment conditions differ and which do not. All three comparisons between pairs of treatment conditions are of interest. A comparison between the bright and mixed strains (4.63 versus 7.13) would indicate whether selective breeding of good learners produces offspring who are superior to "normal" rats. A companion comparison between the dull and mixed strains (9.25 versus 7.13) would indicate whether selective breeding of poor learners produces offspring who are inferior to normal rats. The final comparison between the bright and dull strains (4.63 versus 9.25) examines the difference between the two selected strains of rats. Taken as a set, these comparisons will indicate whether evidence exists for the selective breeding of learning ability (bright versus dull) and whether this effect is found separately for bright rats (bright versus mixed) and for dull rats (dull versus mixed). The main effect of factor B (environment) involves only two conditions, enriched and impoverished, and no further comparisons are possible.

2. (a) 3.50, 4.00, and 7.50. Total number of scores $= 3(8) = 24$. This analysis represents a simple main effect of factor A (strain) at one of the levels of factor B (enriched environment).

(b) 3.50 and 4.00. Total number of scores $= 2(8) = 16$. This analysis represents a simple comparison of factor A (bright versus mixed) at one of the levels of factor B (enriched environment).

(c) There are three sets of comparisons: 3.50 and 3.75; 4.00 and 7.75; and 7.50 and 11.00. Each comparison involves $2(8) = 16$ scores. These analyses represent simple main effects of factor B (environment) at each of the levels of factor A (bright, mixed, and dull strains).

(d)

Environments	Bright	Mixed
Enriched	3.50	4.00
Impoverished	3.75	7.75

Total number of scores $= 4(8) = 32$. This is a factorial comparison involving two of the A treatments (bright and mixed) and the two B treatments (enriched and impoverished). The comparison is represented by a 2×2 data matrix, and the primary interest is in the interaction of the two variables.

(e)

Environments	Bright	Dull
Enriched	3.50	7.50
Impoverished	3.75	11.00

Total number of scores = 4(8) = 32. This is a factorial comparison involving the two *B* treatments and two of the *A* treatments (bright and dull). Again, the primary interest is in the interaction of the two variables.

(f) Bright rats are relatively unaffected by the richness of the environment in which they have been raised, while mixed and dull rats show marked improvement when they are raised in the enriched environment. In addition, the gain for the mixed rats nearly eliminates the difference that was observed when the mixed and bright rats were raised in the impoverished environment.

3. (a) *Formula Development* (see p. 260). Isolate the relevant row of the *AB* matrix. (If the simple main effect involved factor *B*, you would isolate the relevant *column* of the *AB* matrix.) Treat these data as if they were produced from a single-factor experiment rather than from a factorial design. To assist in this translation, change the notational system from the factorial representation to one appropriate for a single-factor experiment. As an example, consider the simple main effect at level b_1:

	a_1	a_2	a_3	Sum
Factorial Symbols	AB_{11}	AB_{21}	AB_{31}	B_1
Single-Factor Symbols	"A_1"	"A_2"	"A_3"	"T"

(The quotation marks around these symbols are intended to remind you that these are special symbols designed for this analysis.) The necessary formulas for this simple main effect, which we will refer to as *A* at b_1, can now be written as follows:

$$SS_{A \text{ at } b_1} = \frac{\sum (\text{``}A\text{''})^2}{s} - \frac{(\text{``}T\text{''})^2}{a(s)} \quad ;$$

$$df_{A \text{ at } b_1} = a - 1;$$

$$MS_{A \text{ at } b_1} = \frac{SS_{A \text{ at } b_1}}{df_{A \text{ at } b_1}}; \text{ and}$$

$$F = \frac{MS_{A \text{ at } b_1}}{MS_{S/AB}} \quad .$$

A similar translation would be performed on the sums at level b_2.

Calculations.

$$SS_{A \text{ at } b_1} = \frac{(249)^2 + (263)^2 + (276)^2}{7} - \frac{(788)^2}{3(7)}$$

$$= 29,620.86 - 29,568.76 = 52.10;$$

$$df_{A \text{ at } b_1} = 3 - 1 = 2;$$

$$MS_{A \text{ at } b_1} = \frac{52.10}{2} = 26.05; \text{ and}$$

$$F = \frac{26.05}{47.64} = .55.$$

$$SS_{A \text{ at } b_2} = \frac{(261)^2 + (173)^2 + (41)^2}{7} - \frac{(475)^2}{3(7)}$$

$$= 14,247.29 - 10,744.05 = 3,503.24;$$

$$df_{A \text{ at } b_2} = 3 - 1 = 2;$$

$$MS_{A \text{ at } b_2} = \frac{3,503.24}{2} = 1,751.62; \text{ and}$$

$$F = \frac{1,751.62}{47.64} = 36.77 \quad .$$

For both F ratios the numerator and denominator dfs are 2 and 36, respectively; only the second F is significant ($p < .05$).

(b) *Formula Development* (see p. 260). Isolate the relevant cells in the AB Matrix that are involved in the factorial comparison. Treat these data as if they were produced from this particular factorial rather than from the overall design. In this example, the component factorial consists of

	Control a_1	Unfamiliar a_2	Sum
Young (b_1)	AB_{11}	AB_{21}	B_1
Adult (b_2)	AB_{12}	AB_{22}	B_2
Sum	A_1	A_2	T

We can now use the standard formula for the $A \times B$ interaction to calculate the interaction of this component formula, remembering that $s = 7$, $a = 2$ (rather than 3), and $b = 2$. We will refer to the interaction of a factorial comparison involving factor A as $A_{\text{comp.}} \times B$. The formulas are as follows:

$$SS_{A_{\text{comp.}} \times B} = \frac{\Sigma\,(AB)^2}{s} - \frac{\Sigma\,(A)^2}{b(s)} - \frac{\Sigma\,(B)^2}{a(s)} + \frac{(T)^2}{a(b)(s)} \quad ;$$

$$df_{A_{\text{comp.}} \times B} = (a - 1)(b - 1);$$

$$MS_{A_{\text{comp.}} \times B} = \frac{SS_{A_{\text{comp.}} \times B}}{df_{A_{\text{comp.}} \times B}}; \text{ and}$$

$$F = \frac{MS_{A_{\text{comp.}} \times B}}{MS_{S/AB}} \quad .$$

Calculations.

	Control (a_1)	Unfamiliar (a_2)	Sum
Young (b_1)	249	263	512
Adult (b_2)	261	173	434
Sum	510	436	946

$$[AB] = \frac{(249)^2 + (263)^2 + (261)^2 + (173)^2}{7} = 32,745.71;$$

$$[A] = \frac{(510)^2 + (436)^2}{2(7)} = 32,156.86;$$

$$[B] = \frac{(512)^2 + (434)^2}{2(7)} = 32{,}178.57; \text{ and}$$

$$[T] = \frac{(946)^2}{2(2)(7)} = 31{,}961.29.$$

$$
\begin{aligned}
SS_{A_{\text{comp.}} \times B} &= [AB] - [A] - [B] + [T] \\
&= 32{,}745.71 - 32{,}156.86 - 32{,}178.57 + 31{,}961.29 \\
&= 371.57;
\end{aligned}
$$

$$df_{A_{\text{comp.}} \times B} = (2 - 1)(2 - 1) = 1;$$

$$MS_{A_{\text{comp.}} \times B} = \frac{371.57}{1} = 371.57; \text{ and}$$

$$F = \frac{371.57}{47.64} = 7.80.$$

The numerator and denominator dfs are 1 and 36, respectively; the obtained F is significant, $p < .05$.

(c) *Formula Development* (see pp. 260–261). Isolate the relevant row of the AB matrix and use the same change in the notational system that we suggested in Part (a). In this case, we are interested in a simple comparison involving the scores obtained for the adult rats (b_2). (We will refer to this simple comparison as $A_{\text{comp. at } b_2}$.) Starting with the sums contributing to the simple main effect at level b_2, the notational change becomes:

	a_1	a_2	a_3	Sum
Factorial Symbols	AB_{12}	AB_{22}	AB_{32}	B_2
Single-Factor Symbols	"A_1"	"A_2"	"A_3"	"T"

(Again, the quotation marks around the single-factor symbols remind us that they are special symbols manufactured for this analysis.) Any single-df comparison can be expressed in terms of coefficients. The necessary computational formulas for a simple comparison can be written in the special notation as follows:

$$SS_{A_{\text{comp. at } b_2}} = \frac{[\Sigma (c_i)(\text{``}A_i\text{''})]^2}{s [\Sigma (c_i)^2]} \quad ;$$

$$df_{A_{\text{comp. at } b_2}} = 1;$$

$$MS_{A_{\text{comp. at } b_2}} = \frac{SS_{A_{\text{comp. at } b_2}}}{df_{A_{\text{comp. at } b_2}}}; \text{ and}$$

$$F = \frac{MS_{A_{\text{comp. at } b_2}}}{MS_{S/AB}} \quad .$$

Calculations.

	Control (a_1)	Unfamiliar (a_2)	Familiar (a_3)
Adult (b_2)	261	173	41
Coefficients	0	+1	−1

$$SS_{A_{comp.} \text{ at } b_2} = \frac{[(0)(261) + (+1)(173) + (-1)(41)]^2}{7[(0)^2 + (+1)^2 + (-1)^2]}$$

$$= \frac{(173 - 41)^2}{7(0 + 1 + 1)} = \frac{(132)^2}{7(2)} = \frac{17,424}{14}$$

$$= 1,244.57;$$

$$df_{A_{comp.} \text{ at } b_2} = 1;$$

$$MS_{A_{comp.} \text{ at } b_2} = \frac{1,244.57}{1} = 1,244.57; \text{ and}$$

$$F = \frac{1,244.57}{47.64} = 26.12.$$

The numerator and denominator df's are 1 and 36, respectively; the obtained F is significant ($p < .05$).

CHAPTER 11

1. *Basic Ratios*

$[A] = 6,056.44$ $[AB] = 6,388.00$ $[ABS] = 6,578$

$[B] = 6,277.33$ $[AS] = 6,222.67$ $[T] = 5,974.52$

Degrees of Freedom

Loudness (A)	$a - 1$	= 2
S/A	$a(s - 1)$	= 15
Rate (B)	$b - 1$	= 2
$A \times B$	$(a - 1)(b - 1)$	= 4
$B \times S/A$	$a(b - 1)(s - 1)$	= 30
Total	$a(b)(s) - 1$	= 53

Analysis Summary Table

Source	SS	df	MS	F
A	81.92	2	40.96	3.70*
S/A	166.23	15	11.08	
B	302.81	2	151.41	191.66*
$A \times B$	28.75	4	7.19	9.10*
$B \times S/A$	23.77	30	.79	
Total	603.48	53		

*$p < .05$

While both main effects are significant, the presence of a significant interaction indicates that the exact relationship for either independent variable depends on the other. We can see this most clearly by examining the simple main effects of either independent variable. For example, it appears that soft passages are less affected by increases in presentation rate than are moderate or loud passages, and that passages presented at fast rates are less affected by the loudness of the passages than are passages presented at slow or medium rates.

2. $[A] = 4,301.50 \quad [AB] = 4,457.00 \quad [ABS] = 4,912$
   $[B] = 4,327.33 \quad [AS] = 4,680.50 \quad [T] = 4,256.33$

Source	SS	df	MS	F
Operation (A)	45.17	2	22.59	.54
S/A	379.00	9	42.11	
Test (B)	71.00	3	23.67	8.42*
A × B	84.50	6	14.08	5.01*
B × S/A	76.00	27	2.81	
Total	655.67	47		

*$p < .05$

The presence of a significant interaction indicates that the tests are differentially sensitive to the detection of differences resulting from the brain operations. While tests b_1 and b_2 do not appear to distinguish among the three treatment groups, tests b_3 and b_4 do. Additional statistical tests will be necessary to determine whether the two groups of animals with brain tissue removed differ from one another on any of these tests. An examination of the data suggests that subjects with the critical area removed do perform more poorly on these last two tests than do subjects with the noncritical area removed. If this observation is borne out statistically, the researcher's hypothesis will be supported.

CHAPTER 12

1.

Load	Meters Pulled
(X)	(Y)

$\Sigma X = 28 \qquad \Sigma Y = 85$

$\Sigma (X)^2 = 140 \qquad \Sigma (Y)^2 = 1,383$

$\bar{X} = 4.00 \qquad \bar{Y} = 12.14$

$\Sigma (X)(Y) = 246$

$SS_X = 28.00$

$SP_{XY} = -94.00$

$b_Y = -3.36$

$a_Y = 25.58$

$Y' = 25.58 + (-3.36)(X)$

2.

	a_1	a_2	a_3	a_4	a_5
Sums	31	70	102	126	167
c_i	-2	-1	0	$+1$	$+2$

$$SS_{A_{\text{linear}}} = \frac{(+328)^2}{10(10)} = 1{,}075.84; \quad MS_{A_{\text{linear}}} = 1{,}075.84;$$

$$MS_{A \times S} = 4.07; \quad F = \frac{1{,}075.84}{4.07} = 264.33 \ (p < .05)$$

$$Y' = .02 + (.66)(X)$$

CHAPTER 13

1. *Regression Line*

$$SP_{XY} = 1{,}746 - \frac{(70)(409)}{16} = 1{,}746 - 1{,}789.38 = -43.38$$

$$SS_X = 400 - \frac{(70)^2}{16} = 400 - 306.25 = 93.75$$

$$b_Y = \frac{-43.38}{93.75} = -.46$$

$$a_Y = 25.56 - (-.46)(4.38) = 25.56 + 2.01 = 27.57$$

$$Y' = 27.57 + (-.46)(X)$$

Test of the Slope of the Regression Line

$$SS_Y = 13{,}285 - \frac{(409)^2}{16} = 13{,}285 - 10{,}455.06 = 2{,}829.94$$

$$SS_{\text{lin. regr.}} = \frac{(-43.38)^2}{93.75} = 20.07$$

$$SS_{\text{residual}} = 2{,}829.94 - 20.07 = 2{,}809.87$$

Source	SS	df	MS	F
Linear Regression	20.07	1	20.07	.10
Residual	2,809.87	14	200.71	
Total (Y)	2,829.94	15		

Prediction is not possible with this set of data.

2. $SS_{\text{residual}} = 482.59$, which compares quite well with the value obtained with the computational formula ($SS_{\text{residual}} = 482.57$).

CHAPTER 14

1.   (a) $SP_{XY} = 61,971 - \frac{(958)(955)}{15} = 61,971 - 60,992.67 = 978.33$

$SS_X = 62,170 - \frac{(958)^2}{15} = 62,170 - 61,184.27 = 985.73$

$SS_Y = 62,753 - \frac{(955)^2}{15} = 62,753 - 60,801.67 = 1,951.33$

$r = \frac{978.33}{\sqrt{(985.73)(1,951.33)}} = \frac{978.33}{\sqrt{1,923,484.52}} = \frac{978.33}{1,386.90} = .71$

(b) $r^2 = (.71)^2 = .50$

(c) $1 - r^2 = 1 - .50 = .50$

(d) $Y' = .44 + (.99)(X)$ and $X' = 32.03 + (.50)(Y)$

Although the r is statistically significant, it tells us nothing about the two means. The question of whether the means differ must be tested separately from the statistical evaluation of the correlation coefficient. The difference between the two means can be tested with the procedures presented in Chapter 8. In this case, the analysis would be treated as a within-subjects design, with two levels of the independent variable (type of test, a_1 = take-home test and a_2 = in-class test) and s = 15 subjects. A significant effect would allow us to conclude that the average performance on the two tests differed. While we could not conclude thus in the present example, since the means are so similar (63.87 and 63.67), we should still pay attention to the two means even though our main interest is in the presence or absence of linear correlation.

CHAPTER 15

1. (a)

Response Category	Psychotherapy	Chemotherapy	Shock Therapy	No Therapy
Improved	$\frac{(3.50)^2}{10.50}$	$\frac{(.50)^2}{10.50}$	$\frac{(1.50)^2}{10.50}$	$\frac{(-5.50)^2}{10.50}$
Not Improved	$\frac{(-3.50)^2}{9.50}$	$\frac{(-.50)^2}{9.50}$	$\frac{(-1.50)^2}{9.50}$	$\frac{(5.50)^2}{9.50}$

$\chi^2 = 1.17 + .02 + .21 + 2.88 + 1.29 + .03 + .24 + 3.18 = 9.02.$

The chi square is significant ($df = 3$, $p < .05$).

(b)

Response Category	Psycho-therapy	Chemo-therapy	Shock Therapy
Improved	$\dfrac{(1.67)^2}{10.50}$	$\dfrac{(-1.33)^2}{10.50}$	$\dfrac{(-.33)^2}{10.50}$
Not Improved	$\dfrac{(-1.67)^2}{9.50}$	$\dfrac{(1.33)^2}{9.50}$	$\dfrac{(.33)^2}{9.50}$

$$\chi^2 = .27 + .17 + .01 + .29 + .19 + .01 = .94 \quad (df = 2, p > .05) \quad .$$

(c)

Response Category	Combined Therapy	No Therapy
Improved	$\dfrac{(5.50)^2}{31.50}$	$\dfrac{(-5.50)^2}{10.50}$
Not Improved	$\dfrac{(-5.50)^2}{28.50}$	$\dfrac{(5.50)^2}{9.50}$

$$\chi^2 = .96 + 2.88 + 1.06 + 3.18 = 8.08 \quad (df = 1, p < .05) \quad .$$

Since one expected frequency is less than 10 (9.50), Yates's Correction should be applied (see p. 382). This adjustment reduces the absolute magnitude of the differences between observed and expected frequencies by .5, that is, $+5.50$ to $+5.00$ and -5.50 to -5.00. The corrected chi square statistic, $\chi^2 = 6.68$, is still significant ($p < .05$).

2. $\chi^2 = 2.50$ ($p > .05$).

3. $\chi^2 = 6.52$ ($p < .05$).

CHAPTER 16

1. $$SS = 62,753 - \frac{(955)^2}{15} = 1,951.33; \quad SD = \sqrt{\frac{1,951.33}{15}} = 11.41$$

For the first score (69),

$$z = \frac{69 - 63.67}{11.41} = +.47 \quad,$$

and for the other scores, $z = -1.20$, $+1.96$, and $+.03$. Percentile ranks $= 68.08$, 11.51, 97.50, and 51.20.

2. For the first case,

$$\hat{\sigma}_M = \frac{12.25}{\sqrt{6}} = \frac{12.25}{2.45} = 5.00 \quad,$$

and for the other cases, $\hat{\sigma}_M = 2.04$, 1.39, and .33.

3. $\hat{\sigma} = \sqrt{\dfrac{1{,}951.33}{14}} = \sqrt{139.38} = 11.81; \quad \hat{\sigma}_M = \dfrac{11.81}{\sqrt{15}} = \dfrac{11.81}{3.87} = 3.05$

$$\hat{\mu} = 63.67; \, t = 2.14 \quad .$$

Lower limit: $63.67 - (2.14)(3.05) = 57.14$
Upper limit: $63.67 + (2.14)(3.05) = 70.20$

4. Lower limit: $63.87 - 4.64 = 59.23$
   Upper limit: $63.87 + 4.64 = 68.51$

GLOSSARIES

Glossary 1

Significant Terms and Concepts

This glossary contains brief definitions of the significant terms and concepts that form the basis for a complete understanding and mastery of the material presented in this text. (See Glossary 3 for a listing of symbols and their meanings.)

AB **matrix.** A systematic arrangement of the treatment sums in a two-factor design.

AB **sums.** Sums of the basic observations in each treatment combination of a two-factor design.

ABS **matrix.** A systematic listing of the basic observations in a two-factor design.

Alpha (α). The probability of committing a type I error. See **Significance level.**

Alternative hypothesis (H_1). The hypothesis that is accepted when the null hypothesis is rejected.

Analysis of covariance. An analysis of variance that accounts for subject differences that existed before the start of the experiment.

Analysis of variance. A statistical analysis involving the comparison of variances reflecting different sources of variability.

Analytical comparison. A meaningful comparison between two or more treatment conditions that are components of a larger experimental design.

Apparent (score) limits. The score values defining the upper and lower limits of an interval in a grouped frequency distribution.

Arithmetic mean. The sum of a set of numbers divided by the number of them in the set.

AS matrix. A listing of the basic observations in a single-factor design.

Bar graph. A pictorial representation of data in which bars are used to represent data from an experiment involving a qualitative manipulation or a frequency distribution of qualitatively different classes of responses.

Basic observation. The score for an individual subject in a particular treatment condition of an experiment.

Basic ratios. The separate quantities entering into the computational formulas for sums of squares in the analysis of variance.

Best-fit straight line. A line representing the linear relationship between two variables that minimizes the degree to which the actual data deviate from the line.

Beta (β). The probability of committing a type II error.

Between-group sum of squares. The treatment sum of squares in a between-subjects single-factor experiment.

Between-subjects design. An experimental design in which subjects are randomly assigned to one of the treatment conditions.

Between-subjects error (term). The error term used to form F ratios reflecting between-subjects sources of variance. See **Mixed factorial design.**

Bimodal frequency distribution. A frequency distribution with two modes.

Block randomization. A method of random assignment in which subjects are balanced over the conditions at the end of each subject assignment block.

Carryover effects. The effects on a subject's performance under one condition of previously administered conditions in a within-subjects design.

Categorical data. Data consisting of a classification of the behavior of subjects into a number of mutually exclusive response categories.

Cell means. The specific treatment means in a factorial experiment.

Central Limit Theorem. A theorem of statistical theory stating that the sampling distribution of the mean approaches the normal distribution in shape as the size of the random sample on which the means are based is increased.

Central tendency. A statistic that describes the typical score in a distribution of scores.

Chi square distribution. A theoretical sampling distribution used in conjunction with the chi square statistic. A different chi square distribution exists for each number of degrees of freedom.

Chi square statistic (χ^2). A statistic based on categorical data in which the observed frequencies with which different classes of responses occur are compared with expected frequencies derived from theoretical or empirical considerations.

Classification variable. An independent variable created by the systematic selection of subjects on the dimension to be studied, for example, intelligence, age, or sex.

Class interval. A range of values used in the grouping of individual scores in a grouped frequency distribution.

Coefficient of alienation. The proportion of variance in either variable X or variable Y that is not linearly related to the other variable.

Coefficient of determination. The proportion of variance in either variable X or variable Y that is linearly related to the other variable.

Coefficients. A set of numbers, one for each treatment condition, that specifies a particular arrangement of treatment means in a single-df comparison. Used in the calculation of the sum of squares for the comparison.

Column marginal means. See **Marginal means.**

Column marginal sums. See **Marginal sums.**

Complete counterbalancing. A counterbalancing arrangement in which all possible combinations of the treatment conditions are included in a within-subjects design.

Completely randomized between-subjects design. See **Between-subjects design.**

Completely randomized single-factor design. A single-factor experiment in which subjects are randomly assigned to one of the treatment conditions.

Completely randomized two-variable factorial design. An experiment in which subjects are randomly assigned to one of the treatment conditions formed from the factorial combination of two independent variables.

Component contingency table. A specialized contingency table used in analytical comparisons conducted in the analysis of frequency data. Used in the calculation of a special chi square statistic ($\chi^2_{comp.}$).

Component deviations. Component parts of the deviation of an individual score from the grand mean; forms the basis for the analysis of variance.

Component factorial comparisons. See **Factorial comparison.**

Component single-factor experiments. Single-factor experiments combined to form a factorial design; the basis for the analysis of simple main effects.

Complex comparisons. A single-df comparison involving the averaging of two or more treatment means.

Computational formula. The formula with which one usually calculates statistics. Involves less computational effort than the corresponding defining formula.

Confidence interval. A range of values assumed with a specified degree of confidence to include a population parameter.

Confidence level. Used in interval estimation to refer to the proportion of times confidence intervals constructed in the same way will include the population parameter.

Confounding of variables. A situation in which one (or more) independent variable(s) varies systematically with the manipulated independent variable.

Contingency table. A two-dimensional matrix used with categorical data to classify subjects jointly on the basis of two variables.

Control condition. A reference condition in an experiment consisting of the absence of a specific experimental treatment.

Control variable. Information about subjects obtained before the start of an experiment that is used to reduce experimental error by means of a procedure known as the analysis of covariance.

Correction for continuity. A correction applied to the analysis of categorical data when 1 degree of freedom is associated with the data matrix.

Correlational data. Data consisting of two (or more) response measures obtained from a group of subjects; used to establish linear relationships between dependent variables.

Correlational research. Nonexperimental research consisting of the establishment of relationships between two (and sometimes more) naturally occurring aspects of behavior.

Correlation coefficient. A measure of the degree of linear relationship between two variables.

Counterbalancing. A systematic arrangement of treatment conditions designed to neutralize practice effects.

Covariance. A measure of the joint variability of two variables.

Covariation of X and Y. The degree to which the X and Y variables vary together; measured by covariance.

Critical region. The range of values of a statistic within which the null hypothesis will be rejected. Known also as the region of rejection.

Critical value. A value obtained from a sampling distribution that specifies the beginning of the critical region.

Data reduction. The process of extracting descriptive statistics from a set of observations.

Decision rules. A set of rules specifying the conditions under which the null hypothesis will be rejected or not.

Defining formula. A formula expressing a statistical operation in a form that preserves the meaning of the concept. Actual calculations are frequently performed with an equivalent but computationally simpler computational formula.

Degrees of freedom (df). The number of independent pieces of information remaining following the estimation of population parameters.

Dependent variable. The response measure of an experiment. Also often refers to the predicted variable in a correlational study.

Descriptive statistic. A numerical summary of a set of scores.

Deviation from the mean. In general, the deviation of a number from the mean of the set of numbers to which it belongs.

Deviation score. The difference between a score and the mean of the set of scores to which it belongs.

Dichotomous classification (or variable). A response variable consisting of only two values.

Differential carryover effects. Carryover effects that depend on specific combinations of treatment conditions and that are not eliminated by counterbalancing.

Directional statistical test. A statistical test that specifies the positive or negative direction of a comparison between two means; a one-tailed test.

Environmental variable. An independent variable in which some aspect of the physical environment is manipulated.

Error of prediction. The discrepancy between an observed score and that predicted by the linear regression line. Forms the basis for the standard error of estimate.

Error term. The denominator term of an F ratio.

Estimation. Procedures permitting the estimation of numerical characteristics of a given population from information provided by a sample drawn randomly from that population.

Expected frequency. The frequency with which a particular type of response will occur on the basis of theoretical or empirical considerations (relevant to the chi square test).

Experiment. A set of procedures permitting the inference of cause and effect. Differential treatments are administered randomly to different groups of subjects (or to the same subjects in a counterbalanced manner) and performance on some response measure is observed and recorded following the administration of the treatments. Any differences observed among the treatment conditions that are not reasonably accounted for by experimental error are attributed to the critical differences in the treatments associated with the different conditions.

Experimental data. Data obtained from experiments; used to establish causal relationships between independent (or manipulated) variables and behavior (dependent variables).

Experimental design. The plan of an experiment, including a specification of the nature of the treatment conditions and the method of assigning subjects to the conditions.

Experimental error. Uncontrolled sources of variability that are assumed to occur randomly during the course of an experiment.

Experimentwise type I error. The probability of committing type I errors over a set of statistical tests.

Explained variability. The proportion of variability in one variable that is linearly associated with another variable. Algebraically equivalent to the square of the product-moment correlation coefficient.

F distribution. A theoretical distribution used in conjunction with the F statistic. A different F distribution exists for each combination of numerator and denominator degrees of freedom.

F **ratio.** A statistical index relating systematic variance to nonsystematic variance. The statistical procedure permitting an assessment of the significance of this ratio is called the *F* test.

F **table.** A table listing the critical values of *F* for different combinations of numerator and denominator degrees of freedom for different levels of significance.

Factor. The term usually refers to an independent variable. Factor *A* is the independent variable in a single-factor experiment; factors *A* and *B* are the independent variables in a two-factor experiment. The levels of a factor are the specific treatment conditions associated with the factor.

Factor analysis. A complicated statistical procedure for analyzing correlational relationships among three or more response measures.

Factorial comparison. A focused analysis of interaction based on a smaller, more meaningful factorial arrangement of the independent variables.

Factorial design. An experimental design that includes all combinations of the levels of two (or more) independent variables.

Fisher Exact Test. A statistical test performed on frequency data when $df = 1$ and one or more of the expected frequencies is smaller than 5 or if the total number of subjects is twenty or fewer.

Frequency. The number of times a given score or response occurs in a set of observations.

Frequency data. Data consisting of the frequency with which certain classes of responses occur.

Frequency distribution. A listing of the frequencies with which particular scores or classes of responses occur in a set of observations.

Frequency polygon. A graphical representation of a frequency distribution of quantitative scores. A line graph that connects points representing the midpoints of successive class intervals and the frequencies with which scores fall within these intervals.

Generalization. The extension to populations of data and conclusions based on samples. See **Statistical generalization** and **Nonstatistical generalization.**

General practice effects. The systematic improvement or decline in performance as subjects receive a series of different treatment conditions in a within-subjects design. Assumed to be the same for all treatment conditions. A potential bias, usually neutralized through counterbalancing.

Goodness of fit. The degree to which observed data correspond to theoretical expectations.

Grand mean. The mean calculated from all the observations in a study.

Grand sum. The sum calculated from all the observations in a study.

Graph. A pictorial summary of a set of data in an *X-Y* coordinate system. For experimental data, the *X* axis is used to denote the independent variable and the *Y* axis is used to denote the dependent variable; for correlational data, both axes are used to denote dependent variables.

Grouped frequency distribution. A frequency distribution based on class intervals containing two or more contiguous scale values.

Higher-order trend. Nonlinear mathematical functions used to describe the effects of a quantitative independent variable.

Histogram. A bar graph used to depict a frequency distribution.

Homogeneity of variance. An assumption of the analysis of variance referring to the equality of the treatment population variances.

Hypothesis testing. The formal process by which a decision is made concerning the rejection or nonrejection of the null hypothesis.

Incomplete counterbalancing. See **Latin Square.**

Independent variable. The variable manipulated by an experimenter. See also **Factor.**

Inferential statistics. Statistical measures and procedures used in making inferences about population characteristics from samples drawn from those populations; consists of hypothesis testing and estimation of population parameters.

Interaction. The outcome of a factorial experiment in which the effects on behavior of one independent variable change at the different levels of the second independent variable.

Intercept of a regression line. A numerical constant in a linear regression equation representing the value of the predicted variable when the value of the independent or predictor variable is 0.

Interquartile range. The difference between two scores, one representing the 75th percentile and the other the 25th percentile; used to define the semi-interquartile range, an alternative measure of variability.

Interval estimate. A form of estimation in which the investigator states with a certain degree of confidence that a population parameter is contained within a particular range of values.

Latin Square. A form of counterbalancing frequently used in the arrangement of orders in which treatment conditions are presented in a within-subjects design.

Least-squares method. The method by which the best-fit straight line is fit to data. Consists of holding to a minimum the sum of the squared deviations of the observed data points from the regression line.

Levels of an independent variable. See **Treatment conditions.**

Linear coefficients. Coefficients permitting the statistical assessment of the presence or absence of a linear trend in the results of an experiment.

Linear regression line. A best-fit straight line depicting the linear relationship between two variables.

Linear regression of X on Y. The linear regression line relating values on the X variable to values on the Y variable. Can be used to predict X from a knowledge of Y.

Linear regression of Y on X. The linear regression line relating values on the Y variable to values on the X variable. Can be used to predict Y from a knowledge of X.

Linear trend. The presence of a linear relationship between an independent variable and the treatment means.

Line graph. A pictorial representation of experimental data in which contiguous points plotted on a graph are connected by straight lines.

Magnitude of factorial effects. Estimates of the size of main effects and interaction in the factorial design. See **Omega squared.**

Magnitude of treatment effects. The "strength" of a manipulated variable. The proportion of the total variance due to the experimental manipulation. Known as omega squared.

Main effect. The overall effect of one independent variable in a factorial design averaged over the levels of the second independent variable.

Marginal means. The means entering into the calculation of main effects in the two-factor design; derived from the AB matrix. Also known as the row or column marginal means.

Marginal sums. Obtained by adding together the AB sums appearing in each column of the AB matrix (column marginal sums) or in each row of the AB matrix (row marginal sums). Used in the calculation of the main effects in a factorial design.

Matched subjects. The term refers to a class of between-subjects designs in which subjects are matched on one or more relevant characteristics.

Matching. Selecting subjects who possess similar characteristics to serve in the different conditions of an experiment; a method for reducing experimental error.

Mean. A measure of central tendency; the arithmetic average. The sum of a set of numbers divided by the number of them in the set.

Mean square. A term for the variances calculated in the analysis of variance. A sum of squares divided by the appropriate number of degrees of freedom.

Median. A measure of central tendency; the score above or below which half the scores lie.

Midpoint of an interval. The center of a class interval; used in the construction of grouped frequency distributions and the drawing of frequency polygons.

Mixed factorial design. A factorial design that contains features of both between-subjects and within-subjects designs.

Mode. A measure of central tendency; the most frequently occurring number in a distribution of numbers.

Modified decision rules. A set of rules for dealing with unplanned comparisons. Involve the decision to suspend judgment when an F falls within the region defined by the critical value of F appropriate for a planned comparison (F_α) and the critical value of F specified by the Scheffé test (F_S).

Multiple comparison. See **Unplanned comparison.**

Multiple correlation and regression. Correlational procedures for dealing with the intercorrelations of three or more variables.

Multiple response measures. The use of more than one response measure in an experiment to provide additional information concerning the influence of the treatment conditions on behavior.

Negative skew. See **Skewed frequency distribution.**

Negative slope. Where the linear relationship between two variables is such that a change in one of the variables is associated with a change in the opposite direction for the other variable.

Nondirectional statistical test. A statistical test that does not specify the positive or negative direction of a comparison between two means; a two-tailed test.

Nonexperimental research. Research lacking a manipulated independent variable. See **Correlational research** and **Observational research.**

Nonlinear relationships. Higher-order relationships between two variables.

Nonrejection. See **Region of nonrejection.**

Nonstatistical generalization. A generalization of research findings to a broader class of subjects and situations based on one's knowledge of a particular research area. In contrast, see **Statistical generalization.**

Nonsystematic variability. Sources of variability that do not affect treatment conditions differentially.

Normal distribution (or curve). A theoretical distribution commonly observed in nature, especially when the characteristic being measured is influenced by a large number of independent factors.

Nuisance variable. A potential independent variable that is not to be manipulated in an experiment and that must be neutralized to prevent confounding with the treatment variable (or variables).

Null hypothesis (H_0). The statistical hypothesis evaluated during the process of hypothesis testing. Usually expressed as the absence of a relationship in the population.

Observational research. The systematic study of behavior as it occurs naturally in the environment. Also known as naturalistic observation.

Observed frequency. The number of observations falling within a particular response category (relevant to the chi square test).

Omega squared ($\hat{\omega}^2$). A measure of the strength, or the magnitude, of a treatment variable.

Omnibus (or overall) F test. An F test evaluating the null hypothesis stating that all the population treatment means in an experiment are equal. If significant, usually followed by additional tests designed to identify the specific treatment conditions responsible for the rejection of the omnibus null hypothesis.

One-tailed test. See **Directional statistical test.**

Orthogonal polynomial coefficients. Coefficients used in a trend analysis of experimental results where a quantitative independent variable is involved.

Overall (or omnibus) null hypothesis. A null hypothesis specifying that all the population treatment means in an experiment are equal.

Parameter. A numerical characteristic of a population. Usually designated by lowercase Greek letters (see Glossary 3).

Percentile (rank). A measure of relative position; the percentage of scores falling below a particular score in a distribution of scores.

Per comparison type I error (α). The probability of committing a type I error for an individual statistical test.

Phi coefficient. A measure of correlation used with data where both variables are dichotomous (have only two values).

Planned comparison. An analytical comparison specified before the start of an experiment.

Point biserial correlation coefficient. An index of linear correlation used with data where one variable is continuous and the other dichotomous (has only two values).

Point estimate. A population estimate based on a random sample; consists of a single value. See **Interval estimate.**

Population. As used in statistical estimation, the term refers to the scores of all members of a specified group, for example, all eligible voters. A sample is drawn randomly from a population to provide estimates of characteristics of the population. As used in hypothesis testing, see **Treatment population.**

Population treatment effects. Treatment effects existing in the treatment populations. See **Treatment effects.**

Population treatment mean. The mean of the scores in a treatment population. Statistical hypotheses are statements about the relationship between the population treatment means of an experiment. See **Treatment population.**

Positive skew. See **Skewed frequency distribution.**

Positive slope. Where the linear relationship between two variables is such that a change in one of the variables is associated with a change in the same direction for the other variable.

Post-hoc comparison. A comparison conducted after the data have been examined. See **Unplanned comparison.**

Power. The probability with which the null hypothesis will be rejected when it is false; defined as 1 minus the probability of a type II error. See **Sensitivity.**

Practice effects. Changes in performance occurring during the administering of two or more treatment conditions to the same subjects in a within-subjects design. The term encompasses general practice effects and differential carryover effects.

Prediction error. The discrepancy between a score predicted from a linear regression line and the score actually observed.

Product-moment correlation coefficient (r). The most common index of the linear relationship between two variables. Ranges from -1.0 to $+1.0$ (perfect negative and perfect positive correlations, respectively); a value of 0 represents the complete absence of correlation.

Proportion of variation due to linear regression. The proportion of variance in either variable X or variable Y that is linearly associated with the other variable. Measured by the square of the product-moment correlation coefficient and algebraically equivalent to explained variability, an index used in linear regression.

Proportion of variation due to linear trend. The proportion of the variation of the treatment sum of squares in an experiment associated with the best-fit straight line.

Qualitative independent variable. Where treatment levels differ in kind rather than in amount.

Quantitative independent variable. Where treatment levels differ in degree or in amount as measured on either a physical or psychological scale.

Random assignment of subjects. A procedure by which subjects are assigned randomly to different treatment conditions.

Randomization. Procedures used to randomize the assignment of subjects to the treatment conditions of an experiment.

Random numbers table. A table of numbers generated by some random process.

Random sample. A sample drawn randomly from a population.

Random sampling. See **Simple random sampling.**

Range. A measure of variability; the difference between the largest and smallest score in a distribution.

Rank-order correlation coefficient. An index of linear correlation used with data where both variables take the form of ranks.

Raw score. The numerical value assigned to the behavior of a subject in a particular treatment condition; also known as the basic observation.

Real (or true) limits. The theoretical upper and lower limits of an interval in a grouped frequency distribution; actual dividing points between adjacent intervals.

Region of nonrejection. The range of values of a statistic within which the null hypothesis will not be rejected.

Region of rejection. The range of values of a statistic within which the null hypothesis will be rejected; also known as the critical region.

Regression line. See **Linear regression line.**

Rejection. See **Region of rejection.**

Repeated-measures design. See **Within-subjects design** and **Within-subjects factorial design.**

Research hypothesis. A hypothesis based on empirical and theoretical considerations that leads to the design of an experiment. The adequacy of the research hypothesis is evaluated during the course of hypothesis testing.

Residual deviation. Deviation of the observed data points from the linear regression line linking two variables.

Residual sum of squares. In within-subjects designs, a sum of squares reflecting experimental error. With correlational data, a sum of squares reflecting the variation not accounted for by the linear relationship between two variables.

Residual variation. Variability reflecting the deviation of observed data points from the linear regression line linking two variables.

Response categories. A classification of responses used to differentiate subjects in a chi square analysis.

Response distribution. See **Frequency distribution.**

Response measure. An index used to measure the behavior being observed by the experimenter; often referred to as the dependent variable. See also **Multiple response measure.**

Response variable. See **Dependent variable.**

Restriction of range. A condition in which one (or both) of the variables in a correlational study is restricted as to its possible variation. The result is a lowered value of the correlation coefficient.

Rounding. An arbitrary method of dropping digits from the results of a calculation.

Row marginal means. See **Marginal means.**

Row marginal sums. See **Marginal sums.**

Sample. A subgroup drawn from a population or larger group of subjects. See **Simple random sampling.**

Sample size. The number of subjects assigned to a particular treatment condition or observed in a sample.

Sampling distribution. A frequency distribution of a statistic obtained from an extremely large number of random samples drawn from a specified population.

Sampling distribution of F. A frequency distribution of the F statistic obtained from an extremely large number of experiments, each consisting of data drawn randomly from treatment populations with identical means and variances.

Sampling distribution of the mean. The frequency distribution of all possible sample means that might be obtained by sampling randomly from a particular population of subjects.

Sampling error. The variability of a point estimate found with random samples drawn from the same population.

Sampling with replacement. A method of random sampling in which subjects (or scores) are returned to the population as soon as they have been selected; used by statisticians in the development of statistical models and theory.

Sampling without replacement. A method of random sampling in which subjects are not returned to the population once they have been selected for inclusion in the sample; used in survey research.

Scatterplot. A graphical display consisting of the plotting of subjects on the basis of scores obtained from two response measures. A useful aid in the analysis of correlational data.

Scheffé test. A correction technique designed to hold experimentwise type I error at a predetermined level regardless of the number of comparisons conducted.

Semi-interquartile range. A range one-half the size of the interquartile range. Often used in conjunction with the median as a measure of variability.

Sensitivity. The ability of an experimental design to detect differences among population treatment means (defined formally in terms of power). For example, within-subjects designs are more sensitive (possess more power) than corresponding between-subjects designs.

Significance level. The probability (α) with which an experimenter is willing to reject the null hypothesis when in fact it is correct. Also known as the probability of making a type I error.

Simple comparison. An analytical comparison used to determine the locus of a significant interaction in a factorial design. Usually undertaken following the analysis of a significant simple main effect or a significant factorial comparison. Also refers to a comparison focusing on the difference between two means.

Simple main effect. The variability among the treatment means associated with one independent variable at a particular level of the other independent variable. An analysis of simple main effects is often undertaken to pinpoint the locus of a significant interaction. Based on component single-factor experiments.

Simple random sampling. A sampling procedure in which each member of the population has an equally likely chance of being included in the sample.

Single-*df* comparison. The analysis of the difference between two means, either of which consists of the mean of a single treatment condition or an average of two or more treatment conditions.

Single-factor design. An experimental design in which a single independent variable is manipulated.

Skewed frequency distribution. An asymmetrical frequency distribution with a "tail" that strings out in one direction. A tail pointing in the direction of larger numbers represents positive skew; a tail pointing in the direction of smaller numbers represents negative skew.

Slope of a regression line. A numerical constant in a linear regression equation representing the change in the value of the predicted variable associated with a unit change in the independent or predictor variable. See also **Positive slope** and **Negative slope**.

Standard deviation. A measure of variability; the square root of the variance. Expresses variability in terms of the original units of measure.

Standard-deviation units. The units in which standard scores (z scores) are measured. The units are raw scores expressed as deviations from the mean divided by the standard deviation.

Standard error of estimate. The square root of the variance based on the deviation of the observed scores on the predicted variable from those predicted from the linear regression line.

Standard error of the mean. The standard deviation of the sampling distribution of the mean.

Standard normal distribution. See z **distribution**.

Standard score. A raw score expressed as a deviation from the mean divided by the standard deviation; a z score.

Statistic. A numerical characteristic of samples.

Statistical generalization. The extension to populations of findings obtained from random samples. In contrast, see **Nonstatistical generalization**.

Statistical hypotheses. Hypotheses specifying relationships between population parameters. Usually consist of the null and alternative hypotheses.

Statistical indices. Numbers used as indicators or measures to describe and summarize a set of observations.

Statistical significance. A finding that is established through the rejection of a null hypothesis.

Strength of linear correlation. The proportion of variance in either variable X or variable Y that is linearly associated with the other variable. Measured by the square of the product-moment correlation coefficient.

Subject sum of squares. Used in the within-subjects design to reflect the consistent variability of subjects who serve in all the treatment conditions.

Subject variable. See **Classification variable.**

Sum of products. The sum of products obtained by multiplying the deviation of a subject from the mean of the X variable by that subject's deviation from the mean of the Y variable. Used in the calculation of covariance.

Sum of squares. The sum of the squared deviations from the mean. Used in the calculation of the variance.

Suspend judgment. To withhold a decision concerning the status of the null hypothesis when the F ratio for a comparison falls within the per comparison rejection region but short of the rejection region specified by the Scheffé test. Part of a recommended method to control experimentwise error in the analysis of unplanned comparisons.

Symmetrical distribution. A frequency distribution that has the same shape in both directions extending from the mean of the distribution.

Systematic bias. A confounding of a nuisance variable (or variables) with the independent variable.

t distribution. A theoretical distribution used in conjunction with the t test and in the establishment of a confidence interval for the mean of a random sample.

t test. A statistical test that uses the t distribution to assess the adequacy of the null hypothesis. Algebraically equivalent to the F test when applied to the analysis of experiments.

Table. A systematic display of the results of statistical calculations.

Task variable. An independent variable in which some aspect of a task is manipulated.

Temporary subject variables. A class of independent variables that change temporarily a subject's behavior in an experiment.

Test of association. See **Test of independence.**

Test of independence. A chi square test of correlation between two classification variables.

Total deviation. The deviation of an individual score from the grand mean of an experiment; used to calculate the total sum of squares.

Total sum of squares. The sum of the squared deviations of all basic observations from the overall, or grand, mean of an experiment.

Treatment combinations. The different treatment conditions administered to subjects in the factorial design; all possible combinations of the levels of the two independent variables.

Treatment conditions. The different treatments collectively constituting an independent variable.

Treatment effects. The differences among the treatment means in the population. A theoretical quantity that cannot be observed directly in an experiment.

Treatment-group deviation. The deviation of the mean of a treatment condition from the grand mean of an experiment. Used to calculate the treatment sum of squares in the analysis of variance.

Treatment-group sum of squares. The sum of squares based on the deviation of the treatment means from the grand mean.

Treatment-group variability. A measure of variability based on the differences observed among the treatment conditions of an experiment.

Treatment Index. A ratio consisting of treatment-group variability divided by within-group variability. More commonly known as the F ratio.

Treatment mean. The mean of the scores of subjects receiving a particular treatment condition in an experiment.

Treatment mean square. The mean square based on the deviation of the treatment means from the grand mean.

Treatment population. The hypothetical scores of an extremely large number of individuals given a particular treatment condition.

Treatment sum. The sum of the scores of subjects receiving a particular treatment condition in an experiment.

Treatment sum of squares. The sum of the squared deviations of the treatment means from the grand mean of an experiment.

Treatment variable. See **Independent variable.**

Trend analysis. The analytical comparisons appropriate for the detailed analysis of the results of an experiment in which a quantitative independent variable is manipulated. Consists of the statistical assessment of linear and higher-order trends by means of orthogonal polynomial coefficients and the general formula for single-*df* comparisons. The most common example is the analysis of linear trend.

Two-tailed test. See **Nondirectional statistical test.**

Type I error. An error of statistical inference that occurs when the null hypothesis is true but is rejected. An error of "seeing too much in the data." See **Alpha.**

Type II error. An error of statistical inference that occurs when the null hypothesis is false, but is not rejected. An error of "not seeing enough in the data." See **Beta.**

Ungrouped frequency distribution. A frequency distribution with a class interval equal to 1.

Unplanned comparison. A comparison not specified at the start of the experiment and conducted after the data have been examined. Also known as a post-hoc or multiple comparison.

Variability. Differences among scores in a distribution. Most commonly expressed as a variance or a standard deviation (the square root of a variance).

Variance. A measure of variability; an average of the sum of the squared deviations from the mean.

Weighted treatment means. Treatment means multiplied by a coefficient specified by a single-*df* comparison.

Weighting coefficients. Coefficients used in calculating the sum of squares for single-*df* comparisons.

Width of the confidence interval. The range of values within which a certain percentage of sample means are theoretically contained. Depends on the variability of the scores in the random sample, the size of the sample, and the level of confidence selected by the researcher.

Within-group deviation. The deviation of the score for an individual subject from the relevent treatment-group mean. Used in the calculation of the within-group sum of squares in the analysis of variance.

Within-group sum of squares. Sum of the squared within-group deviations for all the subjects in an experiment.

Within-group variability. A measure of variability based on the variation of subjects treated alike.

Within-subjects design. An experimental design in which subjects receive all the treatment conditions in an experiment.

Within-subjects error (term). The error term used to form *F* ratios reflecting within-subjects sources of variance. See **Mixed factorial design.**

Within-subjects factorial design. A factorial design in which subjects receive more than one of the treatment conditions. See **Mixed factorial design.**

Within-treatment mean square. The mean square based on the variability of subjects receiving the same treatment condition. Used as an estimate of experimental error in between-subjects designs.

X intercept. The value of the linear regression equation predicting variable X from variable Y when $Y = 0$. The point at which the regression line intersects the horizontal axis (X axis).

Y intercept. The value of the linear regression equation predicting variable Y from variable X when $X = 0$. The point at which the regression line intersects the vertical axis (Y axis).

Yates's Correction. See **Correction for continuity.**

z distribution. The normal distribution expressed in terms of deviations from the mean divided by the standard deviation.

z score. A raw score expressed as a deviation from the mean and divided by the standard deviation. Also known as a standard score. Used to compare the relative standing of scores in different distributions.

Glossary 2

An Overview of the Notational System

Two notational systems are used in this book, one to represent the observations obtained from a single group of subjects and the other to represent the observations and sums of scores needed for the analysis of variance. The notation we use to express the data of a single group of subjects is essentially the standard system used throughout the field of psychological research. In this system, X designates an observation, and the arithmetical operations performed on the X scores are expressed in terms of X; Y represents the second set of observations obtained in linear regression and correlation. The advantage of standard notation is that it produces formulas for problems in linear regression, correlation, and estimation that are familiar to most people who have been exposed to this subject matter elsewhere. On the other hand, standard notation is awkward and confusing to beginning students when it is extended to the data obtained from experimental designs. For this reason, we have used a system of single letters and combinations of letters to represent the individual observations and the various sums needed for the analysis of variance.

Both systems are summarized in this glossary. The glossary consists of three sections. The first section summarizes the standard notation used to represent a single set of scores. The second section summarizes the specialized letter notation used to designate the operations required in the analysis of variance. Where relevant, cross-references note locations in the text where a particular notation is explained more fully. In both systems, numerical subscripts are added where specifying a particular quantity is necessary.

Section III is a comparison of the two systems. This section is intended primarily for instructors who do their statistical thinking in standard notation and for students who have taken other courses or used other texts where standard notation has been employed. Shifting to our notational system under these circumstances can be difficult. Thus, we have placed the two notational systems side by side for direct comparison and translation from one to the other.

I. Notation for a Single Set or Group of Scores (see pp. 23–25)

X (or X_i) = the basic score or observation in a single set of scores on a variable called X.

ΣX = the sum of all the X scores.

Y (or Y_i) = the basic score or observation in a single set of scores on a variable called Y. These scores are paired with corresponding X scores.

ΣY = the sum of all the Y scores.

$\Sigma (X)(Y)$ = the sum of all the products formed by multiplying an X score by its corresponding Y score.

II. Notation for Experimental Designs

A. Single-factor designs
1. Between-subjects design (see Table 4-1, p. 64)
   a. AS (or AS_{ij}) = a basic score or observation in any treatment condition.
   b. A (or A_i) = the sum of the basic scores in any treatment condition.
   c. T = the grand total of all of the basic scores in the experiment.
2. Within-subjects design (see Table 8-2, p. 179)
   a. AS, A, and T are defined as indicated for the between-subjects design.
   b. S (or S_j) = the sum of scores for any subject of his or her performance under the different treatment conditions.

B. Two-factor designs
1. Between-subjects design (see Table 9-3, p. 220)
   a. ABS (or ABS_{ijk}) = a basic score or observation in any of the treatment combinations.
   b. AB (or AB_{ij}) = the sum of the basic scores in any one of the treatment combinations.
   c. A (or A_i) = the sum of the basic scores for all subjects receiving a particular level of factor A. (Levels of factor B are disregarded.)
   d. B (or B_j) = the sum of the basic scores for all subjects receiving a particular level of factor B. (Levels of factor A are disregarded.)
   e. T = the grand total of all of the basic scores in the experiment.
2. Within-subjects design (see Table 11-2, p. 271)
   a. ABS, AB, A, B, and T are defined as indicated for the between-subjects design.
   b. AS (or AS_{ik}) = the sum for any subject of his or her performance under the different treatment combinations associated with a particular level of factor A.

III. Comparison of Notational Systems

The analysis of variance involves the squaring and summing of the raw scores and of critical sums and subtotals. In this section, we compare standard notation with the letter notation adopted for the single-factor and the two-factor designs. In both cases, we describe first in words the scores and sums needed in the analysis of variance and then designate the symbols used to represent these quantities by the two systems. The last two columns of these comparisons indicate how the arithmetical operations of squaring and summing are expressed by the two systems. The letter system expresses these operations with unique symbols (single letters and letter combinations) and single summation signs. In contrast, standard notation uses the same symbol, X, with letter subscripts depending on the design, and multiple summation signs and subscript designations to indicate the classification (or classifications) over which the summations are taken and when they are taken, that is, before or after squaring.

A. Comparison of Notational Systems for the Single-Factor Design

Designated Quantity			Arithmetical Operations[b]	
	Symbols		Symbols	
Words	Standard	Letters	Standard	Letters
1. Individual Score or Observation	X_{ij}	AS_{ij}	$\sum_i \sum_j (X_{ij})^2$	$\Sigma (AS)^2$
2. Sum of Scores for Any Treatment Condition (a_i)	$\sum_j X_{ij}$	A_i	$\sum_i \left(\sum_j X_{ij} \right)^2$	$\Sigma (A)^2$
3. Sum of All the Scores	$\sum_i \sum_j X_{ij}$	T	$\left(\sum_i \sum_j X_{ij} \right)^2$	$(T)^2$
4. Sum of Scores for Any Subject[a]	$\sum_i X_{ij}$	S_j	$\sum_j \left(\sum_i X_{ij} \right)^2$	$\Sigma (S)^2$

[a] Relevant to the within-subjects design only (Chapter 8).
[b] Operations needed in the calculation of the component sums of squares in the analysis of variance. These consist of the squaring of each designated quantity followed by the summing of all such quantities if more than one is present.

B. Comparison of Notational Systems for the Two-Factor Design

Designated Quantity			Arithmetical Operations[b]	
	Symbols		Symbols	
Words	Standard	Letters	Standard	Letters
1. Individual Score or Observation	X_{ijk}	ABS_{ijk}	$\sum_i \sum_j \sum_k (X_{ijk})^2$	$\Sigma (ABS)^2$
2. Sum of Scores for Any Treatment Combination (ab_{ij})	$\sum_k X_{ijk}$	AB_{ij}	$\sum_i \sum_j \left(\sum_k X_{ijk} \right)^2$	$\Sigma (AB)^2$
3. Sum of Scores for Any Level of Factor A (a_i)	$\sum_j \sum_k X_{ijk}$	A_i	$\sum_i \left(\sum_j \sum_k X_{ijk} \right)^2$	$\Sigma (A)^2$
4. Sum of Scores for Any Level of Factor B (b_j)	$\sum_i \sum_k X_{ijk}$	B_j	$\sum_j \left(\sum_i \sum_k X_{ijk} \right)^2$	$\Sigma (B)^2$
5. Sum of All the Scores	$\sum_i \sum_j \sum_k X_{ijk}$	T	$\left(\sum_i \sum_j \sum_k X_{ijk} \right)^2$	$(T)^2$
6. Sum of Scores for Any Subject[a]	$\sum_j X_{ijk}$	AS_{ik}	$\sum_i \sum_k \left(\sum_j X_{ijk} \right)^2$	$\Sigma (AS)^2$

[a] Relevant to the "mixed" design only (Chapter 11).
[b] Operations needed in the calculation of the component sums of squares in the analysis of variance. These consist of the squaring of each designated quantity followed by the summing of all such quantities if more than one is present.

Glossary 3

Arithmetical Operations and Statistical Symbols

Since a relatively large number of symbols has been employed in this text, we have prepared a list of symbols and their meanings. For convenience, the symbols are divided into three categories: (1) symbols used to specify common arithmetical operations and to make specific quantitative statements; (2) Greek letters used as statistical symbols; and (3) Roman letters and English words used as statistical symbols. (The symbols in the latter two categories are listed alphabetically.) Glossary 1 contains definitions of additional terms and concepts.

I. Conventional Mathematical Symbols

Symbol	Example	Meaning
$+$	$X + Y$	X and Y are added.
Σ	ΣX	Summation sign; take the sum of the X scores.
$-$	$X - Y$	Y is subtracted from X.
$\pm$	$X \pm Y$	Two quantities are specified: (1) X and Y are added and (2) Y is subtracted from X.

Symbol	Example	Meaning
( )( )	$(X)(Y)$	X and Y are multiplied.
( )²	$(X)^2$	X is squared; that is, X is multiplied by itself.
/	X/Y	X is divided by Y.
=	$X = Y$	X is equal to Y.
≠	$X \neq Y$	X is not equal to Y.
<	$X < Y$	X is less than Y.
≤	$X \leq Y$	X is less than or equal to Y.
>	$X > Y$	X is greater than Y.
≥·	$X \geq Y$	X is equal to or greater than Y.
√	$\sqrt{X}$	The square root of X.

II. Greek Letters Used as Statistical Symbols

Symbol	Meaning
α (alpha)	The probability of making a type I error; significance level; also refers to the probability of estimating a confidence interval that fails to include the population parameter.
β (beta)	The probability of making a type II error.
μ (mu)	The mean of a population.
$\hat{\mu}$	The point estimate of the mean of a population.
μ_i	The mean of a treatment population.
μ_M	The mean of the sampling distribution of the mean.
Σ (upper-case sigma)	Summation; take the sum of. . . .
σ (lower-case sigma)	The population standard deviation.
σ^2	The population variance.
$\hat{\sigma}$	An estimate of the population standard deviation.
σ_M	The standard error of the mean.
$\hat{\sigma}_M$	An estimate of the standard error of the mean.
$\hat{\sigma}_A^2$	An estimate of the population treatment variance.
$\hat{\sigma}_{S/A}^2$	An estimate of the variance within a treatment population averaged over the treatment populations represented by a single-factor between-subjects experiment.
$\hat{\sigma}_T^2$	The sum of $\hat{\sigma}_A^2$ and $\hat{\sigma}_{S/A}^2$.
χ^2 (chi)	The chi square statistic used in the analysis of categorical data.
χ_α^2	The critical value of the chi square statistic.

Symbol	Meaning
$\chi^2_{comp.}$	The chi square statistic appropriate for analytical comparisons conducted with categorical data.
$\hat{\omega}^2_A$ (omega)	Omega squared; an estimate of the magnitude of treatment effects in the single-factor design.

III. Roman Letters and English Words Used as Statistical Symbols

Symbol	Meaning
a	The number of levels of factor A.
a_i	Any level of factor A; when used with numerical subscript, for instance, a_1, refers to a particular level of factor A.
a_X	X intercept of a linear regression equation predicting variable X from variable Y.
a_Y	Y intercept of a linear regression equation predicting variable Y from variable X.
$a(b)$	The total number of treatment combinations in a two-variable factorial design.
$a(b)(s)$	The total number of observations in a two-variable factorial design.
$a(s)$	The total number of observations in a single-factor design.
A or A_i	The sum of the scores for one of the levels of factor A.
$\bar{A}$ or $\bar{A}_i$	The mean for one of the levels of factor A.
$[A]$	A basic ratio based on the A treatment sums in single-factor and factorial designs.
AB or AB_{ij}	The sum for a treatment condition in a factorial design.
$\overline{AB}$ or $\overline{AB}_{ij}$	The mean for a treatment condition in a factorial design.
$[AB]$	A basic ratio based on the AB sums in a factorial design.
ABS or ABS_{ijk}	An individual observation in a factorial design.
$[ABS]$	A basic ratio based on the individual scores in a factorial design.
AS_{ij}	The basic observation in a single-factor design.
AS_{ik}	The sum for any subject of his or her performance under the different treatment combinations associated with a particular level of factor A in the mixed-factorial design.
$\overline{AS}_{ik}$	The mean for any subject under the different treatment combinations associated with a particular level of factor A in the mixed-factorial design.
$[AS]$	A basic ratio based on the AS scores in single-factor designs and AS sums in the mixed-factorial design.

Symbol	Meaning
b	The number of levels of factor B.
b_j	Any level of factor B; when used with a numerical subscript, for instance, b_1, refers to a particular level of factor B.
b_X	The slope of a linear regression equation predicting variable X from variable Y.
b_Y	The slope of a linear regression equation predicting variable Y from variable X.
B or B_j	The sum of the scores for one of the levels of factor B.
$\bar{B}$ or $\bar{B}_j$	The mean for one of the levels of factor B contributing to the B main effect in a factorial design.
$[B]$	A basic ratio based on the B sums in a factorial design.
c	The number of response categories in a chi square analysis.
c_i	The weighting coefficient used in the analysis of single-df comparisons; when used with numerical subscripts, for instance, c_1, c_2, and so on, refers to the coefficients assigned to particular treatment conditions.
$(c_i)(A_i)$	The weighted treatment sum; used in calculating the sum of squares for a single-df comparison.
Covariance (X,Y)	A measure of the degree to which variable X and variable Y vary together.
df	Degrees of freedom; when used with subscripts, symbol designates the degrees of freedom associated with particular sources of variance and of variance estimates.
df_A	Degrees of freedom associated with MS_A.
$df_{A_{\text{comp.}}}$	Degrees of freedom associated with $MS_{A_{\text{comp.}}}$.
$df_{A_{\text{linear}}}$	Degrees of freedom associated with $MS_{A_{\text{linear}}}$.
$df_{A \times B}$	Degrees of freedom associated with $MS_{A \times B}$.
$df_{A \times S}$	Degrees of freedom associated with $MS_{A \times S}$.
df_B	Degrees of freedom associated with MS_B.
$df_{B \times S/A}$	Degrees of freedom associated with $MS_{B \times S/A}$.
$df_{\text{denom.}}$	Degrees of freedom associated with the denominator term of the F ratio.
$df_{\text{lin. regr.}}$	Degrees of freedom associated with $MS_{\text{lin. regr.}}$ in the analysis of linear regression with correlational data.
$df_{\text{num.}}$	Degrees of freedom associated with the numerator term of the F ratio.

Symbol	Meaning
df_M	Degrees of freedom associated with the standard error of the mean.
df_r	Degrees of freedom associated with the product-moment correlation coefficient (r).
$df_{residual}$	Degrees of freedom for $MS_{residual}$ in the analysis of linear regression with correlational data.
$df_{S/A}$	Degrees of freedom associated with $MS_{S/A}$.
$df_{S/AB}$	Degrees of freedom associated with $MS_{S/AB}$.
df_T	The total degrees of freedom in an experiment.
f	The frequency (or number) of cases falling within a class interval or response category.
f_E	The frequency of cases expected to occur within a particular response category; expected frequencies are derived from theory or empirical information.
f_0	The observed frequency of cases falling within a particular response category in a chi square analysis.
F	The F statistic.
F_α	The critical value of F associated with a per comparison type I error of α; the critical value of F for planned comparisons.
$F_{comp.}$	The F statistic obtained from an analytical comparison.
$F(df_{num.}, df_{denom.})$	The designation of the numerator and denominator degrees of freedom associated with a particular F. In an actual situation, numbers would replace $df_{num.}$ and $df_{denom.}$.
F_E	The expected frequency used as the denominator term in analytical comparisons conducted with categorical data and the chi square statistic; based on the marginal totals of the original contingency table.
F_{linear}	The F statistic for evaluating the significance of linear trend with experimental data.
F_S	The critical value of F obtained by applying the Scheffé correction for experimentwise type I error.
H_0	The null hypothesis; the statistical hypothesis evaluated in hypothesis testing.
H_1	The alternative hypothesis; the statistical hypothesis accepted when the null hypothesis is rejected.
MS	Mean square; a variance in the analysis of variance. Subscripts are used to designate particular sources of variance.

Symbol	Meaning
MS_A	The treatment mean square in a single-factor design; the main effect of factor A in a factorial design.
$MS_{A_{comp.}}$	The mean square for an analytical comparison involving the A treatment means.
$MS_{A_{linear}}$	The mean square for linear trend obtained from experimental data.
$MS_{A \times B}$	The mean square for the $A \times B$ interaction.
$MS_{A \times S}$	The mean square for the error term in the single-factor within-subjects design.
MS_B	The main effect of factor B.
$MS_{B \times S/A}$	The error term for the within-subjects portion of the mixed-factorial design.
$MS_{comp.}$	The mean square for an analytical comparison in a factorial design.
MS_e	The error term for an analysis of variance.
MS_{error}	The error term appropriate for evaluating systematic sources of variance.
$MS_{S/A}$	The error term for the completely randomized single-factor design and for the between-subjects portion of the mixed-factorial design.
$MS_{S/AB}$	The error term for the completely randomized factorial design.
p	Probability; the proportion of times out of 100 that a particular event will occur.
r	The product-moment correlation coefficient; an index of the linear relationship between two variables.
r^2	The square of the product-moment correlation coefficient; the proportion of variance in either variable X or variable Y that is linearly associated with the other variable.
r_α	Critical value of the product-moment correlation coefficient.
s	Sample size; number of subjects per treatment condition; number of pairs of scores in linear regression/correlation.
S or S_j	The sum of the scores for any subject in the single-factor within-subjects design.
$\bar{S}$ or $\bar{S}_j$	The mean of the scores for any subject in the single-factor within-subjects design.
$[S]$	A basic ratio based on the S sums in a single-factor within-subjects design.

Symbol	Meaning
SD	Standard deviation used for descriptive purposes only, for example, with standard scores.
SD_z	Standard deviation of a distribution of z scores; equal to 1.
SP_{XY}	Sum of products; obtained by multiplying the deviation of a subject from the mean of the X variable by that subject's deviation from the mean of the Y variable.
SS	The sum of squares; the sum of the squared deviations from the mean. Subscripts are used to designate particular sums of squares.
SS_A	The sum of squares associated with the treatment conditions in a single-factor design and with the main effect of factor A in a factorial design.
$SS_{A_{comp.}}$	The sum of squares for an analytical comparison involving the A treatment means.
$SS_{A_{linear}}$	The sum of squares for linear trend obtained with experimental data.
$SS_{A \times B}$	The sum of squares for the $A \times B$ interaction.
$SS_{A \times S}$	The sum of squares for the error term in the single-factor within-subjects design.
SS_B	The sum of squares for the main effect of factor B.
$SS_{B \times S/A}$	The sum of squares for the error term for the within-subjects portion of the mixed-factorial design.
$SS_{lin.\ regr.}$	The sum of squares reflecting the variability accounted for by linear regression with correlational data.
$SS_{residual}$	A sum of squares obtained by subtracting one sum of squares from another; often refers to error terms used in the analysis of within-subjects designs and to the variability not accounted for by the linear relationship between two variables.
SS_S	The sum of squares reflecting the consistent variation of subjects in the single-factor within-subjects design.
$SS_{S/A}$	The sum of squares based on the variability of subjects treated alike in the completely randomized single-factor design and in the between-subjects portion of the mixed-factorial design.
$SS_{S/AB}$	The sum of squares for the error term in the completely randomized factorial design.
SS_T	The total sum of squares in an experiment.
SS_X	Used in linear regression and correlation to refer to the sum of squares associated with variable X.

Symbol	Meaning
SS_Y	Used in linear regression and correlation to refer to the sum of squares associated with variable Y.
SS_z	The sum of squares obtained from a set of z scores; equal to 1.
Standard deviation	The square root of the variance; used in hypothesis testing and interval estimation. Also symbolized as $\hat{\sigma}$.
t	The t statistic. Used in establishing a confidence interval of the mean from a sample. Occasionally used instead of the F statistic to evaluate the significance of the difference between two means.
T	The grand sum of all the observations in an experiment.
$\bar{T}$	The grand mean of all the observations in an experiment.
$[T]$	A basic ratio based on the grand sum.
Variance	A variance appropriate for use in hypothesis testing and interval estimation; obtained by dividing the sum of squares by the number of squared deviations *minus* 1. Also symbolized as $\hat{\sigma}^2$.
Variance (X)	Used in linear regression and correlation to refer to the variance of the scores on variable X.
Variance (Y)	Used in linear regression and correlation to refer to the variance of the scores on variable Y.
X or X_i	Used to indicate a score from a single sample of scores; a score on variable X in linear regression and correlation.
X'	A score predicted from the linear regression equation relating variable X to changes in variable Y.
$\bar{X}$	The mean of a single sample of scores; the mean of the scores on variable X in linear regression and correlation.
$\bar{X}_z$	The mean of a distribution of z scores; equal to 0.
Y or Y_i	Used in linear regression and correlation to refer to a score on variable Y.
Y'	A score predicted from the linear regression equation relating variable Y to changes in variable X.
$\bar{Y}$	Used in linear regression and correlation to refer to the mean of the scores on variable Y.
z	A standard score.

Glossary 4

Selected Computational Formulas

The critical and important formulas presented in the text are listed in this glossary. The list is intended to serve both as a summary and as a reference. The formulas have been grouped into the following sets of functional units:

I. Calculations Based on a Single Set of Scores (X Scores)

II. Analysis of Variance: Single-Factor Between-Subjects Design

III. Analysis of Variance: Single-Factor Within-Subjects Design

IV. Analysis of Variance: Two-Factor Between-Subjects Design

V. Analysis of Variance: Two-Factor Mixed Design

VI. Linear Regression

VII. Correlation

VIII. Analysis of Categorical Data: Single-Factor Between-Subjects Design

Equation numbers, specific page references, and, where appropriate, chapter references are provided to increase the usefulness of this glossary. For definitions of statistical symbols, see Glossary 3.

I. Calculations Based on a Single Set of Scores (X Scores)

A. Mean

Equation (2-3)
(p. 25)

$$\bar{X} = \frac{\Sigma\, X}{s}$$

B. Variance and Standard Deviation

Equation (2-8)
(p. 32)

$$\text{variance } (\hat{\sigma}^2) = \frac{SS}{s-1} \quad\text{, where}$$

Equation (2-7)
(p. 29)

$$SS = \Sigma\,(X)^2 - \frac{(\Sigma\, X)^2}{s} \quad .$$

Equation (2-10)
(p. 33)

$$\text{standard deviation } (\hat{\sigma}) = \sqrt{\text{variance}}$$

C. Standard Score (z Score)

Equation (16-1)
(p. 389)

$$z = \frac{X - \bar{X}}{SD} \quad\text{, where}$$

Equation (16-2)
(p. 389)

$$SD = \sqrt{\frac{SS}{s}} \quad .$$

D. Confidence Interval Constructed Around the Point Estimate of the Population Mean ($\hat{\mu}$)

Equation (16-6)
(p. 404)

$$\hat{\mu} \pm (t)(\hat{\sigma}_M) \quad\text{, where}$$

Equation (16-3)
(p. 398)

$$\hat{\mu} = \bar{X} \quad,$$

Equation (16-7)
(p. 407)

$t = $ the value of the t statistic associated with $df_M = s - 1$ for a $(1 - \alpha)$ confidence interval,

Equation (16-4)
(p. 403)

$$\hat{\sigma}_M = \frac{\hat{\sigma}}{\sqrt{s}} \quad\text{, and}$$

Equation (16-5)
(p. 403)

$$\hat{\sigma} = \sqrt{\frac{SS}{df}} \quad .$$

II. Analysis of Variance: Single-Factor Between-Subjects Design

A. Overall Analysis (see Chapters 4 and 5)

Source	SS[a]	df	MS	F
A	$[A] - [T]$	$a - 1$	$\dfrac{SS_A}{df_A}$	$\dfrac{MS_A}{MS_{S/A}}$
S/A	$[AS] - [A]$	$a(s - 1)$	$\dfrac{SS_{S/A}}{df_{S/A}}$	
Total	$[AS] - [T]$	$a(s) - 1$		

[a] Note: $[A] = \dfrac{\Sigma (A)^2}{s}$, $[T] = \dfrac{(T)^2}{a(s)}$, and $[AS] = \Sigma (AS)^2$.

B. Analytical Comparisons: Single-df Comparisons (see Chapter 6)

Equation (6-2)
(p. 127)
$$SS_{A_{\text{comp.}}} = \frac{[\Sigma (c_i)(A_i)]^2}{s[\Sigma (c_i)^2]}$$

Equation (6-3)
(p. 128)
$$MS_{A_{\text{comp.}}} = \frac{SS_{A_{\text{comp.}}}}{df_{A_{\text{comp.}}}}$$

Equation (6-5)
(p. 129)
$$F_{\text{comp.}} = \frac{MS_{A_{\text{comp.}}}}{MS_{S/A}}$$

C. Scheffé Correction for Unplanned Comparisons (see pp. 141–142)

Equation (6-6) $F_S = (a - 1)F(df_A, df_{S/A})$.
(p. 141)

III. Analysis of Variance: Single-Factor Within-Subjects Design (see Chapter 8)

A. Overall Analysis

Source	SS[a]	df	MS	F
A	$[A] - [T]$	$a - 1$	$\dfrac{SS_A}{df_A}$	$\dfrac{MS_A}{MS_{A \times S}}$
S	$[S] - [T]$	$s - 1$	$\dfrac{SS_S}{df_S}$	
$A \times S$	$[AS] - [A] - [S] + [T]$	$(a - 1)(s - 1)$	$\dfrac{SS_{A \times S}}{df_{A \times S}}$	
Total	$[AS] - [T]$	$a(s) - 1$		

[a] $[A] = \dfrac{\Sigma (A)^2}{s}$, $[T] = \dfrac{(T)^2}{a(s)}$, $[S] = \dfrac{\Sigma (S)^2}{a}$, and $[AS] = \Sigma (AS)^2$.

B. Analytical Comparisons: Single-*df* Comparisons

Equation (6-2)
(p. 127)
$$SS_{A_{comp.}} = \frac{[\Sigma\,(c_i)(A_i)]^2}{s[\Sigma\,(c_i)^2]}$$

Equation (6-3)
(p. 128)
$$MS_{A_{comp.}} = \frac{SS_{A_{comp.}}}{df_{A_{comp.}}}$$

Equation (8-6)
(p. 187)
$$F_{comp.} = \frac{MS_{A_{comp.}}}{MS_{A \times S}}$$

IV. Analysis of Variance: Two-Factor Between-Subjects Design (see Chapter 9)

Source	SS[a]	df	MS	F
A	$[A] - [T]$	$a - 1$	$\dfrac{SS_A}{df_A}$	$\dfrac{MS_A}{MS_{S/AB}}$
B	$[B] - [T]$	$b - 1$	$\dfrac{SS_B}{df_B}$	$\dfrac{MS_B}{MS_{S/AB}}$
A × B	$[AB] - [A] - [B] + [T]$	$(a - 1)(b - 1)$	$\dfrac{SS_{A \times B}}{df_{A \times B}}$	$\dfrac{MS_{A \times B}}{MS_{S/AB}}$
S/AB	$[ABS] - [AB]$	$a(b)(s - 1)$	$\dfrac{SS_{S/AB}}{df_{S/AB}}$	
Total	$[ABS] - [T]$	$a(b)(s) - 1$		

[a] $[A] = \dfrac{\Sigma\,(A)^2}{b(s)}$, $[T] = \dfrac{(T)^2}{a(b)(s)}$, $[B] = \dfrac{\Sigma\,(B)^2}{a(s)}$, $[AB] = \dfrac{\Sigma\,(AB)^2}{s}$, and $[ABS] = \Sigma\,(ABS)^2$.

V. Analysis of Variance: Two-Factor Mixed Design (see Chapter 11)

Source	SS[a]	df	MS	F
A	$[A] - [T]$	$a - 1$	$\dfrac{SS_A}{df_A}$	$\dfrac{MS_A}{MS_{S/A}}$
S/A	$[AS] - [A]$	$a(s - 1)$	$\dfrac{SS_{S/A}}{df_{S/A}}$	
B	$[B] - [T]$	$b - 1$	$\dfrac{SS_B}{df_B}$	$\dfrac{MS_B}{MS_{B \times S/A}}$
A × B	$[AB] - [A] - [B] + [T]$	$(a - 1)(b - 1)$	$\dfrac{SS_{A \times B}}{df_{A \times B}}$	$\dfrac{MS_{A \times B}}{MS_{B \times S/A}}$
B × S/A	$[ABS] - [AB] - [AS] + [A]$	$a(b - 1)(s - 1)$	$\dfrac{SS_{B \times S/A}}{df_{B \times S/A}}$	
Total	$[ABS] - [T]$	$a(b)(s) - 1$		

[a] $[A] = \dfrac{\Sigma(A)^2}{b(s)}$, $[T] = \dfrac{(T)^2}{a(b)(s)}$, $[AS] = \dfrac{\Sigma(AS)^2}{b}$, $[B] = \dfrac{\Sigma(B)^2}{a(s)}$, $[AB] = \dfrac{\Sigma(AB)^2}{s}$, and $[ABS] = \Sigma(ABS)^2$.

VI. Linear Regression

A. Equation Predicting Y Values (Y') from a Knowledge of Variable X (see pp. 298–303)

Equation (12-2)
(p. 299)
$$Y' = a_Y + (b_Y)(X), \text{ where}$$

Equation (12-3)
(p. 301)
$$b_Y = \frac{SP_{XY}}{SS_X} \quad ,$$

Equation (12-5)
(p. 302)
$$SP_{XY} = \Sigma(X)(Y) - \frac{(\Sigma X)(\Sigma Y)}{s} \quad ,$$

Equation (12-4)
(p. 302)
$$SS_X = \Sigma(X)^2 - \frac{(\Sigma X)^2}{s} \quad , \text{ and}$$

Equation (12-6)
(p. 302)
$$a_Y = \overline{Y} - (b_Y)(\overline{X}) \quad .$$

B. Analysis of Linear Trend: Experimental Data (see pp. 307–310)

Equation (12-9)
(p. 309) $F_{\text{linear}} = \dfrac{MS_{A_{\text{linear}}}}{MS_{\text{error}}}$, where

$MS_{A_{\text{linear}}}$ = variance due to linear trend, and

MS_{error} = error term for the overall analysis.

C. Analysis of Linear Trend: Correlational Data (see pp. 327–333)

Source	SS^a	df	MS	F
Linear Regression	$\dfrac{(SP_{XY})^2}{SS_X}$	1	$\dfrac{SS_{\text{lin. regr.}}}{df_{\text{lin. regr.}}}$	$\dfrac{MS_{\text{lin. regr.}}}{MS_{\text{residual}}}$
Residual	$SS_Y - SS_{\text{lin. regr.}}$	$s - 2$	$\dfrac{SS_{\text{residual}}}{df_{\text{residual}}}$	

$^a\ SP_{XY} = \Sigma\,(X)(Y) - \dfrac{(\Sigma X)(\Sigma Y)}{s}$, $SS_X = \Sigma\,(X)^2 - \dfrac{(\Sigma X)^2}{s}$, and $SS_Y = \Sigma\,(Y)^2 - \dfrac{(\Sigma Y)^2}{s}$

VII. Correlation (see pp. 344–347)

Equation (14-2)
(p. 346) $r = \dfrac{SP_{XY}}{\sqrt{(SS_X)(SS_Y)}}$, where

Equation (12-5)
(p. 302) $SP_{XY} = \Sigma\,(X)(Y) - \dfrac{(\Sigma X)(\Sigma Y)}{s}$,

Equation (12-4)
(p. 302) $SS_X = \Sigma\,(X)^2 - \dfrac{(\Sigma X)^2}{s}$, and

Equation (13-3)
(p. 330) $SS_Y = \Sigma\,(Y)^2 - \dfrac{(\Sigma Y)^2}{s}$.

VIII. Analysis of Categorical Data: Single-Factor Between-Subjects Design (see pp. 371–381)

A. Overall Analysis

Equation (15-1)
(p. 368) $\chi^2 = \Sigma\,\dfrac{(f_O - f_E)^2}{f_E}$, where

f_O = observed frequency of cases,

Equation (15-3a)
(p. 374) $f_E = \dfrac{(\text{row total})(\text{column total})}{\text{grand total}}$, and

Equation (15-4)
(p. 374) $df = (a - 1)(c - 1)$.

B. Analytical Comparisons

Equation (15-5)
(p. 377)

$$\chi^2_{comp.} = \sum \frac{(f_O - f_E)^2}{F_E} \quad , \text{ where}$$

f_O = observed frequency of cases,

f_E = expected frequency based on comparison contingency table, and

F_E = expected frequency based on original contingency table.

REFERENCES

Anderson, B. F. *The psychology experiment*. Belmont, California: Wadsworth, 1966.

Bailey, D. E. *Probability and statistics: Models for research*. New York: Wiley, 1971.

Bespaloff, A. A corking new wine theory. *New York Magazine,* May 23, 1977, 43–45.

Bresnahan, J. L., and M. M. Shapiro. A general equation and technique for the exact partitioning of chi-square contingency tables. *Psychological Bulletin,* 1966, 66, 252–262.

Campbell, D. T., and J. C. Stanley. *Experimental and quasi-experimental designs for research*. Skokie, Ill.: Rand McNally, 1966.

Castellan, N. J., Jr. On the partitioning of contingency tables. *Psychological Bulletin,* 1965, 64, 330–338.

Cohen, J. *Statistical power analysis for the behavioral sciences*. New York: Academic Press, 1969.

Edgington, E. S. A new tabulation of statistical procedures used in APA journals. *American Psychologist,* 1974, 29, 25–26.

Edwards, A. L. *Experimental design in psychological research*. (4th ed.) New York: Holt, Rinehart and Winston, 1972.

Edwards, A. L. *An introduction to linear regression and correlation*. San Francisco: W. H. Freeman and Company, 1976.

Freedman, D., R. Pisani, and R. Purves. *Statistics*. New York: W. W. Norton, 1978.

Havlicek, L. L., and N. L. Peterson. Effect of the violation of assumptions upon significance levels of the Pearson *r*. *Psychological Bulletin,* 1977, 84, 373–377.

Hays, W. L. *Statistics for the social sciences*. (2nd ed.) New York: Holt, Rinehart and Winston, 1973.

Keppel, G. Association by contiguity: Role of response availability. *Journal of Experimental Psychology,* 1966, 71, 624–628.

Keppel, G. *Design and analysis: A researcher's handbook*. Englewood Cliffs, N. J.: Prentice-Hall, 1973.

Keppel, G., L. Postman, and B. Zavortink. Studies of learning to learn: VIII. The influence of massive amounts of training upon the learning and retention of paired-associate lists. *Journal of Verbal Learning and Verbal Behavior,* 1968, 7, 790–796.

Kerlinger, F. N. *Foundations of behavioral research*. (2nd ed.) New York: Holt, Rinehart and Winston, 1973.

Kerlinger, F. N., and E. J. Pedhazur. *Multiple regression in behavioral research*. New York: Holt, Rinehart and Winston, 1973.

Kirk, R. E. *Experimental design: Procedures for the behavioral sciences*. Monterey, California: Brooks/Cole, 1968.

Kirk, R. E. (ed.). *Statistical issues: A reader for the behavioral sciences*. Monterey, California: Brooks/Cole, 1972.

Kirk, R. E. *Introductory statistics*. Monterey, California: Brooks/Cole, 1978.

Lee, W. *Experimental design and analysis*. San Francisco: W. H. Freeman, 1975.

Lindman, H. R. *Analysis of variance in complex experimental designs*. San Francisco: W. H. Freeman, 1974.

Moses, L. E., and R. V. Oakford. *Tables of random permutations*. Stanford, Calif.: Stanford University Press, 1963.

Myers, J. L. *Fundamentals of experimental design*. (3rd ed.) Boston: Allyn and Bacon, 1979.

Neale, J. M., and R. M. Liebert. *Science and behavior: An introduction to methods of research*. Englewood Cliffs, N. J.: Prentice-Hall, 1973.

Pearson, E. S., and H. O. Hartley (eds.). *Biometrika tables for statisticians,* vol. 1. (3rd ed.) New York: Cambridge University Press, 1970.

Siegel, S. *Nonparametric statistics for the behavioral sciences*. New York: McGraw-Hill, 1956.

Underwood, B. J. *Psychological research*. New York: Appleton-Century-Crofts, 1957.

Underwood, B. J. *Experimental psychology*. (2nd ed.) New York: Appleton-Century-Crofts, 1966.

Underwood, B. J. Individual differences as a crucible in theory construction. *American Psychologist,* 1975, 30, 128–134.

Underwood, B. J., and J. J. Shaughnessy. *Experimentation in psychology.* New York: Wiley, 1975.

Vaughan, G. M., and M. C. Corballis. Beyond tests of significance: Estimating strength of effects in selected ANOVA designs. *Psychological Bulletin,* 1969, 72, 204–213.

Winer, B. J. *Statistical principles in experimental design.* (2nd ed.) New York: McGraw-Hill, 1971.

Wood, G. *Fundamentals of psychological research.* Boston: Little, Brown, 1974.

Author Index

Subject Index